The Magical Years: A Boyhood Revisited is the story of a boy growing up in the Great Depression which ends with his flight from his southwestern Minnesota village womb to enter the Navy Air Corps in World War II. Benjamin revives the angst and wonder of childhood before loss of innocence brought on by immersion in the larger secular world. He vividly describes canning days, family reunions, the terror of dust storms, the ravages of grasshopper plagues, the regimen of garden chores, going to the lake, scavenging for berries and nuts, the hobo culture, and the onslaught of death.

It is the story of every boy who lives through the discipline of an authoritarian yet loving home. His ambivalence toward his father—An "Iron John Father"—is that of legions of young boys. Benjamin poignantly describes the loss of his brother, Dickie, to polio, the "Summer Terror."

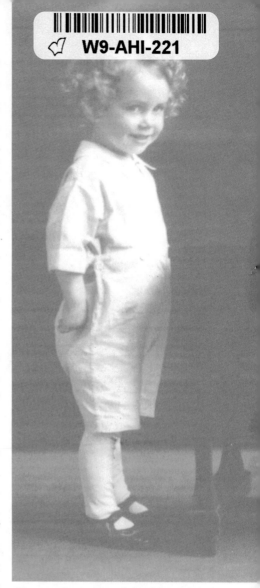

Photo: author's two year birthday from Chapter 3, "Childhood Memories"

It was an era before the onset of the acids of relativism when moral absolutes held sway. Like most families, Benjamin reflects, "we were poor of purse but lived with nobility."

Benjamin writes with frankness and verve, honesty and directness. His descriptions of accompanying his physician-father to farm house calls, avoiding Sammy's, the small town saloon, and participation in the agrarian rite of hog killing are winsomely told. "Puberty and Pimples" records his fear and fascination with girls—the "forbidden fruit."

Church life, summer revivals, simple but centered public school learning, depression-era haircuts and more are recounted. His experience of working for Dutch and French farmers and as a railroad Gandy Dancer are charming, as are the hunting and athletic rites of passage that he endured in the attempt to prove his manhood. Dr. Benjamin's memoir winds down with "the thunder of war" and his desire to escape his rural womb to serve his nation. He closes with a testimony to "the eternal and mythic village," a legacy that is emotional, sustaining and portable rather than simply geographic. Benjamin honors his "our town" community for its values and nurture that led to the success of its offspring.

The Magical Years is the story of a more simple time, one both harsh and richly rewarding, when the heroism of families was pitted against the onslaughts of drought, destitution, disease and depression.

Photo: the author's father from Chapter 39, "An Iron John Father"

Walter W. Benjamin was three years old when the Great Depression began in 1929. Like millions of others, his life was shaped by the decade that followed. The son of a country doctor, Benjamin served in the Navy Air Corps during World War II, received his Ph.D. in ethics at Duke University, and spent most of his career at Hamline University in St. Paul, Minnesota. He is the author of the well-received *War & Reflection*.

"ERA CONDITIONING"

"Author/Professor Walter Benjamin bridges the gap between generations and discovers that the attitudes, values and behaviors he will carry to his grave were shaped by the Great Depression."

Mary Ann Grossmann, *The Saint Paul Pioneer Press*

"The Magical Years" is a splendid achievment and I have enjoyed it enormously. The author gives a beautiful tribute to his family, his hometown, and the society in which he grew up. Yet the portrait maintains its balance.

"Most importantly, Professor Benjamin does a skillful job of revealing the great losses our culture has suffered in its moral spirit, but he does so without playing the scold. His tone of regret for what the youth of later generations have missed is genuine and just right.

"Dr. Benjamin's descriptions of hard and wholesome farm life, of the unifying role the garden and dinner table played in his family, and of the image of his hard shelled father unable to speak upon his son's leaving home for the Navy Air Corps—these are among the vivid impressions that will stay with me for a long time."

D. J. Tice, Columnist, *Saint Paul Pioneer Press* and author of *Minnesota's Twentieth Century.*

"This is truly a remarkable and marvelous book which was written with love, insight, permissible nostalgia, understandable observations and a sense of historical perspective. Dr. Benjamin's story deserves national exposure. Once I got started on it, I found it hard to break away."

Dr. Earl Spangler, Dean Emeritus, Cartage College

THE MAGICAL YEARS:

A BOYHOOD REVISITED

WALTER W. BENJAMIN

EXPANDED SECOND EDITION

Beaver's Pond Press

Edina, Minnesota

Front Cover: Robert and Walter Benjamin, Woman Lake 1937. Photo by Bessie Benjamin

ISBN Number: 1-931646-05-8

Library of Congress Catalog Number: 2001091559

Benjamin, Walter W.
  The Magical Years: A Boyhood Revisited

Includes Bibliography, Index, and Table of Contents

1. Autobiography
2. The Great Depression
3. Twentieth Century History

4. Agriculture
5. World War II
6. Minnesota History

Cover Design and Art: Steve Harmon
Editor: Douglas C. Benson
Production Editor: Milt Adams
Copy Editor: Marjorie G. Benjamin
Publisher: Beaver's Pond Press
Photo Credits: Pipestone County Historical Society, Sogn's Studio, Iowa State University Press, and the author's personal collection
Interior Design: Mori Studio

2nd Edition: January 2002
Printed in United States of America

05 04 03 02 01   6 5 4 3 2 1

Beaver's Pond Press

5125 Danen's Drive
Edina, Minnesota 55439-1465
(952) 829-8818
www.beaverspondpress.com

DEDICATION

Isn't it queer: there are only two or three human stories, and they go on repeating themselves as fiercely as if they had never happened before; like the larks in this country that have been singing the same five notes over for thousands of years.

W. Cather, *O Pioneers!*

These reflections are dedicated to two dear and gracious persons, one living, one dead. I owe more than words can tell to Marjorie Prescott Benjamin, my wife and soul-mate for over 45 years. She has virtue enough for a dozen women. Beyond raising our four children, she has had careers in half a dozen different vocations, from teaching school to real estate, teaching fashion design to literacy tutoring. Whatever hidden talent or success I have achieved in life has come to fruition largely due to her love, compassion, and steadfastness.

Bradley Kent Benjamin, our second son, was a sweet and gentle lad, whose untimely death due to the Furies, has left a scar that no reconstructive surgeon can efface. He was a child of God, compassionate, without guile, a lad untimely born and too sensitive for our harsh and turbulent times. As a history major, he read some of the early chapters of these memoirs and urged me to complete the project. Brad was deeply attracted to the glorious American Experiment and identified with our Nation's heroes. Each month he changed a folio of portraits of our nation's presidents that stood on his dresser.

St. Paul states faith is a trust in God's promises and in the acceptance of things not seen. In faith, we can hope that in God's mysterious grace, Brad may even now comprehend this Depression history and the saga of the family tree he so deeply loved.

TABLE OF CONTENTS

PREFACE

Tell me the landscape in which you live, and I will tell you who you are.

Jose Ortega y Gassett

Most American historians agree that the Great Depression, 1929-1939, played an enormously significant role in the shaping of the American character. My own character also was molded during that decade, while I was growing up in a small southwestern Minnesota prairie town. As a youngster I had little existential knowledge of the woeful economic conditions of that era. In spite of those conditions and, even discounting the nostalgia that may come with moving into the autumn of life, I believe my boyhood circumstances were incredibly rich. Being poor is only partly a financial issue. Most of the families I knew who lived in those straightened circumstances were incredibly rich in spirit, in character, and in moral capital. The majority of the households in my town were governed firmly by the family values that are so contentious in public discourse today.

I wrote *THE MAGICAL YEARS: A BOYHOOD REVISITED* so that my children and grandchildren, as well as a wider audience, could gain perspective in viewing that era. The Great Depression is gone, not only economically, but more importantly, in the attitudes and values it generated. I return again and again to the memories that were shaped within my prairie home and village because I am convinced they imparted something of enduring value. Much that shaped the Depression era pattern of life—farming practices, threshing crews, educational methods, country physicians, railroad work, recreation, family life—is now gone. But I am firmly convinced that there is much that should endure if individuals, families, neighborhoods and our nation are to remain vibrant and strong.

Because of the rampant cynicism, violence, nihilism, and other social pathologies that affect American life today, I would have to state that I fear for my grandchildren. But I am comforted in knowing that this apprehension is to some extent a generic attitude, a repetitive and innate angst that afflicts every generation as it passes over the horizon of history.

The Great Depression engendered within me the attitudes, values, and behaviors that have shaped my life and that I will carry to the grave. Most are positive and I cherish them—the enjoyment of family activities; discipline and thrift; a respect for law, authority, and property; prudence; a love of family, church, neighborhood, and country; a hopeful realism regarding the future. Others are, perhaps, less admirable—an intense fear of destitution, an inability to "let go," a tendency toward moralism and workaholism, an emphasis on law rather than grace, a suspicion toward outsiders and those who are different, and a lack of ambiguity regarding morality and the human condition. It wasn't until I grew to manhood that I realized how indelibly marked the Depression generations of my parents and grandparents were by the pessimism, fatalism, and resignation of the time and how much had brushed off onto my generation.

Even superficial behaviors are deeply ingrained—turning out lights in empty rooms, bathing and showering using a modicum of tepid water, setting the thermostat low, saving slivers of soap, searching for bargains in order to save a few pennies, being reluctant to discard old, worn out items. Grant Wood's classic painting, *American Gothic*, is not far off the mark in portraying both the external and the internal character of those whom I knew during my adolescence.

The majority of my genetic line tried to follow the Genesis dictum— "Be ye fruitful and multiply, and fill the earth and subdue it"—as faithfully as the Hebrew patriarchs. Shakespeare's third sonnet which warns, "Die single, and thine image dies with thee," was taken with the utmost seriousness by my Tribe. Therefore, because our numbers are legion, it is dangerous to write a story of intimacy and personal reflection. Different memories, moreover, edit in diverse ways. Many who will read this have been witnesses to the events that I am about to chronicle; their different recollections may be proportional to their numbers. It should be remembered, however, that the angle of vision determines what one sees, feels, and recalls. Undoubtedly, some may say, "That isn't the way I remember it." From Homer to Winston Churchill, from Heroditus to the historians of the Vietnam War, the problem of the memoirist has been difficult.

Writing during one's gray-haired years is, in fact, fraught with danger. "Old age is by nature," says Cicero, "rather talkative." Moreover, "One who speaks about his own books," Benjamin Disraeli mused, "is almost as bad as a mother who talks about her own children."

Undoubtedly, there may be members of our extensive Tribe who view the following record through a different prism. So be it. Existentialist philosophers such as Sartre and Camus remind us that it is a cardinal transgression to treat that which is concrete, individual, and personal as if it were abstract, universal, and generic. In human affairs subjectivity, not objectivity, is truth; there is no pure, universal, or correct story of a human pilgrimage.

According to Emerson, "there is properly no history, only biography." Oliver Wendell Holmes reminds us that historic continuity with the past is not an option, but rather it is a duty and a necessity. Nevertheless, respect for the past, however pious, should never be idolatrous. What I have written, therefore, is "true for me," though different visions and remembrances are not necessarily antithetical. Indeed, they may be complementary. Historians agree there is no objective or unbiased view of the affairs of human beings. We act and are acted upon. We see life through our own particular and personal window and we, of necessity, choose to select, remember, and record impressions that are particular as well as universal.

Memory is the diary, according to Oscar Wilde, that we all carry about with us. What follows is my attempt to be faithful to that remembrance.

It will be obvious to the reader that the author has a devotion to tradition, biography, ethnic memory, and history. "To know nothing of what happened before you were born," wrote Cicero, "is to remain ever a child." To study history liberates us from the present, from the idols of our own market-place. It can emancipate us from the falsities of the past as well. Those who are ignorant of history are usually, without knowing it, enslaved to a fairly recent past. Nonetheless, I am cognizant that a man who leaves memoirs, whether well or badly written, leaves intimate, psychic grist for a future psychologist's mill. But that is a risk that must be taken. I have enjoyed this labor of love. It is my hope that it fulfills Joubert's adage, "All that is good in man lies in youthful feeling and mature thought." Nevertheless, "Life must be lived forward," as Kierkegaard reminds us, "but can only be understood backwards.

ACKNOWLEDGMENTS

> To deprive elderly people of their bogeys is as brutal as snatching from babies their big stuffed bears.
>
> L.P. Smith

These reflections on my childhood and youth began over 10 years ago with episodic jottings. I wanted to mine and record the subterranean mother lode of my memories before something happened to my physical or spiritual self. Although the selective bibliography indicates part of my preparation for this task, for the most part, what I have recorded has come from my mental memories, like Minerva came full-blown from the head of Zeus.

I am greatly indebted for the services of my editor, Mr. Doug Benson, for his keen management and judicious oversight of my text. Moreover, his renaissance knowledge of historical detail has been helpful at many points. I also owe much to Steve Harmon for his exceptional skill in providing the artistic design of the cover and his creative use of the Depression-era and family photos. I also want to extend my deep appreciation to Jack Caravela, President of Mori Studio, for his professional skill regarding the layout and design of my book. Milt Adams, my energetic publisher, secured the necessary technical data and people to bring this project to a successful conclusion. My wife, Marjorie, gave yeoman service as the copy editor of the manuscript. Her gimlet-eyed scrutiny was often performed in the car during the long and boring travel to Arkansas and Oklahoma via Interstate #35.

I am in debt to the Pipestone Historical Society, both its former head, Mr. David Rambo, and its present director, Mr. Chris Roelfsema-Hummel, and their able assistants. Both made available to me relevant issues of *The Pipestone Leader*, *The Pipestone Star*, photos, and other materials relating to Pipestone county and the Great Depression. I also appreciate the permission by the Iowa State University Press to use several of their photos from Carl Hamilton's *No Time at All*.

I want to thank my former student at Morningside College, Chuck Draper, editor and publisher of *The Pipestone Star*, for his continued support of the Pipestone County Museum. Periodic visits to Pipestone and class reunions down through the years have refreshed my memory as have conversations with my good friends Les Kallsen, Neal Knudtson, Steve Hicks, Will Walz, Jack Lambert, and many others.

Earl Mahoney, too, has been helpful in giving me a perspective on the 1920s and 30s before I came into awareness. Although they have not been directly involved in this endeavor, discussions through the years with my brothers, Robert and Roger Benjamin, and my sisters, Martha Unke and Mary Bowen, have given me insight into our common past and our family tree. Conversations with Mother about the Tribe of Benjamin during the years before her death were invaluable, as have been annual reunions at Hutchinson with my many cousins. Conversations with many relatives at Kee Nee Moo Sha Resort on Woman Lake also have been beneficial. I also want to express my appreciation to our daughter, Barbara, for selecting the title of these memoirs. Until I wrote this book, I did not realize that the title is usually the last thing an author decides. While the angst of the Depression was pervasive and crippling, Barbara suggested that the majority of children, whatever the condition of their lives or the historical epoch in which they live, look at the world through a wondrous, enchanting prism. If true, at one time perhaps all of us had a bit of the charm and pride seen in the faces of my brother and the author, whose photo graces the cover of this volume.

Like Ivory soap that purports to be "99 and 44/100 percent pure," this account of my origin and early life is largely true both as to the data and my recollections. In this I am literary kin to H. L. Mencken, the bard of the *Baltimore Sun*. Mencken's genial caveat regarding his autobiography was that it contained some "yarning" and was "not always photographically precise," and that there were undoubtedly "some stretchers" in his reflections. I have, therefore, taken a few literary liberties and have changed a number of names of classmates and others to respect their privacy and that of their families. Individuals such as the Italian butcher, Mr. Tarango, and Karl Olson are inventions constructed to help carry the story line. The saloon, "Sammys," did exist in Pipestone, albeit that was not its name.

I am grateful for the coterie of teachers, farmers, church members, neighbors, pastors, and others who left indelible and precious deposits on my mind.

INTRODUCTION

I want to go home
To the dull old town,
With the shaded street
And the open square;
And the hill
And the flats
And the house I love,
And the paths I know—
I want to go home

Home, Paul Kester

I was born in Pipestone, Minnesota on October 10, 1926 just as the second quarter of the 20th century was getting underway. Two days later the weekly newspaper, *The Pipestone Leader* ($1.50 per annum) proclaimed the event: "A son was born Sunday to Dr. and Mrs. W. G. Benjamin, at the Ashton Memorial Hospital." The 17 word announcement was but one of over 90 items in the "personals" column and was sandwiched between "Mr. and Mrs. P.C. Goembel returned Tuesday from a business trip to Minneapolis" and a misplaced ad, "Fourteen photographs for the price of a dozen during the balance of October at C.E. Sogn's Studio."

Mother had ensured the Sunday delivery by ingesting a solid dose of castor oil tempered by orange juice. It was the same birthing ritual that brought on the contractions of labor for all of her six children, a ceremonial she employed to make certain her husband, not one of the other local physicians, would be attending her. An innate sense of modesty, combined with her view of the limited and modest abilities of the other Siouxland practitioners (an evaluation obviously picked up from Father), prompted her action. I cannot help but believe Father was pleased.

Several page-one headlines overshadowed the announcement of my birth: "F.H. Burgert Company Going Out of Business" (a pre-Depression casualty?); "Hiawatha Area Council to Meet Here Thursday" (the village elders knew our Indian connection meant money?); "Young

Men Confess Burglaries: Sentenced" (law and order are alive and well in the Heartland?); "Escaped Lunatic Found in Jasper" (no "politically-correct" medicalese then—a spade was called a spade); "Pipestone Woman in Trouble at Omaha: Alleged to Have Passed Forged Checks," (obviously the moral bedrock of Pipestone had a fissure or two).

On the national and international scene, events both weighty and foreboding dominated the news:

* Stalin continued the killing of millions of kulaks to complete his collectivization of Soviet agriculture.

* US Marines landed in Nicaragua following an uprising led by General Augusto Cesar Sandino.

* Teaching of the theory of evolution was prohibited in the public schools of Atlanta.

* In Germany an embittered World War I veteran was in prison writing *Mein Kampf.*

* Henry Ford introduced the 40-hour work week to boost the ailing automobile industry.

* Significant books published were: Carl Sandburg's, *Abraham Lincoln: The Prairie Years*; Will Durant's, *The Story of Philosophy*; William Faulkner's, *Soldier's Pay*, Ernest Hemingway's, *The Sun Also Rises.*

In the month I was born, the verdant summer fields turned to autumn's amber. The life cycles of crops and animals were the great cogs upon which the farm year turned. Villagers and farmers alike spoke in the cyclical accents of the centuries—of a killing frost, the heft of the wheat and barley, their hopes for an extended Indian Summer, the provisions needed for the coming winter—and looked forward to the celebration of Thanksgiving when "all was gathered in."

The world into which I was born seemed Eden-like. The Great War was a distant memory and America had "returned to normalcy." In that care-free era I ascended the primordial infant curve—teething, being weaned, learning to walk, outgrowing diapers. At the age of two, adorned with beautiful six inch-long blond curls, I would have my picture taken at Sogn's studio.

But before I learned to tie my shoes, Wall Street crashed, a cataclysm that shook the foundations of both our nation and the world. The economic bedrock of America was shattered and the Great Depression began. The ten lean years that followed shaped my life.

The Quartzite rock outcropping from the Coteau des Prairies. It was here that our family picnicked and I camped out overnight with my friends. As a boy I dreamed of courageous explorers and heroic Indian warriors. Later this spot was included in the Pipestone National Monument.

1. The "Mountains of the Prairie"

There were giants in the earth in those days; and also after that, when the sons of God came in unto the daughters of men, and they bare children to them, the same became mighty men which were of old, men of renown.

Genesis 6:4

The grand simplicity of the prairie is its peculiar beauty, and its occurring events are peculiar and of their own kind.

Memoirs of My Life, J.C. Fremont

I have noticed in my life that all men have a liking for some special animal, tree, plant, or spot of earth. If men would pay more attention to these preferences and seek what is best to do in order to make themselves worthy...they might have dreams which would purify their lives.

By The Power of Their Dreams, Brave Buffalo, Sioux

The first 18 years of my life were spent almost entirely within the womb of a mile-square village that numbered approximately 5,000 inhabitants. Pipestone, Minnesota, rested upon and drew a precarious existence from the undulating, semi-arid plains of the southwestern portion of the state. Located one mile south of the sacred shrine of the Empire of the Sioux, its name came from the red sedimentary rock that Indians used in creating their peace pipes, or calumets. According to legend, the soft stone had been stained red through centuries of tribal bloodlettings. In more recent times, however, peace was assured by annual encampments. Pipes were filled with kinnikinnick (a mixture of wild tobacco and the dried inner bark of the red willow) and smoked as pledges of tribal concord.

The first white man to record his trip to the quarries was fur trader Philander Prescott in 1831. In the summer of 1836 the noted artist and writer George Catlin visited the site. He recognized the fragility of the Native American culture which, under the hammer blows of the westward-bent immigrant hordes, would soon be no more. He recorded this unique but passing panorama—the nobility of Indian life and costume—in magnificent color. Catlin also was impressed by the stark and rolling hills, what the French called the *Coteau des Prairies,* which can mean "highland of the grasslands" or "mountains of the prairie."

"Man feels the force of illimitable freedom—his body and mind both seem to have entered a new element, as expanding and infinite as the boundless imagery that is spread around him." The elevation of the *Coteau* ranged from 1700 to 2000 feet above sea level, the second highest area in the state. It was a great midwestern watershed: rain falling on the east side of the Coteau ended up in the Mississippi River; that on the west slope ultimately trickled into the Missouri. The bedrock was formed 1.5 billion years ago, and I could put my fingernails in the grooves or striations that had been formed by the massive glaciers moving over the rock.

In 1838 the Nicollet-Fremont cartography expedition spent a week at the quarries and cut the names of their party into the Sioux quartzite ledge by the Winnewissa Falls. While camping overnight by their inscription, I imagined what it must have been like to be alive during those days. The thought of penetrating into the wilderness filled me with awe and stimulated visions. Rapture seems to be related to geography. Just as the English moors generate melancholy, my prairies stimulated mystical ecstacy. I remembered reading that in 1846 Francis Parkman had observed that a herd of buffalo being chased by Indians was like the black shadow of a cloud passing rapidly over swell after swell of the distant plain. To join an expedition, see virgin vistas, fight against Indian warriors, confront the vagaries of nature, shoot bison, explore the unknown—all these images and more flooded up into my conscious mind. I needed some heroic test of manhood. I fought sleep in my bedroll not far from where I envisaged giants had stalked the land in those days.

Only a quarter-mile south of the Nicollet inscription were the Three Maidens, rocky descendants of a 50-foot granite boulder that had been carried down from Canada by a continental glacier during the last ice age and had been split into pieces during thousands of freeze-thaw cycles. According to Indian lore the spirits of the maidens required offerings from visiting tribes before permitting them to quarry the sacred stone. As darkness crept into my tent, images of red men arose to trouble my dreams.

On such nights I was dimly aware that I slept on the sacred soil of a vanished but noble race. I thought about the courageous but tragic chiefs such as Sitting Bull, Red Cloud, Yellow Wolf, Cochise, Geronimo, and Chief Joseph as they fought for their way of life against overwhelming odds. The chief of the Santee Sioux, Little Crow, had been shot but a few miles from the Hutchinson homestead where Father had been born.

As school children we were taught to commit to memory parts of Longfellow's "Song of Hiawatha," of which the following is the most famous stanza:

On the great Red Pipe-stone Quarry,
Gitche Manito, the Mighty...
On the red crags of the quarry
Stood erect, and called the nations,

"...Bury your war clubs and your weapons,
Break the red stone from this quarry,
Mold and make it into Peace-Pipes...
Smoke the calumet together,
And as brothers live henceforward!"

But the Land of the Sioux Empire was no longer in the hands of the Indians. Like other pre-literate, pre-metallic societies, the Native Americans had little conception of territorial ownership. They fought frequently over women, sometimes over hunting rights, and often for prestige and revenge. But their limited numbers—estimated at only 600,000 at their most populous—imposed little need to fight over land. Without territorial acquisitiveness, lacking cannons or wheels, they were relatively helpless before the repeated tidal waves of Europeans, "those of the pale faces," who came with Winchester repeaters, Conastoga wagons, plows, barbed wire, and "smoking iron horses."

I empathized with their trail of tears and wished that there had been more critics like Theodore Frelinghuysen. "The Indians listened to our professions of friendship. We called them brothers and they believed us," lamented the Senator of New Jersey. "We have crowded the tribes into a few miserable acres and it is all that is left to them of their once boundless forests, and still, like the horse-leech, our insatiated cupidity cries, give! give! give!"

The tale of our continent's conquest is a great American epic; it is also a great American tragedy. Two utterly irreconcilable styles of life came into conflict. Our history simply repeated a confrontation as old as agriculture—settled people simply cannot comprehend the fulfillment that the roaming existence brings to the migrant pastoralist and the hunter. The East was settled by agriculturalists; why should the West be any different? "What is the right of a huntsman to the forest of a thousand miles over which he has accidentally ranged in quest of prey?" asked John Quincy Adams. "Shall the field and valley, which a beneficent God has formed to teem with the life of innumerable multitudes, be condemned to everlasting barrenness?" Later, General Phil Sheridan applauded the slaughter of the buffalo or, as he put it, the "Indian's commissary." He exhorted the buffalo hunter to "kill, skin, and sell" until the animal was exterminated. Only then could the prairies be "covered with speckled cattle and the festive cowboy." A buffalo holocaust was a precondition for that indigenous beast's replacement by Longhorn and Whiteface cattle. Indians faced a tragic choice between dependency on the reservation or an ultimately futile armed resistance. The latter could lead to death. But in the words of Crazy Horse to the rabbit-hearted who chose the former—"slaves to a piece of fat bacon, some hardtack and a little sugar and coffee"—that choice would kill their souls.

This diorama of the quarries at the Pipestone National Monument shows Indians quarrying the soft, blood-red sedimentary rock. The escarpment at the rear was created by a large prehistoric inland sea.

Hindsight now allows us to confess one of the cardinal injustices of our history. It was an era, as historians now muse, when "space overpowered time." Space, not time, movement, not stasis, is the dimension in which Americans have lived since Plymouth Rock. Our official symbol may be the American eagle, but our real totems are the trailer hitch, the golden arches, the mobile home. Had the immigrants come in driblets rather than as a tidal wave, and had they taken mincing little steps westward rather than strides more akin to the long jump, there might have been enough time for accommodation, for touching, learning, exploring, feeling, and adjusting to one another's cultures.

Then our whole nation faced West, and ever since, we have been driven by a loose, "let-me-at-the-horizon" lope. The Homestead Act of 1862 made Minnesota land available for the asking. One could obtain 160 acres by paying a ten-dollar filing fee and then living on the land and farming it for five years. Manifest Destiny was in control; the settling of the West was just another chapter in the triumphal march of the invincible Anglo-Saxon race. No force on earth could have stopped the westward surge of the pioneers. Good, cheap land was a magnet whose pull reached back through Europe and into Russia. The multitudes were restive—militarily conscripted, religiously coerced, over-populated, hide-bound by restrictive laws and traditions. They wanted release from autocratic regimes that shackled their spirits. Free land—a farm in the family, the dream of European peasants for hundreds of years—was the New World's great gift to the old. William Stoughton, a Boston pastor, claimed that "God sifted whole nations that He might send choice grain over into this wilderness."

Most of those who joined the western tide were peasants or the younger sons of small farmers. Joined with our own restless citizens of the eastern seaboard, they constituted the greatest mass migration in history. Their credo was that of the later Kansas populist, Jerry Simpson, "Man must have access to the land or he is a slave."

When cultures as different as those of the Native Americans and the Europeans collided at 90 miles an hour, demonizing took the place of understanding. The "garbage of Europe," in the words of Eric Hoffer, was having a love affair with America. Our immigrants were proving what the common man could achieve when the shackles of caste and autocracy were broken. But the price of emancipating the Anglo Saxon was the destruction of the Indian's cosmology as well as his body and spirit. The Earth was the Native Americans' Mother and aliens had violated her. When the aliens suggested that Indians should give up their bow, lance, and nomadism for the plow, spade, and hoe, the response was that digging in the dirt was unmanly. Besides, "Shall I take a knife," cried a chief, "and tear my mother's bosom?"

The hope expressed in the letter of President Jefferson, carried by

Lewis and Clark during 1804-06 was read to the Indian nations from St. Louis to the Columbia River; alas, it never came to pass:

> It is so long since our forefathers came from beyond the great water, that we have lost the memory of it, and seem to have grown out of this land, as you have done…We are all now of one family, born in the same land, & bound to live as brothers; and the strangers from beyond the great water are gone from among us. The great Spirit has given you strength, and has given us strength; not that we might hurt one another, but to do each other all the good in our power.

It would be well, then, neither to idolize the Indian (Longfellow and Rousseau) or demonize him (General Custer and 19th century popular culture). Indian tribes, like European nations, had their particularistic virtues and vices. Captain Meriwether Lewis thus was able to draw judgments based on empirical evidence. He liked some (Nez Perce, Shoshones), admired others (Wallawallas), pitied some (Mandans), and feared a few (Blackfeet). There are no people, ancient or modern, without original sin and hubris. Indians had all too human faults—scalping ("taking coup"), stealing, ill treatment of women—that tempered their virtues of endurance to pain, hunger and cold, fine horsemanship, and adaptation to a harsh environment. In truth, there was no Native American Garden of Eden that the white man destroyed. Both before and during the Westerning movement of "those with the pale faces," the Indian nations were on the warpath against each other.

"The Indian adopted all of the White man's vices," went a widely held popular adage, "and none of his virtues." But Thomas James, one of the early Mountain Men, admired Indians. He reported having seen the "finest specimens of men," chiefs with the dignity of princes and the eloquence of orators, and braves with the "valor of the ancient Spartans." Yet white men labeled them as "heathen" and infected and poisoned them with smallpox, T.B., and fire water. "You rot your grain in tubs," mused a chief, confused over the strange manner of liquor-making by the palefaces. The Indian viewed our work ethic as slavery and our worship of land and mammon as evil. Work was the invention of an alien civilization. It was not work to roam the prairies and hunt bison. It was not work to gather chokecherries and pound them into jerky and make pemmican. As hunters and gatherers, Indians were convinced they had not yet tasted the apple and thus had not been expelled from the Garden. The Nez Perce chief, Smohalla, when asked why his "lazy" young braves with strong bodies did not do manual labor, answered: "My young men shall never work. Men who work cannot dream, and wisdom comes to us in dreams."

While our western spaces were being filled, there never was enough time for understanding and acculturation. Diaries of the settlers who took the Oregon Trail speak of having to leave Missouri in mid May to avoid getting caught in the snow of the mountains. The sound of the frontier pulsed with calls to "hurry up," "move-'em-out," "make 20 miles a day," "get the best land." "I must walk toward Oregon," mused Henry David Thoreau in feeling the pulse of the nation. "That is the way the nation is moving." "Trying to stop American immigration," opined the Texan, Stephen F. Austin, "is like trying to stop the Mississippi with a dam of straw."

It took Europeans a millennium or more to subdue their wilderness. But in North America, thanks to our technological wonders—the steel plow, the Colt six-shooter, the windmill, barbed wire—it took less than a century.

It was not only Native Americans who suffered during the westward migrations. A study of women's overland diaries finds not a single wife who initiated the idea of moving, while nearly a third actively objected. Fear was the ever-present companion of most pioneer women. The vastness of the unexplored reaches, the inhospitality of the wilderness, the lack of institutional and human aid and comfort when disaster came—these were terrifying things to gentle souls whom fate had not rough-hewn for pioneering. Thousands of frontier women died in childbirth, or went insane, or turned to the comfort of a dark religion, or simply longed for the more settled communities of our eastern seaboard or their European womb. Many saw the seascape grasslands as demonic—troll-possessed, without a place to hide, beyond the reach of church and God. There was an adage that the plains were great for men and dogs but hell on women and horses. Yet these women and their husbands toiled and suffered and even died that their children might inherit the promise. In time the dangerous, trackless seas of grasslands were replaced with fenced, innocent, garden-domesticated places.

I often wished I could have lived during the heroic time of Indians, Lewis and Clark, bison without number, Mountain Men, and French voyageurs. A race of Homeric heroes lived then; fearless men, men of a staunchness unknown in my day. I thought of the wide plains and the wagons moving across them like centipedes. The only physical barriers to the pioneers in this part of the country were the tall native grasses—Big bluestem, switchgrass, Indian grass, and timothy. Ever moving toward the sunset, the colonists heard the chest-high prairie grasses sing, "tish-ah, tish-ah" in protest as their wagons pushed through. The track that was left behind was like the wake of a boat—except that instead of widening out astern it closed in again. Settlers saw the prairie as a rolling sea or ocean of grass—they steered by the stars in their prairie schooners. They could imagine no other metaphor, since many of them had lately seen the Atlantic. Those with a romantic and poetic inner eye experienced an epiphany—the prairie vistas looked like music, like Kyries of grass in harmony.

In spite of its flat and treeless character, the land of the *Couteau de Prairies* was fertile. The constant dying, decomposition, and renewal of the grass roots over the millennia had created soils far richer in organic matter than the soil in forestland, where tree roots transferred most nutrients into the trees.

The "westerning" or "great settling," as historians called it, was over long before I was born. As early as 1877, for every Indian in the West there were now nearly 40 whites. There was no place left to settle, every place was taken and filled in. Long columns of settlers had bumped up against the Pacific shore, hating the ocean because it stopped them. By then the immigrant hordes had passed through Ellis Island and scattered the length and breadth of the land.

The prevalent impression made upon a stranger to the southwestern corner of Minnesota during my childhood was that of loneliness and isolation. Light and distance, sky and horizon, are the dominant themes of the prairie. A region shapes the reality of its inhabitants, and a seascape of grassland usually reflects a sense of estrangement. Both in its external and internal characteristics, my world paralleled that visualized by Andrew Wyeth's painting, "Christina's World." A young woman sitting on the prairie, with body contorted and face averted, looks wistfully at a weather-beaten barn. The rest of the canvas is vacant. My world, like Christina's, was one of empty spaces wanting to be filled. Like Christina, I longed for color, life, and tempo to drive out that which was forlorn and abandoned. Like the rest of the painting, the rolling plains were nearly vacant, cut periodically by ravines or creeks where enough moisture would allow such indifferent timber as the worthless cottonwood and willow to grow. It was a world of extremes, of burning summers and paralyzing winters. The wind was seldom gentle and drove the rain, snow, sleet, or dust in horizontal slants. The old-timers of Pipestone said there was a silver lining in our harsh climate—"It keeps the riffraff out." The *Coteau des Prairies* offered constant reminders that we were often powerless over circumstances.

Fifty years before my birth hordes of immigrants had entered this immense prairie, many of them lured by the enticements of railroad companies, which would not make money by running trains that traversed vacant prairies. "You can lay track to the garden of Eden," said the head of the Northern Pacific, "but what good is it if the only inhabitants are Adam and Eve?" Hence, they plastered Europe with circulars—OPPORTUNI-TIES! UNDISCOVERED RICHES! FERTILE SOIL! A MILD CLIMATE! Exaggerations were the rule, not the exception. Posters did not depict the brute American frontier of European sketches and wood carvings but rather showed what looked like paradise. Some claimed the presence of railroads increased the rainfall—that the concussion of the air and rapid movement of the engines affected the electrical conditions of the atmo-sphere. Hence the myth that rain was said somehow to follow the plow. The Santa Fe Railroad boasted that there was a "rainline"—a front edge of an ever increasing rainfall—that moved at about 18 miles a year, just ahead of newly created settlements. Immigration bounty-hunters were paid so much a head to attract settlers. Pastors and priests often played the role of Pied Piper and led their entire villages from Germany and the Scandinavian countries into the New Land.

In the two decades after the Civil war more new U.S. soil was brought under cultivation than in the previous two-and-a-half centuries. The idea behind the Homestead Act was the Jeffersonian ideal—that a nation of small, independent farmers would be the ideal foundation for democracy. The tidal wave of newcomers from abroad simply wanted the chance to rise from peasanthood to proprietorship. They had hoped to inhabit the rich and moist land of the east, and knew that with every step they took toward the setting sun an imperceptible forfeiture of future prospects and hope would occur. Yet, these new sodbusters knew that the rolling prairie of southwestern Minnesota was no worse than what they left behind on Russia's steppes or in Sweden or Ireland or Germany. Refusing to proceed further to the West, they put down roots every five or ten miles, establishing communities which in time human-ized the emptiness.

The majority had to build houses without timber, burn fires without wood, and carve furrows in a soil so matted and tough that an ordinary plow would often snag in the sod or skitter across its surface like a stick over ice. Many lived under canvas or in sod houses until they could save enough money to bring in—by ox cart—lumber for a house. The best way to build a "soddie" was to burrow into the side of a hill, preferably on the south side. The soddies were well-insulated against the cold and the heat but they were dark, leaky, and sections of the roof would occa-sionally collapse. Snakes, centipedes, ground squirrels, gophers, and other burrowing creatures often intruded. Settlers draped muslin from the ceilings in the vain attempt to keep dirt and mud from dropping onto the table and beds.

All the elements made homesteading in Pipestone county difficult. During summer droughts the thermometer might rise above 100 degrees and hover there for days on end, charring a pioneer's corn crop as effectively as a blowtorch. In winter, when temperatures sometimes plunged to 40 degrees below zero, horrendous snowstorms struck so suddenly that a man might lose his way between his house and barn and freeze to death. Summer hailstorms could be almost as destructive, flattening crops and often battering the pioneers themselves with hailstones. It reminded some of hearing the survivors of General Pickett's charge at Gettysburg relate their stories of facing canister shot. Old-timers spoke of hailstones the size and weight of croquet balls; of cattle being killed while grazing in open fields, as if they had been shot dead with cannon balls. An occasional Minnesota monsoon, a "gully washer," would grab the topsoil and carry much of it to the Gulf of Mexico in seven days.

And then there was the wind. It blew ceaselessly—winter and summer, night and day—averaging 16 miles an hour. It was a low, stupefying moan that drove many Pipestone sodbusters to distraction. A popular joke had it that, "When the wind stopped, the chickens fell over." In this land without trees the Rocky Mountains provided the nearest windbreak. About every decade a horrendous drought would grip the land. Dry, scorching winds would blow in from the southwest, further desiccating the land, and the ground would break open with two-inch wide cracks. "Black rollers" would wheel in from South Dakota and sandblast everything with soil as fine as baby talcum powder. "Between Amarillo and the North Pole," went a popular saying of my youth, "there is nothing to stop the wind but a barbed wire fence." Dust and dirt would pile up like drifting snow in a winter blizzard and completely bury a fence in a single night.

As a child I would often see tumbleweeds bouncing across the landscape, racing just ahead of the wind. Father said they blew in from South Dakota. One of his farmer patients told him dust had gotten in his flour dough and as a result his morning biscuits tasted like "they'd been made down in the ground at the bottom of a prairie-dog burrow." Many cottonwood trees that once shaded farms had long since died, their bark blown off, their trunks polished by the wind so that they looked like the silvery, stark "hanging trees" that I read about in Western novels. "When you get the feeling that the whole world can see you but no one is watching," mused an old settler, "you have come to the grasslands of North America." A few must have considered the irony in Walt Whitman's praise of the prairie states as "a newer garden of creation."

But the Pipestone sod-busting immigrants held on and survived. In time, spider webs of railroad lines followed. Within a few decades, this overwhelmingly horizontal world was punctuated by small cultural oases. Grain elevators, the great secular cathedrals of the plains, began to rise, standing stark white and red against the sky. The spires and towers of churches seemed almost toylike and puny against their bulk. The silos and the church spires together, however, testified to the basic needs—bread and spirit—of the human condition.

Norman Rockwell could have found a dozen character types for his *Saturday Evening Post* covers in Pipestone. Grays and browns rather than bright colors predominated, for we were too far north of the tropics for the intensity of tone and hues found further south. The drabness of the community was, fortunately, broken by almost a dozen private and public buildings of character. In spite of the poverty that existed at the turn of the century, Pipestone citizens had sacrificed greatly to create edifices with architectural embellishments that expressed the dignity of the institutions they housed and that honored the public realm of the city. The Roman Catholic and Presbyterian churches, the First National and the Pipestone National Bank, the Calumet hotel, the original city hall (now the Pipestone County Museum), the Carnegie public library (now Senior Center) and the public school were impressive structures. Most were built in Gothic or Romanesque style. They were lovingly constructed by stone masons who laboriously chiseled and laid the Sioux Quartzite and trimmed with the darker stone that came from the quarries of nearby Jasper.

Our county court house was especially impressive. From a plinth above an immense quartzite building of Renaissance Revival design, a giant gesturing woman, Lady Justice, kept her balance and surveyed her realm from a height of over 120 feet. The building's four-sided dome was covered with copper sheathing weathered to a beautiful greenish gray. No expense had been spared in its construction. With its immense windows, steps, doors, pillars, and massive foundation stones, it seemed to me to be a peaceful castle, a legal Gibraltar that stood for everything good, right, and true. Whenever I walked to Sunday School across the city block upon which it stood, I was awed by its presence. Intuitively I felt that it validated my existence and seemed to convey a message that I was part of something large, holy, and timeless. It gave me an historical connectedness to the past and the future. It seemed to sanction the American Experiment of which I dimly perceived I was a part.

Another unique feature of Pipestone was its poured-cement, silo-type water tower. (Standing 132 ft. high, it remains one of two—its near twin is in Brainerd—in existence.) It had a dozen small one-by-two-foot sized windows, that spiraled up the outside, revealing the existence of an internal staircase. Its barrel top looked like a Paul Bunyanesque, crenelated jelly glass. As a child I would watch for it when our family came home from the Twin Cities on highway 23. Shortly after we left Holland, at a distance of over five miles, it would gradually rise up from the horizon like a prairie light house. Like a medieval peasant beholding the spire of his cathedral from afar, I was inwardly comforted when I saw it. It was one of many talismans of my home and security.

Pipestone had a four-block long main street and four feeder-line railroads—the Great Northern, Milwaukee, Chicago Northwestern, and Rock Island. The buildings along Main Street had been built during the heady days of the late 1890s of quartzite, brick and brown stone. Most of them had two stories: commercial spaces below, professional offices and apartments above. But such was the constricted historical imagination of the founders that the streets were labeled just that, "streets" and "avenues," and were identified with numbers. With my love of history, I wished they had picked out presidents, scientists, explorers, and military heroes.

Our streets were bordered with green ash, hackberry, Chinese elm, Russian olive, and cottonwood trees, about the only species that could survive on the mere 26 inches of rain that fell during a year.

All of the pre-World War II neighborhoods in Pipestone had sidewalks. Because I loved to roller-skate, I now appreciate the fact that city fathers of that era had not been as tight as modern developers. I knew all the wide cracks and uneven slabs that were a skater's nightmare within a four-block area around our house. Shoe skates were unknown then, and would have been an impossible luxury even if they had existed. Along with my friends, I wore clamp-ons and carried my skate key on a string around my neck. When my skate came off or I misjudged an uneven slab, the only option was to bail out and take a tumble in the grass. Like all of my friends, I carry many old scars from my years of roller skating without helmets or elbow and knee pads.

Although I did not know it then, growing up in the 1920s and 1930s in Pipestone was ideal for adolescent maturation. I was too young to know that such a place might have cramped an adult's restless mind. Nor did I know that during my birth, Sinclair Lewis, writing about Sauk Centre in *Main Street, Babbit,* and *Arrowsmith,* was depicting the very people who would nurture, educate, and set me on the path of life. *The Baltimore Sun's* Henry Mencken, too, was calling my mentors "the booboisie." But for me, Pipestone meant stability, order, discipline, peace, protection, and love.

Fortunately the inter-war period was free from many movements and causes that can overstimulate and induce cynicism in those of tender sensitivity. Under Presidents Coolidge and Harding, America "returned to normalcy" after having pulled Europe's chestnuts out of the fire. We had fought the "war to end all wars." In microcosm, I was left alone just as our country, in macrocosm, wanted to be left in international isolation. The world of my childhood was devoid of class conflict, the din of TV, corporate-dictated two-year moves, easy divorce, one parent homes, race riots, four-letter words in public, nudity, Beavis and Butthead, latch-key kids, incest, drugs, battered women, abortion, gays and lesbians, illicit drugs, R- and X-rated movies, and all the other modern phenomena that serve today to make so many children fearful of their future. Men opened doors for women, rose when women entered a room, and did not eat with their hats on. "Stress" existed only as a dictionary word; "burn-out" simply didn't exist. Few people would have known what you meant if either word was used in conversation.

The language of the technological and information-age revolution was several decades away. Words, phrases, and acronyms such as "internet," "web site," "gigabyte," and "Ram" wouldn't exist until the 80's or, if they existed, they would have a totally different meaning. In my world a "mouse" was a rodent. A "byte" would have been corrected by my spelling teacher to "bite." Neither Father nor an engineer would have understood the word "virus" as presently used in medicine and computer science.

A stable, sacred and civil foundation supported life in Pipestone. Civic and Religious holidays—Lincoln's and Washington's birthdays, Easter, Memorial Day, Flag Day, July 4th, Labor Day, Armistice Day, Thanksgiving, and Christmas—punctuated a tribal life that was harmonized with the cosmic cycle. We lived at the behest of Nature's bounty. Most conversations began or ended with reference to the weather, for much of our behavior was governed by the rain, wind, and sun. Proximity to the elemental forces produced a humility born of human finitude. In spite of good soil and machinery, fertilizer and prayer, and labor from dawn until dusk, there was a great deal that lay outside of human control. Even the best of intentions and backbreaking labor could not guarantee a good crop. A modest fatalism was an antidote to any tendency toward hubris, for bounty or want, fertility or drought, cancer or longevity, was often a matter of grace rather than works.

There was, of course, a modicum of gossip. Critics of village life decry its openness to those with inquisitive souls, prying eyes and elephant ears. There were citizens, to be sure, who took delight in the misfortune of others and who relished passing on a juicy story over their morning coffee or the backyard fence. But Pipestone gossip was essentially democratic—unfortunate events happened to everyone sooner or later, and sin and tragedy were great social levelers. For every finger-wagging individual who accusingly said "tisk-tisk" there were three sympathetic souls who said, "That's too bad" or "What a shame." An individual or family could not hide very much—certainly not birth, sickness, death, divorce—from the all-seeing community eye. Gossip was one way for Pipestone folk to manifest their solidarity. The tales of Pipestone I remember from my youth were morally instructive: e.g., pride goes before a fall, and humor and hope are necessary to get through life. At bottom, gossip conveyed the body of common experience that provided guidance for our response to set-back, sickness, suffering, and death.

A couple of dozen church, professional and business leaders governed the life and manners of the community. The school board, the Kiwanis, the Masonic Order, the ministerial alliance, and the city council were the organs through which they exerted quiet control. Whatever evil might have been floating about in southwestern Minnesota at the time, they were determined to keep it out of Pipestone. Despite our belief that ours was one of the friendlier towns in Southwestern Minnesota, outsiders sometimes were treated like aliens, and differences in dress, accent, manners, or values were often regarded with suspicion.

From 1929-1939 unemployment and soup lines were tragic, omnipresent fixtures of urban life. Rural and small town folk suffered also, but were not as visible as the poor in metropolitan areas.

2. THE GREAT DEPRESSION: 1929-1939

THE VIEW FROM WASHINGTON, DC

The test of our progress is not whether we add more to the abundance of those who have much; it is whether we provide enough for those who have little.

Franklin D. Roosevelt, *Second Inaugural Address* (January 20, 1937)

From the age of three to thirteen years, my inner subjective history was shaped by the external events of the Great Depression. Before the onset of World War II, no episode of the previous hundred years except the Civil War so deeply impressed itself upon the thoughts and attitudes of Americans.

The Great Depression is one of the most neatly demarcated events in our history. It began in New York City on a series of days in October 1929, and ended decisively on December 7, 1941. The storm broke on what historians would later call "Black Thursday," October 24, 1929, when blocks of shares went down the river in lots of ten and twenty thousand. Five days later came the deluge, when investors, including bankers and legions of small-timers, could not meet margin calls. Before the plunge you could buy a dollar stock for ten cents; then, Wall Street was a casino without any federal safeguards in place. Westbrook Pegler called the "Coolidge prosperity" of spending and speculation, the "Era of Wonderful Nonsense." The economic Everest of 1929 was a mountain of credit on a molehill of money.

Everyone was hurt in the Crash—corporations, millionaires, bankers, taxi drivers, professors, farmers, coal miners, janitors, chorus girls. By creating a plausible vision of capitalist ruin, the Depression had made prophets of revolutionists who had been dismissed as crackpots only a few years before. The very Puritans who had seen the hand of God in the Coolidge prosperity now saw in the Crash the backhand of his judgment. Pulpits groaned with the forgotten warnings from Psalms 49:6-7: "They that trust in their wealth, and boast themselves in the multitude of their riches; None of them can by any means redeem his brother, nor give to God a ransom for him."

The financial gurus cautioned against panic. A senior partner at Morgan Trust opined that "there has been a little distress selling." A Boston investment trust placed an ad in *The Wall Street Journal* that read: "S-T-E-A-D-Y Everybody! Calm thinking is in order. Heed the words of America's greatest bankers." But they were whistling in the dark. Days turned into weeks and weeks into months and still production data spiraled downward. The drop in stock value was astonishing. Within a few weeks after the October 1929 Wall Street crash, investors had lost a sum approaching the national cost of fighting World War I.

In our era of wall-to-wall credit cards and guarantees that protect depositors, it's hard to convey the sheer panic that a nationwide bank run could cause in a time without those supports. In 1933 a depositor could lose his entire life savings if other customers got to tellers' windows first and the bank ran out of cash and had to close its doors. "Don't tell my mother what I'm doing," a banker in one Depression-era joke exclaimed. "She thinks I'm playing the piano in a sporting house." Later, the popular movie, *It's A Wonderful Life,* starring Jimmy Stewart dramatized the infectious terror of a full-blown bank run.

Across the nation factories stood idle. Steel stocks plummeted from ninety dollars a share down to nine; auto companies let half of their workers go. Newly finished skyscrapers stood empty, and having a secretary was deemed a luxury. The Depression blighted nearly everyone except the very poor who had nothing to lose. "Poverty is a soft pedal upon all branches of human activity," wrote H.L. Mencken, "not excepting the spiritual." Well-dressed men who told their wives they went out to look for night work were cadging dimes and quarters. The great and the small warmed their hands over fires in steel barrels and sold pencils and apples on street corners. The country was delighted to hear that John D. Rockefeller couldn't pay his servants—something he always did in cash—and had to ask them to wait a few days. A new class of men, the hoboes, "down on their luck" as the saying went, took up lodging in empty box cars and camped at railroad sidings. Truckers had nothing to truck. Farmers left their crops in the field because the cost of harvesting was more than the crop was worth. Banks were failing every hour of the day, and gold and currency were being withdrawn at an appalling rate. Millionaires-turned-paupers were jumping out of skyscrapers or turning on the gas jets.

Meanwhile legions of prophets sprang to the attack via the radio waves. Victims of this economic catastrophe needed to blame someone—

some group or malevolent cabal—for destroying their chance to achieve the American dream. A Roman Catholic priest, Father Charles Coughlin, at first a gushing supporter of FDR—who termed the New Deal as "Christ's Deal"—turned on the "Franklin Double-Crossing Roosevelt" when he reduced crop production in the midst of hunger. Millions of bewildered men and women sought solace and solutions in Coughlin's weekly paper, *Social Justice.* The messages of hate and suspicion Coughlin directed against political elites, blacks, and Jews stimulated thousands of letters each week to pour into his Shrine of the Little Flower in Detroit. Later Coughlin left Michigan for Louisiana and became a major outrider for the Kingfish, Huey Long. He itinerated throughout the south, even outdoing the fundamentalist shouters: "Let's pull down those hugh piles of gold until there shall be a real job, not a little old sow-belly, black-eyed-pea job, but a real spending-money, beefsteak-and-gravy, Chevrolet, Ford-in-the-garage, new suit, Thomas Jefferson, Jesus Christ, red-white-and-blue job for every man!" The money changers, Coughlin said, had been driven from the temple only to have taken up lodging in the White House. Yet many influential people claimed the priest as their confidant—Roosevelt, Joe Kennedy, Clare Booth Luce, Bing Crosby, Eddie Rickenbacker, and Ezra Pound among them—even if later on, they disavowed his support. In the 1930s, Coughlin achieved the kind of prominence that a more benign and circumspect Billy Graham would attain in the last three decades of the century.

In California a dentist, Dr. Francis E. Townsend, had concocted a get-rich-quick "Share Our Wealth" formula: let the printing presses hum and send every old-age pensioner a monthly check. Townsend speakers showed their bourgeois values when they said their program would make jobs for young people and take them out of their "cigarette-smoking, whiskey-drinking, road-side-petting hell of idleness." In New Orleans Huey Long showed signs of dictatorial ambitions until an assassin's bullet ended his life. The search for a Satan, whether in the form of elephant, donkey, or Wall Street octopus, was all too common in the early Depression years. Everyone, it seemed, had an opinion on who the villains were and had a sure-fire blueprint for prosperity.

But on the Great Plains we had to contend with an unending drought that continued through much of the 1930s. Unrelenting westerly winds withered the wheatlands and buried farms to their windowsills in vast drifts of topsoil and dust. On the worst days cars had to turn on their lights at high noon and the Knudtson home across the street was but a shadowy image. A wag told of a gopher that was digging a hole and when the wind died down, it found itself six feet in the air. Biblical "fundies" proclaimed the end of the world was at hand. Woody Guthrie's memorable song, "So Long, It's Been Good to Know Ya," conveyed a similarly pessimistic message, albeit in a secular mood. It was the decade of the "Dirty Thirties," of summer days when the western sky billowed with frightful "black rollers" that gyrated over land and sky. Father told mothers to wrap their infants in damp muslin during the days of "black blizzards."

In April of 1934 a giant dust cloud, black at the base and tan at the top, rose up out of the western plains and moved east. It left dead birds and rabbits in its wake and drifts six feet deep against the sides of barns. Those in its path thought the end of the world had indeed come and went to churches to await the Second Coming. A month later a dust storm blew all the way to New York City and blocked out the sun for five hours. Business men came home from work in an eerie half-light not unlike that of an eclipse. During winter we referred to the combination of snow and blowing dust as "snirt" storms. From the pulpits preachers declared that an Old Testament God had sent "the whirlwind by day and the darkness at noon" as His judgment against the hubris of over-planting the prairie land.

President Calvin Coolidge's successor, Herbert Hoover, the famous engineer who had fed Europe's destitute after World War I, was blamed for both the weather and the moribund economy. In *Gold Diggers of 1933,* Hollywood portrayed Hoover, the rich, and the upper social classes as prejudiced and foolish. In the movie, marching World War I soldiers were faded into jobless men marching on a soupline, as Joan Blondell sang:

Remember my forgotten man,
You put a rifle in his hand,
You sent him far away,
You shouted, "Hip Hurray!"
But look at him today.

Democrats piled all the blame on the President who once had been the most honored man in the world. His postwar relief organization had saved some 15 million Europeans from starvation. "I wish we could make him President of the United States," FDR had said of Hoover in 1920. "There could not be a better one."

Hoover's bitter legacy included "Hoovervilles"—shanty towns of tin and wood—along the rivers of our large cities. Homeless folk on park benches tried to keep warm with newspapers, known as "Hoover blankets." And a "Hoover flag" was an empty pocket, turned inside out as a sign of destitution. People laughed over the story of hitch-hikers who zoomed across the country in five days by displaying the sign, "Give me a lift or I'll vote for Hoover." In the 1920s America's railroad companies had purchased 1,300 locomotives a year. In 1932 they didn't buy a single one. Of the 14,000 residents of Donora, Pennsylvania, a steel town, exactly 277 had jobs. Toward the end of 1932 banks were foreclosing on a thousand homes a day.

Trying to find ways to end the Depression, Hoover often worked 18 hours at a stretch; during that time he lost 25 pounds and his hair turned white. But deficit financing was anathema to him, as it was to most economists at that time. Hoover was committed to free enterprise, self-help, and the goal of a balanced budget, but the situation seemed to have outrun those remedies. When he left office there were 13,000,000 unemployed and in the bread lines. Intellectuals were increasingly supportive of Karl Marx's critique of capitalism in *The Communist Manifesto:* "Pauperism develops more rapidly than population and wealth." The Depression was a war whose casualties received no eulogies, medals, or parades and achieved no final victory.

Were we on the brink of revolution? We will never know, because a redeemer from a highly cushioned life in New York took over the presidential helm in 1933. With a pedigree from Groton and Harvard and an income to match, Franklin Delano Roosevelt was a million light years away from the life and death of the average American family.

For several dizzy years America had a flirtation with socialism and Roosevelt was an administrative dictator, albeit a benevolent one. The poliomyelitis that had struck him at age 40 (he had a burly upper body, a bull-like neck, but stick-like legs), seemed not to have affected his energy level: in a frenzy of activity he established the Works Project Administration (WPA), the the National Recovery Act (NRA), the Tennessee Valley Authority (TVA), the Civilian Conservation Corps (CCC), Social Security, and attempted to pack the Supreme Court, and more. At last there was action and movement rather than political stasis and hand-wringing in the nation's capital. The WPA even had a Federal Art Project that employed 5,000 artists across the country at a salary of $95 a month. They created murals, sculptures and paintings, taught community art classes to millions, and produced 2 million posters from 35,000 designs at a cost of about a dime each. The murals depicted workers and farmers, usually with heads that looked as if they had been carelessly carved out of soap, and with bulging muscles reminiscent of the sinews of lions and bulls in Assyrian bas-reliefs.

Roosevelt's nasal voice, his up-angled cigarette holder, his sense of humor, his dog Fala, and especially his activist wife, Eleanor, drove conservatives wild. During his famous "fireside chats," his voice—languid one moment, theatrical the next—dripped with the accents of Groton, Harvard, and centuries of blue blood. Yet no president had ever communicated better with ordinary people. Roosevelt had a flair for homely analogies, such as comparing Lend-Lease aid to Britain with loaning your neighbor a garden hose to put out a house fire.

Finally, the gloom of the Hoover era began to lift and many began to believe the Democratic campaign quatrain of 1932 was more than just a song:

> Happy days are here again,
> The skies above are clear again,
> Let us sing a song of cheer again,
> Happy days are here again!

Roosevelt had correctly understood the national mood. "The country needs," he said in 1932, "bold persistent experimentation. It is common sense to take a method and try it. If it fails, admit it frankly and try another. *But above all, try something.*" He was simply acting on the advice of Alexis de Tocqueville, who said in *Democracy in America,* "I cannot but fear that America may arrive at such a state as to regard every new theory as a peril, every innovation as an irksome toil, every social improvement as a stepping-stone to revolution, and so refuse to move altogether for fear of being moved too far."

Roosevelt used the presidency to champion the people's needs. He knew, as did Aristotle, that poverty is the parent of revolution and crime. "Nothing is more dangerous than discontinued labour," warned Victor Hugo. "It is a habit lost. A habit easy to abandon, difficult to resume." But capitalists despised FDR, even though he saved their system by deliberately failing to balance the books. In the end his was a revolution fueled not by violence but by bookkeeping and lawmaking, a revolution in which the power of politics replaced the power of business. Still, after 10 years Roosevelt's goal of full employment in peacetime still eluded him, as it has every government, whatever its ideological stripe. In 1939 there were still ten million unemployed.

The fusillades of H. L. Mencken attacked the triumphant FDR, whose whiff of bogus collectivism filled him with disgust. FDR was the "Führer" and the "Quack," who surrounded himself by a "rabble of impudent nobodies" whose appeals to class envy and hatred had turned the government into a "milk-cow with a 25 million teats." Roosevelt evoked fits of paranoia in the rich and the conventional. The following are a few of the epithets they used: a Svengali, a Little Lord Fauntleroy, a pledge-breaker, a socialist, a tyrant, the Violator, the Embezzler, a simpleton, a shallow aristocrat, a Fascist, a Communist, a "subjector of the human spirit," a modern Political Juliet who made "love to the people from a White House balcony."

A number of economists believe the Great Escape from the decade-long Great Contraction was retarded by FDR himself. Roosevelt pleaded for private investment to stimulate the economy, yet his rhetoric undercut potential investors' confidence. Business leaders sincerely believed the government was in evil hands, preparing the way for socialism, communism, or some other variety of anti-Americanism. Roosevelt had railed against the "economic royalists," a "new industrial dictatorship," and the "magnates of organized money." In 1936 he boasted that "organized money" unanimously detested him and declared, *I welcome their hatred.*

But Hitler did what FDR could not. The great irony of the Depression is that Hitler saved the reputation of the New Deal and the Roosevelt presidency. When the first war orders came in from the British and the French, the steel mills began to belch smoke again. Unemployment virtually disappeared as conscription pulled more than 12 million potential workers into the armed forces. Soon, the breadlines were a thing of the past.

THE VIEW FROM PIPESTONE, MINNESOTA

Neither *The Pipestone Star* nor *The Pipestone Leader* took notice of the Wall Street Crash of October 24, 1929. Caught up in city and county issues, the heartland proved to be provincial and insular. But week after week, month after month, relentless and ominous as a Sioux drumbeat sounding the gathering of its warriors, the Depression droned on. On many Saturdays in the early 30s, hundreds gathered on the steps of the court house for a farm sale. Indeed, *The Leader* stayed in business during the early 30s largely by printing legions of farm foreclosure notices. Throughout the Depression farm values plummeted. In 1935 a beautiful quarter- section of land (160 acres) could be had for $3,800. Insurance companies, not banks, held farm mortgages at that time.

During the winter of 1932, militant farmers, organized by the toughest agricultural union, the Farmer's Holiday Association, prevented dozens of foreclosure sales. Phone lines were cut to help keep bids low. In Woodbury County, Iowa, the audience held the bid for a farm to

$11.75, and then forced the holder of the mortgage to sign a note accepting that amount as settlement. After stopping a dairy truck, Holiday protesters slathered butter over U.S. Highway 75; passing vehicles would hit the patch and slide smoothly into a ditch. Chicken farmers were getting as little as three cents a dozen for their eggs. In early 1933 an Iowa farmer named August Weger sent five calves via rail to Chicago. Instead of a check he got back a bill for $1.98; the selling price of the livestock didn't cover the cost of shipping and feed.

"Farmers are ready to do anything," the president of the Wisconsin Farmer's Union told a Senate committee. "I almost hate to express it, but I honestly believe that if some of them could buy airplanes, they would come down here to Washington to blow you fellows all up."

After his re-election in 1934, Minnesota Governor Floyd B. Olson suggested what was needed was "not just a new deal, *but a new deck."* No one doubted his radicalism after he gave the Farmer-Labor party's convention speech in March, 1935. "Now I am frank to say," he declared, "that I am not a liberal. I enjoy working on a common basis with liberals for their platforms, but I am not a liberal. I am what I want to be—*I am a radical.* I want a definite change in the system. I am not satisfied with tinkering. I am not satisfied with patching. I am not satisfied with hanging a laurel wreath upon burglars and thieves and pirates and calling them code authorities or something else."

It was tough to be a sheriff then. During a farm auction a noose was sometimes hung from a barn door. At other times a phalanx of grizzled and steely-faced farmers might press the lawman into a corner and suggest that he call off the sale. On other days a festive spirit prevailed and a bloodless "penny auction" took place. Even the auctioneer might play along:

"How much am I bid for this horse?"

"Three cents!"

"I'm bid three cents. Do I hear a higher bid?"

"Five cents!"

"Hey guys," the smiling autioneer might say, "Don't you know that I'm working on commission?"

When the bidding reached fifteen cents or so, the crowd might chant, "Sell It, Sell It," or "Close the Bidding!" Afterwards, the auctioned items would be returned to the owner. The heavy hand of social censure effectively dampened the ardor of many an outsider bent on making a killing off a farmer down on his luck.

When a farm was repossessed, families were often allowed to stay on the premises if they paid a nominal rent.

Even when crops were good, grasshoppers were an omnipresent threat. Earl Mahoney, an octogenarian and long-time Pipestone resident, reflected, "I personally have witnessed a horde of grasshoppers completely destroy a 40-acre field of corn in two hours. When they were through, the field looked like a field of broomsticks. They darkened the sky so that I could stare directly at the sun without sunglasses." Some claimed "hoppers" ate the paint off houses and clothes off the clotheslines. The government furnished poisoned bran for 25 cents a bag. Farmers were supposed to dig ditches around their farms and lace them with the poison. Nothing really worked. "When one died," went the saying, "a thousand came to the funeral." Chickens ate hoppers until they loathed them, though on most farms it was hoppers or nothing.

As the Depression deepened, barter increasingly took the place of money transactions. No one gave credit; a merchant would have had no way to replace his stock had he done so. Mr. Dibble of the Chevrolet garage would often accept a team of horses in partial payment for a car. If they were in bad shape, he would put them on a farm to flesh them out and have them shod before putting them up for auction. Merchants accepted corn in trade, but since it was only worth ten cents a bushel they would burn it in place of coal. In the early 1930s Father entered into an agreement with Mr. Bowman, our Methodist Sunday School Superintendent. He purchased a Guernsey cow known as a "good milker" which Bowman housed, fed, and milked. It supplied enough milk for both of our families and Bowman sold the surplus to other households. It was a creative, win-win solution for both families. Through it all, there was a sense of solidarity that grew out of common suffering. When President Roosevelt declared his March 1933 "bank holiday," Mr. Fellman, president of the Pipestone National Bank, secretly brought the payroll of the Chevrolet garage to Mr. Dibble so that his workers could be paid. In spite of hard times, crime hit an all-time low and most people did not lock their homes or cars.

The Great Northern railroad canceled two trains in 1931. In 1932 the salaries were cut for the sheriff, county superintendent, county attorney, highway engineer, and other public officials. The public school teachers joined them in taking further reductions in 1933 and 1934. Even Cupid's arrows went astray as the Depression increased—the number of marriage licenses dropped from 92 in 1930 to only 40 in 1931. Pipestone's premiere clothing store, Geyermans, went into bankruptcy in 1934.

Now and then militancy surfaced. There were occasions when children would climb on top of coal cars and throw chunks of coal down to their parents. In 1935 a band of farmers drove starving horses and cattle up the steps of the capital in St. Paul to dramatize the pathology that stalked the land.

Prices seemed reasonable—ladies' silk dresses were advertised at $7.95, men's wool shirts at 87 cents and men's suits and overcoats at $9.95. A dime got you into a movie matinee. In 1937 Father charged $20.00 for a tonsillectomy; Dr. Fred Yseth, our dentist, billed $9.00 for a gold crowned tooth; and two teeth could be filled for $3.00 Two years after the Crash, the price of winter wheat had plummeted from $1.37 to 25 cents a bushel. Reasonable or not, however, few people had the money to buy.

Salaries ranged from $27.50 to $35 a week for secretaries, mechanics, or newspaper typesetters for a 48 to 60 hour week. Of course, there was no medical coverage or vacation with pay. Mahoney remembers that most people were grateful to have a job and understood that their employers worked longer hours than they did in order to keep their businesses in the black. Although Plato held that poverty was the "parent of meanness and viciousness," the Roman philosopher, Lucan, believed privation was the "mother of manhood." While there's probably support for both views, most citizens of Pipestone retained their civility during the Depression.

Relief committees were formed to receive and distribute food, clothing, and wood for winter fuel. Indians were put to work on the roads. Farmers who had a team of horses were paid $1.50 for a day of work improving the roadbed. Truckloads of potatoes were given gratis to the needy and baseball games were played for a "charity fund." On occasion Kiwanis members dined on bread and milk and each member gave 35 cents to the Pipestone Relief Fund. Pipestone was a microcosm of what was happening in the Washington, DC, macrocosm.

Pipestone county always contributed its share of the 84,000 men who worked in the Civilian Conservation Corps (CCC) from 1933 through 1942 at 112 camps across Minnesota. "All the workers did menial jobs," reflected Earl Mahoney, "but they accomplished many projects that benefitted the community." Paid $30 a month ($25 had to be sent home) the "boys" as they were called, were furnished with room, board, and clothing (often old Army uniforms from World War I). They planted millions of trees; constructed museums and restored historic buildings; improved state parks; built bridges, fish-rearing ponds, and lookout towers; dug wells and septic tanks; fought fires; contoured land; and more. Their work changed the face of the nation and brought badly needed hope to legions of the depressed. Decades later author Jim Mitchell, reflecting on his CCC experience in *A Nickel for Bread*, mused

"I am puzzled as to why our nation has not embraced the Corps' basic concept: universal service as a down payment for citizenship." Conservatives (even *Chicago Tribune* founder Colonel Robert McCormick) and liberals lauded the program.

The Works Project Administration (WPA) workers built some beautiful cut stone quartzite bridges and the dam at Split Rock Creek State Park, just south of Pipestone. The project created an artificial lake, thus partly compensating for the fact that the glaciers did not leave our county with a natural one. The W.P.A. masons also built our municipal swimming pool, which is now on the Historic Preservation Register. These programs put money into circulation so that families could buy groceries and pay their bills. Nevertheless, because some men had poor work habits, I parroted Father's scorn of such "make-work" projects and said that the WPA stands for "We Piddle Around."

Those on welfare—the Depression term was "on relief"—tried to hide this humiliating fact from their neighbors. But there was no mistaking government surplus food, which came unlabeled. By not having labels, those boxes of prunes, rice, and cornmeal and cans of grapefruit juice shouted "government handout" as clearly and as embarrassingly as if they'd been stamped with huge red letters. Children who pulled their wagons home from the store with such commodities were told by their parents to cover the food with their jackets so as not to be publically shamed as Pipestone "no-account" failures.

Social activities were limited so there was little pressure for students to outdress each other. Everyone had a dress or shirt and pair of trousers to wear to class; those who had a warm wool jacket and a sturdy pair of shoes as well felt fortunate. A ticket to the movies cost 35 cents, popcorn, 5 cents, admission to the Playmor dance pavilion, 10 cents. "With such high prices," mused Earl Mahoney, "we were very selective about who we asked for a date." With gasoline at 20 cents a gallon, few families could afford to go for a Sunday drive in the country. Softball was popular because an entire team could be outfitted for a modest fee, but everyone was expected to chip in 10 cents to help pay for the lights.

A popular, though probably apocryphal, story of the era illustrates something of people's attitudes about stretching a dollar. It seems an FBI man had confiscated a counterfeit $20 bill and asked that the hotel manager place it in the safe until he left in the morning. The manager needed some cash to pay for repairs on his car. So, not knowing the bill was bogus, he borrowed it. The garage owner accepted the bill and immediately went to the grocery store and used it to buy food for his family. The grocer used the fake twenty to pay a bill at the hardware store, whose owner turned around and purchased some things from a traveling salesman using the same $20 bill. The salesman checked in at the hotel and paid for his room with the counterfeit bill. The hotel manager finally put the bill in the safe and returned it to the FBI in the A.M. Everyone used a single counterfeit bill to transact $100 worth of business without using legal tender.

For the most part, the Depression brought out reserves of altruism and generosity, but occasionally it called forth hubris and meanness. One day a neighbor asked one of my friends what he had for lunch. "Macaroni and cheese," he replied. "Is that right?" she replied as her nose seemed to lift a bit toward the heavens. "We had fried chicken at our table." Fortunately such remarks were rare because even well-to-do folk felt some compulsion to "talk poor."

One cannot read the record without an admiration for those who lived through the 1930s, the "dark night of the soul" of America. "Because the future seemed so uncertain," remembered Earl Mahoney, "we were carefree. We simply knew that things had to get better." Few people thought of retirement; poverty was so pervasive that most assumed they'd have to work until they were taken by the Grim Reaper. In spite of everything, humor did not die. "I went through the 30s with nothing," reflected an old codger, "and still have most of it left." An elevator had a sign—"Shelled Corn, Eight Cents Per Bushel: Ear Corn, 10 Cents Less!" The worthies in a local tavern loved to tell the story about a man who broke his back trying to carry 10 cents worth of oats. But I was too young, innocent, and protected, to know what was happening across the land. Much later I came to realize that my community had been made up of unheralded, stolid and strong people, citizens with great moral reserve, who never lost hope when want and penury stalked the land.

During the dust storms of the '30s, 1,400 counties in 22 states were "burned out, blowed out, and boiled out." A Kansas woman wrote in her diary:

My heart seemed to leap into my throat; I felt sick and weak. I went back into the house, hastily covered the table with newspapers and an old cloth, covered the water pail, covered all the unwashed cooking utensils, made my bed and spread an old denim comfort over it; next I put on an old stocking cap to protect my hair, an old jacket to comfort my shaking body, and sat down by the kitchen range with my feet on the oven door. The room soon filled with dust haze through which the coal-oil lamp made a pale light, and for the first and only time during the dust storms, I abandoned myself to an orgy of weeping.

I pose before a spinning top for my second birthday, October 10, 1928. It was almost exactly one year before the beginning of the Great Depression. My romper suit and white stockings were characteristic of that time.

3. CHILDHOOD MEMORIES

Oh would I were a boy again,
  When life seemed formed of sunny years,
And all the heart then knew of pain
  Was wept away in transient tears!
When every tale Hope whispered then,
  My fancy deemed was only truth.
Oh, would that I could know again,
  The happy visions of my youth.

Last Song, Mark Lemon

My memory bank is a chest of golden treasures—the nostalgic reminiscences of my childhood. It was a time:

… When the acrid yet sweet perfume of burning leaves hung thick in the fall evening air.
… When people didn't lock their doors at night.
… When, upon hearing a sound in the sky, we pointed and shouted excitedly, *"Look, it's an airplane!"*
… When every boy had a crew-cut, butch, flat-top, or buzz haircut.
… When Burma-Shave signs ("If Necking On The Highway Is Your Sport—Trade In Your Car For A Davenport") marched alongside our roads.
… When children weren't herded off to "organized" activities, but instead they had to plumb their own creativity.
… When the passage of time was punctuated by church bells on Sunday and the town's 10 P.M. curfew whistle each night.
… When bib overalls, the universal dress for boys, were handed down from brother to brother and not artificially "aged."
… When milk came in glass bottles and, if left out and frozen, would wear a paper hat five inches above the bottle.
… When summer evenings were filled with children's games: "pumb-pumb, pull-away," "red light, green light," "kick-the-can," "hop-scotch," and "capture the flag."

... When we fell asleep and awakened to the gentle cooing of mourning doves.

... When crickets serenaded us at the end of a hot August day.

... When the entire town gathered in the high school auditorium on Friday night to cheer on the basketball team.

... When the changeover from knickers to long pants was the ritual recognition that a boy had reached adolescence.

... When upon walking to school we avoided stepping on sidewalk cracks, lest we "break our mother's back."

Our home was a substantial four-bedroom frame edifice on a 200 foot lot on the southwest edge of town, a block and a half from the hospital, easy walking distance for Father to make his evening rounds. The house was cream color with brown trim and stained green shingles that substituted for siding on the attic gables. A broken cement driveway led up a gentle rise close to the north side of the house before it spread into the apron in front of a detached double garage. Three seven-by-three-foot heavy doors had been hinged together and moved accordion-like to the side on rusty rollers. Only Father could move them.

In spite of an impressive exterior, the house had its share of problems. The basement was always damp and regularly flooded during a heavy rain. One corner was walled off and contained a cistern. During a rain we were to wait ten minutes, then run outside to turn the downspout levers, allowing the water to enter the cistern. The wait allowed the rain fall to flush the topsoil blown in from South Dakota from the roof and gutters so that it would not end up in the cistern. Even so, the cistern had to be cleaned periodically. We would climb over the edge, drop into the black void, and shovel the accumulated muck into buckets to be hauled out to the garden. No one had water softeners. Mother used the soft, pale brown rain water to wash clothes in the Maytag wringer machine that stood before the double, dark gray laundry tubs. Invariably damp and dark, to my child's mind, the basement took on the character of a depressive medieval dungeon.

A basement recreation room contained a ping pong table where I began learning the skill that ultimately would lead to a championship in the sport at Hamline University.

At the center of the basement—between the washing machine, recreation room, stairs, furnace, and old coal bin—stood a wood-burning stove. It was Mother's altar for her summer canning ritual. During peak season its black stovepipe would glow cherry red as the unending garden bounty found its way to the basement. Almost every wall was lined from floor to ceiling with shelving. Quart jars were filled during the summer, only to be gradually emptied during the following nine months. The Thanksgiving hymn stanza, "all is gathered in, ere the winter storms begin," had real poignancy for my family. I felt good running down the basement steps before supper to get a quart jar of food that I had helped prepare months earlier.

My older brother, Bob, and I roomed together in the southwest bedroom. Its modest 8-by-10 foot size necessitated double-decker bunks. Father had wisely bought a New England rock maple set of fine quality. Because of my recurring nightmares, I was relegated to the bottom bunk lest I leap out of the top bunk and injure myself. A desk, bookshelf, and chest completed the bedroom ensemble. We kept our minuscule Depression-genre wardrobe of faded but clean clothes in a tiny closet whose cramped ceiling was tucked against the roof line. By the time we reached the eighth grade we had to stoop over like the Hunchback of Notre Dame in order to enter our closet.

Nevertheless, by Depression-era standards, the house was spacious even for a family with five children. Walls were lath and plaster and the trim and built-in buffet displayed a generous use of dark oak. There were front and rear entryways, a side door, a large kitchen, a half-bath, and living and dining rooms. A screened-in front porch was wonderful for sleeping on hot summer nights. Air conditioning was unknown. During the summer we simply opened all the windows in the evening and closed them and drew the shades in the early morning to keep the house cool. We knew a lot about passive heating and cooling and energy conservation long before they became fashionable.

The back yard was bordered by the garage, lilac bushes, and a buckthorn hedge. It was our private bower that sheltered us from the prying eyes of the neighbors. Flagstones of quartzite and pipestone led to a large grape arbor, where we ate supper on hot evenings. Other paths curved behind the garage to a rock garden surrounding a 10' by 6' kidney-shaped pool. Three feet in depth, it held plantings of cattails and water lilies, as well as a few sunfish and goldfish that rarely lasted long. Transplanted Moccasin flowers and other wild flora did well in the shady, moist soil under a Wealthy apple tree next to the pool. A running hose atop a five-foot rocky structure at the back of the pool created a miniature waterfall. Wren houses, a twelve-unit martin house, honeysuckle and spirea bushes, blue and black spruce, a sweet-smelling catalpa tree, apple and flowering plum trees, and other flora completed the secluded Benjamin Eden.

Behind the garage was a tall but non-descript box elder tree. It was an ugly thing, not at all comely and symmetrical like our evergreens, elms, and hackberries. I had nailed several boards in sturdy crotches to form a seat 35 feet above the ground. It was a leafy womb to which I could retreat, dream, and indulge my fantasy life. Sheltered from the world and with a green apple in my hand, I could ponder the future and have a conversation with my soul. I would occasionally talk to my favorite tree, it being my only audience. Of course, the box elder never answered back, but sometimes I had a feeling that it was trying its darndest to say something to me. And I knew that if it could talk it might have said something like: "Please don't nail anymore wooden seats on my limbs," "Water me well during the hot August days," and "Please don't ever move away and leave me."

Labor-saving technology was quite limited, so normal household chores—preparing meals, doing laundry, cleaning—were enormously time-consuming, especially for larger families. Like many upper middle-class families we addressed this issue by employing a series of "hired girls." After being subjected to a physical examination by Father to make sure our family would not be infected with some hidden disease, a new girl moved into a small bedroom with a half bath just off our kitchen. My parents wanted someone who had "no highfalutin' ideas," a "no-nonsense type of girl," who "knew what life was all about." For as long as a girl was with us, she was treated "like family," celebrating our good fortune and weeping with us in grief.

Like Thomas Jefferson, Father considered the farm the ideal incubator for the cultivation of character and discipline. Ethnically, his preference favored either the Dutch or Germans. "You could do worse than to marry a Dutch farm girl, Neb(my family nickname)," went his common refrain, "She won't run off to Hollywood on you." Biology was destiny. It was unnatural and foolish to think a woman could escape it.

Given their limited options, our hired girls enjoyed a good life—board and room, free health care, paid vacation time, certain days and evenings off, and, considering those times, an adequate salary. It was their substitute for college, a rite of passage for poor girls between leaving home and getting married. I remember Ann, Alice, Jean, and Anesha. They had plenty to do because the Benjamin babies, six of them, came like clockwork, every two and a half years. (Although I never had the courage to ask how they did it, I think my parents could have taught modern couples a lot about family planning.)

Food preparation, cleaning, sewing, mending, canning and other chores went on from dawn to dusk. Depression-era Pipestone did not have deli markets, fast-food emporiums, super markets, or yellow pages where goods and services in almost infinite variety could be found and ordered via the telephone. I never remember Mother reading a book during daylight hours; there wasn't time. She made our own laundry soap from scraps of fat and lard. Laundry and diapers were done in the Maytag wringer washer, hand-rinsed twice, carried up the basement stairs, and hung on a five-wire clothes line in the back yard. The wringer was a fearsome thing that could break a lot of fingers or wrists if you weren't careful. On sub-zero days the steam would billow off the clothes as they were carried outside and pinned to wire lines. They came back freeze-dried and stiff as boards. Miracle fabrics such as the polyesters used in drip-dry clothes were unknown. We had only cotton and wool. From my earliest years, I was taught how to press my pants by putting a damp cloth over the legs. wore a freshly starched white shirt every day. (They were double-starched: a thin starch was used for the body of the shirt, a thicker one for cuffs and collars.) All cottons to be ironed were sprinkled with soft rainwater, rolled up, and left for a day or so to ensure that the dampness was uniform throughout. Every cotton item was ironed or "mangled." Most of the neighborhood women thought Mother was too fastidious because she ironed or mangled T-shirts, sheets, towels, wash cloths and even socks. She could not deny her German genes.

In autumn, the most arduous job was putting up the storm windows. We would lug the heavy six-by-three-foot frames with their thick panes of glass up from the basement, hose them off and wipe them down under Mother's supervision. "I don't want to look through dirt all winter," she would exclaim. We would match the numbers inscribed on the window frames with those on the storm windows and then begin the installation. (If a window was warped or had been repainted, sometimes it wouldn't fit and we'd have to shave the sides with a wood plane.) The second-floor windows were hardest. We'd push them up a long ladder; then it took courage and brute strength to grasp the bottom of the storm and lean far enough back from the ladder to get the upper brackets to catch on the hangers at the top of the frames. After the storm windows were up, we would stuff rags into any cracks to keep the wind and the Dakota-born soil from the "black blizzards" out of the house.

In the spring we would roll up the rugs, carry them outside, and beat a year's accumulated dust out of them. The curtains came down, were washed, starched, and stretched on frames and dried on the south side of the house.

In the winter quilt frames often dominated the living room for a week at a time. Old wool suits, coats, skirts, and pants were cut into pieces, sewn together, then placed against batting and tufted into place to finish a patchwork quilt. Other garments were cut into strips, rolled into balls and crocheted into oval rugs. It was fun to guess the origin of a color: "There's my pants...is that Aunt Bessie's coat?...that's Bob's old jacket...where did that red and blue piece come from?"

In the winter Bob and I would turn off the radiator in our bedroom and open the window to prove we came from hardy Anglo-Saxon stock. Some mornings there would be six inches of snow on the floor.

The bathroom was always warm because the chimney came up one side. When we were very young sometimes our family would collectively dress there. I was amazed at how adroitly Mother could put on her undergarments beneath her night gown. The common bathroom was an admirable, if low key, medium of sexual education. Now, with our two or three bathroom homes, children rarely see their parents undressed or partially clothed. My parents were always modest, but their behavior indicated a matter-of-factness, not a shameful or a puerile interest in the body and its functions. The bathroom door lock never functioned until Bob fixed it years later in preparation for bringing Betty, his wife-to-be, home. He knew that neither his Father nor his brothers respected closed doors.

Father exhibited a physician-induced frankness about the body. "What if Mrs. Stuven sees you?" went Mother's reprimand as she quickly pulled down the shades as he undressed in front of the window. "If she's a lady, she won't look," was his retort. "And if she's not, *I don't give a damn.*" However mild, it was one of the few times I remembered him using an expletive.

Dr. John Benjamin (center) and his wife, Elizabeth (at his left), pose with their family at their "Fairy Glen" homestead near Hutchinson in 1894. Robert is seated at the left.

Martha Jane ("Mattie") Benjamin and her seven children several years after the death of her husband, Robert. My father stands next to his sister, Bessie, in the back row. I never knew my paternal grandparents.

4. English Roots: From Barrington to Benjamin

Death is in such strange contradiction to life that it is no matter for wonder that we recoil from it, and turn to remembrances, and find recompense in perceiving that those we have loved live in our memories as intensely as if they were still before our eyes.

The Bending of the Bough, George Moore

Father always bragged about the quality of his ancestors—the Tribe of Benjamin as he put it—forgetting the wisdom of Plutarch that "It is indeed a desirable thing to be well descended; but the glory belongs to our ancestors." However, because his parents died before I was born, I was deprived of one set of grandparents. Robert Gleave Benjamin (1854-1906) died of heart failure when Father was thirteen. Robert's wife, Martha Jane McBroom (1864-1923) died of pneumonia when Father was thirty. Father's grandfather, Dr. John Benjamin (1823-1902), was a graduate of London Medical College, although he was more interested in homesteading, farming, and church organizing than in practicing medicine. (Such was the knowledge of medicine at the time that his training, probably taken at a proprietary school, lasted no more than six to twelve months.)

According to the lore of the Tribe, during the 18th century Dr. John's ancestors had carried the impressive and lordly name of *Barrington*. As nominal and inactive Anglicans, they had been converted to Methodism by one of John Wesley's lay preachers, legions of whom itinerated throughout the United Kingdom. Historians believe that the Wesleyan movement saved England from the kind of violent upheaval that later devastated France by giving dignity, discipline and status to the underclass that served as the human fodder of the Industrial Revolution.

One of the converted Barringtons, possibly Dr. John's grandfather, therefore, petitioned his magistrate for a Biblical name that symbolized his new spiritual estate. They agreed on Benjamin as a close match, but the name change subjected future generations to periodic queries as to whether the Benjamins had Hebrew origins.

Two years after John landed in Boston, his betrothed, Elizabeth Garner of Flint, North Wales, joined him and they were married on June 5, 1851. In 1855 they moved to Rockford, Illinois, and started a furniture business. Whereas the public story has it that he was wiped out by the financial panic of 1856-57, the private account suggests that his partner absconded with his money.

Dr. John came to Hutchinson, Minnesota, by ox-cart in the spring of 1857 and lived in a tent until his log cabin was completed. An older brother had been an alcoholic, and Dr. John had told Elizabeth that "we will go to the new country and travel so far west that there won't be any pubs." He quickly became known as one of the leading citizens of his new community. Dr. John knew the Sioux chief, Little Crow, and prescribed medicine for his family as well as inviting him for dinner on several occasions. During the Sioux uprising in 1862, Little Crow warned John and his family that he could not control his "young bloods" and urged them to seek safety in the Hutchinson stockade.

Thanks to the subsequent warning of another friendly Indian, Good Charlie, John and Elizabeth and their three children vacated their homestead, "Fairy Glen," just in time. From the stockade, Elizabeth could see the Sioux dancing around her burning home, some clad in her own garments, many of which she had brought from England. Some of the marauders were Indians she had nursed and fed during the previous winter. Everything was lost—either burned or stolen. The frontier aphorism seemed true: "In peace, their best friend; in war, their worst enemy."

Life in the stockade lasted two weeks. It was crowded, food was scarce, and sanitation was inadequate. Dr. John was in charge of a make-shift hospital and managed to save twenty-three wounded men from the battle of Acton without loss of "life or limb." Elizabeth, too, cared for the ill, stopping long enough to give birth to a daughter. Sadly, they lost a two year old son to "intestinal troubles."

Over 800 settlers were massacred during the uprising. Three months later an observer watched as 38 of the "savages swung into eternity" from a Mankato, Minnesota scaffold. Five times that number might have been executed had not the Civil War absorbed the attention of the government. Through it all, the feeling of Dr. John and his family toward the Indians remained humane, compassionate, and forgiving.

Years later the interaction of the Sioux with Dr. John, and with legions of other farmers, was recreated in the Great Seal of Minnesota. A straw-hatted ploughboy plows up the prairie while a red man gallops off into the sunset, thus symbolizing the triumph of agriculture over nomadism. The motto above the seal, *L'etoile du Nord*, is French for "The Star of the North." I suspect Dr. John would have rendered it simply as "Northern Toil." An updated Great Seal today might show a farmer in a pickup driving into the setting sun as a suburbanite parks in front of a new K-Mart.

Later, after Little Crow was killed and some Hutchinson boys were mutilating his ears and nostrils with firecrackers, Dr. John recorded in his diary:

> These indignities I considered inhuman, and with the assistance of Mr. Sharp we buried the body in an open grave and covered it with gravel. A cavalry officer, using his saber, dug into the grave and severed the head from the body. I was informed by my children of his actions and hastened to meet him and inquired his authority for this act. He replied that it was none of my (expletive) business.

Family photos of the Benjamin clan homesteaders remind one of Grant Wood's "American Gothic." The images depict people for whom laughter came hard, for whom life was hardly a lark. One picture shows Dr. John as a rotund gentleman with a white Colonel Sanders-type beard sitting in a rocking chair surrounded by his grown children. Father was fond of quoting his grandfather's comment to his mother: "Mattie, Mattie, what a wonderful thing you and Robbie have done! Five boys! Five sons! My name and the Tribe of Benjamin will never die out in the New Country!" He neglected to mention his two granddaughters, Bessie and Blanche. Dr. John was not unlike an Old Testament patriarch for, in an agricultural setting, children were an important measure of wealth. He agreed with William Burke that "people will not look forward to posterity who never look backward to their ancestors."

Upon the death of grandfather Robert, my grandmother, Martha, was left as the sole guardian of and provider for seven children aged one to seventeen years. A somber mood settled over the family as they faced a fearsome future. A wealthy brother from Chicago, Walter McBroom, wanted to adopt Bessie because they had lost a little girl of the same age. "We will get along somehow," Martha answered. "The family will stay together." Martha's brother did not offer financial help.

But Martha was both resourceful and efficient. Her favorite saying was "Make your trip count both ways," meaning, if you carried something from the home (ashes, a pail of slop, etc.), on the return trip you should bring wood, corn cobs, milk, water, or eggs. With her children's help, she made the best of her situation.

George, 17, Bessie 15, and my Father, at 13, were responsible for the farm operation. The day began at 5 A.M. with such chores as milking the cows and feeding the other farm animals, followed by a breakfast of oatmeal or corn meal mush and a mile walk to school. After school there were more chores, dinner, and homework before bedtime. In spite of the regimen, Father had time for football and track. The seven children did well, considering their rural poverty and the loss of their father at a tender age. The strength of character, mutual support, discipline, and sacrifice that kept them on track was nothing short of amazing.

By today's measure, Father's family was poor. Yet all seven children achieved some education beyond high school and several entered the classical professions. All were active Methodists and served with yeoman selflessness in volunteer agencies dedicated to enhancing the economic and moral improvement of their communities. Father and his brother, MacBroom, became physicians. George stayed at the homestead after earning a B.S. in agriculture. Arthur attended Moody Bible College in Chicago and studied to become a missionary, but the poor health of his wife prevented him from doing so. Instead, he joined his father-in-law in Hutchinson as an owner-manager of a paint factory and wallpaper store.

Uncle Arthur manufactured paint under the regional label, *G.F. Nemitz & Son,* a company started by his father-in-law. Uncle Art taught me that oil-based paint should be made up of at least 50% solids—pigment, titanium, and oxides. The vehicle of good paint was pure linseed oil. These ingredients were expensive, and shoddy producers, knowing that the average person was ignorant about what constituted good paint, scarcely included them.

In the basement of Arthur's shop were large 50-gallon cement-like mixers that blended the ingredients together. Dozens of fist-sized stones at the bottom of the mixers pulverized the pigment into a fine powder. Uncle Art enjoyed telling the story that shortly after the Second World War a "fly-by-night" painting outfit swept through central Minnesota. During the war there had been neither the labor nor material available for painting, so many farmsteads had a run-down, weatherbeaten appearance.

"They hoped to pull a fast one on some gullible farmers," Uncle Art recounted. They wanted to buy my good paint at a significant discount and spray it on barns. They weren't even going to wire-brush the wood first. They wanted my good name but *Nemitz Best* paint would have been sprayed over cobwebs, dirt, blisters, and manure."

"How can you put my quality paint through a nozzle?" he queried.

"You don't have to worry about that," came the answer. "Hell, we'll thin it down with gasoline!"

Uncle Art gave them the "bum's rush." It was the era before latex paint, and paint thin enough to be sprayed through a nozzle was as worthless as whitewash. After a couple of rainstorms, most of the color would be on the ground. By standing on principle, he lost a sale of over 1,000 gallons.

After beginning a career in banking, Ben discovered he would rather work outside and became the president and CEO of his own trucking firm.

The two sisters, Bessie and Blanche, entered the traditional professions open to women at that time—teaching and nursing. Bessie spent nearly her entire career as an eighth-grade math teacher in South St. Paul. Noteworthy among her students was the future governor of Minnesota and perennial presidential candidate, Harold Stassen. While Bessie remained single, Blanche married late in life.

Blanche was a spunky sort whose depression-engendered thrift enabled her to crowd 200 words onto a post card. She blamed some of her emotional problems in later life on her brothers tossing her in the horse trough when she was a child. At one time she lovingly cared for 23 cats, "the orphans of alleys," until the Minneapolis Humane Society intervened.

Father and George alternated going to the University of Minnesota and running the farm. Family support was deep. After the death of Martha, all six children signed over their interests in the farm to George because, as the oldest, he had done the most to keep the farm intact while they were young.

Four of the five brothers served in the Army. George and Father remained stateside in the National Guard during World War I. Arthur and MacBroom, however, were engaged in several major battles as members of the American Expeditionary Force. They rarely spoke of the carnage they witnessed. Mac was an ambulance driver and could only shake his head and choke up when he thought about the slaughter.

While the virulence of the worldwide 1918 "Spanish" flu pandemic killed 21 million people, over twice as many as were killed in the Great War. "Influenza annihilated soldiers of all nations as viciously as machine guns," Mac told me. "Troop ships became floating coffins." Ten thousand Minnesotans died that year. Unlike some contagious killers such as AIDS, flu is easily passed from one victim to another through the air and there were no preventive "flu shots" in 1918. Years later, Mac served as a medical doctor in World War II with the rank of major.

Father's university education was very discontinuous. At one point he took time out to teach for a year or two in a one-room rural school house. At other times he took charge of the farm while George attended the university. He also had to give a day or two a month, as did most farm boys, to "work on the roads" during the Spring and Fall. The work was done gratis because the county had little money. The county furnished a horse-drawn blade and scoop; farmers provided horses, manpower and shovels.

In later years, Mother confessed to having observed the manifestation of a "wild gene" in the Benjamin family tree. In those days lineage was deemed to count for more than it does now in the endless "nature v. nurture" debate. She implied that however bright, some members of the Benjamin clan did not have the pragmatic and stolid qualities that characterized those of the German Bedell/Bohn lineage; in fact, she had observed utopian and visionary qualities in her husband's genetic line. The Benjamin family homestead, for example, was always mortgaged and Uncle George went from investing in turkeys, to hogs, to dairy cows, to this new crop to that new seed. It seemed like at each reunion of the Tribe of Benjamin, we would dutifully leave the house to review a new project that George was certain would be successful. He was forever seeking an agricultural will-o'-the-wisp that would make him a gentleman farmer. His unrealistic and esoteric ventures, like the the octagonal brick house that grandfather Robert had built, seemed to be rooted in deeply eccentric dreams and visions. Uncle George never really quite made it.

The farm that had been Father's *axis mundi* always had a nobody-really-cares, run-down-at-the-heel character about it. The grove, for example, was a dumping ground for rusted-out machinery, old wire fencing, broken boards, and other farm detritus. The buildings needed paint; sagging fences, loose boards, and broken windows all cried out for attention. Later I realized that the homestead was probably like New Harmony, Brook Farm, and other utopian communities that philosophers had started in an attempt to purify human nature by linking soil and soul. George seemed kin to many other philosopher-farmers who would rather intellectualize about the wonders of farm life than milk cows and shovel manure. But Mother didn't really judge him, nor was she malicious in her observations. As a Benjamin, he just wasn't fortunate enough to have Teutonic genes.

Years later my opinion of Uncle George mellowed a bit. I learned that, as a result of his agricultural courses, George and Father began to test each cow for the quantity of milk, along with its protein and butter fat. A cow that didn't produce quality milk in sufficient quantity was "culled" from the herd and shipped off to the slaughter house. The old time farmers who were "set in their ways" laughed at the Benjamin "upstarts." It wasn't long, however, before the Benjamin boys had the reputation for having the best herd in McCloud county. Moreover, in time I came to realize that George should have been in the classroom rather than behind a plow or in a barn. He was happiest when in his study reading a book. For a time he was a county extension agent in Western Minnesota. He would have made a competent professor of agronomy at the University of Minnesota.

I also heard subtle references to another uncle here or a relative there who couldn't "quite get it together." Not that my parents were gossips. Far from it. They simply, like the sage Hebrew author of Proverbs, drew their moral lessons from life. One relative, for example, was a pack-rat and never missed an auction nor came home empty-handed. Upon depositing his booty, he would remark, "That will come in handy someday." But it never did. His farm looked like an overgrown junk yard. Mother saw the Benjamin clan, unlike her side of the family, as good talkers but short on doing. To be loquacious about worldly dilemmas, they believed, was identical to solving them. Benjamins were Renaissance Men, experts on everything. It was a sin to confess, "I don't know." One of my cousins once had a business card listing himself as a consultant in two dozen different fields. He thought he could do everything, which probably really meant, he could do next to nothing. We were, as Eric Hoffer would say, "men of words," not pragmatic "men of action."

As I grew older I became more tolerant of some of my strange, whimsical, and quaint relatives. Their odd-ball manners were strangely attractive. By then I had learned from John Stuart Mill that "eccentricity is always found where strength of character has abounded; and the amount of eccentricity in a society has generally been proportional to the amount of genius, mental vigor, and moral courage which it contained." Moreover, Oliver Wendell Holmes' observation that "insanity is often the logic of an accurate mind that is overtaxed" could not be discounted. In spite of Mother's suspicions, I ceased to worry over my genetic progenitors.

My grandparents, Jesse and Kate Bedell shown with their only child, Mabel, my mother. 1903.

Mother's Graduation photo, University of Minnesota, 1922.

My grandparents and "Skippy" in the 1940's.

5. MATERNAL LINEAGE: BEDELLS AND BOHNS

> Do not shorten the morning by getting up late; look upon it as the quintessence of life, as to a certain extent sacred.
>
> *Counsels and Maxims,* Arthur Schopenhauer

Mother was the only child of Jesse Bedell and Kate Bohn. A family record has two Bedell brothers coming from England "early in the history of the United States." The brother "our family is descended from" crossed the mountains and settled on a farm near Factoryville, Pennsylvania. It was there that Grandad Bedell was born on January 2, 1871; he died in California on April 11, 1957. For a time family members eked out a living by farming on the rocky Appalachian soil and peddling apples and meat products in Scranton. Later many members of the family secured more stable employment with the Pennsylvania Railroad. Jesse came from a large family of nine children.

As a child I would sit on his lap, entranced by stories of his education in a one-room school house and the pranks he used to play. He boasted of walking three miles to school carrying a lunch pail filled with a combination of cold corn bread, leftovers, cabbage, biscuits, and beans. Sometimes there might be dried fruit.

Toilet facilities at the school were primitive. On the first day of classes, the teacher would announce, "Now if you boys 'want to do your business,' you go over here to the woods on the south, and if you girls 'want to take a walk,' you go over here to the woods on the north." Later there was an outhouse for both boys and girls—with a partition between the two sides. In those days you didn't say you had to go to the restroom. You said, "I have to empty my ash pan." One day Jesse went out to the privy and realized there was a girl on the other side, so he got a board and reached under the seat and gave her a swat on her bottom. While Grandad's grades were but middling, he ranked at the head of his class as a prankster.

He loved to tell me stories of "thrashing" effeminate, milk-toast teachers and of tying down the school bell clapper so classes couldn't begin. Favorite nighttime pranks were bringing a calf into the school and overturning outhouses. Once he "boxed the ears" of the school bully and earned the praise of his peers. Teachers were single then and were boarded-out among farm families to keep township taxes low. Jesse's antics must have driven several teachers out of the profession. He left school before the eighth grade but one would never know it from his grammar and penmanship or from his accounting, farming, and financial acumen.

On August 3, 1894, at the age of 23, Jesse wrote in a small notebook, "Today I am going way out west and if I like it best, I'll make my home away out west." Perhaps he had heard the oft-repeated statement of Henry David Thoreau: "Eastward I go only by force; but westward I go free…I must walk toward Oregon…And that way the nation is moving." He left home with only $20 and a gold watch. He found a job in a flour mill at Elmore, Minnesota (on the Iowa border) at $40.00 a month and slept on a cot in the grain elevator to save on expenses. Within a year his rectitude of character and work ethic were such that he bought the flour exchange in Bancroft, Iowa, trading it in 1899 for the elevator in Irvington, a few miles farther south.

It was a time of frenetic land speculation. "Throw a stone into any crowd and you will be sure of hitting a real estate agent" was a common adage. Through it all Irvington settlers had acquired a reputation for keeping their word in business affairs, a standard that Jesse Bedell admired. "There are enough people slack about paying their debts without my being one of them" was a motto he practiced religiously. "The firm of Bedell Brothers (Jesse later sold a half interest to his brother B.D. Bedell) runs the elevator and deals in lumber and tile," according to Reed's **History of Kossuth County**. "*This business is conducted on the square*, and the proprietors as a result have made friends of their many customers."

Like legions of others, Jesse embodied the Horatio Alger boot-strap epic of success and Horace Greeley's advice that the West was where young men would find their fortune.

He was a handsome man of classic facial features, ramrod straight at six feet, two inches tall, with a full head of silver-white hair. He loved games of all kinds and was a great tease. Pinching my knee cap between his thumb and four fingers he would exclaim, "This is where the Dutchman keeps his money." In retirement he would play mill, checkers, or cards with me. (Once when the Methodist pastor came for an unannounced visit, my Grandparents swept up the cards and threw them under the couch. Even I knew our pastor wasn't that judgmental.)

Grandad neither knew about—nor would he have cared about—modern child-rearing philosophies that agonize over the potential damage to fragile egos of children who are denied continual positive stroking. In our games and contests, he almost always won. Life was too serious to allow a stripling to believe he could master a grown man.

Jesse was almost painfully shy. Sensitive, proud, and somewhat boyish to the end of his days, Grandad tended to keep to himself and eschewed gregariousness. Nevertheless, he was a man of noble bearing, one from whose taut, severe, lawyer-like face the love of someone else could suddenly shine forth. He embodied the adage of Francis Bacon, "virtue is like a rich stone—best plain-set." Grandad had a regimen, an ethic, and a routine synchronized with nature and the land, a form of self-sufficiency that he would not sell at any price. Yet, he seemed a man of some loneliness and inward suffering, gaunt, tough, abstemious, keeping his physical and spiritual hurts contained, living a life satisfied with simple pleasures until brought down by a stroke, like a towering Norway pine, when he and Grandma were wintering in California.

"Put your money in land, Neb," he would repeat again and again. "It can't burn up, blow away, get lost, or be stolen from you." Both he and Will Rogers exclaimed "God isn't making any more of it, you know!" His own primary investments were in land and that friend of widows and orphans, Bell Telephone.

Even during his retirement years in Pipestone, he would always arise at 5 A.M. to do yard or garden work. I thought his gardens were magical until I was old enough to be assigned to weeding them. Then they became inventions of the devil. His yard was manicured like a golf course. Not given to small talk or much socializing, he drew his raison d'etre from nature. Grandad was entranced by the wonder of growth, the pungent smell of earth and the clean feel of dirt on his hands. He lived by the motto of the anonymous author, "Count that day lost whose low descending sun, views from thy hand no worthy action done."

Jesse Bedell knew and lived the old joke about wisdom: What was its secret? Good judgment. And the secret of good judgment? Experience. And the secret of experience? Bad judgment.

Jesse met Kate at the Bohn family restaurant at Bancroft, Iowa. Kate Bohn was born on Christmas, 1871 and died on February 2, 1964. The Bohns had emigrated from southern Germany shortly after her birth, and a large family photo shows Kate as a babe in arms. After her death, Mother found a customs declaration that had been carefully altered by ink eradicator, indicating the family came to America with eight rather than nine children. Mother surmised that Kate was traumatized by the anti-German feeling during World War I and, fearing deportation, reduced the family number to establish her birth-right citizenship. Grandma Bedell died at 93 years of age, not the 89 years to which she claimed! So great was her fear that she never confessed the subterfuge to her only child and carried the secret to her grave.

Kate landed Jesse by the time-honored means of culinary artistry— her apple pie was reputed to be the best in the county. Later a potential marital conflict due to Kate's Catholicism was avoided thanks to the insensitivity of the priest who baptized Mother. Though the temperature was below zero, the vicar insisted on pouring cold water over Mother's head. Holding Mother's damp head close to her during the buggy trip back to the farm, Kate vowed not to go back to the Catholic Church. At least, that was the story for public consumption. Intuitively, she may have known that her Catholicism might have caused problems with Jesse.

Occasionally Father would teasingly interrogate his in-laws, with questions that bordered on the malicious, as to why they did not have more children. He might as well have queried the four faces of Mount Rushmore, for he never got an answer. Their Victorian privacy would not even let a physician son-in-law be entitled to such intimate details of their life. Unable to best him by verbal fencing, their stony silence conveyed to Father that his question was out of bounds.

Kate Bohn Bedell ran to type—a classic German stolid-type of woman, both in her outward and inward being. Forced to leave school during the middle grades because of family poverty, she nevertheless knew her figures, had an excellent writing hand, and excelled in domestic science. She followed the New England Puritan maxim: "use it up, wear it out; make it do, or do without." She was a stoically strong woman who could have survived a half dozen trips over the Oregon Trail. She could have handled a brace of oxen on the journey as well as any trail master. In her early 80s, she was still jumping like a teen-ager into a fishing boat without taking an offered hand.

Like her husband, she never cried that I was aware of and was never depressed, or out-of-sorts. Her bond with her only child and daughter, Mabel, my mother, was a thing of beauty and fidelity. Kate was content at home and there was no evidence that the suffragette movement had touched her life. She knew that her role in the economy of the family was complementary to, and as important as, that of her husband. Jesse, in turn, showed her great respect. Intuitively I knew they loved each other very much although, given the canons of the era, they were not public with their affection. As I grew into manhood I realized how fortunate I was in having behind me several generations of honest, hardworking ancestors.

The lives of the womenfolk of both my Bedell and Benjamin genealogy were consumed by hard, endless, and dirty labor. They kept the farm and hearth alive. Behind every man with a hoe was a woman nursing, washing, and counseling. In their early years they lived without electricity, gas, plumbing, and central heating. Homes were bereft of refrigerators, radios, telephones, automatic laundry machines, or vacuum cleaners. Lacking indoor toilets, each morning they had to empty, scour, and deodorize the bedroom slop jars. For baths, laundry, and dishwashing, they hauled pails of water from the yard pump and heated it in the kitchen on cob-burning stoves. They boiled laundry in tubs and scrubbed it until their knuckles were raw, then hung it out to dry by hand.

Ironing was done by lifting three inch thick, ship-like, six-pound weights heated on the stove top. My farm-reared ancestors scrubbed floors on hands and knees, thrashed rugs with carpet beaters, killed and plucked their own chickens, baked bread, made most of their own clothing on treadle-operated sewing machines, darned stockings, made jelly and relishes, polished the chimneys of kerosene lamps, lamp-blacked the stove and flues, yet they still found time to tend geraniums, dahlias, lilacs, hollyhocks, and peonies that grew around their houses like colored embroidered lace around a doily. At twilight, their menfolk drifted back from the fields, dirty, exhausted, and steaming. They toiled like serfs and their sleep was not unlike a deep coma.

Almost everything Grandma Bedell's family consumed was produced from scratch by them. A 19th-century recipe for roast pig from one of her cookbooks reads, "wash (the pig) well in cold water, and cut off the feet close to the joints...Take out the liver and heart...Put the pig on the spit and place it before a clear, brisk fire...rub it frequently with a feather dipped in sweet oil." Little was packaged or processed. "This soup will require eight hours to prepare," begins a recipe for Mock Turtle or Calf's Head Soup. From a recipe for Tomato Catsup: "Mix the seasoning with the tomato pulp; let it boil slowly during four hours. Then take it out of the kettle, and let it stand till next day..." In less than a century, cooking has declined from one of the most important concerns in a woman's life to one of the least. While my Grandmother Bedell may have understood food to be the essence of survival and saw her cookbooks as the tools of her trade, today's woman often turns to cookbooks for entertainment, escape, and fantasy.

In comparison to my family, my own Grandparents were not overtly religious. Table grace, Bible readings, references to God or Providence never arose in ordinary discourse. They practiced a form of individual morality and self-reliance without a theological substratum; the Benjamin Franklin virtues without John Wesley:

It is hard for an empty sack to stand upright.
Plough deep while sluggards sleep.
Never leave that til tomorrow that which you can do today.
He that goes a-borrowing goes a-sorrowing.
Whatever you have, spend less.
Idleness and pride tax with a heavier hand than kings and parliaments.
Vessels large may venture more,
  But little boats should keep near shore.

The Bedells never joined a church. Was childhood indoctrination and fear of perdition—"There is no salvation outside the Catholic Church"— the obstacle? We never found out. Although they weren't pious in daily life and never formally attached themselves to the Methodist Church, they were regular in their Sunday attendance and in their giving. Perhaps they feared Father's censure if they did not conform.

Grandad Bedell was shrewd in business. Rumor had it that he sold farm land in July when the corn crop looked its best and then sealed the contract by asking for the crop at harvest time. He liked land with a gentle slope to the south; the consequent higher soil temperatures allowed for early spring planting. In his grain elevator office, in a sun-drenched spot near a window, he made inconspicuous marks on the oak floor that replicated a sun dial. When there was a lull in chewing the fat with his town cronies, he would exclaim, "I'll wager a piece of pie and coffee that I can tell the time closer than anyone here." With bets in, he would call the telegraph office for the exact time. He never lost, nor was his intrigue ever discovered.

Sometimes his teasing backfired, however. Once he bet Fred Bohn, Mother's cousin, who had received a .22-caliber rifle for Christmas, that he "couldn't hit a barn door" with it. When the nine-year old Fred promptly accepted the 25-cent bet, Jesse immediately opened the door edgewise to Fred. Surprisingly, Fred hit it. Grandad Bedell was the genetic origin of my love of teasing.

The Bedells lived in Irvington, a town of fewer than 100 people, until Mother was old enough to attend high school. Their home, a well-constructed two-story frame house on the northwest corner of the village, still stands, surrounded by the now-sizable pine trees planted as saplings by Jesse. His lawn perfectionism, precluded Mother's having a swing, because her feet might have scuffed the lawn. A branch of the Des Moines River flowed only 500 feet away and a favorite summer pastime was catching carp, catfish and redhorse.

Grandad Bedell was one of the first persons in Kossuth County to own a nice car. He also had a wild streak in him. One afternoon, while driving from Irvington to Algona, he asked Mother, then ten years old, to watch the speedometer to find out how fast his new 1910 Buick would go. With clouds of dust billowing up behind them, Mother's bonnet blew off, and the dial read 64 before Jesse took his foot off the accelerator.

Mother's chores as a girl included feeding the chickens, gathering eggs, pumping a fresh pail of water for every meal, and going to the neighbors' farm to get a quart of milk every day. She also had to pick potato bugs off potato leaves and drop them into a can of kerosene.

Mother's grammar school was a one-room school house in which all eight grades were taught together. The teacher arrived first and started a fire with laths and coal. The boys brought a pail of drinking water from a block away and everyone drank from a common dipper. The library consisted of 30 books but there was never any homework because of the chores the children had to do at home. Whippings were administered by the teacher as necessary with two laths tied together. Every Saturday Mother took her piano lesson in Algona by catching the freight train, which pulled one passenger car along with its load of freight. The round trip fare was ten cents.

The Princess dress, navy blue with plaid stripes, was the fashion of the era. There were six tucks at the waist and a big hem. As Mabel grew, the hem was dropped and the tucks were taken out one by one. In its final incarnation, the waist was cut and a six inch strip of scrap material was added. A white pinafore was worn over the skirt to hide the strip and keep the dress clean.

When Mother entered high school, the Bedells moved to Algona. They built a home with a quantity of lumber that would build two houses today. It was classic middle-class Victorian with wide overhanging eaves, plenty of ginger-bread at the gables, a three-sided porch, massive wooden pillars, quarter-sawed maple trim, and leaded-glass windows. While she was in high school Mother experienced the jingoism and hatred of the Hun that accompanied World War I. At night gangs of rowdies daubed yellow paint on the homes of German families, causing many to change their names. One day, following the dictates of her teacher, Mother and her classmates gathered up their German language books, marched to a nearby field and burned the books. That was the end of instruction in Deutsch in Algona.

Basket socials were a major fund-raising tool used by churches and schools. Every woman and girl would fix a box supper for two people. The boxes were auctioned off by the pastor or teacher. A girl usually would tip off her boyfriend as to the ribbon or color of her box in advance so that he could bid on it and the two of them could eat together. Spirited bidding between two or three contestants might cost the winner $10.00 for his supper. Once a boy named Elmer was sweet on Mother and paid $6.50 for the box he thought was hers. Mother never told me whether she tricked Elmer or he simply got confused. In any case, the box was that of an obese married woman, with her husband and their seven kids. Elmer had indigestion that night and didn't speak to Mother for a month.

Recreation for Mother's family was wholesome, family-oriented and noncommercial and included picnics, swimming, fishing, and gathering nuts and berries. Mother's love of making jams and jellies began when she was a child and continued until her death. Years later, while on vacation at Kee Nee Moo Sha, our family's favorite resort in northern Minnesota, she received more enjoyment from gathering blueberries, pin cherries and chokecherries than from occupying a chaise lounge on the beach. During her early 80s, while living in the Minneapolis suburb of Fridley, she often prepared hundreds of jars of jam of 15 different kinds for an annual neighborhood boutique. Such was the reputation of "Mabel Benjamin jams" that they always sold out on the first day.

Mother's closest bonds in Algona were formed as a member of the Campfire Girls. The girls were impressive in their blue skirts, white middy blouses and red kerchiefs. She kept up her friendship with former members well into her 80s and often visited them in their retirement homes in Florida and Arizona.

*My father and his four brothers. From left to right: George, Walter (father),
Arthur, MacBroom, Ben. ca. 1911.*

6. THE UNIVERSITY OF MINNESOTA: STUDY AND FINANCES

The formation of right habits is essential to your permanent security. They diminish your chance of falling when assailed, and they augment your chance of recovery when overthrown.

An Address to Students, John Tyndall

Mother went to the University of Minnesota, St. Paul Campus, to major in home economics because of the influence of a Campfire Girl friend, Rachel Hickman. The year after she moved from home to spend her freshman year in a dormitory, her home moved back to her. At age 47, Grandad Bedell sold his elevator and he and Grandma bought a home at 1800 Iglehart Avenue in the Midway district of St. Paul.

The reason for this abrupt transition was never divulged. Was concern for their daughter the reason? The Horatio Alger stories and Protestant ethos of that era held that our urban Sodom and Gomorrahs, filled as they were with crime, John Barleycorn, and Catholics, were inhospitable environments for the pristine souls of rural youth. There were thousands of stories of how saintly Sallys and virtuous Virgils lost their morals, manners, and money in American Vanity Fairs.

Then again, perhaps, the move had a less protective inspiration; they may have moved simply because Jesse's brother Fred lived on Iglehart Avenue. Or it may have been that they were lonesome for their daughter. In any event, the transition must have been traumatic. The Bedells left a village of 4,000 to live in a metropolitan city of 300,000, giving up the expansive vistas of Iowa for a small house on a 40-by-120 foot lot.

Before my grandparents moved to Pipestone in the late 1930s, Jesse spent 15 years taking the streetcar down to Paine, Weber, and Jackson to watch the stock market quotes come over the wire. He found a community of retired folk who loved to chew the fat about everything from the weather to politics. He also spent plenty of time with his first love—tending the garden and fruit trees he had established in their yard.

The Bedells' one attempt at investing in St. Paul commercial real estate, two six-flat apartment houses on Snelling Avenue a block north of Hamline University, proved to be a disaster. One day an entire stucco-covered wall fell off one of the buildings and, fearing a lawsuit, they dumped both at a significant loss. Nothing like that had ever happened to good Iowa topsoil!

Father and Mother met at the Wesley Foundation of the First Methodist Church next to the University of Minnesota. For Father the Foundation was a weekly oasis that broke the arduous monotony of study and work. It provided a home away from home with its Sunday routine of program, dinner, and recreation. Decades later he repeatedly and generously gave to the Foundation, grateful that it had brought Mother and him together and had humanized his educational rite of passage.

Father's first year at the University was difficult. His lodging, a room in the basement of the home of the dean of the medical school, leaked gas fumes, and the noise from the children upstairs interfered with his studying. After he received two "pink slips" (deficiency notices) at the end of the first quarter, he moved and his grades improved. He had not told anyone that he planned to be a medical doctor. Some of his class-mates had done so with great braggadocio, only to flunk out and creep back home with, as he said, "red eyes."

Later he confessed that he was only a one-talented, not a ten- talent-ed student, and that he had made it through medical school on effort rather than innate ability. He agreed with Thomas Edison that genius was 90% hard work.

During his junior and senior years, 1916-18, Father kept a financial log. His resources were meager and he had to practice his credo, "waste not, want not." Daily and monthly entries, either "Dp."(deposits) or "Ce."(credits), were made in ink and in an uncharacteristically legible script for a future physician. September 4 began with $3.51 "cash on hand"; by the end of the school year in mid-June, he had spent $290.32 and earned $193.10. The difference of $93.71 was made up in small checks from home or loans from sister Bessie or brother George. Bessie was especially generous, and her loans increased from $5.00 to $10.00 and even $20.00 during his first year in medical school. These were significant amounts for a Mankato normal school graduate who had just started teaching. Father paid her back with interest the moment he began earning money in his practice.

While in school he earned $20.00 a month stoking the furnace and sweeping out Willard Hall. Other income came from yard work, working at the state fair, and bussing dishes at the student union. Financial bonanzas that came his way in medical school included $150.00 from a Gilfillan Fund Loan and a National Guard check of $44.50.

His attention to financial detail was impressive. Nothing was too small to record. He embodied the proverb, "pay attention to the pennies and the dollars will take care of themselves." The financial litany was monotonous: "post card, 1 cent," "car fare, 5 cents," "breakfast, 5 cents," "crackers, 5 cents," "haircut, 25 cents," "shoe repair, 25 cents." And so it went. There were four entries for "shoe repair" during the two years but none for a new pair of shoes. So rare was what might be called frivolous spending, that such entries seem to leap from the page. During two years there was only one entry for "peanuts, 10 cents," two for "candy, 20 cents," and one for "ice cream, 30 cents."

On the other hand there are regular weekly entries listing "SS (Sunday School), 5 cents" and "church, 10 cents." He made regular pledges of $1.00 a month to the YMCA building fund and gave to its prison relief fund and other charities, and he subscribed to *The Christian Herald.* His correspondence with his mother, brothers, and sisters must have been extensive because each week records significant amounts for postage.

Recreation was largely noncommercial—skating, hiking, hay rides, picnics—although there are a number of entries for "symphony tickets, 25 cents." In sum, his financial logs reveal an abstemious student, rotating between church/Wesley Foundation, classroom, and janitorial duty. His values remained intact as he progressed toward his degree. He followed the Benedictine motto, "to work is to pray," and lived a form of "inter-worldly asceticism"—an abstemious existence outside of cloistered walls. He was a workaholic before the word was invented to denote a disease, and he would have viewed as preposterous the belief of some contemporary behavioral scientists that those who worship their work are preoccupied by thoughts of death. He only knew that during the time he had, he wanted to make the most of his talents and give something back to God and mankind. A loyal Methodist, he would have answered with a loud "Amen" to the charge John Wesley put before his lay preachers: "Be diligent. Never be unemployed. Never be triflingly employed. Never trifle away time; neither spend any more time at any one place than is strictly necessary."

Father in his National Guard uniform worn during his service on the Mexican border.

My parent's wedding photo, 1800 Iglehart Avenue, St. Paul. July 1, 1922.

7. The Mexican Border Service and Marriage

Villa epitomized the Mexicans' love of machismo and had become
the Latino version of Robin Hood, looting the rich, rustling their cattle,
and giving to the poor. (Although) a folk hero, he was also a cold-
blooded killer who "could shoot down a man point-blank, showing no
more emotion than if he were stepping on a bug."

The Great Pursuit, Herbert Molloy Mason, Jr.

During the summer of 1918, at the age of 25, Father was on the Rio
Grande border in Texas as a member of a Minnesota National Guard
field artillery unit. Pancho Villa, a Mexican "bandito," took advantage of
American involvement in France, and was making periodic raids to rus-
tle cattle. Although Father was exempt from the draft because of his
medical studies, he and his brother George had joined the National
Guard out of a sense of patriotism. He kept a diary that began with their
departure by train on July 17, 1918, and ended on September 4, after
hearing a rumor that they were to break camp and return.

It was a great "break out" experience for Father, the first time he
had left the Land of 10,000 Lakes. Unaware of his agricultural myopia
and Minnesota jingoism, his journal reveals he judged everything he
saw through a Hutchinson prism.

It took over a week to get to the Rio Grande and they experienced a
train wreck in transit. Father's powers of observation were perceptive if
biased: "Iowa land does not compare with Minnesota"—a judgment he
conveniently forgot years later when he invested in Iowa real estate. He
carefully recorded the agricultural panorama as it slipped by his train
window. His knowledge of crops, land, soil management, animal husbandry, trees, and shrubs was phenomenal. Occasionally he grudgingly
admired Southern bounty and the modernity of cities such as Dallas.
On occasion the train stopped long enough for him to seek out a YMCA
or Methodist church. He was impressed with Southern hospitality.

The Rio Grande encampment was cut out of a mesquite grove that
was home to abundant lizards, tarantulas, snakes, flies and other
insects. Heavy rains turned the soil into gumbo and, with no fighting

and little entertainment, his bete noire was boredom. After the initial novelty of the military experience wore off, Father had a hard time keeping up his spirits. The entries in his diary declined both in quantity and in quality as the summer progressed. The Army truism—"Hurry up and wait"—was proving to be true.

As a private first class, Father was the orderly to Captain Sherman and was in charge of his correspondence, horse, and uniforms. "Capt. Sherman called me to his tent to ask me if I understood the duties of an orderly," his entry on August 1 read. "When I told him that I did not, he endeavored to explain. However, I decided not to exert myself too strenuously on behalf of any army officer for 'pull,' not work, counts here." He complained of the torrential rains, the knee-high muck, and the parching sun. Worst of all, he "caught the bloody diarrhea," an affliction that plagued him on and off for the rest of his life. The war on the Rio Grande had to do more with the elements than with a renegade Mexican.

Father and George always went to church or attended a YMCA service on Sunday. They fraternized with high-minded, clean-living guardsmen and stayed clear of the gamblers, boozers, and fornicators. Father's religious values were rock-hard and stayed with him the rest of his life, yet one finds little moralizing in his journal.

His log abruptly ends with the rumor that they would be rotated home upon the arrival of the New York National Guard. As a postscript, Father copied a bit of doggerel written by an anonymous soldier stationed on the Rio Grande 30 years earlier.

The devil, we're told, in Hell was chained,
 And a thousand years he there remained;
He never complained, nor did he groan,
 But determined to start a hell of his own
Where he could of his own torment the souls of men
 Without being chained in a prison pen.
So he asked the Lord if he had on hand
 Anything left when he made the land.
The Lord said: 'Yes, I had plenty of land,
 But I left it down on the Rio Grande;
The fact is, old boy, the stuff is so poor
 I don't think you could use it in Hell any more.'
The devil went down to look at the truck
 And said if it came as a gift he was stuck,
For after examining it carefully and well,
 He concluded the place was too dry for Hell.

So in order to get the stuff off his hands,
   The Lord promised the devil to water the lands;
For he had some water, or rather some dregs,
   A regular cathartic that smelled like bad eggs.
Hence the deal was closed and the deed was given,
   And the Lord went back to his home in heaven;
And the devil then said, 'I have all that is needed
   To make a good hell' and him he succeeded.
He began to put thorns on all of the trees
   And he mixed the sand with millions of fleas;
He scattered tarantulas along all the roads,
   Put thorns on the cacti and horns on the toads,
He lengthened the horns on the Texas steers,
   And he put an addition on the jack-rabbits' ears;
And he put a little devil in the bronco steed,
   And he poisoned the feet of the centipede.
The heat in the summer is a hundred and ten,
   Too hot for the devil and too hot for the men.
The wild boar roams thru the black chaperelle
   It's a hell of a place he has for a hell,
The red pepper grows on the banks of the creek
   The Mexicans use it in all that they cook.
Just dine with a grease fire then you will shout,
   'I've hell on the inside as well as the out!'

Upon graduation from medical school in 1920, Father took an internship year at Minneapolis General Hospital. Mother graduated from the University with honors with a degree in home economics in June of 1922, and although Father loved to kid her about her degree from "cow college," he was secretly proud of her academic accomplishments. It was a tough degree, involving chemistry with pre-medical students, aesthetics, and upper-level biology courses. She was good in foreign languages, especially French. Moreover, she had good business sense. Had she lived two generations later, when the lives of women had a wider orbit, she could have been the CEO of her own company.

Mother never seriously dated a man other than Father and, in spite of his kidding about being sweet on a beautiful red-haired nurse—"Neb, how would you have liked to have red hair?"—I doubt that he had dated anyone else, either. In the Puritan ethos of their upbringing, a serious kiss betokened an imminent engagement.

On July 1, 1922, they were married at the 1800 Iglehart home decorated with hundreds of moccasin flowers that George had gathered from a Hutchinson swamp. Although Mother had attended Trinity Avenue

Methodist Church three blocks away, her parents were not members there and this may have been the reason why they did not have a church wedding. The newlyweds left the next day for Rochester, where Father began the second of a three year residency in general surgery. They found a duplex to rent but later on moved to a small two-bedroom house. Father's stipend was $50 a month.

Mother began to keep a record of their expenditures. The week of July 9-15 reveals that their expenditures for food amounted to $5.27. Included was 30 cents for steak, 15 cents for "stew" and 25 cents for two pounds of prunes. After acquiring a dozen Mason jars, sheet music, a six-by-nine-foot piece of linoleum, two rugs, medicine, four bars of Ivory soap, and a clinic dinner, their expenditures came to $26.85 for the week. Her home economics major immediately began paying thrifty dividends. After the electric bill skyrocketed to $11.00 the first month because of the electric stove, she quickly switched to a kerosene appliance, a Ward's special that cost only $6.00.

Looking west on Main Street, Pipestone, Minnesota during the 1920's. Father's medical office was on the second floor of the Pipestone building (left) and could only be reached after negotiating a long and dark staircase.

8. MEDICAL PRACTICE AND FAMILY RITES OF PASSAGE

Father was always proud to have taken a residency in surgery at the medical mecca, the Mayo Clinic. Autographed photographs of the famous medical brothers, Will and Charlie, were prominently displayed in his Pipestone office waiting room. He loved to repeat the anecdotes of the famous pair and was proud to have mastered state-of-the-art gall bladder and goiter surgery of that era. Because salt was not laced with iodine at that time, large disfiguring neck tumors were common, and he loved to point out to me the fine, almost invisible scar that his sutures left on the necks of his patients. Father was not afflicted with medical modesty. Nonetheless, there was more substance to the "Physician and Surgeon" under his name than there was to the other Pipestone doctors. From my friends I discovered that he was the "most expensive" doctor in town. When I questioned him about it, he said with considerable heat, "I did not come to Pipestone to be the cheapest doctor in town."

Although he was invited to stay on at the Mayo Clinic, Father decided to locate in Pipestone because of an intense, diabetic little man by the name of Ed Trebon. In his elevator shoes Trebon was barely five feet, three inches tall, and was possessed of the megalomania that often affects undersized men. He had been trying for years to get his wife pregnant and had come to the Clinic for advice. There were few infertility experts then, and his contact with Father, a resident in general surgery, had something of a serendipitous quality about it.

Sinclair Lewis would have hated Trebon for, as the editor-publisher of *The Pipestone Leader,* he was a fervent booster of the small town. Perhaps as a compensatory mechanism for his diminutive stature, he drove the largest car in the county, a Buick. Trebon also owned a 12-horse Johnson outboard motor, a monstrous engine at a time when most people rowed their boats. His employees considered him one of the best employers in town but were on notice that anyone who referred to him as "Shorty" would be summarily fired. It was Trebon, claiming later that Father had saved his life during a diabetic coma, who persuaded Father to come to Pipestone.

"Doc" (Father hated to be called by this layman's term of endearment, but always let it pass), "there would not be a surgeon of your skill within 50 miles of Pipestone," trumpeted Trebon. "You can't believe the medical incompetents we have. Why, I wouldn't let those quacks touch my dog. Besides, Pipestone is the garden spot of southwestern Minnesota. We have everything you would want." That's the official story—Father was persuaded by Trebon's entreaty.

The real reason Father chose to practice in Pipestone, however, may be more subtle. Father probably feared the big cities. He had been suckled on Horatio Alger stories in which virtuous farm lads lost their character and moral compass in the urban fleshpots. American cities were the lair of liquor and bootleggers, jazz and Sunday golf, wild parties, crime, divorce, and other temptations too numerous to mention. The Hutchinsons and Pipestones of the world were more controllable, family-oriented communities that prized and cultivated caring and personal relationships. Then too, he may have feared being a member of a multispecialty group where critique, research, review, and judgment by peers would have been unceasing. Or he may simply have wanted his family to be free from the clannishness and clique-ridden Rochester medical community. Father kept his own counsel and never told us whether any other than Trebon's entreaty influenced his choice of location. He did, however, prize the autonomy of a medical entrepreneur, where he could give orders, not take them. Pipestone, therefore, promised to be an ideal place for his profession, his family, and his personality to flourish.

Trebon's overture to Father was the onset of a bond that lasted until the Trebons moved to California in 1938. Father and Ed Trebon were a Depression-era, tall-short, "odd couple," physician and publisher, two of the dozen or so pillars of Pipestone. Together they became the guardians of our culture and the stimulus to all positive community developments. In 1937 the Benjamin and Trebon families took a four-week eastern vacation. I was 11 at the time and remember Father and Trebon in the office of Senator Henri Shipstead pressing for the conversion of our "Shrine Park" to the status of a national monument. "Senator," exclaimed Ed, "you have to push this legislation through. Without it, gangs of rowdies will destroy the Indian heritage." The bill passed without delay.

Sociologically, the twenty years before World War II was a good time to practice medicine. An expanding medical and technical armamentarium had not as yet driven a wedge between the patient and the healer. Physicians were considered to be members of the family by their patients and were often ascribed near saintly qualities. For their part, patients lacked today's near-religious fanaticism about their health and longevity. The loss of vital force was deemed as natural and inevitable. "John," Father could say, "You are getting old and your body just isn't functioning as well as when you were young." Father's expertise as a medical pedagogue undoubtedly paralleled his skill as a body mechanic.

The town trinity of authority—attorney, pastor, physician—had not yet suffered the erosion of status and deference that happened after the war. Few protested the canons of *nobless oblige:* the requirement that professional status be accompanied by a refined and virtuous character and conduct. Medical care was still largely paternal, not technological and, if you lived beyond 65 years of age, it was attributed to divine grace rather than medical heroics. There were few second opinions or 1,000-mile train trips to discover some medical Lourdes. The classical professions were a serving class, not self-serving, and few of their members minded that their private life was open to public scrutiny. Most considered it a small price to pay for a life that helped set the moral tone of their village.

Father arrived in Pipestone in September 1924 and rented an office on the second floor of the "Moore Block," a building now listed on the historical register. The building was graced by a dozen gargoyle-like stone carvings, and I wondered whether they added to the anxiety of the children who came for his ministrations. In Europe, medieval cathedrals and churches were ringed by gargoyles and grotesques whose function was to keep evil and unclean spirits at bay. Father may not have wanted to neglect any potential help in launching his medical career.

Mother joined him a few weeks later with two month old Bob in a rented house at 525 West Centennial Street. His ad appeared for the first time in the November 18 edition of *The Pipestone Star,* whose professional listings included five M.D.s (including a "Dr. E.S. Perrigo, M.D. Homeopathic Physician-Surgeon, office at residence"), an osteopathic physician, a chiropractor, five dentists, two veterinarians, and a "Mrs. William Gaskell, 'practical nurse.'" Father must have been mortified that all the doctors listed "physician *and* surgeon" after their names, since he was the only one who had specialty training in general surgery. He had to convince a lot of gullible folk how to tell a true from a false healer.

In addition to Ed Trebon, the new Ashton Memorial Hospital must have exerted some influence on Father to locate on the sacred turf of the Sioux. It had "an operating room with a pure white finish...an X-ray room with one of the most modern machines for this line of work, a well-equipped sterilizing room, 16 two-bed rooms, two single-bed rooms,

Pipestone Gargoyles

Pioneer sculptor Leon H. Moore left a legacy of stone faces in the downtown Historic District

"Hiawatha Emerging from the Woods"   "Court Jester"   "Mirth"   "Northwind"

"Moses"   "Hiawatha"   "Baphonet"   "Babe"   "A Knowing Wink"

During the early years of his medical practice, Father had his office in the "Moore Block." Pioneer sculptor Leon H. Moore left a unique legacy of 14 Duluth Sandstone relief sculptures, often called gargoyles, that embellish the north and west facades. I often wondered whether they added to the anxiety of children who were his patients.

Pipestone Gargoyles

Pioneer sculptor Leon H. Moore left a legacy of stone faces in the downtown Historic District

"Man-in-the-Moon"   "Pensive Face"

"Eve"

"Guardian Angel"   "Bawl-Baby"   "Lion"   "Disgust"

° Pipestone Preservation Postcard   79602

and two wards each having four beds…all are light and pleasant." The U. of M. Medical School's Dean Lyon spoke at the November 18th dedication and complimented Pipestone on employing the "new ideal of democracy in its financing, with private benevolence being joined with public funds."

Ever the optimist and confident of his future earnings, five years later, in 1929, Father built a three story office building of light brown brick that measured 30 by 110 feet. He took out a large term insurance policy in case tragedy struck. With considerable bravado, he called it the "Pipestone Building." It had a bit of everything—five commercial offices on the first floor, space for a dentist and Father's five room office on the second floor, and seven apartments on the rest of the second and the third floors. There were no elevators. Father's office required a 23-step climb up a dark staircase. Long before handicap accessibility laws were enacted (today OSHA would have closed him down), that obstacle must have been an effective screen against any patients who were malingerers or came for frivolous complaints. Also, Father may have wanted to be on the second floor away from the prying eyes of the passers-by.

Grandad Bedell came down from St. Paul as a volunteer "straw boss" of construction. Years later Father occasionally suggested that Grandad must have been "asleep at the switch" because certain features of the building were not up to code. Ultimately, the Pipestone Building was a financial albatross, for something was always going wrong with it. Pipes burst, toilets overflowed, ceilings leaked, paint peeled and flaked, and apartments were either too cold or too hot. Within a few years, having been introduced by his father-in-law to the fecundity and investment potential of Iowa land, Father realized the building was a drag. However, he often used it as an instrument of family pedagogy. With my brothers and sisters, I was regularly called upon to clean and paint the boiler and laundry rooms, a job I greatly detested. Fifty years after its construction Mother sold the building for $60,000, the same price it had cost to build in 1929.

For all its faults, Father's office was probably the state of the art for a small town in the 30s. He would oscillate between the two 12-by-16 foot examination rooms at the front of the building. One of the rooms had his desk in a corner and it doubled as his office. A six-foot-tall medical "breakfront" contained the simple instruments—speculums, oscilloscopes, reflex hammers, tongue depressors, an instrument sterilizer, etc.—for examining patients and peeking into body cavities. Segmented glass-fronted book cases contained the basic medical texts of that era on surgery, internal medicine, pediatrics, and obstetrics. Each room had a three-foot-square curtained alcove where patients disrobed. As a child I would play on top of the examination table and wonder about the purpose of the circular metal stirrups at the corners. Whenever I stood on the scale, I was depressed by a large wall chart that compared height to weight. The projections must have been done by a corpulent actuary. No matter how much I ate, I was always woefully underweight.

The 16-by-22-foot waiting room had large windows on the east that allowed the sun to warm the goldfish in a large aquarium. It sat on a Mission Oak table and entertained both young and old as they sat uncomfortably on a dozen mahogany-stained, straight-backed birch chairs and waited their turn to see the doctor. Another table contained outdated magazines whose quality, nevertheless, was slightly superior to those in Peterson's barber shop. In one corner sat a large oscillating fan, which would be turned on only if the temperature rose above 90 degrees. On the opposite wall, the benign yet imposing faces of Will and Charlie Mayo looked down from their framed photos and gave their medical imprimatur to the scene. Their blessing, "With Best Wishes to Walter G. Benjamin, M.D.," followed by their signature, seemed analogous to the pope's portrait sanctifying a humble sacristy and ministrations of its priest. They seemed to assure patients that "You Are In Good Hands," a theme that State Farm Insurance would pick up decades later.

A small lab, an office-reception area, a store room, and a half bath completed the office space. Father was able to do routine blood work and urinalysis. In the early years he kept a small pharmacy and sold expensive pills at cost but doubled the price of the cheap ones.

His two faithful assistants—Opal Brennan and Freida Becker—stayed with him for over two decades. Opal met the public with a smile and kept the books, while Freida was a registered nurse and office manager of exceptional ability. Freida was a tall, rangy type of woman whose Teutonic genes wouldn't allow her to take any guff from either her boss or his patients. Had the Olympics of that era had a woman's volleyball team, Freida could have been its premier spiker. She had a reach that exceeded that of Father's by a foot and could pull a two-gallon bottle of cough syrup off an eight-foot-high shelf as if it were cotton candy.

Posters warning patients against the lure of "socialized medicine" were prominently Scotch-taped to the wall by the receptionist's window. It was the era of paternalism. Father believed he knew not only what surgical procedures and drugs were best for his patients; he wanted to write their political prescriptions as well. During the Depression, the American Medical Association was controlled by entrepreneurial, small-town physicians and it reflected their basic conservatism. Father viewed the intrusion of government into medicine as a social cancer that would ultimately undermine medical quality and destroy both patient and physician autonomy. "My patients don't care who delivers their mail," he would comment, "but I know that they don't want to be forced to go to a physician-bureaucrat!" As the Depression deepened, he grudgingly understood the need for Blue Cross and Blue Shield as pre-paid insurance hedges against bankruptcy. But he constantly lamented the ever-increasing paperwork that such programs required.

Even though physicians during the Depression-era did not practice under today's omnipresent threat of malpractice suits, Father detested members of the legal profession. To my knowledge, he was sued only once. Even though the case was settled in his favor out of court, he was depressed for weeks. It was as if a member of his family had turned prodigal. He never recited a retinue of "lawyer jokes" such as: "What is the difference between a lawyer and a catfish? *One is an ugly, scum-sucking bottom feeder,* the other is a fish." Like many, he felt that attorneys exacerbated rather than healed conflict between humans. Although Pipestone attorneys took him into their confidence regarding their medical condition, he never reciprocated. His estate, will, and other legal work was done by attorneys far from Pipestone.

Father would have laughed at Shakespeare's aphorism in *Henry VI,* "The first thing we do, let's kill all the lawyers," without recognizing that it was uttered by Dick the Butcher—an unschooled, irrational, buffoonish peasant who was part of a rebellion to overthrow the king and lawful government. What he feared and loathed in lawyers was probably a reflection of what we fear and loathe in ourselves: anarchy. Father overlooked the fact that lawyers are supposed to uphold law and order, not threaten it.

The practice of medicine in the Depression-afflicted towns of the Heartland was almost always solo, competitive, and exceedingly territorial. Like the village butcher, baker, and candlestick maker, physicians, too, guarded their turf like a mother wolverine protecting her den. With women consumed with *kuche, kinder,* and *kierke,* medicine was a male-dominated profession. Financially physicians were middle class. Most had entered the guild out of humanitarian motives; some simply wanted to escape the farm, mill or mine and thus raise their social status. Father often told me that he knew three physicians in the county who had died as paupers.

Father intuitively knew that while medicine was a science, acquiring a practice was an art. He knew and observed the Hippocratic dictum, *primum non nocere* (first, do no harm); wherever a physician cannot either cure or control disease, he must do nothing to harm the patient. From the viewpoint of the last third of the 20th century, the Depression-era medical armamentarium was miniscule. Father's ability to do much harm, therefore, was limited. He knew that fashions in therapy may have some justification, but that fashions in diagnosis have none. He followed the advice of the father of American medicine, Sir William Osler:

> Care more for the individual patient than for the special
>   features of the disease.
> Don't touch the patient—state first what you see.
> One of the first duties of the physician is to educate
>   the masses not to take medicine.
> Half of us are blind, few of us feel, and we are all dead.
> One finger in the throat and one in the rectum make a
>   good diagnostician.
> Jaundice is the disease that your friends diagnose.
> To talk of diseases is a sort of Arabian Nights
>   entertainment.
> Look wise, say nothing, and grunt. Speech was given
>   to conceal thought.

Fees for office visits and house calls were modest—$3.00, $5.00, and $10.00. Surgery for an inflamed appendix or the removal of a gall bladder cost $50 and $75, respectively. Our family was modestly middle class, like most teachers, farmers, teachers, pharmacists, lawyers, and small businessmen. No one drove a fancy car, wore designer clothes, or vacationed in exotic, far-away places with strange-sounding names. Father may have remembered a statement of Dr. Will Mayo—"We want to pay our physicians well, but we don't want to see their children lolling on the beaches of Florida"—that encouraged an abstemious life-style. By the 1960s, however, because of family thrift and Father's investments in Iowa land, our family would have been categorized as "upper middle" in class rank, although he tried to hide it. Medicine became one of the affluent professions only after World War II with the exponential growth of the medical armamentarium that necessitated specialization and allowed more intrusive intervention.

Although medicine was his mistress, Father assumed responsibilities for the Pipestone common good in many other organizations as well. He was a pillar of our Methodist church, president of Kiwanis several times, a member of the school board and the Shrine Association.

With Mother, he was a member of the Current Events Club for almost 35 years, a club whose programs were presented by its members.

STATEMENT

No._____.   Pipestone, Minn., *8-1*_____192 *8*

M   *Mrs Frank Waters*
     Pipestone Minn

IN ACCOUNT WITH

Ashton Memorial Hospital

Room Days at $4.50 per day				
Room *3* Days at $3.50 per day	*10*	*50*		
Ward *22* Days at $2.75 per day	*30*	*25*		
Nursery *23* Days at $1.00 per day	*23*			
Use of Delivery Room $	*5*			
Use of Operating Room $				
Anesthetic $	*5*			
Surgical Dressings $	*10*			
Medicine $	*1*	*50*		
Board for Special Nurse. Days at $ per day				
X-Ray				
Laboratory	*2*			
Telephone	*87*	*25*		
Byckf	*87*	*25*		

When Patricia Waters was born in Ashton Memorial Hospital in 1928, Father recommended that her mother, Mrs. Frank Waters, remain in the hospital for some minor surgery. This copy of the bill indicates that a 22 day stay cost $30.25. Patricia stayed in the nursery for 23 days for 23 dollars. The entire bill including the delivery room, surgical dressings, medicine, anesthesia, and laboratory amounted to $87.25.

9. The Richness of Not Having

Our home at 808 Third Avenue Southwest was four blocks from the public school and seven from the Methodist church and Main Street. We were only a thousand feet from prairie land on both the west and the south. We seldom asked for a ride to go anywhere; instead, we walked or rode our bikes. Our home was on a substantial 200-foot lot and was surrounded by gardens and grass. In 1933, my parents lured Grandad and Grandma Bedell to Pipestone by giving them a corner lot, kitty-corner to us, on which to build their house. Otherwise, gardening would have been our Waterloo. Like the proverbial rooster whose "cockadoodle doo" greets the morn, Grandad never gave up his farm-honed habits. He was always in the garden when we got up. His yard was the envy of the neighborhood and he zealously practiced most of the proverbs of *Poor Richard's Almanac*.

Grandmother, too, was frugal and thrifty. A third of the metal was worn off her tablespoons from stirring, but she wouldn't throw them out. When she cracked eggs she would get every last bit of egg from the inside of the shell with an index finger. After she had used a spatula to clean the batter out of a mixing bowl, the bowl barely needed washing. I would laugh at her common refrain, "Jesse, eat this or I'll throw it out." He always did. Behind his back we called him the human garbage can.

Unlike our parents and grandparents, I was not traumatized by the Great Depression. I was too young to know that tragedy stalked the land, that millions of people were losing homes, businesses, and farms. It was an era before entitlements, Social Security, and safety nets. Thoreau's observation that most people "live lives of quiet desperation" was never more true than during the tragic '30s. Unemployment was a terrible affliction that many viewed as a reflection on one's character. Being unemployed meant that one had not incarnated the Puritan verities—"Waste not, want not"; "Save your nickels and they will turn into dollars"; "Where there's a will, there's a way"; "Put overalls on your dollars and make them work for you." At a deeper level, the book of Proverbs, classical economics, and the ethos of Social Darwinism reinforced the dogma that property and character, virtue and affluence, went together. The spirit of scarcity and thrift, I believed, was like the law of gravity. Income differentials in Pipestone were modest. Anyone could consider himself either rich or poor. It depended on one's point of view.

Our gardens, therefore, were a substantial hedge against future want. Idle land was analogous to a barren womb. We had a screen of flowers—iris, tulips, and peonies—on the street side of the cultivated area. But the heart of our gardens grew just about everything listed in the seed catalogue—corn, carrots, parsnips, tomatoes, strawberries, raspberries, asparagus, lettuce, cabbage, gooseberries, squash, pumpkins, ground cherries, even gourds that we would shellac for decoration or sell house-to-house from our wagons.

Because the saga of Johnny Appleseed decreed that apple trees were the blaze marks of civilization (government surveyors laying out Jefferson's grid upon the prairie often planted apple seeds to mark section lines on the ocean of grass), our garden had a dozen apple trees. There were Duchesses and Pattan Greenings for baked apples and pies, Wealthies for eating, sweet Anisms for sauce, Iowa Beauties, Strawberry and Whitney Crabs for pickling. We wrapped their trunks with old clothes in the winter until they grew too large for hungry rabbits to gnaw comfortably.

Several times we picked tender dandelion greens to cook or walked rural roadsides in search of wild asparagus. I suspect such tasks were designed to increase our moral capital rather than a product of economic necessity. Christian stewardship dictated that good land should not lie fallow. And did we grow beans! One summer I helped Mother and Grandad Bedell snip, wash, cut, and can 178 quart jars of green beans. After that I couldn't eat a green bean for years.

Mother's pride and joy was her 30-by-40-foot asparagus bed. A periodic dose of salt water kept the weeds down but did not harm the deep asparagus roots. Mother knew when the tender purple-tinged noses, their leaflets overlapping like fish-scales, had poked far enough out of the ground to be dug with the special asparagus cutter. I gagged at those green spears even though Mother said they were good for me. Happily, the asparagus season didn't last long; by July the beds were clouded over with feathery forms of stalks gone to seed and the roots needed the rest of the summer to regain their vigor if we were to hope for a good crop the following year.

When county fair time approached, Grandad Bedell and Mother showed me how to select five uniform apples, tomatoes, beets and/or other fruits or vegetables for entry in the prize competitions. After great indecision, I would select the final five, polish and arrange them on a tray, and hope for the best. I received third prize one year for my beets; another time, my crab apples won second prize. To see a ribbon by my tray of apples was ecstasy. The prize was two or three dollars, but more important than getting the money was seeing my name in the paper. I was angry that some farmer from Jasper with a foreign-sounding name entered produce in every category and usually won 70% of the prizes. He didn't give kids a chance.

As the dog days of summer came to an end and our garden turned brown, Mother would announce that "the Colorado peaches are in." I never knew what was so magical about a Colorado peach, but she would buy a dozen lugs and we would can them, along with purple plums and pears. Sometimes we would can them whole with the pits in for flavor. I never appreciated the taste of home-canned fruit and vegetables until after I'd left home.

One of Father's Depression-era decisions—we called it "the Chicken Coop Venture"—went sour. Zoning laws were nonexistent then, and Pipestone families seemed to have just about everything but swine in their back yards. Chickens, Father believed, would produce a synergistic trinity—meat and eggs for our diet, discipline for his children, and manure for the garden. "Do you promise to take care of them?" he queried. "That means gathering the eggs, feeding them regularly, and cleaning the coop once a week."

"Of course," Bob, Martha, and I answered in unison. "Pretty please with sugar on it, we will dearly love our chickens." To be sure, our knowledge of chickens, having come from picture books, was incredibly romantic. We knew they went "peep peep," were cuddly, had pretty feathers, and we thought they could fend for themselves by picking up their food from the ground. Later we were shocked to learn they pecked and suffocated each other to death and defecated altogether too frequently. We simply avoided the unpleasantness that dropped all too frequently from their rear ends.

A small Quonset hut was duly hauled to the edge of the garden, where a fenced-in area was constructed. I had looked through picture books of chickens to form an opinion regarding the pedigree we should get. Naturally, I selected the most fanciful and colorful breeds I could find. It was hard to decide among New Hampshires, Buff Orphingtons, Rhode Island Reds, Barred Plymouth Rocks, Silver-Grey Darkings, and Black Minorcas. Mother reminded me that some of the exotic breeds I was considering did not exist within 1,000 miles of Pipestone. "Those are exhibition, show birds you are looking at," was her pragmatic response. "The birds you want wouldn't last a week out of their hot-house environment. You need more than pretty feathers to make a good layer." In the end, she made the decision, and we got 20 White Leghorn pullets.(Her decision may have been determined by what was available from the farmer who deducted the birds from his medical bill.)

Meanwhile, I read up on chickens. Mediocre as I was in math, I hoped to impress my classmates with my chicken knowledge. I discovered that all domestic chickens were related to *Gallus gallus,* a red jungle fowl native to India and Southeast Asia. I learned that the Romans routinely tossed grain to chickens before major battles. If the birds devoured the grain, it was considered a good omen. Since chickens ate as eagerly then as now, it is not surprising that the Romans conquered the world. I learned that any hen that didn't lay at least 250 eggs a year wasn't paying its dues and should give up its life for soup or Sunday dinner.

During the first week, we kids bonded closely with our beloved chickens. Our garbage can remained empty as we carried potato peelings, leftover oatmeal, bread, table scraps, lettuce leaves, burnt toast, apple cores and whatever else we could scavenge for our precious birds. "Please," I begged Mother, "we've got to have more garbage!" For the first month our chickens ate better fare than did the Depression poor. Unknowingly we were ahead of our time. Our birds were not cooped-up in factory farms like today, l00,000 to a building, confined from seeing the sun, scratching, and strutting their stuff in the open air. No sir! Bob and I were sensitive to the feelings of our cherished birds. Since our chickens could move in and out of their coop and fenced-in yard as they desired, our operation could have been called "moderately free range."

When the eggs began to appear, we fought over who could gather them. But before long the novelty wore off. Watching chickens eat, fight, lay eggs, and poop affected all the excitement of watching grass grow. The manure piled up, eggs went ungathered, the chickens were fed and watered only sporadically. The chickens began to be confused. Using the board game Monopoly as a metaphor, these creatures had enjoyed a wonderful sojourn of living it up on Boardwalk, had been evicted, and now inhabited a slim-pickings ghetto on Baltic Avenue. Their fare had changed from caviar and filet mignon to corn meal mush—and even that was available only irregularly. We began to detest cleaning out the coop on Saturdays because it cut into football and soft-ball practice.

Besides, chicken manure was bad enough in a static state. When swept or shoveled, its odor and dust made our eyes weep and stuffed up our noses. The only relief I had was occasionally finding an old rotten egg behind a bale of straw to pitch on the roof of Vance (we called him "Pants") Peterson, a kid in the neighborhood I didn't like.

Father's grand trinitarian design linking discipline, diet, and fertility had fallen prey to the law of unintended consequences. Mother was doing our chores and the coop had become the focus of family discord. Father was right—the children he had sired had no "staying power." We were "good starters but poor finishers." My parents decided to return to the tested and much more reliable method of getting chickens and eggs: obtaining them from a farmer "working off a bill." I was ecstatic when Father decided to cut his losses and shut the operation down. I gladly got out the hatchet and helped Grandad Bedell dispatch the survivors. Their magnificent genes had attested to the Darwinian thesis of the survival of the fittest—they had persevered through our months of indifferent care and had survived our chicken holocaust. But instead of being honored and set at liberty, they went to the block. Afterwards, I tore off their feathers with gusto and helped Mother stuff their body parts in glass jars for canning. The coop was hauled off to the farm.

Every spring I was reminded of "the year of the chickens." I inwardly thanked them for their sacrifice, for the vegetables were always large and lush where they had enriched the soil during their short sojourn with us.

My boyhood home at 808 Third Avenue in Pipestone. Our extensive and productive gardens extended far to the left of this photo.

10. Canning Days, I

Just as the liturgical year punctuated the church calendar with Lent, Easter, Pentecost, Trinity, and Advent, so the Benjamin summer was punctuated by canning days. Unlike liturgical events, however, the dates for the canning ritual were determined not by the calendar but by the vagaries of weather and pests: rain, sun, grasshoppers, worms, and blight among them. (Canning days rarely fell on a Monday for that was wash day.) Only a radical nonconformist would hang out laundry on any day but Monday.

Although we grew some vegetables on large lots across a vacated alley behind the alley, our primary garden was immediately south of the house. This 90-by-140-foot space was bordered by the Morgan's picket fence on the south and ours on the north. Beautiful gladiolas, peonies that grew to the size of basketballs, iris, tulips and other perennials nicely framed the garden on the east, the street side, while a dozen-and-a-half fruit trees bordered it on the back. The soil was rich beyond compare. Our gardening was done before horticultural science produced aseptic, odorless, granular fertilizer that looked like colored sand in a polyethylene bag. Father, nostalgic for his boyhood years and odors, each year had several loads of manure dumped on our lawn and garden by a farmer working off a bill. This annual ritual had brought our soil to such a state of potency that the seeds literally exploded from the ground.

To Father the scent of manure was like a perfume, but his agrarian compulsion made the neighbors very angry. Several former farmers who lived within three blocks of our house had retired to the city to escape hardships of which the smell of manure was a reminder. Spring rains made the stuff especially pungent, and the odor could clear out your sinuses, however badly they might be clogged. My friends loved to taunt me on my way to school: "Geez, do you Benjamins love crap," and "Do you have sh.. for breakfast too?"

In the late 1940s, when I brought Marjorie Prescott, my wife-to-be, home on Spring break from college for her first visit, my Father put her to the test. An eight-foot pile of sheep manure had been dumped in the garden prior to her arrival. She resisted the thought that her visit and the pile were related. Marjorie, a city girl, swallowed hard, put on some of my sister Martha's old clothes, held her nose, and reluctantly grabbed a shovel. Father graded her efforts as "C minus." Years later she confessed that that day was one of the more difficult tests she'd had to face to earn her laurels as a member of the Tribe of Benjamin.

I honed my expertise regarding fertilizer as a child whenever our car passed a particularly odoriferous farm. I would screw up my face, look accusingly at my brothers and sisters, roll down the window, and mumble "WHO LET ONE?" The intensity of their protestations of innocence was the clue as to whether the smell originated inside or outside the car.

In time, I began to realize odor was a sign of excellence. Sheep manure won hands down, followed by that of hog, chicken, cow, and horse. Father's sadistic streak became apparent in that he always had it delivered when it was moist and never asked the farmer to spread it. Our Easter vacation was always clouded by the chore of having to spread the stuff.

Unfortunately, the rich, fresh fertilizer nourished noxious weeds as well as luscious vegetables. Daily our rows of vegetables, like miniature green soldiers in perfect dress parade, welcomed me as, with my file-sharpened hoe over my shoulder, I marched to rescue them from attack by Roman wormwood, buckhorn, smartweed, lambs-quarters, foxtail, johnswort, pigweed, sorrel, piper-grass, crabgrass, ragweed, quack-grass, and dandelions. With a repetitious up-and-down oil-well pumper motion, I chopped the weeds and turned their roots upward to the sun. If they had a single fiber of shade or drop of moisture, it seemed they would turn the other side up and be green as a leek again in two days.

But our garden castle's enemies included fauna as well as flora, and it was almost impossible to raise a secure drawbridge against them. In the classic anvil-and-hammer military tactic, moles and worms of a dozen varieties wreaked their havoc from below while crows, bluejays, grackles, rabbits, squirrels, and woodchucks coordinated their attack from the soil and air above. The names of our creepy crawlers were endless: bean beetle, cankerworm, corn ear worm, wolf spider, snail slug, Harlequin bug, potato leaf hopper, squash bug, Mormon cricket, cucumber beetle, Japanese beetle, stink bug, chinch bug, sow bug, and, of course, the omnipresent grasshopper.

Not all bugs were bad. Mother told us never to kill ladybugs, tiny round, orange, humpbacked critters with a voracious appetite for aphids, scale, mealybugs and mites. Whenever I found one I would carefully pick it up and bring it up close to my face and sing softly: "Ladybug, Ladybug, fly away home. Your house is on fire and your children will burn!" I was always amazed that by the time I had finished, the ladybug had "heard me" and flown away.

It was tough on my ego to be defeated by bugs and worms: it gave me a sense of hopelessness regarding gardening. Depression-era gardeners didn't have the chemical armamentarium that is available today for those who aspire to a green thumb. Then, pre-emergents, DDT, systemic fungicides, Round-up, Malathion and other bug blasters and weed killers that one day would provide "Better Living Through Chemistry" were only a dream.

A woodchuck could nibble a hundred-foot row of tender bean sprouts in a night. Rabbits could do almost as much damage but were not so methodical. However, they worked the year around and would chew the bark off smooth-barked trees in the winter if we didn't wrap the trunks. Pipestone birds seemed to have a preternatural intelligence. One summer we tried warding them off with a scarecrow, but it failed miserably; grackles and jays roosted on its arms. Our Pipestone birds seemed to be members of an ornithological mensa society. Add to the foregoing enemies of gardeners everywhere the threats of rust, smut (a fungal disease that turns plants black), blight, early frost, hail, and drought. It defied logic why year after year, we waxed optimistic for our gardens the moment spring began warming the earth.

Father often required that I cut a bushel of dandelions every day. A foot-long dandelion cutter had a sharp "V" at the end so that I could cut the roots off several inches below the grass. No matter. Dandelions were the flora equivalent of the blue ribbon survivors of the fauna world—cockroaches. As long as a snippet of root remained they would be back in a week to haunt me. Filling a bushel basket with this noxious weed was a daunting task. Often times, before Father could examine the success of my labors a hot sun might wilt a basketful down so that I was six inches short of my quota. Sometimes I put straw or empty tin cans in the bushel and covered them with a thin veneer of dandelions. Fortunately, I never got caught.

A "Canning Day" began with an announcement by Mother at supper: "Papa says that the beans are ready for canning. TOMORROW, WE WILL CAN THE BEANS!"

It was an *ex cathedra* pronouncement born of years of experience and detailed knowledge of the agrarian cycle. Timing was everything. Of course, we would "can the beans" many times during the summer because different varieties matured at different times. Besides, it would have been a violation of Puritan dogma not to save every morsel God's good soil provided.

Though Father determined the timing, Mother reigned over the harvest and canning process. Father, the patriarch, had no knowledge to countermand this matriarchal arrangement, which was one of several significant areas in a small town economy where women held sway and men had to stand aside. Moreover, an efficiency expert would have discovered a fine economy of scale. Mother commanded the kitchen and garden forces. Grandfather Bedell, Bob, Roger, and I were the field hands, while Mother, Grandmother Bedell, Martha, Mary, and the hired girl were the inside operatives.

The night before the big day, we would carry cartons of empty quart jars up to the kitchen from the basement. Mother would carefully run her finger around the top of each jar, making sure each was smooth enough to make a good seal. Some were fitted with glass tops that were compressed with a stout wire mechanism pushing down on a rubber ring between the top and the jar itself. A new technology involved Kerr brass lids, whose soft rubber seal would be compressed with a screw top.

We went to bed early on the eve of a canning day so as to husband our energy for the demands of the morrow. We picked the corn, beans, and tomatoes early in the morning, both to avoid the heat of the afternoon and to maximize the freshness of the produce. We could never beat Grandad Bedell into the garden. The fresh earth had a primordial magnetism for him; he intuitively knew it was the source of all wealth and power. By 6:00 A.M. he always had a bushel basket full of whatever had to be canned ready to be carried into the house.

Our small, screened back porch was the site of the first stage in vegetable processing. We all wore no-nonsense, old-fashioned aprons that came up high in front and tied in back—there wasn't a frilly fashion apron in the house. We would sit with large earthenwear crocks between our legs. The glaze on their edges had been rubbed off years earlier by countless honings of paring knives.

Green beans had to have their ends snapped off. (I suppose that's why they were called snap beans.) Sometimes they were tough and stringy and had to be lined up in bunches and cut into half-inch lengths.

Corn had to be shucked and have its silk removed. As I've noted, effective herbicides and pesticides hadn't yet been invented, and often I would yell, "Ick, I got a smutty one" and my hands would be covered with a grayish black goo. Many of the ears were wormy, but Mother would salvage as much of the ear as she could. Everbearing strawberries were picked several times during the summer; they were mixed with sugar and then frozen. Parsnips were topped and left in the ground all winter and could be eaten the next spring. Small crab apples were canned whole, but our prized Wealthies were peeled and quartered. We would impale them on an apple peeler and, with a few turns of the crank, produce a peeling that resembled an apple-peel Slinky. Sometimes the curlicue peeling was almost a yard long. We would make believe it was a snake, wiggle it through our teeth, and chew it down.

Grandmother disdained even such rudimentary technology. She would sit for hours hand-peeling apples; her skill, honed during the Depression-era, produced paper-thin peelings. Nothing was wasted. Apples on the ground, windfalls, although wormy and bruised, were salvaged and turned into cider or apple sauce.

Beets and rutabagas were always washed and sliced before being canned. Carrots were topped and buried in sand in a four foot high Red Wing clay crock in the basement; we enjoyed fresh carrots well into March. Although we grew some potatoes, most were dumped into two large basement bins by a farmer working off a bill. By mid-winter they would start turning soft and we'd have to pull off the sprouts that grew out of their eyes. Of the many kinds of squash that we grew, the Hubbard was Mother's favorite. They were monstrous things, the largest of which weighed up to 40 pounds and were almost three feet long. They looked like greenish-gray hogs lying amidst the vines. Their hard, crinkled skin was like the bark of an elm tree, and it often took a blunt end of an ax to break them open. Inside, their succulent orange meat was sometimes four inches deep. After steaming the squash, we would scrape the meat down to the rind and pack it in jars. Sometimes the seeds were dried in the oven and saved for next year's planting. In the winter Mother often decorated the top of a squash casserole with a dozen marshmallows. I always tried to get a marshmallow, because it sweetened the squash.

Everyone in town had a few clumps of rhubarb in the back yard. Commonly called pie plant, it was the poor man's vegetable. It needed no fertilizer or cultivation, and its broad leaves began to appear almost as soon as the snow melted in the spring. We were fortunate that most of ours was the ruby red variety. The stalks were smaller, but they were sweet and, when cooked into a sauce, had a beautiful deep red color.

Some years we had enough ground cherries to make into sauce or jam. They grew on small bushes and simply dropped off when ripe. Inside the paper-thin hexagonal covering, there was a beautifully translucent, yellow-orange berry with an incredible sweetness. We ate as many as we put into the pail.

Outwardly, our community was pacific, but underneath this surface calm, a desperate competitive struggle was waged. Everyone in town understood that the prize for horticultural excellence automatically went to whoever produced the first ripe tomato. Come late July, the question, *"How are them tomatoes of your'n coming? Ya picked any yet?"* displaced the usual inquiries about the weather. It was the central query along Main Street, in the churches, indeed, at every social gathering. It was a major embarrassment to have to mumble, "Nope, ain't had any yet. Think mine might be set back a bit by that frost in June or else the nematodes is gettin' at 'em." One would rather break wind in public than have to admit to a set-back with one's tomatoes. The agricultural elect would gloat and feign sympathy: "Really? Too bad. What variety did you plant? Were they set back by the frost? Too bad. I picked six yesterday. They was real beauties. Had 'em last night for supper."

To be last in the tomato race in Pipestone, to have miserable, ping-pong-sized green tomatoes still on the vine when your neighbors were feasting on red, luscious fruit the size of softballs was about as close to being forsaken by God as a Methodist could come. Sometimes the winners would rub it in with, "Let me know if you could use some. We got more than we can eat."

Tomatoes were started from seed in paper cups set on window sills. When they had grown to two or three inches high, they were transplanted to a garden cold frame, a 4-by-6 foot wooden enclosure covered by an old storm window. The hothouse effect accelerated growth by warming the soil and protecting the fragile plants against the cold night air. When the plants were eight inches high, we would wrap their stems in paper to protect them against cutworms and transplant them into the garden in rows a yard apart. Each was encircled by an old gallon can, both ends of which had been cut out. This was to protect their tender stalks from the wind, worms, and weeds as well as to provide a little reservoir for water. Every morning Grandad Bedell would fill a large galvanized tub with water to be warmed by the sun. Later, he'd sprinkle the sun-warmed water on his precious plants with the diligence and tender care of a priest christening an infant with holy water. He and Mother methodically inspected each plant for bugs, grubs, sun scald, blight and other pestilences. If they encountered an enemy, they immediately employed a variety of sprays and powders to launch a vigorous counterattack. Never mind that the active ingredient in their weaponry was arsenic; the important issue was winning the tomato race.

Once the tomatoes started ripening there was no stopping them; one may as well have tried to stop a charging bull with a BB gun. Grandad Bedell could pick a bushel before breakfast every day of the week. Sliced tomatoes the size of saucers graced the table for every meal except breakfast. It never occurred to us to boil them down into catsup or tomato paste. Only Italians did that and, since Italians were Catholic, their food was suspect, not quite American. Occasionally, Father and I would take a salt shaker into the garden and eat tomatoes right off the vine.

In spite of the frenetic pace of canning and eating, we never were able to keep ahead of the tomato tidal wave. Sometimes my friends and I would have tomato fights to reduce the torrent. We took sacks of the fruit to give away at church to no avail; everyone else was trying to get rid of tomatoes too. What in early summer had been intensely desired now became a terrible burden. We were caught on the horns of a dilemma—God's command to "waste not" conflicted with His immeasurable bounty, gifts that we could not possibly use. Our pride and joy, the garden, began to generate guilt feelings.

With the first hard frost, the torrent ceased. Inwardly, I think my parents, too, welcomed the end of the growing season. By that time there wasn't an empty jar in the house. Even so, with the prediction of a frost, Mother would send us on one last foraging expedition, to pick the last green tomatoes so they could ripen on the window sills.

Of all our garden produce, tomatoes were the easiest to prepare. They were blanched, that is, immersed in hot water for a minute, then skinned and canned whole. Corn was easy, too. We would pick dozens of ears before the morning dew was gone and quickly husk them before their sugars turned to starch. Mother would carefully inspect each ear for silk, worms, or smut. After blanching the good ears, we would simply slice the kernels off with a sharp knife. Grandmother was slow. I could do four ears of corn to her one, but I invariably cut into the ear, gouging out pieces of cob and sometimes leaving rows of kernels. Her ears were so immaculate there wasn't enough left to interest a fly. She would finish each ear by scraping the cob with the back edge of her knife until there was nothing left on it.

We canned some corn, but most of it was packed into plastic containers and taken to our locker at the freezer plant downtown. It would keep for years; liberally laced with butter when it was finally consumed, it tasted like fresh corn on the cob.

Among the many things we canned, Mother's bread-and-butter pickles were a favorite. We would thinly slice the cucumbers (or "cukes" as Grandad called them), mix in celery seed and just the right amount of onion, and let them soak for a day or two in a special kind of vinegar. We ate them on everything. Mother would glow at a church pot-luck supper when women would exclaim, "Aren't those Mabel Benjamin's pickles?" Or, "You better take some now. They won't last long."

There was little variation in the canning ritual. Mother was high priestess before her spotless electric four burner altar. A steady stream of produce from the back porch was examined, washed, peeled, cored, and diced, halved, or quartered to best use the capacity of each jar. Her long artistic fingers could finesse peach or pear halves into a quart jar so that they were an aesthetic delight to the viewer. I thought it a waste of time, since the only exposure a jar would have to the world would be in a damp cellar. Sometimes I would protest the Olympian standard she demanded with: "Isn't that good enough?" "If a job is worth doing," she would respond, "It's worth doing well." Grandad and Grandma would silently nod their heads in assent.

On the stove four containers boiled continuously: One was used for pan sterilizing the lids and jar covers, another for blanching the fruit; the stove's two twelve inch burners held two four-gallon cast aluminum pots in which the jars of produce were boiled before sealing. Our kitchen took on the atmosphere of a Turkish bath, and the sink overflowed with Burpee Big Boys. Jars were lowered and raised with tongs from the steaming pots, timed by Mother's calculations on a nearby pad. After lifting them out she would let them cool a bit on a dish towel on the counter, then use a thick towel to protect her hands as she screwed down the top to make a good seal.

The steam that arose around her reminded me of the bubbling mud pots of Yellowstone National Park that I had seen as a child. Mother used the back of her hand to brush back strands of her hair that had been loosened by the steam. Yet she never complained of being tired, and her thin, piano-delicate fingers, could hold hot jars that would have blistered mine.

The morning after canning we'd carefully wash the 40 to 70 jars, label them, and carry them to the basement. If the jars had fully sealed, the Kerr tops would be dented or concave from the partial vacuum.

Those that hadn't sealed well would be placed in the refrigerator for earlier eating. (It was harder to tell if the jars with glass tops and rubber rings had sealed tightly; if they hadn't, we'd know months later when we saw mold on the top of the fruit.)

Mother knew who were the good providers among her peers and where they stood in the Pipestone home economics hierarchy. We loved to repeat the story of a hard-working man whose wife had left him. He was caught one summer canning peaches with THEIR SKINS ON! When chastised for this canning sin he retorted, "Next winter when I eat them peaches, I'll have a damn sight more time to take their skins off then than I do now!"

Each year in late August and early September, I looked forward to our annual weekend trip to Iowa to pick black walnuts and wild grapes. For Grandma Bedell and Mother, it was an enjoyable step back into their childhood. We found walnuts in their greenish-brown husks on the forest floor along a branch of the Des Moines river. We would scoop them up by the bushel and lay them out to dry on our basement floor before storing them. In the winter we would remove the husks, crack the nutshell with a hammer and tease out the nutmeats with a crochet hook.

Wild grapes grew along broken-down fence lines. In good years there would be 15 to 20 small grapes to a stem. It seemed miraculous that Grandma and Mother's alchemy could turn something so bitter, and made up almost entirely of a seed and skin, into something that tasted so wonderful. They'd boil large caldrons of grapes into a mush that they then poured out into large squares of cheesecloth. The opposite corners would be knotted together and the resulting bundles slipped over a broom handle and allowed to drip. (Grandma was so frugal she would add water to her residue and do the process a second time. Even Mother wasn't that economical.)

In the final step, the rich juice was made into jelly or canned. Mother knew just the right amount of Certo to add so that the jelly would set. The juice was put into empty glucose bottles Father brought home from the hospital. On a hot day, the deep purple juice, mixed with water and sugar and poured over ice cubes, was delicious beyond compare. I had heard that Greek gods drank ambrosia to gain immortality, but I doubted if even it could taste so sweet. This wild grape juice was our Benjamin soda pop, the only colored sugar water allowed in the house at 808 Third Avenue.

We all needed a second wind in late summer to take care of fruit from the West—purple plums, peaches, pears, apricots. We bought them by the crate and processed them into jars with Germanic efficiency. Mother knew which varieties had the best flavor and when the price would be the lowest. Although we canned Washington and California peaches, her favorites were the late Colorado peaches. They were the best. Maybe it was the mountain air. She usually left a pit in the jar for flavor.

"Work" during the Depression was not limited to work for wages; it included homemaking, child care, cleaning, cooking, gardening, canning, sewing, and household repairs. Today a consumer culture reigns, and money earned "at work" buys many, if not most, of the goods and services we used to create for ourselves. Modern Americans occupy themselves less and less with the basic chores essential to keeping body and soul and homestead together. Of course, this provides some personal liberation, but there is a trade-off: I believe work had more meaning and probably more satisfaction when we lived amid the final fruits of our labors rather than working for somebody else's enterprise and paying someone to grow food, paint the house, make our clothes, and raise our children.

Because the drought had killed or stunted many trees or shrubs, Arbor Day was a solemn if secular rite during the 30s. In early May, every school child was given a three-foot twig of a tree, usually a hackberry, Russian Olive, or green ash, to take home and plant. We were admonished to water our trees every week and to wrap the trunk with rags or chicken wire before the winter. Rabbits easily girdled smooth-bark trees but had a difficult time getting purchase on those with rough bark.

Of course, few of us would hang around Pipestone long enough to enjoy the beauty and shade of those childhood plantings. I had remembered, however, a story about Napoleon, who wanted to plant trees along French roads to shade his marching troops. "But Marshall," was the rejoinder of a staff officer, "It will take 30 years for the trees to grow enough to accomplish that." But Napoleon commanded: *Yes, indeed, so we must start at once!"* Decades later, when I returned with my children and grandchildren to 808 Third Avenue, I was gratified to see the results of one of my plantings—a 60-foot-tall hackberry whose trunk was nearly three feet in diameter.

With the ending of the "dog days" of August and the influx of the cool breezes of September, the garden that had been so verdant in June began to resemble a lunar landscape. It was a mass of dried vines, stalks, rotten vegetables, rusted cans, exposed roots, and holes. Its exhaustion paralleled our own. The land would soon begin its slumber under a white winter mantle until called to life again by spring rains, the warming sun, and the spade.

My summer bondage to the soil, while intense, was only temporary. Ancient poetry and mythology suggest that husbandry was once a sacred art. Living within and adjusting to the ceaseless cosmic cycle provided, curiously enough, a mysterious form of freedom.

Without knowing it, I had been a part of a ritual of generations. It was sad that there was no festival, no procession, no rite (not even our cattle-shows and Thanksgiving) that celebrated my activity and reminded me of its sacred origin. Intuitively, however, I knew I was connected to a powerful if humble legion of tillers of the soil that predated the Hebrews, Greeks, and Romans. With that bond and knowledge, I felt secure. By next April I would be renewed and expectant once again.

12. Hunting; Rite of Passage to Manhood

You must know that there is nothing higher and stronger and more wholesome and good for life in the future than some good memory, especially a memory of childhood, of home. People talk to you a great deal about your education, but some good sacred memory, preserved from childhood, is the best education. If a man carries many such memories with him into life, he is safe to the end of his days.

The Brothers Karamazov, Fyodor Dostoyevsky

A trinity of rites of passage—hunting, athletics, fighting—confronted rural lads during the Depression. My modest stature caused me to eschew the third, and a fourth—impressing one's peers with sexual exploits—was alien to my moral principles as well as psychologically difficult because of my innate shyness. Therefore, I had to concentrate on the first two. Father taught us the use of firearms at a very early age and our home always contained a variety of rifles and shotguns. Guns were not associated with violence and murder. Nor was there in their use any attempt to prove oneself a "macho man." They were as necessary to male maturation as a basketball, softball glove, hockey stick, whiskers, or a first sportcoat and tie. I probably would have agreed with the philosophy of the National Rifle Association had I known of its existence.

When things were slack around the home and I felt that I had done my chores well enough to pass Father's demanding scrutiny, I would take a single-shot .22 and our Chesapeake Bay retriever, Skippy, and wander down the right-of-way of the Great Northern railroad that passed within three blocks of our house. I would shoot at tin cans, crows, grackles, bottles, and rabbits. (Though we never ate rabbits for fear of tularemia.) Unlike some of my friends, I never shot at the glass insulators on the telegraph line. There was a stiff fine if you got caught.

Alone with Skippy and my rifle, my fantasies knew few limits. I would lie on my back along the grassy slope of the railroad right of way, gaze at the scudding cotton-puffy clouds as they drifted across the sky and dream of future conquests over the forces of evil. Indians, Germans, gangsters, Italians, robbers—all things demonic fell before my unerring aim. Depression era gangsters such as John Dillinger, Pretty Boy Floyd, Bruno Hauptmann (kidnapper of the Lindbergh baby) and others had received great media attention. My childhood reverie ran riot. In my fantasies, I always out-drew them and gunned them down. I imagined myself rescuing a drowning girl, thwarting a bank robbery, saving my parents from kidnappers or from President Roosevelt's evil policies, rescuing my sisters from our burning home, even assassinating Hitler or Mussolini. For such exploits I pictured myself receiving status, love, rewards, and medals. At a deeper level, I hoped my life would count for something and leave a mark on history through some great heroic deed. In my Dick Tracy-like grandiosity it seldom entered my mind that I could find a purpose in life simply attending to daily and familial duties that fulfilled common and ordinary needs.

I usually was shocked out of my reverie by Skippy's whining and licking my face. I'd hear the 6 P.M. town siren and hurry home in order not to be late for supper.

Hunting was an important means of bonding with my Father, brothers, friends, and other men in Pipestone. We joined our mythical ancestors, the hunter-gatherers, in the primitive, noble and male ritual of securing game to nourish the family. Game secured by means of the hunt, like vegetables from the garden, was far richer in symbolic overtones than pork chops or a beef roast purchased at the market. Hunting was both a therapeutic release and an occasion for parental mentoring. Father would quiz me on varieties of hay, hogs, cows, beef cattle, and birds. I began to differentiate between dozens of kinds of trees and shrubs and discovered what type of berries, nuts, and roots were edible in case I ever had to live off the land. I learned to size up a farmstead and judge the quality of the farmer by the placement of buildings, the windmill, feeding lot, windbreak and general ambiance.

Pipestone was still close enough to its frontier roots to view hunting as a rite of passage from the status of "mother's boy" to that of "father's son." Intuitively, I knew that Father, as one of the community's patriarchs, would closely monitor my behavior for any sign of weakness. If I broke, cried, or didn't "measure up" during the hunting ritual, I was still my mother's boy, not yet ready to join the male collectivity of fathers and age-mates of the community core. I had to endure with grace the discipline that my patriarchal Father meted out in order to earn the right to be his son.

Besides initiating my rebirth as my Father's son, the hunting drama also helped me master my violent drives—destructive impulses that placed me in opposition to my Father and his law. My Father, seemingly competent in all things including hunting, was enviable and also admirable: a pillar of strength. He spread an umbrella of security over me under which I temporarily took shelter. Gradually, I gained sufficient skills to become my own hunter/achiever, moved away from Mother, and could declare myself to be a distinct person.

Hunting was a great democratic and egalitarian leveler. It taught the skills of observation, independence, calculation, and planning. All of my friends had shotguns and rifles of various gauges and calibers. We practiced the rules of safe hunting and always "broke" our shotguns and emptied the chamber before crawling under or through a fence. It was rare to see a "NO TRESPASSING" sign. Unlike the British preserves restricted for the English noblemen, in Pipestone county hunting was an equal opportunity activity. Everyone in our hunting fraternity would have agreed with the nun in Chaucer's *Canterbury Tales:* "ya've not of the text of a pulled hen / That saith that hunters ben not holy men."

Divorced from a symbiotic relationship with nature, some ecologists today are repulsed at the supposed "barbaric slaughter" of "innocent" animals. They know the idealized, not the real, animal. In a strange inversion of value, a few may even prefer animals to humans. They see only noble human qualities in their pets while injecting only the beastial in their fellow human beings. And how strange it is to apply "innocence" to a being without free will.

Like the ancients, however, I had an empathetic relationship with nature. Hunting was not considered ugly. We accepted the cosmic and classical scale of being that allows higher beings to responsibly use the lower forms of life. The culture in which I was reared was immersed in a 4-H Club ethos. Intuitively, I knew Darwin to be right long before I read *The Origin of Species* and *The Descent of Man.* I respected the creature that gave itself up for food and sport. Long before I studied the sacrificial cultus of the Old Testament, I existentially knew the symbolic meaning of blood, atonement, flesh, and the bounty of Nature.

How I looked forward to hunting season! Even as a small child, too young to shoot a gun, I had sprinted through the corn rows like a trained field dog, spotting the birds, flushing them up, and running down those that were wounded. I would collect empty shotgun shells— red Super-X, green Kleenbore, blue Peters—and sniff the exotic aroma of burnt powder, slip them over my fingers and click them together like miniature castanets.

At the age of 12 I started my hunting apprenticeship with the smallest shotgun made—a single-shot .410—then progressed through the .20-gauge to a .l6-gauge doublebarrel. Some of my friends used .12-

gauge weapons, but since Father had a .16-gauge Browning automatic, I didn't feel I needed anything larger.

I approached every fall with eager expectation. I longed to match wits with deer, pheasant, ducks, grouse, and rabbits by joining the hunting fraternity. Hunting seemed to moderate the authoritarian father-son relationship and created a more egalitarian bond. The compliment, "Good shot, Neb," would warm my heart for days. I was thrilled by the stalk and admired the cunning of an animal that could double back between the line of walkers and remain incognito while we walked past. It was not sinful to kill if one played fair. Rules concerning gun loads, hours, season, and size were strictly obeyed. This assured that enough game would survive for the coming year. A winter with deep snow and long periods of subzero temperatures would kill far more game than hunters could and starvation or freezing was a far more cruel death than a clean kill. Hunters, not arm chair sentimentalists, scattered corn for pheasants, helped restock lakes, and cut browse for starving deer. We despised the "pot fisherman" who kept small fish or the "meat hunter" who shot hen pheasants or fawns.

One fall, deep in the woods, I came upon a large buck from which only a magnificent rack of antlers and a hind quarter of venison had been salvaged. A light dusting of snow covered the carcass. "What a waste," I thought. Ridicule and social ostracism prevented such behavior in our group and enforced ethical hunting.

I began "road-siding" pheasants with Father when I was five years old. Many times we would go out for a half-hour before supper. I was warned to keep my eye peeled and taught that if I spotted one it wasn't enough to cry out, "There's one!" I learned to give as much specific and detailed information about the place, cover, and number of birds as I could so those with guns could perform at maximum efficiency. "There are two cocks about two hundred feet back on the right," I would shout. "They are 30 feet from the fence line in that clump of milk weeds." The car would grind to a halt and Father would pull out his .16-gauge Browning automatic from a half-zipped case and blaze away. (Once he touched the trigger before he got the gun out of the car and blew a hole in the floorboard of his Ford. Father found it easy to forgive himself for such a lapse; had it happened to me, I would have been subjected to a 30-minute lecture.) As the season wore on, the birds spooked more easily and flew off as soon as the car slowed down or stopped.

I walked the corn fields long before I was old enough to carry a gun. The worst farmers had the best hunting fields: weedy with short corn. Even so, I often felt as if I were walking through a forest. Sometimes I would almost step on a pheasant that was trying to hide. Skippy had not been trained to hunt, so I ran down wounded pheasants myself, wrung their necks, and hung them proudly from my belt. Later we would stick the tail feathers of cock birds in empty shell casings and use them as missiles.

Sometimes a group of 20 or 30 of us would walk an entire section of 640 acres in South Dakota. Because many farmers had gone into defense industries, much land was left fallow. The pheasants sometimes took flight by the hundreds and seemed to darken the sky. We always got our limit. Afterwards, the hunting group might come to our house for oyster soup, ping-pong, and story-telling.

During a trip, whenever we hit a pheasant we always stopped, picked it up, and threw it in the trunk. Later mother would cut out that portion that was too badly bruised to eat. The advantage of game hit by our car was that I didn't have to worry about biting down on some lead shot when eating the bird. One morning in 1936 on a trip to Minneapolis we had a "ten-strike." East of Gibbon on Highway #19 a dozen Peking ducks had waddled up out of the ditch and on to the road. Father had slowed down to about 50 mph going through the small village and had resumed putting "leather to the pedal." (He was a fast but careful driver.) Since it would have been dangerous to take evasive action at 65 miles an hour, Father plowed right through the middle of the flock. "Uncle" Charlie Hickman turned around and shouted, *"Nice going, Doc, you got three of 'em!"*

The undercarriage of cars then rode higher than today, and the bumper had snapped their necks without damaging the meat. Father braked to a stop and quickly performed a "boot-legger" turn. We sped back and "Uncle" Charlie and I jumped out, gathered up the weighty carcasses of the beautiful birds and threw them in the trunk. Since there wasn't a farm within a half a mile of the scene of the "crime" (later the event was called "The Peking Waterloo") we had no idea where the ducks had come from. Had we known to whom the ducks belonged, we later rationalized, we would have stopped and paid the farmer for the damage to his flock. As it was, the next Sunday we had a wonderful duck dinner, a real rarity during the Depression.

Searching for game in Alaska in 1957. Our August-September trip was the "mother of all hunting trips" and I secured a moose, Dall ram, caribou, and grizzly bear. We religiously "packed out" all of the meat that we possibly could.

13. DEER HUNTING: PRIMORDIAL BOND OF FATHER AND SON

My first deer hunting experience was traumatic. I was in the ninth grade when I went with Father, a Dutch farmer by the name of Van Bockle, and his twelfth-grade son. We drove all night to a cabin near International Falls. As we drove through the darkness, the radio kept us company with its weird seasonal personifications—*"When The Buck's Away, Shop at Betty's Lonely Doe Sale."* For the last fifty miles the deer were like cattle grazing along the edge of the road. Van Bockle wanted to "fill out" right then—"Come on, Doc, let's get ours right now!" Several times the Hollander opened the car door while we were moving. But "shining deer" by artificial light was illegal and I was proud of my Father for refusing to stop. That night we rested easily, knowing we would have a fine hunt the next day.

But I had significant obstacles to overcome. Small for my age, it was difficult for me to negotiate the hunting area, a burned-over peat bog. The snow was deep and the burn holes were filled with water thinly crusted over with ice. I was up and down all day, falling through the ice, wet and cold to my waist. The second day I was "on stand" with the temperature at about zero. It was hard to look for deer when I was flailing my arms and stomping my feet in an attempt to stay warm. Besides, I had a single-shot shotgun with slugs that I had never used before. After four days, I had not shot my weapon and had seen only one deer a mile off.

I was afraid we would go home skunked. I dreaded going back to school and having the refrain, "Didn't you get one? Did you get 'buck fever?'" stuck in my ear. A successful hunt was a badge of manhood. It would have been difficult to convince my friends that there was a lot of luck in hunting.

To prevent the trip from being a total loss, the Dutchman took a .22 caliber pistol during a lunch break and shot 20 pure white snowshoe rabbits. They had not seen a human before and he could walk right up to them. They were big and fat, about the size of a medium-weight dog. That evening Van Bockle and his son skinned the rabbits in our cabin. The son held the hind legs as the bloody pelt was stripped off, the gore and entrails dripping into a large galvanized wash tub. Father was at the stove preparing a deer heart and liver that some other hunters had given us. The sights, sounds, and odors of the rabbit blood and offal, the steam rising from the boiling heart and the liver sizzling in the frying pan assaulted my senses.

I went to the table bravely. For my age, I prided myself on my gastronomic tolerance. Until then I had only gagged on asparagus and liver—not bad for a thirteen year-old. I had heard that the French considered rabbits a gastronomical delight and I did not want to sully the good Benjamin name in front of strangers. But this was a test few boys my age would have won. The battle was lost before I even sat down. I was desperately hungry but the ambiance was so bizarre—sweaty human bodies, blood and guts of rabbits nearby, the nauseous aroma of potatoes, onions, rabbit, liver, and heart—that I was fated to lose. The others ate with gusto and I choked down what I could, knowing of the physical demands of the morrow.

Later that night as I shared a double bed with Father, I awoke in a cold sweat. My body became rigid, feverish, and began to shake. Suddenly, before I could lift my head from the pillow, a volcano of poorly masticated rabbit and deer organs surged up from my innards. I barely had time to turn my head as a missile of vomit hit the cottage wall and cascaded to the floor. Mercifully Father, seeing my distress, cleaned up the mess. At home I would not have gotten off so easily.

I remained in bed the next day as our troop, now depleted by one-fourth, ventured forth in yet another unsuccessful foray. Two days later we broke camp with only the bloody, stinking rabbits as emblems of our hunting artistry. To prevent the trip from being a total waste, we picked up 300 pounds of russet potatoes, a good buy at two cents a pound. But the fine potato dust filtered through the sacks and made me nauseous. We crept back into Pipestone under cover of darkness without deer decorating our front fenders. What a shame. I had yet to prove my manhood. I told my friends I had a great time and skipped the details.

I was 15 when I shot my first deer, a six-point buck that had followed several does out of a clearing. That was his undoing, for I was fortunate in getting a good shoulder shot from a distance of 200 feet. The buck gave a great leap but went only 50 feet before collapsing in the deep snow. In an epiphany of both wonder and dread, I slowly walked up to the magnificient animal and looked down at what my marksmanship had wrought. It was an awesome moment and I must have been as immobile as a statue for at least two minutes. Then I let out a war-hoop, *"I got a buck! I got a buck!"* and within 15 minutes Father appeared. He was pleased but tried not to show it. I expected him to dress-out my deer but instead he handed me his hunting knife, razor sharp, and pulled the buck over on its back. Several times I had witnessed his surgical technique on deer (as well as on our Thanksgiving turkeys), and I hoped he took greater care with his patients in the operating room.

"Grab his genitals," Father commanded, "and cut around them. Then slice up his belly, and make sure you don't nick the stomach or the gut or you will ruin the meat." My hands were covered with sticky blood up to my elbows. "Cut around the rectum and pull it through. Careful you don't cut yourself!" I worked feverishly deep within the body cavity as the warm gore created steam when it met the cold November air. Following Father's directions, I cut open the diaphragm, reached up and severed the esophagus and windpipe and then turned the buck over to get rid of the entrails. The lungs were a beautiful pale pink and, had I shut my eyes, they would have felt like I had my hands in tapioca pudding. Father said my shot had destroyed the aorta and that the buck had not suffered. I felt good about that. Hunting lore also dictated that the scent glands on the two rear feet had to be cut off to minimize the venison becoming too strong. We saved the heart and liver and impaled them on a forked stick.

Then the tough part began—dragging my kill three-quarters of a mile to the road—an ordeal that took two hours. I tied a rope to the antlers and Father and I each grabbed an end. I was drenched in sweat by the time we got out even though other members of the party heard us coming and helped the last 300 feet. They patted me on the back and congratulated me. In spite of the cold, I had left my sleeves rolled up to show my bloody hands and arms. Symbolically, I considered them a close equivalent to the Army's Purple Heart.

Our worst hunting disaster came to be known as the "para-typhoid" trip. Twelve members of the Benjamin Tribe—uncles, brothers, friends, and "hangers-on," as my Father called our non-genetic relatives—lived for five days in the unheated attic of a mink rancher near Ray, Minnesota. It was bitter cold with temperatures rarely rising above zero. We took our meals with the family and slept on mattresses on the attic floor. Our bathroom was a two-holer at the end of a snow-packed path, 100 feet behind the house.

At dinner, after the first day of hunting, the *piece de resistance* was lemon meringue pie. The dinner and dessert having been wolfed down, coffee drunk, and exploits of the day's hunt recounted, we went to bed. Sometime in the dark of night, I awoke to muffled cries of pain, heavy breathing, loud flatus, belching, moaning, tossing and turning. Then it struck me. My belly began to churn. Each of us at first, believing that we alone had been stricken, tried to bear the suffering in silence. But as minute by minute the volume of our distress increased, it became clear that a plague had crippled our entire hunting party.

When I began to hear swearing I knew that the situation was desperate. Today's four-letter words were not allowed by my parents. It was barely permissible to say "Jeez," "Hell," "Damn," and "Crap." So when I heard someone cry out in the darkness, "Judas H. Priest, where in the hell is that f...ing commode!" I knew that the situation was desperate. We plunged down the stairway in our one-piece woolen long underwear with the back flap already unbuttoned ready for action. Some never made it and stopped somewhere on the path; others, finding the two holer occupied, detoured behind the shanty for relief. A few had to repeat the trek half a dozen times that night, fearing frostbite less than fouling themselves. The fact that some were not successful was evident from the increasing degradation of the atmosphere in the attic as the night progressed. The only window was nailed shut.

In retrospect, our routine that evening seemed to have been a combination of a Laurel and Hardy routine and John Balushi's *Animal House*. By sunrise the churning of our collective bowels had moderated, undoubtedly because they had been fairly well emptied out: tribal members then began to trace the etiology of the malady. After a heated debate it was agreed that the delectable but unrefrigerated lemon meringue pies had spawned a para-typhoid organism. The diagnosis, right or wrong, could not salvage our hunting trip. Some of us were not well for days; others had recurrences at home. We did not sue. Neither did we ever go back.

One of our most humorous yet potentially tragic episodes came during rabbit hunting. Jackrabbits had excellent fur that was made into parkas for our airmen, and the American Legion organized Sunday hunting parties where the animals were slaughtered by the dozen. Jackrabbits were big as spaniels, and when I held one up by the ears, his length extended from my armpits to the ground. Good pelts brought $1.25, an excellent price. But unlike the lowly and tamer cottontail, jacks were difficult to shoot. They zigzagged at over 50 miles an hour over difficult terrain. You could hit them with a .22 rifle if they were sitting still, but it took a shotgun if they were running. At night you needed a spotlight to get them in your sights. The difficulty was getting close enough.

One cold January night in 1941, Bob, Les Kallsen, and I piled into Father's Ford to get some jacks. Father drove slowly down gravel roads, swiveling his spotlight from side to side. We hoped to catch a jack out in a field in the beam. Bob rode shotgun while Les and I were in the back seat, shivering with cold, our shotguns half cased. "There's one," I shouted, "at 10 o'clock, 600 feet out on the plowed field!"

Father shifted into second gear; the Ford charged down the road-side ditch and lurched up onto the plowed field. The snow tires screeched as they tore through the ice and frozen black clods of dirt. "Don't let him get away," we screamed as Father tried to manipulate the spotlight with his left hand and drive and shift with his right. (I think Father could have qualified to drive a Sherman tank in one of Patton's elite battalions.) We were trying to get close enough to the jack so we could exit with all four guns blazing. Like Bob and Les, I was lovingly yet nervously caressing my weapon.

All at once there was a deafening "KAH BOOM" in the car. Acrid smoke filled my eyes and stung my nostrils. I couldn't see outside the car and wondered how Father could see to drive. For a split second I imagined we were in combat and that our Jeep had hit a land mine. Full of apprehension I began checking my legs for blood and then my gun. I noticed that Bob and Les were furtively doing the same. Father kept driving after the jack. After what must have been a full minute, he said in a voice that had been conditioned by repeated medical crises to remain calm:

"Bob, did your gun go off?"
"Nun...nun...nun...nun...NO, Dad!" cried Bob.
"Neb, did your gun go off?"
"Nun...nun...nun...nun...NO, Dad!" I groaned.

Then I heard a wee little voice I didn't recognize at first. *"IT...IT...IT...IT...WAS ME, DOC!"* said Les in the strangest falsetto I had ever heard. "Are you all right?" *"I...I...I...THINK SO!"* replied Les as he started to massage his legs. The smoke gradually cleared. Father kept after the jack. We didn't stop. Father had shifted into high and was making turns that would do an Indianapolis 500 driver proud. Les had been sitting behind Father when his .12 gauge shotgun discharged. He had succumbed to "jack fever," an aberrant form of "buck fever." Several dozen number 6 shot pellets had barely missed Father's buttocks and medical bag. The jack got away. Our hunting became rather desultory the rest of the night; we had had our peak experience for the day. We dropped Les off, said goodnight, drove home, put the car in the garage, and went to bed without looking at the collateral damage to the Ford. Father did not blame Les. Nor did he harangue us with moral lessons to be drawn from the experience. He knew the event needed no reinforcement or embellishment.

In school the next day, Les was still a bit shaken and pale from the experience. He reported that Ada, his step-mother and a nurse, had checked Father's car in front of the hospital. She told him how lucky he had been. I don't remember Les ever accepting our invitation to go rabbit hunting again.

For all of my love of hunting, however, I didn't particularly like the meat. Pheasant was good, duck passable. Venison was difficult to choke down. It was full of gristle and stringy, and when the fat got cold, it would stick to the roof of my mouth. Because it wasn't processed immediately after being shot, its flavor was too strong. Unlike many hunters today we did not mix it with pork and grind it into hamburger. I hated to admit I didn't like it for fear of endangering my status as a hunter. It was unmanly not to like what you had shot. After I was married, we ate it more to help the slim budget and as a pedagogical tool for our children rather than for enjoyment.

My brother, Dickie, at 10 months. Polio was the scourge of children during the Great Depression. After being sick for only 48 hours, Dickie died of "the Summer Terror" shortly before his second birthday.

14. FAMILY TRAUMA: THE SUMMER TERROR AND THE ACCIDENT

Rieux could feel himself at one with them...these plague-stricken people...We learn in a time of pestilence, that there are more things to admire in men than to despise. But there was no final victory, only what had to be done in the never ending fight against terror...for the plague bacillus never dies or disappears for good.

The Plague, Albert Camus

It is better to drink of deep griefs than to taste shallow pleasures.

William Hazlitt

It was not only poverty and unemployment that parents feared during the Great Depression. Each summer Father and Mother faced the great crippler of little children, polio, which stalked the land during the dog days of July and August. Poliomyelitis, polio's scientific term—from two Greek roots, *polios* (gray) and *myelos* (marrow)—was a demonic disease that attacked a child's spinal cord and caused paralysis. Every neighborhood had at least one child with a twisted stick of a leg encased in metal braces.

As the long, hot days began, our family routine changed. We were scrupulous in washing our hands and avoiding crowds. The age-old remedy of isolation strained community bonds. We avoided crowds and shunned playmates for fear they might carry contagion. Theaters were shut down, Sunday schools closed, swimming pools drained, the county and state fairs canceled. Families who could, left for farms or lakeside cottages.

Despite these precautions, no one was safe from polio, not even the family of a doctor who had trained at the Mayo Clinic. Neither Father's personal connections nor his medical skills held sway over the Terror.

I was not quite four, so my recollections are fleeting, but I remember the day I was playing in the sandbox with my two-year-old brother, Dickie. He had very blue eyes and lots of curly hair for one so young. Being an older sibling, whose natural role is to torment the younger, I filled his diapers with sand and made him cry.

But one day Dickie suddenly became, as was said in those days, "cranky." He would not calm down and ran a high fever. The law prevented Father from admitting him to our 20-bed hospital for fear of contagion. In desperation he called a former classmate who was practicing pediatrics in Minneapolis; after a late-night drive, the doctor arrived at our house. I was supposed to be asleep, but I could hear Father and the specialist talking and Mother crying. They put Dickie on Mother's dressing table, gave him some ether to put him to sleep, and performed a spinal tap, which revealed that bulbar polio had invaded his brain. Less than 48 hours after he'd become cranky, Dickie was dead.

The law required that anyone who died of a contagious disease be buried within 24 hours in a sealed, metal casket. No more than 15 people could attend the funeral. Dickie was buried in a small, galvanized steel coffin in our family plot at Hutchinson. After Dickie's death, we visited his grave every year on Memorial Day to adorn it with spirea and tulips from our yard.

As they returned from Dickie's funeral that evening, Father and Mother could see light coming from every window in the house. Something was wrong. Anna, our hired girl, greeted them at the door with news: "Bobbie," she said in a frightened tone, "started getting cranky this afternoon." Mother broke down and cried as Father ran up the stairs to join a physician colleague with my brother.

The Summer Terror had struck again.

Grasping for hope and any remedy that might stem the onslaught against our family, Father frantically sought blood from any child who had survived polio. After many fruitless calls, he finally persuaded a farm family whose child had recovered from polio to give a few ounces to Bobbie. No medical evidence suggested that the transfusion would be beneficial, but when one's personal world is collapsing, desperate responses follow. Bobbie was driven to the University of Minnesota hospital where, after some paralysis, he fully recovered.

It was assumed then that for every child who got sick with polio, at least 100 were infected with the virus, yet managed somehow to resist it. Many children became ill with high fevers and headaches; most of them got well. But for a few, their temperature would go down for a day and then shoot up again. That was a bad sign. Physicians called it the "dromedary type" because there would be humps of high fever. The apprehension and shaking hands of some parents meant they could scarcely read their children's thermometer. A high reading often set off panic and hysteria.

The Minnesota newspapers covered polio like they reported sports, recording the daily tally of the number of cases confirmed. On some August days the number reached 50; some years the total number of cases came close to 4,000.

Mother often wondered why I was spared. She surmised that Dickie had caught polio from some neighborhood children who had played with him in the sandbox several days before he became ill. But I was there too! She gave thanks for an early September frost that, although it devastated our gardens, brought an end to the Summer Terror. When I was a teenager, she took me into the bedroom and lifted the scarf from the dressing table where the doctor had examined Dickie and showed me where the ether had marred the varnish. She never had it refinished. Along with a few photos, a pair of booties, and a locket of hair, it was a talisman of the most devastating moment in her life. Like every woman who has lost an infant, Mother had gained a child of immortal youth.

The Summer Terror revealed the truth of Kierkegaard to my parents: "it requires moral courage to grieve; it requires religious courage to rejoice."

In the early 1960s my wife, Marjorie, and I thought of Dickie as we watched our grade-school children, Barbara and Mark, swallow a few drops of Salk vaccine. My eyes filled with tears. The advent of a new medical ritual could make them, and all future children, forever immune to the Summer Terror. We and other parents would never again be fearful with the warming of the earth. Our children would never see homes marked with the "sign of Cain"—QUARANTINED—that we had hurried past. Neither would they see their classmates, as I had seen mine, dragging crippled limbs along, their legs as thin as sticks and burdened with cumbersome metal braces. We would never again have a president like Franklin Delano Roosevelt, struck by the Great Crippler in the prime of life, a master at statescraft but physically impaired. The March of Dimes would have to turn to other concerns.

Each generation has its own peculiar Terror—be it in the form of polio, the mushroom-shaped cloud, or Aids—that stalks the land in its time. The "good old days" were not always all that benevolent. Polio was but one of many diseases—typhoid, tuberculosis, rickets, St. Vitus' Dance, rheumatic fever, smallpox, scarlet fever—that are almost non existent today. Parents no longer fear that their children will be taken from them by infectious diseases; rather, that they will be maimed by accidents, promiscuity, liquor, or drugs. Back then, dozens of diseases, true destroyers of children, lay in wait to carry them away and medicine was all but helpless to intervene. Couples no longer have to have eight or ten children in order to have four or five reach adulthood.

Sometimes I think of how courageous my parents were, and indeed all parents, to live through the Summer Terror. Generations of parents prayed for magic potions that would save their children from mysterious diseases. Legions of tombstones bear witness to how long they waited. Sometimes I grow sad thinking of the countless numbers of Dickies whose lives and genius were fated never to unfold.

Years later I read about the 500,000 causualties the British Army suffered during the Battle of the Somme in 1916. An entire generation of German, French and English boys were killed during the Great War. I realized there were a legion of older Dickies whose untimely and sudden death came not alone through disease, but also through accident, pestilence, and war.

> Remember that he was, with thankful heart,
> The bright, the brave, the tender, and the true.
> Remember where he is—from sin apart,
> Presence with God—yet not estranged from you.
> But never doubt that love, and love alone,
> Removed thy loved one from this trial scene,
> Nor idly dream, since he to God had gone,
> Of what, had he been left, he might have been.

My mind, like that of most children, was like a *tabula rasa*. My subconscious was deep-dyed by traumatic moments. One cold winter morning when I was three, I awoke to the plaintive cry of "Bobbie...Nebbie ...Bobbie...Nebbie." Was I dreaming? The voice seemed familiar yet strange, near yet far off. I got up and went downstairs. Mother was on the sofa wrapped in a quilt quietly crying. As she hugged me fiercely I could feel cold and strange metal and straps beneath her robe.

Dr. Rider, Father, and Mother had been in an accident during the early hours of the morning. They had attended a medical meeting in the Twin Cities and, while driving home, Dr. Rider had fallen asleep at the wheel. The Buick had gone through the guard rail on highway 75, fifteen miles north of Pipestone.

"We had just enough momentum to break through," Mother said, "and I remember counting the times we rolled over—one, two, three— each time hoping it would be the last." She described how the car ended up on a frozen creek bed, 40 feet below the road. "I screamed...Walter! Walter! Walter!" Just when she feared the worst, Father answered matter-of-factly, "What do you want?" He had been asleep in the back seat, wrapped up in a buffalo robe and had only a slight cut on one ear.

The big Buick was on its side. Mother had a broken collar bone and severe bruises. Dr. Rider, his back broken, was in bad shape. Father wrapped them up against the below-zero weather and then, guided by a yard light, walked to a farm a half-mile away. "It seemed like an eternity that he was gone," Mother said softly. "Dr. Rider was getting numb, in pain, and wasn't answering me. My job was to keep him awake. Finally Father came back with a farmer, a team of horses and a hay wagon. We laid Dr. Rider on some hay but he screamed as we bounced over the plowed fields."

The dents in the Buick were pounded out, new glass was installed, and the torn upholstery stitched back together. For as long as we kept that car, however, I would look at the cuts in the fabric and think about the fragility of life, of Mother's feelings, the events of that night, and how close I came to losing a parent or even becoming an orphan. Whenever we drove by the accident site on the way to tobogganing, I thought of the car rolling over and over and tensed up as the car went by the fragile barrier. I was grateful that my parents had survived and I was not left alone in a fearsome world.

Father was on much better terms with physicians in neighboring towns than he was with his fellow Pipestone practitioners, probably because their medical turf did not intersect they were not a threat to each other. His favorite was Dr. Rider, who was born and trained in Germany and who practiced surgery in Flandreau, South Dakota. They would often consult and do surgery together. Rider was a man of renaissance interests who, following a lengthy tour through Italy, Germany, and England in the spring of 1939, delivered his reflections before Kiwanis.

Rider didn't just talk about his positive impressions of the surgical skills of his European peers; he also defended the social benefits of Fascism. Like many people of that era who held isolationist sentiments, he allowed moralism to dull his critique of totalitarianism. Mussolini, Rider said, had "eliminated the beggars," whereas in London "15 to 20 street walkers could be found on Piccadilly" within blocks of his hotel. The Fascists made the trains run on time; the *autobahn* was impressive, and Hitler had promised every family a Volkswagen. Rider said that in Vienna all medical professionals had been completely won over by Hitler; during hospital rounds, patients had to stand by their beds and give ringing "Heil Hitlers," with physicians responding in kind. "It was very dramatic," Rider commented, ignoring the fact that the salute symbolized loyalty to the Nazis. Asked repeatedly, "Why was Franklin D. Roosevelt making it so hard for Hitler?" Rider found the question difficult to answer.

In those days Colonel Charles Lindbergh was one of the most

admired citizens in the United States and had accepted a medal from Adolf Hitler. As late as 1941, in a speech in Des Moines, the Lone Eagle castigated the Jews and accused them of pushing America into World War II. Tragically, Rider fully supported Charles Lindbergh's isolationist stance and his admiration for Germany. Its gross domestic product was increasing, unemployment lines were gone, factories were humming, and the German burgher had a new bounce in his step. Although profession-ally competent, Rider ignored the storm clouds in *Mein Kampf*—"The one means that wins the easiest victory over reason: terror and force." Likewise he was deaf to Benito Mussolini's assertion that "We have buried the putrid corpse of liberty," Hermann Goering's, "Guns will make us powerful; butter will only make us fat," and Baldur von Schirach's, "He who serves our Fuhrer, Adolf Hitler, serves Germany, and he who serves Germany, serves God." Rider was in denial as to the portents of the Nazi brownshirts as they sang and goose-stepped outside his Munich hotel window: "Today all Germany is ours. Tomorrow the whole world."

In times of crisis, Germany, more than any other Western country, capitulated to an instinct as old as mankind—the proclivity to opt for a savior. Besides, Hitler had built an impressive network of autobahns and made the trains run on time. Like legions of cultured intellectuals, he denied the essentially irrational nature of Nazi doctrine, which stressed blood, sentiment, and instinct rather than reason. When chaos threat-ens, the majority of citizens of any nation will always allow unity and order to trump freedom and independence. Totalitarian regimes, unlike democracies, don't allow litter or panhandlers on the streets.

When war came, Rider lamented that "it was senseless, just a new episode in Europe's age-long struggle for power and new boundaries. Leave European problems for Europeans and their representatives of greed, drum-beaters and their self-seeking politicians."

Rider's view was difficult to fathom because while he was in Munich he found all hospitals were *"Judensaal"* (free of Jews), and he discovered a Jewish home for the sick and interviewed patients who complained that their illnesses came from concentration camp experiences. Whatever Rider's professional and medical competence, like many citizens of that era, he wore moral blinders. Most foreign observers visiting Germany and Italy in the 1930s expressed admiration and even envy when reporting the new spirit of optimism in the fascist regimes. They preferred social order, albeit purchased at the price of totalitarian coercion, to the discord of democratic freedom. Rider's reverence for German culture trumped his moral capital.

Shortly after Rider's talk, either due to his trip or his views, the FBI questioned Father as to Rider's loyalty to his adopted land. Father was upset for days. He may have thought Rider was naive, but that hardly made him disloyal.

15. HOME MANAGEMENT AND THE HOBO

The Great Depression completely dominated the cultural ethos in which I grew up. Although our family was never threatened by poverty, as were millions across the land, Father had to adjust his fees to the level of his patients' income. Because more than half of his patients were farmers, a great deal of payment in kind—milk, butter, eggs, ducks, chickens, pork, and beef—came to our home. Once I cut off the heads, scalded, plucked and helped can 25 stewing hens. Mother disdained the scrawny eight-week old chickens sold in the stores. "They are nothing but skin and bone and don't have any flavor. I prefer an 'old biddy' every time." I was fascinated to watch the chickens bounce around the yard for 10 seconds after being guillotined. When halves of hogs and quarters of beef were carried down to the basement, I got a practical course in anatomy as I tried to find the joints with my knife to cut the carcass apart.

Home freezers were unknown; in the winter our roasts and steaks went into a metal box against the north side of the house. Every Saturday I would dig away the snow and ice and come up with an appropriate joint for our Sunday dinner. Sometimes I had to make several trips before my selection met with Mother's approval.

Mother's German ancestry decreed that much of our pork should be ground up, mixed with spices, and stuffed into casings of hog intestines. While filling the slimy intestines, I vowed never to eat them. But months later, when these curled white tubes were removed from quart jars, browned, mixed with mashed potatoes and sauerkraut, I devoured them. It was an old German recipe that Grandmother Bedell had passed down to Mother.

During the Depression there was a great demand for seasonal labor, much of which was supplied by an army of drifting men called hoboes. (Over the years the terms applied to wanderers and the unemployed have been confused until all meaning has been lost. A bum was a local man who did not want to work. A tramp was a wanderer of the same kind, but a hobo was a wandering worker and essential to the nation's economy. Depression-era hoboes, for the most part, did not suffer from the multiple pathologies of today's urban homeless underclass.)

Although associated with the Depression era, hoboes began "riding the rails" much earlier. After the Civil War, many unemployed soldiers without families became loners, men without homes. America was expanding westward with the railroads, and short term employment was to be found along the railroads. When work fizzled out, they hopped a train (without tickets) for another site further along the tracks.

(The origin of the term "hobo" is not entirely certain, although there are at least three possibilities. The Latin "*homo bonus*" means good man; Civil War veterans were "homeward bound;" and finally, this group of young men willing to work were called "hoe boys" doing agricultural work.)

During the '30s hoboes had a national organization and a code of conduct. Crime was almost nonexistent, and those who were "down on their luck" had a great deal of respect for each other. The residential "soft touch" was marked with a form of hobo art on mailboxes, sidewalks, or gateposts. A piece of chalk or grease pencil did the trick. Hobo Depression "art" was father of the World War II "KILROY WAS HERE" cartoons wherever GIs and sailors went. There were many prominent men who were proud of their hobo "knock-about" days; among them, film writer/director Richard Brooks, Charlie Chaplain, Chief Justice William O. Douglas, Clark Gable, Woody Guthrie, Emmet Kelly, Louis L'Amour, Art Linkletter, Jack London, James Michener, and Red Skelton.

Every year around the middle of August, the National Hobo Convention meets in Britt, Iowa (population 2,133 in 1999), a tradition that dates back to 1900. Each summer this Iowa community fetes the free-spirited travelers with a parade, carnival, Mulligan stew feast, coronation of a king and queen, and a large flea market.

In the days before the big combines it was the hobo who shocked the grain. They picked up the eight or ten bundles dropped by a binder and stacked them butt first on the ground so that later they could be picked up for threshing. Many hoboes would start working the harvest in Texas and follow the ripening and golden ocean of grain as the summer tide moved through Oklahoma, Kansas, Nebraska, Minnesota and the Dakotas. During harvest season, when the demand for farm labor was great, freight trains allowed the hoboes to ride gratis. Since the railroads were to ship the harvested grain, it was in their interest to see that labor was available.

Mixed in with these harvest hoboes were college boys earning money for school or working to get in shape for football. By and large they were Anglo-Saxon and Irish, with a few other immigrants of European extraction. As the Depression deepened, a different kind of drifter came into Pipestone. The carefree, cheerful attitude of the earlier hobo was lost and we began to experience a more serious and often frightened wanderer. There were at least four or five men for every job, and finding work was like a game of musical chairs.

The criminal element was small. During the Depression the poor rarely stole, and when they did, it was petty theft—something to eat or perhaps an item of clothing to keep them warm. The hungry men were without power, without leverage, and were often vulnerable to any kind of bully and were constantly accused of crimes they rarely had committed. While our hoboes may have been objects of compassion they were seldom feared. The vast majority were simply "down on their luck" and not addicted to booze, money, sex, or drugs.

During these knockabout years our midwestern hoboes created a repertoire of song and poetry that was passed down by word of mouth. I enjoyed singing some of their songs—"Hallelujah, I'm a Bum," "The Bum Song," "The Dying Hobo," and "Big Rock Candy Mountain"—as I walked to school. My friend Neal Knudtsen was good at memorizing some of their quatrains:

> I've juggled a tray in a New York cafe,
> Hopped bells in a hotel in Chi.
> I've carried a pack down the B&O track,
> And hopped Red Ball freights on the fly.

We shouted out the words in a sing-song of cadence but, in our youthful innocence, were completely oblivious to the pathos of the message.

> I've clerked in Kansas City,
> Sold insurance in St. Paul,
> Peddled books in Dallas, Texas,
> And gone hungry in them all.

Occasionally a hobo would come to our back door and ask if there were any odd jobs that needed to be done. He had dropped off the Great Northern two-and-a-half blocks away from our home as the engineer slowed for the station. Most wore blue jeans and had a coat of the same denim material. A Confederate soldier-type bedroll started at the top of the left shoulder and curved around the back and ended at the right hip. They had clodhopper shoes and the majority wore an old flat-brimmed Stetson-type hat. Their bodies had been ravaged by the artillery of time. Their faces reminded me of dried beef and the outside corners of their eyes were drawn down with the hooded lids of age. But however bright and piercing, their eyes were deeply set in their sockets and instead of sweetness in them, I perceived a deep sadness. Life had not gone well with them. Lines fanned out from the corners of their eyes and often framed a sad smile. The character in Frost's poem— "And nothing to look backward to with pride/And nothing to look forward to with hope"—seemed to profile their internal condition. Some of the drifting men who came smelled a bit sour but I did not find it unpleasant. Their strong bony wrists and hands were often gnarled and knotted and seemed as hard as a hackberry branch. However deeply impressed I was by their physical appearance, it was the hobo's quiet dignity and manner that was especially poignant to me. I pitied their poverty, but they did not seem to be impoverished.

Popular attitudes found it agreeable to romanticize some of the criminal element. Woody Guthrie's 1939 song, *"The Ballad of Pretty Boy Floyd,"* mythicized bank robbers as Robin Hoods who gave to the poor:

> There's many a starving farmer the same
> old story told
> How the outlaw paid their mortgage and
> saved their little home.

Guthrie's closing verses made the point many others left unarticulated in their romanticization of criminals:

> Yes, as through this world I ramble,
> I see lots of funny men,
> Some will rob you with a 6-gun, and
> some will rob you with a pen.
> But as through your life you'll travel,
> whenever you may roam,
> You won't never see an outlaw drive
> a family from their home.

Such songs, especially in an agricultural society, allowed people to maintain the myths and "the vision of a just society."

No one I knew in Pipestone agreed with Nietzsche's cynical assertion that "beggars should be abolished. It annoys one to give to them, and it annoys one not to give to them." Mother always fed the hoboes that came to our door. Rachel Hickman made a nice ham sandwich for a hobo one day but then saw him go behind the garage. After he left she found he had trimmed all the fat from his ham. Her husband, Charles, didn't think the drifter was that hungry for having wasted all that "good fat." He had been eating it all of his life and it hadn't hurt him any.

I marveled that the hoboes always ate the asparagus, beets and some other vegetables that caused me to gag. Too young and naive to know that my scrutiny might embarrass them, I would sit at the other end of the kitchen table and watch them eat. They had good table manners and respectfully addressed Mother as "Ma'am" and always said "Thank you" when they left the table. Poverty had not eroded their civility. Their clothes may have been old and faded but I remember that they were fairly clean. Mother would pay them if she could find extra work for them to do; it was against my parent's principles to give anyone money without work. Thoughtless charity was "compassion that killed the soul." Sometimes there was enough work for two or three days, in which case they would unsling their blanket roll and sleep in our basement or garage. My parents may have drawn some tight Puritanical lines against some people and classes, but I never remember a negative word against a hobo.

I was impressed by their quiet dignity. Hitchhikers picked up by Father often apologized to him for their condition. Unlike many of the homeless today, our hoboes did not seem to be afflicted by mental illness, alcoholism, or drugs. They had been set adrift by hard times or some minor personal failing and had gravitated to live on the periphery of family life. They were dressed and groomed as well as their financial circumstances allowed. The deeply etched lines in their weathered faces seemed to be "character crinkles." They did not carry signs advertising "Will Work For Food," but if they had, the money would have been spent for bread and not liquor or drugs. They came from and returned to a world beyond my comprehension. I often wished I could make their sojourn with us easier. When I compared their clothes with mine, which were clean and pressed, I began to feel guilty. I had a security unknown to them. At night before dropping off to sleep, I wondered what life had done to them, where they had come from, and what might happen to them after leaving our home. Our hoboes never took anything or said anything unkind.

Sometimes hoboes occupied an old shack by the Great Northern railroad tracks just outside the city limits. A few hoboes got day-old bread from the bakery or eatshops or anywhere they could get something to add to the pot of mulligan stew often cooked in a gallon can picked up along the way. They would chop wood, sharpen scissors or unload a car of coal for 10 cents an hour. Often their only cover at night was a sheet of the building paper used to line box cars that hauled grain. Under those conditions cleanliness was next to impossible for long.

The Depression was the origin of my thriftiness. The line between being stingy and thrifty, miserly and saving, is a difficult one to draw. The Depression is the source of my feeling guilty about spending money on luxuries, throwing away left over food, discarding clothes before they are worn out, wasting hot water, burning unneeded electric lights, having more shoes or clothes than I can use, having the house temperature above 68 degrees…the list is endless!

Mother usually made lye soap several times a year. Because we did not have a fireplace, Mother had to buy commercial lye. Like many Iowa farm families, Grandma Bedell dumped the winter's hardwood ashes into a big V-shaped hopper. In the spring buckets of water were poured over the ashes until pure lye ran into a trough underneath. Mixed with fat meat, stale grease, and sometimes even bones, the lye and grease were then cooked "thick as thickenin' gravy." At the proper consistency the vile smelling stuff was poured into a shallow wooden crate lined with paper. When cool it was cut into squares.

If the mixture was poured while it was still jellylike, it was called "soft soap." Thus, the expression "Don't let them soft-soap you." Mother let her soap rest for six weeks before using it since, it was claimed, "fresh-made soap takes the skin off'n yore hands." It looked much like Fels-Naphtha and I suspect Grandma Bedell used it for lathering up a dirty horse or cleaning up the privy. Mother claimed store-bought soap couldn't hold a candle to her lye-made soap. Everyone who made it claimed it would "eat up everything except the steel pan it was made in." Some Pipestone women used it as a sure cure for skin diseases such as impetigo. Mother restricted its use to our clothes, since it was too strong for our skin.

The psyches of my parents were also scarred by privation, both actual and potential. The possibility of penury was omnipresent. Money spent on movies, soda pop (Father called it "colored sugar water that makes millionaires"), candy, tobacco, and liquor moved one closer to the void. Even if I could afford them, frugality was necessary for character formation. Until leaving home, I rarely saw a movie. On Sunday it violated the Sabbath; on week days, it was wasteful. It was a heads Father won, tails I lost proposition. Even now, a half century later, I feel uneasy seeing a film on Sunday. The sensate values of many of today's youth, too, make me uneasy. Since many have never known privation, I wonder if it would be difficult for them to give up spending $7.00 for a movie, $3.00 for popcorn, and $2.50 for "colored sugar water" should hard times return.

The effects of the Depression were not all bad. During those years, people tended to draw closer together, and there was less social differentiation. Because the role of the state was modest, the bonds of creative compassion that linked extended families were often tighter than they are now.

The lack of a governmental safety net also encouraged self-reliance. There was no automatic preferential treatment for the poor because respect had to be earned, as by adherence to a moral code. The poor were not viewed solely as the helpless victims of circumstance, absolved of accountability, or excused from moral dereliction on the grounds that poverty carried with it a presumption of innocence. Indeed, there seemed to be a recognition that expansion of state power would weaken the moral and social ties of families. (Which is just what has happened. Today, families are insular and include single parents, divorced parents, childless couples, same-sex couples and numerous other configurations; then, the definition of "family" had normative connotations: father, mother, children was the terrestrial pattern of the celestial Trinity.)

The Depression was a time before Dale Carnegie and Norman Vincent Peale had discovered the importance of self-esteem. There was shame attached to anti-social behavior. "Shameless" behavior was eschewed lest we live at the level of primitive primates. Stigmas were real and had social shock value. The application of terms like *bastard, tramp, slut, bum* and other terms was a form of social "tough love" that warned people to stay within behavior channels that enhanced the common good. "What if *everybody* did that?" was a mantra repeated ad nausem by mothers everywhere because they believed that "outlandish," "perverse," and "degraded" behaviors were pathogens to the body politic. Shame forced us to know and remember our failures and thus acted as a pedagogue. Good parents, teachers, physicians, and pastors were necessarily and properly "judgmental." It came with their calling.

My Pipestone mentors were not especially concerned that I "feel good about myself." They would have done me a terrible disservice if they had showered me with undeserved approval. Self-respect could not be conferred; it had to be earned by risking failure and disappointment. Stigmas, shame, judgment, rules, and high standards, were necessary to firm up the internal values—civility, industry, honor, deference, self-restraint—held indispensable to personal governance and to a democracy. Given the eternal tension between responsibility and rights, the focus of that era was on responsibility and accountability.

My Mother, the full-time homemaker, would have argued that she had greater freedom than many mothers today. She never felt compelled to work for another car, set of drapes, carpet, or furniture suite. Nor did she view her home as a prison or domestic work as indentured servitude. Her major in home economics was respected because the public knew the family was the cardinal character-shaping institution in society. No one doubted the aphorism, "the hand that rocks the cradle rules the world." Nor did she spend time worrying about whether as a woman, she was being "fulfilled." She would have laughed had anyone told her she was an unconscious victim of a guileful "patriarchy." She had precious little time to worry about the internal state of her psyche because she was fully focused on the needs of her family, neighbors, church, and community.

Nor did she have to trade any part of her motherhood for the presumed freedom afforded by a day-care center or baby-sitter. No one could have convinced her that her freedom and the "good life" were attained outside rather than within the home. She was her own boss, had a loving and faithful husband, paid the bills, invested her own money in stocks and bonds, was proud of her skills, and raised five loving and loyal children who showed every promise of "making something of themselves." She was always "there" for her children and this is probably the reason that none of the five of us was ever in any serious trouble.

The Depression reduced the cardinal vice of the affluent, according to Thorstein Veblen, that is, "conspicuous consumption." The bonds between those suffering privation were stronger than those that link the affluent. Moreover, they were comforted by words of Jesus—"Blessed are the poor for they shall be filled." The few privileged families in Pipestone were largely incognito, for it was most unseemly to flaunt one's wealth. The suffering of so many prompted the fortunate to live abstemious lives. The well-to-do were "fat of purse but thin on living." At times I was shocked at the size of the estate left by someone thought to have fallen on lean times. Although our family could have afforded a Buick, Packard, or Cadillac, Father always drove a Ford, and Mother, an Oldsmobile. Nobody, it seemed, would admit to being either poor or rich—everyone was middle class.

Money had a strange power. It was necessary to have enough of it to keep the wolf from the door, yet it could possess one's soul and lead to damnation. It had a fascination, a magical quality about it, and we struggled not for it alone but for the security it could provide. In church I learned what Christ said about the danger of riches. In the pew, I looked up at Father. Would Christ consider him rich? Would being rich in spirit cancel the dangers of being rich of purse? I wondered how rich you had to be to be damned. Did Christ have our family in mind? I worried but suppressed my fears. Our middle-class status was the result of work, virtue, and thrift. Besides, we were very charitable.

My life was filled by moralisms that answered the enigmas of worldly fortune. They were the legalisms of life's road. The proverbs of Ben Franklin's *Poor Richard's Almanac* and the stories of Horatio Alger were secular scriptures. The refrain: "If at first you don't succeed, try, try, again," had many variations but the theme was always the same.

As my life expanded, I began to realize the Victorian moralisms of my parents did more to salve consciences than answer human needs. The Templers, a poor family that lived only four blocks away, served as a symbol of improvidence and lack of moral rectitude. Their house was poorly painted, their children undisciplined, and their yard full of weeds and broken toys. We were told again and again to mind our ways or we "might end up like the Templers." But as I grew older, I began to view the Templer family in a more kindly light. The oldest son had joined the CCC and sent money home to his parents. Years later I had heard that he had died in France as a member of General George Patton's Third Army.

As time passed I realized that my parents knew little about the Templers; that they used the family as a crude pedagogical teaching tool to increase the capital of our character. I began to see there were "deserving" and "undeserving" poor; that there were superhuman forces that often crushed those who had the best of intentions. Untimely death, sickness, and poverty were not always the consequence of sin or lack of will, but of polio, a bad genetic deck of cards, corporate insensitivity, of drought, and fate. The Biblical verse, "The Fathers have eaten wild grapes and the children's teeth are set on edge," reveals our autonomy can be destroyed by cruel determinisms. The admonition "There, but for grace of God, go I" rang true. To be born into a family such as mine was to be given a pearl without price.

Although I have learned that life is too complex to be governed wholly by the simple moralisms of my youth, looking back I consider them preferable to the nihilism and cynicism of our present era. Since children are by nature expectant and optimistic, it is best to inculcate in them the notion that virtue is rewarded. It is healthier to emphasize the capacity to change circumstances than to accept the sociological fatalism of victimization. When I came home with a low grade, my parent's response was "you are not studying enough" or "you are not cutting the mustard" rather than "the school is failing you." I was not allowed to claim the role of victim or to feign dependency. I would be accused of an alibi if I used a sentence that had "if only" in it. I affirmed my idealism well into my teens. It was only after my Navy Air Corps experience and reading Reinhold Niebuhr, my theological mentor, that I became a "tamed cynic." It is best to move from idealism to modest or hopeful realism. Few teenage cynics, in my experience, ever become idealists or, for that matter, achieved much success in later life.

At eight years this was my first hair cut by our barber, Mr. Peterson.
Since he and Father bartered their services, Peterson cut my hair very
short to lengthen the time between visits. We called a haircut, "getting
our ears lowered".

16. Depression Era Haircuts

Until I was eight years old Mother cut my hair with a hand-operated clipper. I sat on the toilet seat in the bathroom or on a chair in the kitchen. She pinned a dish towel around me so that, in my little white cassock, I must have looked like a diminutive Cistercian monk. She got out the old Montgomery Ward clipper, oiled it up with Singer's sewing machine oil, and began my monthly torture. She held my head with one hand and whacked away with the other. The session was rarely painless, for sometimes she moved the clippers faster than she compressed the handles. The result was torture. I would scream, "It's pullin, Mother!" at least a dozen times a session. "Take it easy, my hair is coming out at the roots! Please! Aren't you done yet?" Had there been a social worker in town, she could have heard my screams three blocks away and may have called a child abuse specialist.

Mother's haircutting expertise didn't hold a candle to her wonderful culinary skills. I would have deep grooves in my hair where the scalp was visible. But since the juices of testosterone had not begun to rise, I didn't care that much. Mother would never apologize for scalping me. Depression haircuts weren't supposed to be perfect. "It would have been better had you sat still instead of being a wiggle-worm," she'd say, adding, as an afterthought, "Remember, it will always grow out." Getting a "professional" haircut for a kid was just throwing money away.

In fact we didn't really throw any money away even when I finally was liberated from the torment of Mother's tonsorial efforts and started "getting my ears lowered" at Milt Peterson's Barber shop under the Pipestone National Bank. We never had to pay because Peterson was working off a bill.

Outside Peterson's shop a number of village worthies would be sunning themselves, with their bodies inclined forward and their eyes glancing along the line this way and that. Or else they were leaning against the wall of the bank with their hands in their pockets as if to prop it up. Their ears caught whatever was in the wind. As Thoreau observed in the village of Walden, these were the "coarsest mills" in which all gossip was first rudely digested or cracked up before it was emptied into finer and more delicate hoppers within doors.

Like every passer-by I had to run the gossip gauntlet. Most of the seniors would give me a Mona Lisa twitch of a smile, complemented by an almost imperceptible nod of the head. As a shy youngster I hurried by, wondering what comments they would make about me after I was in the shop. In addition to the cafes, barroom, post-office, and grocery, the barber shop was one of the five pentagon points within which the tattle victuals of Pipestone were chewed and metabolized.

Peterson would zip up the back and across the top of my head with his electric clippers to give me a buzz, heinie, flat-top, or crew-cut. It was a no-nonsense cut, a junior version of the US Marine Corps' "high and tight." My scalp was open to the sun and wind and ideal for being in athletics.

I was in the chair less than three minutes. Since I was a non-paying customer, he never used soap and a razor to trim around my ears as he did for his adult clients. I wondered how many 15-cent haircuts it took to pay for delivering a baby and who got the best deal in this familial barter. Father occasionally complained that he got "skinned" by Peterson. But it was his own fault. As his hair became gray he tried to mask his aging by asking the barber to give him a "high and tight." Then too, Peterson may have wanted to increase the interval between haircuts of his non-paying customers.

Norman Rockwell would have felt at home in that barbershop. The six-sided, one inch square, little black and white tiles of the floor were so covered with hair that I doubted whether Milt swept up the place more than once a week. He wasn't lazy. Rather, he wanted his customers to think he was terribly busy. Scenes from Brown and Bigelow calendars looked down on us—Remington's Indians, the Grand Canyon, George Washington at prayer in the snow of Valley Forge or Crossing the Delaware on Christmas Eve, Bald eagles, the White House, Civil War battle scenes, and the like.

The most impressive picture was Otto Becker's 1895 lithograph of General George Armstrong Custer's "last stand" at the Battle of the Little Bighorn. It was a magnificient scene, even though it reeked of the sentiment of Manifest Destiny, frontier mythology, and the superiority of the Anglo Saxon. The "Son of the Morningstar," as the Indians called Custer, was flailing away at the "red skins" with his sword in one hand and shooting his six gun with the other. Custer's famous yellow, shoulder-length locks were streaming in the wind. Even with my rudimentary knowledge of the West, however, I observed that some the "savages" looked more like Apaches or Aztecs carrying Zulu shields than the Sioux I had studied. Moreover, there were too many war bonnets in the picture. Becker had probably put them in because they added color to the bleak Montana landscape. Whether technically correct or not the magnificient scene provided a horrifying lesson in the art of scalping. A fierce coppertone warrior with a knife between his teeth knelt on a cavalryman's back ready to peel away the top of his head. The Anglo features of the trooper were being metamorphized into that of an Oriental. The picture was titled: "Revered Even By His Savage Foes."

A 12-point buck that Peterson had shot surveyed the scene with his glass eyes. Milt said "them eyes kin foller you from the door to the chair." But try as I might, I never saw them move. Reading material consisted of dog-eared old issues of *The Farm Journal, Outdoor Life, The American Legion,* and *Field and Stream.* Steam pipes hung from the ceiling and kept up a hammering drum beat expanding and contracting while keeping the barber cave warm in the winter.

Retired farmers and pensioners used Peterson's shop as a social center and a gossip distribution point. Unlike old thoroughbred studs that retired to a life of siring Kentucky Derby champions and leisurely grazing bluegrass, retirement was especially tough on farmers "put out to pasture." They had given up being lord over 160 acres and a Monopoly board full of buildings. Now most were shoe-horned into a two-bedroom townhome set precariously on a quarter of an acre with a 12-by 20-foot dab of garden in the back. Whereas they used to roam free over their kingdom, now they were underfoot of the missus. Neighbors who used to be a half mile away now were across the street or 15 feet away on either side of their house. Their farm homes had never needed shades; now shades were a necessity, lest strangers peek into their bedrooms or see them squatting on the commode.

Retired farmers were supposed to frequent the cafes in town, give free advice, breed irises or roses, watch the polls during schoolboard elections, go fishing, or work part-time in the hardware store. Primogeniture allowed a few to jump in their pick-ups each morning and drive out and help out their son on the "home place." Most still wore their Oshkosh-By-Gosh bib overalls, only now they did not get soiled by the muck of the hog-or-cattle yard. Their badge of manhood and acceptance—muck and smell—was forever gone. It was quite a fall from grace and autonomy. I surmised it was something like a four-star general being stripped of his ribbons and being reduced to the rank of private. It almost seemed as if they had been disconnected from life support. Like over-traumatized rats that curl up in a corner and die with their feet in the air, retired farmers seemed like aliens who were living on borrowed time.

On each of my visits to Peterson's, the discourse had a boringly predicable pattern of nursing grievances against a mysterious *"They."* As in, *"'They* are raising taxes again," or *"'They* are throwing money away on welfare," or *"'They* are keeping the price of hogs so low that an honest man can't make a living," or *"'They* are keeping the interest on money so high you can't get a loan." There were always demonic *"theys"* outside our agrarian Eden that prevented life from being beatific. Or again, the "big shots in The Cities are taking all the gravy." Once the talkative Peterson asked a visitor to town how he would be trimmed. The uppity outsider answered, "In silence!" The barber shop crowd spoke of the incident for weeks. The glue of common grievances seemed to hold them together more than their positive commitments.

Milt had a coterie of regular customers who came in three times a week for a shave. He would hone his six-inch straightedge razor to a fine edge with a yard-long leather strop that dangled from the barber chair. The test for sharpness was by touching a hair to the edge. I was always on pins and needles when an old codger bared his grizzly throat to Peterson's blade. Some of their necks reminded me of those of a tom turkey, only fatter. Sometimes I thought I detected a Parkinsonian-like tremor to Milt's hand. Those retired farmers had more faith in their barber than I had. One slip and they would have gushed out blood like one of the hogs they had butchered.

Now and then Peterson was called upon to shave a dead person. He didn't mind the job, because he could charge double his fee for a live client. He took extra special care, because his finesse would be on display before the entire funeral crowd. "I don't mind shaving a dead person," Milt mused. "They lay a whole lot stiller than my live customers, but it's tough trying to talk to them. Sometimes you get kind of lonesome."

When he'd finished my haircut, Peterson would dust me off and then rub a liberal dose of Butch wax on his hands to keep my flat-top at attention. Unlike his adult, cash-paying customers, he would never bring me a mirror and slowly turn the chair for approval of his handiwork. Anyway, what did a kid know about the fine art of cutting hair? "On the bill" customers got short shrift. Later I would apply more greasy kids' stuff to help my hair defy gravity. A farmer once told me my hair looked slicker than deer guts on a doorknob. As I entered high school and my hair grew longer, I employed Vitalis Liquid Hair Groom, Vaseline Hair Tonic, Wildroot, or "a little dab will do ya" Brylcreem.

Sometimes I could get a 16-ounce bottle of Rose Hair Oil for 39 cents. It had a good smell to it that gave a deep sheen to my hair. I silently hoped that it would attract the girls. But Mother complained it left a stain on the pillowcase.

As I got older I realized hair is the ultimate vanity. Like my friends, I allowed my hair to grow longer and I would spend half an hour in the bathroom to primp, fuss, curl, and smooth my forelock. At times I needed to dip my comb into Mother's wave set to make my hair stay in place just so. "If truth is beauty," Lily Tomlin once said, "how come no one has their hair done in a library?"

This abandoned farm home is characteristic of those Father served prior to World War II. During some nights he would have to get out of bed as many as three times to go on his "missions of mercy."

17. THE FARM HOUSE CALL

Keep the faculty of effort alive in you by a little gratuitous exercise every day. That is, be systematically ascetic or heroic in little unnecessary points, do every day or two something for no other reason than that you would rather not do it, so that when the hour of dire need draws nigh, it may find you not unnerved and untrained to stand the test.

Psychology, William James

Illness is the night-side of life, a more onerous citizenship. Everyone · who is born holds dual citizenship, in the kingdom of the well and the kingdom of the sick. Although we prefer only to use the good passport, sooner or later each of us is obliged, at least for a spell, to identify ourselves as citizens of that other place.

Susan Sontag, *Illness as Metaphor*

Before World War II, scarcely a night went by without Father making one or two house calls between midnight and 7 A.M. Sometimes, awake at night, I would hear a predictable sequence: a telephone ring, quiet talking, sounds of Father dressing, footsteps descending the staircase, the slam of the front door, the opening of the garage door, the engine of the Ford coughing and catching fire, and the squeak of tires against the hard packed snow as the car was backed out. Rarely was I awake when he returned. From my bed I wondered at the fortitude and sense of duty behind those nocturnal missions. After the war, night calls diminished as patients were educated to go to the hospital, where an expanding technology could do more for them.

Father always wanted one or more of us to accompany him on farm calls after supper. He rarely got an ecstatic, "I'll go!" because tagging along invariably meant listening to a moral monologue and a long wait in a cold car in a smelly farm yard. He parried all my excuses. Yet, once aboard and on our mission of mercy, I enjoyed listening to the monologues. As farms flashed by, reduced from vastness to insignificance by our speed, Father's head would regularly pivot in an arc of 180 degrees and he would offer a continuous horticultural and moral commentary on the progress of farm work, the condition of the animals in the pastures, the size of the house, barn, garden, grove, weeds, and the state of repair of the fences. Father had seen but a small fragment of the world but he wasn't hesitant to make rather sweeping judgments. Like him, I believed the globe was little more than Pipestone county writ large. I viewed the universe through a Benjamin-and-Pipestone prism. All people should worship, believe, and follow our moral code. The lessons of life and nature were plain to all who had eyes to see. I nestled into my seat in the certainty that our home, village and life were secure.

Father believed that a good farmer would invariably have a good farm. A poor-looking farm betrayed the farmer's personal failures. He saw farming as an unforgiving way of life and was less than indulgent about weedy fields, dirty and broken equipment, delinquent children, poor animal stock, and run-down fences. Intuitively, he perceived a symmetry between farming and medicine. A farmer who cannot manage his homestead is akin to a patient who lets his body get out of shape.

I was amazed at his knowledge of people who lived within a radius of 15 miles of Pipestone. He and Mother kept straight the Scandinavian, German, English, and Dutch folk who were spread throughout the county. The dozens of different Johnsons, Olsons, Petersons, and Millers, and the Dutch Vander-whatevers, could be located with precision: "You go four miles north from the Trotsky turn-off and then two-and-one-half miles west. It's the farm with the broken-down sheep shed in front of the Chinese Elm grove that is half dead." To physical directions they could add a genealogy and a judgment regarding whether they were "good farmers"; that is, whether they paid their bills, had well-mannered children, were thrifty, successful, and conservative, church-goers, and voted Republican. Character was everything.

Father was prepared for any eventuality. He always bought a Ford with a spotlight on the left side so he could pick out names and addresses at night. Snow tires went on the car November first and didn't come off until the middle of April; they gave off a piercing whine at high speed. The gas tank was never allowed to fall below half full in the winter and the trunk, along with his home delivery obstetrical bag, contained logging and tire chains, extra blankets, sand, and wood blocks. Sometimes we got stuck in snow drifts or slid into the ditch when the spring rains turned dirt roads to gumbo. I would wrap myself in a blanket and wait in the car while he walked to the nearest farm to get a farmer and a team of horses to pull us back onto the road. Alone in the empty darkness of night, minutes seemed like hours. Anxiety chilled me as much as did the cold wind whistling through the door frames. I would sing to myself to keep it at bay. I was warned not to play the radio too much for fear of running down the car's battery.

To identify his homestead in the blackness of a winter's night, a farmer usually placed a lantern in the window. To make certain he had the right place, Father would rotate the handle of the Ford's spotlight and zero it in on the mailbox name. (He could have competed for accuracy, I believe, with most of our B-24 Liberator bomber waist gunners on their daily runs over Hitler's Germany.) The Ford would wheel into the farm yard, where strange and foreboding outbuildings loomed up out of the darkness. To a sensitive and impressionable youngster, it was a scary and awesome place.

If the temperature fell below zero, I was allowed to come into the farmhouse kitchen. Father's reception both astonished and comforted me. The farmer's ruddy, weather-lined face bespoke gratitude as he exclaimed, "Thanks so much for coming, Doc." Father would take off his coat and enter the bedroom of the sick patient. He practiced the advice of Aeschylus—"Words are the physicians of a mind diseased"— and Pindar's observation that the "best of healers is good cheer." I would stay in the kitchen with the other members of the family and warm myself around the massive, cob-burning kitchen stove. In my shyness, I would put my hands between my knees and look at the linoleum. I enjoyed the cookies they usually offered me, but because they tried to draw me out, the price was psychologically high. Because I was bashful, I would usually rebuff their queries with a simple "no" or "yes."

Father seemed to enter the sick room with a grave demeanor indicating to his patient he felt for him. But he left with a cheerful countenance so the sick man would think his case was not that serious. Sometimes the door of the bedroom was open and I could hear the muffled conversation. "Eric, I think you might do better in the hospital," began a typical interchange.

"But Doc, isn't there a possibility I might linger too long?" came the weak reply.

"That's always a possibility," Father said gravely.

"Ya know, if I did that, Louise might lose the farm and that would be a terrible thing."

"I understand," Father answered, "and I'll leave the decision up to you. In the meantime, I want you to take these pills." Father would shake some pills from his medical bag and put them in little envelopes, and write out the dosage.

"Now be sure and don't take too many of those green ones, Eric. That might not be good for you." In cases like Eric's, Father was always more somber and less talkative on the way home. Life had to be endured. Nature fought for you until it turned against you. Father knew that illness is the night-side of life, a more onerous form of citizenship. He held dual citizenship, in the kingdom of the well and in the kingdom of the sick. Like Hippocrates 2500 years earlier, Father knew that death should be considered the enemy until it clearly presents itself as a friend.

Unlike physicians today, Father viewed his patients as belonging to one of two families: that of his genetic lineage, the other the Pipestone extended household. Thus, the psychic strain doubled when illness and death occurred. He rushed off not to a generic "confinement case," but a specific "Elaine Johnson who was having a baby in a farm home near Woodstock." Father never said, "I have a gall bladder up at the hospital" but rather, "Ed Smith is suffering from gall stones." Although Father could not perform many of today's technical miracles, he had greater moral authority than today's physician. By presence, word, and the laying on of hands, he showed that he cared. However, it would have been dangerous, indeed superhumanly impossible, for him to take upon himself the entire suffering of the county. Such a burden would have destroyed him. Father had to have the proper amount of armor—a professional covering that revealed empathy, but not sympathy. The former expresses concern and caring while keeping feelings on a tight tether, while the latter often unleashes emotionalism that might compromise medical objectivity. Psychologically, Father was in a dangerous profession. Those who were impersonal and distant were poor healers; those too susceptible to the demons of disease of their extended family and patients often turned to booze and drugs. As a rule, Father did not violate the autonomy of his patients by telling us information that was private. But occasionally there were "teaching moments" that I would never forget. Once he came into the house after a home visit to one of our community pillars, a comparatively young man of 40. Father had told him he had about a month to live. "The pity of it all, the pity of it all," the man had cried as Father held his hand. "For me life is over. I have been so busy building my business. I am going to die and my three sons are strangers to me. I should have known that life is fragile and precious."

Unlike today's "health care providers," Depression-era physicians had the satisfaction of not charging, or simply canceling the bills, for their services for the legions in straitened circumstances. During the '30s Father did not charge for at least one-third of his professional services. Physicians joined their professional counterparts, the clergy, whose services and self were often given *sola gratia*.

On the other hand, Father had little patience for those who had the ability to pay but chose not to do so. If there was no response after several entreaties, he turned their bill over to a collection agency. Mrs. Gladys Anderson was one of the best. She reminded me of a pleasant Aunt-Jemima type, the stereotypical grandmother. I wondered how this saintly woman with such a kind face was able to leverage money out of legions of professional "dead-beats." But Mother said Gladys' manner and persistence convinced many slackers to "own up" to their financial responsibilities. Father was especially critical of those who were spendthrifts, especially if he discovered they were the denizens of the saloon. "I don't want money that is legally mine going for liquor," he often remarked.

In 1930 a German farmer canceled a large bill by giving Father a beautifully carved, 30-hour, Bavarian cuckoo clock. Father hung it at the bottom of the stairs and each morning when he came down for breakfast, he would pull up the three heavy acorn weights. When I was awake at night, I would often hear it strike. In spite of the blackness of the night, its solemn tones seemed to convey to me that all was well and secure in my precious homestead. On the quarter, half, and three-quarters, I would have to guess what hour it was because the bobwhite sounded only on the hour. Two-and-a-half feet tall, it was hand-sculpted of black walnut and had the traditional scene from a German fable: a large black crow at the top of the frieze is eating grapes while a handsome fox looks longingly upward, hoping for a misstep so that he will garner his daily meal.

Like physicians of every era, occasionally Father had to bear the onus of medical finitude and personal failure. When medical judgment or prognosis proved to be wrong, his finely honed super-ego often turned inward and became punitive. If a patient was not doing well or died, he often had a soliloquy with himself: "Am I doing the right thing?" "Did I miss something? "Why didn't I catch it earlier?" "Perhaps I should have referred her to a specialist in the Cities or at the Mayo Clinic?" These private interrogatories were as natural as they were unremitting, for the practice of medicine, whether in primitive or in technical times, is always an art as well as a science. But there were no answers from a medical Mount Sinai that helped ease the pain of his soul.

The loss of Betty Mehling in 1943 was especially tragic. She was a year behind me, a classmate of Les Kallsen and Neal Knudtson. Betty was a farm girl and everything parents would wish for their daughter–intelligent, positive, modest, bubbly, outgoing, cute and curvaceous. But Betty had come to Father with a bad stomach ache. She hadn't been able to "keep anything down" for several days. Father was frustrated because he couldn't pin down the diagnosis. I remember him coming home one evening and, in a medical version of blaming the victim, remarked, "She's just a spoiled kid!" But Betty was "going sour" in a hurry. Father had no other choice than to do exploratory surgery.

The finding: *Intussusception.*

Even now, more than 60 years later, intussusception is a difficult condition to diagnose and in an acute stage patients, like Betty, often die from it. It is a rare condition where the small intestine "telescopes"—somewhat like pushing the finger of a rubber glove into itself. The enfolded segment obstructs passage of intestinal contents, endangering local blood supply of the tissues, and immediate treatment is crucial. Without it, infection ensues, which soon closes off the intestinal tract. Symptoms are sudden, severe, sharp abdominal pain associated with nausea and vomiting.

In the early 1940s, Father was not unlike a medical David fighting a demonic Goliath. Compared to today, his "medical sling" held only "tiny pebbles." Once a massive abdominal infection set in, Father could do little. At that time Britain's Sir Fleming was about to cross one of the most monumental of medical thresholds—the discovery of penicillin. The sulfonamide drugs and the whole array of "miracle" medications were discovered during the Second World War and the years that followed. Fate had been terribly cruel to Betty. Her disease had come too early. Had Betty come down with this ailment a few years later, she undoubtedly could have been saved.

Father was in a funk for days. A member of his extended family had died. For a Kantian inner-directed individual like Father, self-recrimination was a terrible taskmaster. Moreover, in solo practice there were no colleagues to whom he could have unburdened himself and eased his pain. In small communities, doctors and pastors, physicians respectively of the body and of the soul, often had to bear their crosses in isolation. Today with C.T. scans, M.R.I's, ultra-sound and more, discovery of that condition and thousands more would have been routine.

Les Kallsen and I walked over to the home mortuary to see Betty. While I had observed a few of my elderly relatives in their respective coffins, this was the first time I had seen one of my peers. Perhaps the artistry of the mortician during the Depression was a pale copy of what it is today. I was stunned by Betty's appearance. She was a Madame Tossaud cadaverous wax figure without any color. Betty was pale, thin, and shrunken. A few days of sickness and suffering had mutated a beautiful young girl into a form we could scarcely recognize. It was a shock to suddenly realize the fragility of life, with Betty's bubbly personality and charm gone forever.

Les and I rubbed our eyes and inwardly wept. It may have been the first time that, as a couple of adolescents, we realized life had a tragic dimension. I put my chin on my chest and looked at my shoes so that no one could see my red eyes. Les and I walked home without saying a single word. In June our high school yearbook had a black border around the photo of our dead classmate.

Some other of Father's medical failures were actually a bit humorous. On one occasion an obese German lady, Gertrude Baak, brought her two-year-old son, Adolph, to the office to be circumcised. Mrs. Baak, unfortunately, appeared "out of sorts," having negotiated the 19 steps of the dark staircase with no little difficulty. Moreover, little Adolph was not cooperating, probably because of a premonition of what was going to happen to his "little Willie." Our Ashton Memorial Hospital seemed to hold a certain mystique for Gertrude, and she wondered why the procedure was not done within its hallowed precincts. But Father had a full waiting room and simple office surgery was routine for him. As his office nurse and Gertrude pinned the child to the examination table, Father whipped out his scalpel and, *zip-zip-zip,* the foreskin of Adolph's little penis was removed forthwith.

Have you ever heard a Chester white boar being "stuck?" Adolph's screams would have shattered the finest Waterford crystal.

Father had administered a shot of Novocain, of course, but it seemed that Adolph was psychologically advanced for his age. Like men of mature years, he viewed his "wetter" as his most precious possession. Father's patients were exceedingly discombobulated by the "bloody-murder" screams that thundered through the solid oak door into the waiting room. An observer reported that several immediately got up and canceled their appointments. Later it was reported that Adolph's howling could be heard three blocks away at the Dibble Chevy dealership. A patron of Sammy's, Pipestone's saloon, opined over his Grain Belt that the little tyke had the lungs of a future circus carny.

Of course, many medical professionals tend to have a tin ear when it comes to the wailing of kids, especially those they consider "spoiled rotten." Crying, screaming, and protest is something that has to be endured by those who practice on medical turf. Later, Mike Baak, a hell-for-leather type trucker and the father of Adolph, confronted Father on Main Street and chewed him out for subjecting his son "to torture." Perhaps Mike assumed that circumcision is painless only when done within the sterile confines of a hospital. Undoubtedly, Father's rejoinder was as follows: *"Mr. Baak, don't you dare tell me how to practice medicine. And I promise not to tell you how to drive your truck!"*

Another hiatus in Father's medical knowledge had to do with birth control. In 1946 a newly married couple, Mr. and Mrs. Elmer VanCliben, entreated Father regarding his wisdom on family planning. Elmer had recently been discharged from the army and faced four years of college. Understandably, the couple wanted the enjoyment of conjugal bliss without the possibility of a pregnancy during their early years of financial struggle. Never one to admit to any blank spots in his medical knowledge, Father told them about the rhythm method and sent the Dutch newlyweds on their way. The charge? "No professional fee. You're nice kids. Have a good time!"

The result? A baby boy 10 months later! The VanClibens were "fit-to-be-tied!" In checking with their Catholic friends, they discovered, *"Doctor Benjamin's advice was totally wrong!"* Father had not mentioned anything about condoms ("rubbers"), diaphragms, coitus interruptus, spermicidal jellies, or inter-uterine devices (only in the late '50s was "the pill" invented). Sometimes during his darker moments, Elmer wondered whether Dr. Benjamin had tricked him, since he knew that Father believed in large families. I am certain Father didn't willfully misinform the VanClibens since that would have been a clear violation of both medical ethics and his own moral code. Rather, Father's attempt at medical omniscience betrayed him. Perhaps, as wordsmiths now propound, "there may have been some 'cognitive dissonance'." A zealous hater of the "Roman" Church later on told them, *"Wise up! The rhythm method is a form of Vatican roulette!"*

It was nine years before the VanClibens had their second child.

Father did, however, draw some lines with regard to fecundity. When the county nurse informed him that an Irish farm woman, Mrs. Kit O'Brian, was overwhelmed by having nine children in 15 years, he sent the wearied woman to the University of Minnesota for a hysterectomy. "Some husbands are real brutes," he said sadly, "and have no sense of when 'enough is enough'."

Once during a violent snowstorm in 1929 that blocked all the roads, Father hired a horse-drawn sleigh and drove 15 miles to a farm in Lone Rock Township in South Dakota for a "confinement case." He had a raccoon coat and Hudson Bay blankets to keep him warm. At times the visibility was limited to 30 feet. In gratitude, the parents christened their newborn, *"Walter Benjamin Ellefson."* Father knew the truth of Galen's aphorism, "He cures most in whom most have faith."

During the famous November 11, 1940 Armistice Day blizzard, Father was fortunate to escape with his life. Stan Morgan's essay "I Silently Thanked God For Being Safe," in *All Hell Broke Loose: Experiences of Young People During the Armistice Day 1940 Blizzard,* details the events of their close call while duck hunting at Dead Coon lake, 35 miles north of Pipestone. Dr. Fred Yseth and Louis Steinberg were the other members of the foursome. After Morgan's 1939 Studebaker Commander burst a radiator hose upon slamming into a monstrous snow drift, Father and the others got out of the car and followed a fence line. Visibility was less than 10 feet. "It seemed as though within just a few minutes," Morgan recalled, "we had become engulfed in a raging, blinding blizzard." After going a half mile, by sheer luck they bumped into a barn where two members of the Schuler family were milking. They lived in the Schuler's basement for three days and two nights and tried to help with the chores. On November 13 they shouldered their guns and trudged eight miles on top of 10-foot snow drifts to Tyler where Tracey Hicks picked them up. On the way home "we observed that only the cross-arms of the telephone poles along the highway showed above the snow banks."

Father never said much about the harrowing experience. He knew how lucky he was to be alive, but he felt guilty for getting caught and not being better prepared.

His M.D. seemed to stand for "minor deity." Patients' invocation at his arrival and benediction at his leaving was heartfelt and warm. It was the Golden Age of medicine; golden not because of financial reward or technological wizardry, but because of the rapport, status and satisfaction a doctor received from immersing himself into the lives of his patients and their families.

Today we need such contrived occasions as "Take Your Daughter To Work Day" to try to bridge the chasm that separates our suburban bedroom communities from our urban work sites. Legions of children now know almost nothing about what their parents do outside the home, but I never was in doubt as to the work-a-day world of my Father. The private and public, personal and professional, social and vocational worlds were intimately linked. However, with that knowledge came a burden. Because I intimately knew what my Father did, and heard his plaudits on every hand, I wondered whether I would ever be able to walk in his footsteps.

18. FATHER'S BLACK BAG

The desire to take medicine is perhaps the greatest feature which distinguishes man from animals.

Sir William Osler

The symbol of Father's authority was his black bag. It was a big, solid, no-nonsense case of smooth black leather reinforced with plywood. Carried by two leather handles, it weighed 12 pounds fully loaded. Its corners were reinforced by leather patches riveted into place, and the two shoulders opened opposite each other on lengthwise hinges.

On one side were two compartments, one filled with dressings and the other with syringes. A subcompartment contained needles, sutures, and a flip-open black case filled with vials of the injectable and oral drugs and medications likely to be needed in an emergency.

The bag's opposite shoulder opened on two chrome-plated containers for tongue blades and cotton, two types of catheters, and a plastic hemocytometer kit for evaluating blood cell count. The main compartment had a stethoscope, a triangular reflex hammer, a box of brittle finger splints, and an ophthalmoscope, its black lacquer worn through by tens of thousands of handlings.

But the greatest mystery was contained in two dark brown leather cases holding the entire pharmacopoeia of the era in 30 glass bottles with metal screw caps. The drugs ranged from such potentially dangerous narcotics as Morphine Sulfate "(Warning: May be habit forming, POISON)" to relatively innocuous analgesics such as Codeine, Sodium salicylate, and Upjohn throat tabs. As a child I saw those bottles as little soldiers with different colored uniforms standing at attention. When their caps came off, exotic odors attacked my nostrils, odors so strange that I could not possibly doubt the healing potency of their source.

Of all the contents of the black bag, the one capable of bestowing the greatest and fastest comfort was a shiny brown urinary catheter. Our sophisticated society may be unaware that acute urinary retention ever existed, but on many occasions Father would arrive at a farm house to find an elderly man in agony because of it. A simple passage of the slender tube brought instant relief and surpassing gratitude.

Another bag was rarely taken out of the trunk of the Ford and was therefore more mysterious to us. It was made from rich Gladstone leather and had a more rotund shape than the rectangular black bag. It was the obstetrics bag Father used for "confinement" cases. Now in the museum of the Pipestone County Historical Society, it contained forceps and other instruments used to perform difficult deliveries.

One circular steel instrument, resembling a carpenters brace and bit, had tiny sharp teeth that could be rotated and was for trepanning followed by the crushing of the skull of a baby that was stuck in the birth canal. Such instruments had been used by shamans, mid-wives, and medical priests since the Bronze Age. I often wondered about those tragic moments in dark and isolated farm-home bedrooms when agonizing decisions were made as to who would live and who would die. It was a time before medical backup, ambulances, and today's menu of medical specialization.

At home the black bag was always next to the front door. The telephone would ring, Father would throw on his coat and rush out the door with his precious bag, anticipation and good will pouring out of him. His mission of mercy was as much personal as medical. How could he seem so confident with such paltry tools? He had no antibiotics, no effective antihypertensives, no diuretics, no hormones, no antiarrhythmics, few antacids, and only a few good pain drugs and sedatives.

Such a paltry armamentarium! To be sure, Father's medical intervention far exceeded the 19th century quatrain: "Howe'er their patients may complain/Of head, or heart, or nerve, or vein/Of fever high, or parch, or swell/The remedy is Calomel." Compared to that snake-oil hucksterism, medicine had advanced light years by the 1930s. Nevertheless, at that time a woman could still die in childbirth; a child could die of strep throat, whooping cough, or meningitis; and anyone could perish from appendicitis, pneumonia, TB, heart failure, or a host of other ravages for which treatment is now considered routine.

Because Father knew his Depression-era armamentarium was exceedingly modest, he constantly preached preventive medicine to his family and his patients. Long before research proved the validity of the seven health virtues—no smoking, no or modest liquor consumption, no snacking between meals, a minimum of seven hours of sleep a night, daily exercise, keeping weight down, maintaining a balanced diet—he knew their practice led to a better and longer life. It was far cheaper to keep your health than try and buy it back once it was lost. For example, he taught me never to put my hands on a public railing or the door or knob of a public toilet. He would push the door open with his elbow or grasp the knob with a clean handkerchief. It is a practice that I follow to this day.

The limited number of therapeutic arrows in Father's medical quiver forced him to hone his professional persona to a fine edge. When science was exhausted and medical artistry was all he had to offer, he was the incarnation of noblesse oblige: empathetic without being common. In manner, conduct, word, and bearing, he was a medical maestro who was able to calm the existential terror brought by disease and death.

During the Depression physicians and clergymen helped people endure often heavy, joyless lives and kept people from feeling alone in the world. By doing so, doctors and clergymen developed a real bond of affection for their clients. Sometimes the bond of endearment took a stern counsel for a misdirected life. Other times it was composed of nothing more than pleasant conversation or a pat on the back. Either way, doctors and clergymen exerted a powerful effect on people's lives.

When asked for advice about life, Father gladly talked to his patients although in a manner and in a spirit that is almost incomprehensible today. Often he would put his instruments aside, assume a more thoughtful mood, and discuss issues with an almost relaxed indifference to any scientific purpose. His wisdom was not a "treatment" in the contemporary sense of the term. The slightly condescending tone of his voice would probably be an insult to today's egalitarian and democratic sensibilities. Nevertheless, he was a distinguished and urbane person deigning to illuminate the less well-educated—certainly not today's technician empowered solely by his narrow scientific expertise.

When Father's patients asked for his advice about life, they did not expect the wisdom they received to be confirmed by experiment. They simply listened to him and gradually and unconsciously followed his prudence. His education and social status combined with the propensity of every human being to believe in something, allowed his untested sagacity to grab hold of a patient's mind. Father influenced his patient's thinking and satisfied their demand for answers to life's problems, simply by stoking the religious instinct to believe.

Today many people see the medical professional as too busy and too science-oriented to care about the everyday problems of patients. A young doctor recently confessed, "Every day I pray, God spare me from an *enigmatic case!*" He viewed patients who might want to talk to him about their secret struggles as a souce of trouble. They interupted the brisk flow of patients through his office. When today's physicians talk about the problems of life with their patients they usually have one eye on the diagnostic categories of mental illness. Rather than exploring life's issues philosophically, doctors wonder whether a whining patient has a form of depression that needs to be treated with medication. Today the writing of a prescription is often a sign that a doctor wants closure on an engagement or examination with a patient. The result, of course, is "cookbook" medicine where the practitioner worries too much about efficiency and time management. Alas, in the mind of his patient, a doctor has been reduced to the status of a tradesman, such as a plumber or electrician—someone whose work calls for little depth of human understanding. Tragically, many patients have experienced this change and are repelled by it.

Though Father's own pharmacopoeia was modest, he detested the quacks who preyed on the purses and gullibility of his patients. They were like wolves that circled a pack of buffalo, ready to pounce on weakened members of the herd. Father saw himself as the loyal guardian of empirical medical science. Occasionally during his house calls he would see some ancient and useless tonic or potion on his patient's nightstands: Hostetter's Celebrated Stomach Bitters, Lydia Pinkham's Herb Medicine, and Dr. Kilmer's Oceanweed Perfect Blood Purifier Heart Remedy, to name a few.

Father fought a two-fronted medical battle: he had to cure or control disease, or at least keep company with his dying patients, and at the same time protect them from the medical masqueraders and charlatans. Most of the chiropractors, homeopaths, naturopaths, herbalists, and others (they always put "Doctor" in front of their names, rarely the abbreviation of their superficial degrees) were simply con artists who took advantage of vulnerable people by reciting apocryphal tales of "healing." When a patient left Father's medical guardianship, he took it as a personal affront betraying a lack of faith in him. When a long-term patient turned apostate, it was akin to a pillar of the Methodist church succumbing to Mormonism.

He especially detested a clinic of chiros (chiropractors) in Canton, South Dakota, who were, in his terms, nothing but "gut washers." Their fliers warned of a "Build-up of toxins and poisons" in the body. The procedure they used to address this alleged build-up was popularized in the late 19th century by the inventor of corn flakes, "Doc" Kellogg of Battle Creek, Michigan. His "health spa" became the mecca for tens of thousands of sufferers of undifferentiated complaints. Kellogg claimed that our intestines, like water or sewage pipes, are constantly becoming encrusted with gunk. Only a regular "flushing out" of the bowels (by passing a tube up through the anus and rectum into the colon and forcing warm water through it) would restore one to health. Once a patient, a farmer near Edgerton, reported he felt "ever so much better" after receiving his first "high colonic irrigation"—that was the fancy chiropractic term given to the procedure. "Doc Flusher told me," the farmer protested, "that all kinds of crud came out—festering corn flakes and even rancid bits of cheese—that could have been caught 'up there' for 10 years. They had been poisoning my system for years."

Father didn't know whether to laugh or cry. He may have felt the warm water was a substitute for those whose libidos, not bowels, were stopped up. Jane, another patient turned apostate, stopped taking her medicine and began a regimen of aligning her body with the earth's magnetic field with her head pointing toward the North Pole. Barnum and Bailey were right—fools were born every minute. Nevertheless, it hurt when your medical authority was questioned, when patients no longer saw you with a nimbus around your head. Shades of medievalism! Father wondered when they would turn to bleeding, bat dung, Jordan River water, prayer cloths, and leeches.

During our trip to Washington, D.C. in 1937, we stopped for several hours at a small town in Ohio to watch a quack who specialized in treating arthritis. Quack or not, his reputation was widespread: we counted license plates from more than 20 states in the parking lot. We found "Doc Metacarpal," a self-proclaimed healer with magic hands, in an outdoor pavilion perched on a swivel chair strategically placed at the hub of eight aisles that converged on him. With his white shirt sleeves rolled up to his elbows, Metacarpal seemed to be a genial old fellow. He offered a greeting to each patient and then, taking hold of an offered foot or hand, made a gentle twist and pronounced a benediction: "This will make you better." He then rotated 45 degrees to the next patient. Metacarpal charged a dollar for every three-second ministration; a "nurse" in a starched white uniform collected the greenbacks.

Metacarpal was running a medical "Wheel of Fortune." It was nice and clean—no billing, no prescription pads, no drugs, insurance forms, red tape, litigation, hospital bureaucracy, or snooping I.R.S. folk to contend with. Father recorded this Lourdes for arthritics with his Eastman Kodak 16-millimeter camera. I'm not sure whether he sent the films to the A.M.A. for investigation. He was so angry I was surprised he could hold the camera steady. We calculated that Metacarpal would make a million dollars every six months.

In medicine, as in other areas of life, the "good old days" weren't as good as nostalgia suggests: quacks and charlatans practiced with impunity, while dedicated physicians like Father had to practice medicine without specialized nurses, clerical staff, sophisticated laboratory tests, and MRIs, and they usually charged only what patients could afford. On the other hand, Father enjoyed some advantages today's doctors might envy: he did not have to have a nurse present during a gynecologic examination as a precaution against being charged with sexual assault. He knew nothing of practice protocols dictated by insurance companies; nor of OSHA regulations; hazardous waste disposal; mountains of paperwork required by HMOs, PPOs, etc.; $40,000 malpractice premiums; or the constant need to be updated in state-of-the-art surgical technology. Ironically, the very technology that has wrought medical wonders and extended lives, has also driven a wedge between physicians and their patients. Father's successors can perform medical marvels but the price—a diminished moral authority in the eyes of patients—has been high.

The dignity of medical practice that Father knew has almost disappeared because doctors have been transformed into "providers," not physicians. Patients whom he knew existentially now are "consumers of medical services." Today a gap of painful consequences has been opened between what people want and hope for from medicine, and what it can actually give them. The Depression was not an era of unquenchable wants and never-satisfied hopes stimulated by constant hype of new and expected medical breakthroughs. Medicine had not then turned its face, on request, against those human conditions that testify not of illness or bodily failures, but the absence of some perceived good that some human beings want: a better appearance (cosmetic surgery), an enhanced sense of well-being (Prozac), or greater height (human growth hormone). No genetic scientist then cried, "Foward to Methuselah!" with the faith that research might stop aging and lead to 200-year life spans. If Father were living now he could not have adjusted to the contemporary shape of medicine.

Once, while trailing Father as he made his hospital rounds, we stopped before the beds of two, frail, bird-like, little women. He stood between their beds as each grasped one of his hands as though it were a line from the lifeboat of a sinking ship. Their heads were upturned, eyes wide with expectant trust and hope. He introduced me, chatted quietly with each woman in turn, and stroked their foreheads in a manner reminiscent of a priest giving last rites. Later, in the hall, I asked: "When will they get well?"

"They will not be getting well," he said with a deep sadness. "They have no place to go. Each one will die soon. We will care for them until that happens."

Like most physicians Father had a greater fear of disease and death than did his patients. Procedures that he would recommended for his patients, he deferred for himself. Because of the untimely demise of his father, he feared he was genetically programmed for an early death. When Fred Niebauer, a friend of the Bedells, suffered from a fast-growing cancer, his comment was, "I don't think I could ever endure something like that." As chemotherapy became ever more widely used to combat cancer, he often judged the side-effects of treatment worse than ravages of the disease. He practiced wellness and holistic medicine long before they became popular, eschewing fatty foods, coffee, rich deserts, and all forms of liquor and tobacco. When a friend judged that his hobby of taking 16 millimeter home movies might be expensive, his retort was, "Not really; that's where my liquor and tobacco money go." He kept his weight down by taking two-mile walks each evening before retiring. Until he suffered from a cerebral-vascular accident when he was 76, he looked 15 years younger than his age.

A patient's view of my Father as they entered his office/examination room. He hand wrote all their medical records. For the few who had "social" diseases, he invented his own secret code to protect their privacy.

19. EXPERIENCING MEDICAL TREATMENT

Hygiene is the only useful part of medicine, and hygiene is rather a
virtue than a science. Temperance and industry are man's true remedies;
work sharpens his appetite and temperance teaches him to control it.

Emile, or *Education,* Jean Jacques Rousseau

Sometimes Father allowed me to come into the operating room to
watch surgery. (He never bothered about getting informed consent
from the patient undergoing the scalpel.) I experienced what philosophers called ontological shock, an awe and reverence analogous to what
a medieval peasant might have felt upon stepping from the profane
world of his sheepyard into an incense-laden church sanctuary. I experienced a "Wholly Other" realm of existence.

Like a peasant humbled by bread and wine turned into flesh and
blood, I stood transfixed as Father, the medical priest, garbed in surgical vestments, performed the mysterious rites that would make his
patient whole. Medical anasepsis and ritual scrupulosity are not that far
apart. Both theaters eschew ordinary language for Latin and medicalese, respectively. Priests, religious and medical, were lords over their
respective sanctuaries and stood apart lest they be contaminated.

Father's sense of medical territoriality was strong. In the
Depression-era, medicine, like economics, followed an individualistic
ethos; there were no group practices in a town the size of Pipestone.
Father enjoyed being a medical loner, a Marlboro country physician,
but he wanted little competition on his turf. As he became older, he worried that his medical lambs might stray to another fold and often spoke
about the "loyalty" of his elderly patients. Father rarely did surgery with
other Pipestone physicians. Instead, he invited Dr. Garrett Beckering
from Edgerton or Dr. Rider of Flandreau, South Dakota, to assist him.
Since they did not directly compete for patients with him, they were not
a threat to his practice.

Father was particularly estranged from Dr. John H. Lohmann, a
Catholic physician who lived with his large family in a large modern

home a block from the Methodist church. Scarcely a Sunday went by that Father did not make a comment about the Lohmann "sheep shed" as we drove to church. Once, when Beckering and Reider were unavailable, Father was forced to avail himself of Lohmann's modest surgical skill to attend to the thumb Father had crushed in a car door. The result was a less-than-perfect, deeply grooved nail which, for years afterward, Father pointed to as a sign of Lohmann's limited abilities with the scalpel.

My first experience with surgery came when I was four years old and had my tonsils removed. It was during Christmas vacation and the snow was deep. Mother packed a small valise and I struggled through the waist-high drifts to the hospital. At the desk, I stammered forth with the lines I had rehearsed at home: "I'm Nebbie Benjamin. I have come to have my tonsils out this morning."

The nurses helped me into my pajamas and put me to bed. Later Father appeared and I was wheeled into surgery. As the mask was put over my face, I was told to count as long as I could. The ether was poured on to the gauze but the smiling faces of the nurses above me gave no comfort. I was being suffocated. All I could do was scream, "DADDY! DADDY! DADDY!..." I awoke back in my room with a burning throat, but the smiles and plaudits of the nurses, "you were a brave little guy," more than made up for the pain. After a night in the hospital I returned home in triumph and was given all the ice cream I could eat.

Without exotic cures, prevention was emphasized. When I was young every winter morning I would run into my parent's bedroom, lie down and alternate putting my feet against my Mother's chest. She would roll down long brown stockings over my long winter underwear nearly up to my crotch and secure them with safety pins. However necessary for warmth, I detested wearing "Long Johns." Moreover, spring did not come when we spotted the first robin tugging at an angleworm. Nor was winter over when we saw a mysterious V in the sky of Canadian geese heading north. It arrived, officially in the Benjamin household, when Mother finally relented after days of our pleading, to let us go to school without wearing long underwear.

Our "union-suits"—full-legged, full-armed, and fitted with a necessary "drop seat"—were cumbersome, scratchy garments that never seemed to fit. Their only color, battleship gray, hid Depression era dirt, a feature that extended the time between launderings. I wore Bob's hand-me-downs that were woefully stretched out of shape. There were always a baggy three-inches that pushed out around my shirt cuffs. The ankles, too, were stretched due to the fact that Mother had often caught us without having put on the detestable garment. When that happened,

I would scream, *"I don't have time. You are forcing me to be late for school!"* Mother would counter, "I would rather you be late than to have to go to the hospital with pneumonia." In protest, I pulled it on over my shoes. By looking in the mirror, I was mortified that the drop seat hung down at least four inches below my bottom. I was afraid someone might accuse me of carrying a "load" in my pants.

In late February I would begin to clamor to put aside this cocoon of servitude, inconvenience, and social discomfort. Days passed. My pleas fell on unheeding ears as the earth continued warming. But weather was on my side and finally Mother made her *ex cathedra* pronouncement: "Bobbie, Nebbie, and Martha: you do not have to wear your long underwear tomorrow." Her voice sounded like a heavenly chorus. But it came with a warning: "Remember, if we get a cold snap, you may have to put them on again."

I stepped outside during a crisp April morning, no sensation ever quite duplicated that shiver as a fresh breeze rushed up my pant legs and touched my groin. It was stimulating, even brisk. But I didn't complain. Our ice and snow were gone! The hated cocoon and encumbrance of winter was laid away in mothballs until next November.

Every day we had to fill the humidifier pans on the radiators to aid winter breathing. Chest colds were treated with a mustard plaster, a mustard-impregnated muslim cloth that covered one's chest and made it feel like it was on fire. But this simple remedy, like the hot pad and warm oil used for ear aches, bitter old fashioned licorice and a salt water gargle for sore throats, steaming for colds, and hot packs for sinus and eye infections was remarkably effective.

Amid our various medical experiences, a few were traumatic. Bob received a single-shot .22 rifle at Christmas when he was nine years old. After we had opened our gifts, Father left for the hospital, promising to instruct us on gun safety and the art of weaponry upon his return. A short while later, we heard a sudden shriek from the upstairs bedroom: "I SHOT MYSELF! I SHOT MYSELF!" Bob came running down the staircase and threw off a shoe. He had shot himself through the fourth toe. Unknowingly, he had performed a most delicate procedure. All of us Benjamins share a genetic defect, a crooked fourth toe inherited from the Bedell/Bohn side of the family. It was a trait that Father had great fun teasing Mother about. Bob's unerring aim had straightened out the toe. But his rifle surgery treated only the phenotype, not the genotype. His progeny, like ours, would continue to manifest two crooked toes.

At seven, I fell out of a tree while reaching for green apples and tore a gash in my left arm. Father asked me how it happened as he stitched me up. I compromised the truth by saying it had happened in the box elder tree. I didn't feel too bad about lying because I had planned to repair to a favorite perch in the box elder tree to eat the forbidden fruit.

When I was in the sixth grade I broke my left collar bone playing touch football. Both Bob and I dislocated our shoulders, he while playing football and I while wrestling.

The most serious accident—it could have been fatal—happened when Roger was knocked down by a road grader. Only six years old, he was throwing stones in front of the scraper blade, watching them tumble to the side. But he was so absorbed that he forgot about the grader's big rear wheel, which rolled over his left arm. At the time, Mother and I were in the Twin Cities for my monthly visit to the dentist to have my braces adjusted. When we returned that evening, Father detoured Mother from the ritual of reviewing her sleeping children. In the morning we were told about the frightful mishap and trooped out to the hospital to see Roger. He looked awful. His arm was twice its normal size and his face was puffy and black and blue. He was under sedation and could hardly open his eyes. For weeks afterwards he wore a shoulder cast with a brace that held his arm out at a right angle.

As children of a physician we were routinely subjected to vitamins, cod liver oil, various elixirs and tonics, and ultraviolet sessions at the office. While their placebo effect was marvelous, their medical efficacy was questionable. All through grade school years, cod liver oil could only be had in liquid form. It was a nauseating concoction with the viscosity of axle grease. As Mother's unerring hand moved a tablespoon of the yellow stuff relentlessly toward my mouth, I would hold my nose with my left hand while with my right I kept ready an orange juice or Kool Aid chaser. Sometimes I was so quick on the draw that Mother had trouble getting the tablespoon out of my mouth. No matter: the cod liver oil coated the lining of my mouth and esophagus like a thick layer of glue. The mantra, "It's good for you" helped not at all.

When my chest was congested because of a cold, I was subjected to mustard plasters. Mother would liberally slather mustard on my rib cage and then cover it with layers of muslin. Within a few minutes, I felt as though a red hot 36-pound cannon ball from one of the guns of Admiral Horatio Nelson's flagship Victory was on top of my chest. In vain I pleaded with Mother to stop the torture: *"I can't breathe! It's burning a hole in my chest!"* My protestations always fell on deaf ears. My body was captive to an antiquarian but Puritanical, "no-pain, no gain" moralism. Mother maintained it was a necessary poultice that produced a "healthy" heat that drew out and loosened the phlegm. "The longer you can endure the heat," she warned, "the better off you will be." A time-honored remedy for sinus congestion was "steaming," breathing the vapors of boiling water through an inverted cone made of cardboard.

Father was captive to a number of unconventional rituals. Before he wore a new pair of socks he would rip out all of the elastic because he feared it would constrict the veins, a condition that might lead to edema. As a result his socks were usually at "half-mast." Before going to bed I would sometimes see him take each one of his toes, vigorously rotating each of them this-way-and-that to maintain the strength and range of motion of each digit. "God never intended that our feet be encased in shoes where our toes don't get any exercise," he would proclaim. I wondered if I faithfully practiced his ritual if I would be able to climb trees like an orangutan.

Father knew that our hands were a major source of bacterial contamination, and he warned us against biting our nails or putting our fingers in our noses, ears, or mouths. Once he came back from a meeting of the Southwestern Medical Association with a new story about an event in the men's room. He observed that a visiting British physician washed his hands first before walking over to the urinal to void. Upon being quizzed by Father about his inversion of a traditional health pattern, the Englishman said with some heat: *"Sir, I know for certain where this organ (pointing to his penis) has been. I'm not certain what contamination these (lifting up his hands) have touched!"*

During the long winter months we endured periodic "sun baths" by ultra-violet treatments both at home and at the office. Additional benefits were that they kept our acne in check and mitigated against the development of false modesty—any member of the family might stick their head in the door and yell, "It's time to turn over!"

While not of a serious life-threatening nature, there were a number of kid diseases that were embarrassing. Ringworm, "the itch," began with a small red spot that enlarged and then erupted into a gooey, scaly, itchy mess. The tiny burrowing mites circled around just under our skin. Their favorite site seemed to be the back of the hand, neck, or hair. Once afflicted we needed the fortitude of Job not to scratch at them. Father's treatment was a smelly yellow sulfur-type salve covered by a gauze bandage. There were gradations of social status associated with kid ailments. While anyone could get ringworm, the town gossips assumed it was caused by those who avoided soap and water. Their censorious attitude was as bad as "the itch."

Lice seemed to be a "kissing cousin" of the ringworm. Our Doughboys in World War I had lice, which they called "cooties," because they could not wash and change clothes. Occasionally the school nurse would examine the scalp of one of my classmates for head lice. Whether the kid's scalp was immaculate or contaminated, the word would spread: *"Elmer's got lice. Stay away from him!"* Kids were cruel. Elmer would be destroyed socially within a few minutes. More often someone we didn't like would be seen scratching at an armpit or his crotch. The word went out: *"Butch has got the cooties! Butch has got the cooties!"* It was futile for Butch to protest. Cooties were the leprosy of the·Depression era playground.

As the children of a physician, the five of us were always subjected to taking a lot of pills. Later I realized that most of what we consumed had only a placebo effect. But Father religiously dictated that we promptly swallow whatever he doled out, even if some of the pills appeared to us to be the size of a robin's egg. He liked to tease Mother because she couldn't swallow a "simple little pill" and had to mash hers between two spoons and mix it with jam. As a protection against its abuse by children, Father believed that medicine should always have a vile taste. "If pills were sugar-coated," he believed, "children would eat them like candy and many would die as a result."

My parents knew that approximately 70 percent of medical complaints were psychosomatic (the term in the 30s was "functional") rather than physical or organic. They were properly conservative in terms of medical intervention. In most cases, if an ailment was left alone (like the bark of a tree growing around a properly trimmed limb), the natural healing powers of the body would take care of the indisposition. Mother was always worried, however, about the aggressive ministrations of Rachel Hickman in treating her children's belly aches. "Her medicine of choice is always a large dose of castor oil" she worried. "One of these times she is going to trigger a simple case of appendicitis into a ruptured appendix. Peritonitis will set in and she will lose her child."

Although our genetic heritage fortunately gave us excellent teeth with hard dentine, we were taught to brush them after every meal. We could use baking powder as well as toothpaste but were advised that it was the length of our brushing rather than the taste of the soap that mattered. Nor was the tongue ignored. Father told us that it was the origin of bad breath and that the scum that collected on it was the seedbed of all kinds of germs and pathogens. I would vigorously brush my tongue every night and watch it turn from a trashy gray to a bright pink.

As far as bowel habits were concerned, we were instructed to "listen to our body" and religiously go "number two" during a set time each day. In an attempt to aid nature's timing, Father decreed that each of his offspring consume the number of breakfast prunes that corresponded to his or her age. Father's dictates regarding prunes was as rigid as the Decalogue. Had the California prune growers known about Father, they would have given him an award. Regarding other dietary practices, we were "hard-core" carnivores. Drawing upon her knowledge of nutrition, Mother believed that animal protein provided minerals and other important nutrients that could be gained in no other way. Present day vegetarians would have been ridiculed as "grazers" and taunted for their naive and faddish philosophy.

My brothers and sisters and I regularly violated our parents' rule against snacking between meals. To do so we had to live off the land, and we anxiously awaited the time when green apples would be large enough to eat. Another favorite snack was sheep sorrel. It grew to two or three inches in height, had triangular-shaped leaves and small light yellow flowers. It had an acidic taste, but when I was hungry, I ate it by the handful. I would put a bunch in my mouth, close my teeth and open my lips, and scissor off the leaves as I pulled out the stalks.

We rarely ate out as family; Father's suspicious nature did not trust the cleanliness of restaurant kitchens or the personal hygiene of cooks or waitresses. Evidence abounded from his practice that they might carry bugs he did not want transferred to his loved ones. When we did eat out, we carefully placed our silverware on a paper napkin so it would not be invaded by the unseen microbes lying wait on the table top.

At home, I never came to the table without first washing my hands with Lava—the Benjamin family soap of choice. To bite our nails was a crime close to fornication. Like medieval knights guarding a castle drawbridge, we were directed to fortify all of our bodily openings against foreign contamination.

Once a friend, Clark Hickman, gave me a pair of bathing suit trunks that he didn't want. Before I could put them on, Mother threw them into the Maytag washer with a large bar of her homemade lye soap with the warning, "You can never be sure what Clark has been up to."

Father was a great tease and often put Mother to the test regarding her ability to catch a pint bottle of tonic or cod liver oil. "Catch!" he would shout from the vestibule as he underhanded a bottle across the living room with a flat trajectory. She was lucky if the toss was from only 10 feet away. Most often it was closer to 20. I never saw her drop one. She knew what it would do to the carpet.

One summer in the mid-1930s, Mother went to the Mayo Clinic to have her gall bladder removed. Grandmother Bedell went with her as did Father who observed the surgery, but we children had to remain home with the hired girl. I worried a lot and imagined the worst. Though a child, I knew that surgery at that time was anything but routine. "If there was nothing to worry about," I wondered, "why had she gone to Rochester rather than enter our hospital?" Spontaneously, a beautiful experience developed involving Bob, Martha, and me. We imagined we were present with her in the hospital and wanted to thank her for her sacrificial love for us. An unconscious yet collective act of grace began to take shape. Chores that had been considered loathsome were done joyously and in a spirit of vicarious love. We experienced a metamorphosis from child servants to true sons and daughter. The cocoon of the "letter of the law" was transformed into the butterfly of the "spirit."

Knowing we could never repay her for everything she had done for us, we nevertheless heroically tried for the impossible. From morning to night we watered the lawn, cut dandelions, trimmed shrubbery, hoed the garden, dusted furniture, and vacuumed rugs until the entire house and yard were in as close to a state of perfection as three children could bring them. Gone were the side-wise glance comparisons and typical whines "I did more than you did," "That's your job not mine," or "You didn't do your share."

After three weeks Mother returned, and we went down to welcome her at the train station. The conductor did not have a portable step, and stepping down two feet from the train caused Mother obvious pain. Father lashed out at the conductor for his insensitivity. Later a letter to the president of the railroad company extracted an apology. As the railroad physician for three of the four railroads that came through Pipestone, Father felt he could throw his weight around. Long before assertiveness training became fashionable, I learned that I should neither endure an injustice passively nor be afraid to take my complaints to the top, when possible.

Memorial Day, 1940, at Hutchinson in the backyard of my Uncle Arthur. From left to right: Walter, Robert, Martha, Father, Roger, Mother, Mary.

20. THE FAMILY ALTAR—THE DINING ROOM TABLE

> In later life as in earlier, only a few persons influence the formation of our character; the multitude pass us by like a distant army. One friend, one teacher, one beloved, one club, *one dining table,* one work table, are the means by which his nation and the spirit of his nation affect the individual.
>
> Richter

My parents and we five children, when we were at home, ate nearly every meal together at our dining room table. Our almost religious observance of rigidly-set mealtimes—7:30 A.M., 12:00 noon, 6:00 P.M.— was violated only on those occasions when a medical emergency intervened. Almost every meal was served in the dining room on a tablecloth. (Even poor families restricted oilcloth to the kitchen table.) At breakfast we commenced eating only after observing a time-honored breakfast ritual: a short Bible reading followed by a passage from the *Upper Room* and a blessing. Naturally, Father served as high priest. On Sundays and special occasions a real linen tablecloth, purchased by Father during a 1930 medical trip to Belfast, Ireland, graced our table. Each of us had a napkin ring that held a cloth napkin, which we were expected to keep reasonably clean for a week. Each of us had a specific place at the table, with Father at the head and Mother at the foot. We were expected to come in suitable attire, hands washed, and behave in a manner reflective of Benjamin values and etiquette. If my hands were noticeably dirty, I had to wash again, with Lava, until they were clean.

Our Depression-era meals were nourishing if a bit monotonous. Epicurean interests were secondary to the need to stoke the stomach for our daily physical regimen. Mother fixed hot breakfasts, rotating cooked oatmeal, rye, Malt-O-Meal, and Cream-Of-Wheat. Occasionally we were allowed to have corn flakes, Grape Nuts, or Wheaties, "The Breakfast of Champions," but Father considered cold cereal to be a poor value—"those boxes contain mostly air, and I don't want to pay for that"—and deficient in calories. Our toast was always slathered with jam or apple butter that we had put up the previous summer. The tedium of the fare was broken by a grace note of brown sugar or puffy soft raisins that Mother had soaked overnight.

Lunch was a hot dish or a sandwich and soup with a dish of canned fruit for dessert. The main meal of the day was supper and consisted of meat, salad, mashed potatoes, bread, and a vegetable. Mother usually wore her apron to the table. More than just a protection garment, it was a symbol that she had been active in preparing the meal and had not just microwaved a frozen box (such trays were not available then). Once a week we had cake or ice cream for dessert as a welcome break from canned peaches, pears, or apricots. Although Mother and Grandmother Bedell could make a huge array of prize-wining pies, during my childhood such delights rarely graced our table because Father believed they were hard on the digestive system. In later years he relented and even had an occasional cup of coffee with his pie.

On weekends we children joined in the food preparation. On Saturdays I often enjoyed making an upside-down cake. I would arrange pineapple circles and maraschino cherries on the bottom of the rectangular cake pan, carefully pour a brown sugar and butter mixture over them, followed by the batter. When baked and inverted, my creation was, in my opinion at least, a thing of wonder. We took turns making cookies on Saturdays and, within reason, Mother would let us choose the recipes. On Sundays we fought to be chosen to mash the potatoes in the Mixmaster. I was careful to thoroughly pulverize the boiled potatoes before adding whole milk; otherwise, there would be lumps in the potatoes and I would receive a gentle reprimand at the table.

The Sunday sacramental fare of our evening meal was always the same—toasted cheese sandwiches, hot chocolate, canned applesauce, and popcorn. We thought it strange that Father poured cream on his applesauce—it curdled instantly—but he said he was just helping his stomach get past the first stage of digestion. The pace of the meal and tone of the conversation were set by my parents. Each of us was expected to contribute to the conversation out of our daily experience of school, music, work, and sports. It was considered bad form to vent feelings of anger, depression, frustration, or criticism toward anyone within or outside the house. I never dared tell my parents that "I'm having a bad day," or "I'm not a morning person," or "Mr. Olson, my math teacher has it in for me." Father's automatic rejoinder would have been, "Are you making up alibis again?" Emotions were fine as long as they were kept on a tight tether. Unlike some contemporary families, the Benjamins countenanced no childhood tyrants at the table—or anywhere else. We repressed our hurts, fears, and traumas. My parents would have pooh-poohed the claim that catharsis or ventilating feelings was necessary for psychic health.

Father presided over our board not unlike a genial Marine drill instructor. God help us if our shoulders slouched or we put our elbows on the table! *"Get those shoulders back!"* or *"Take your elbows off the table"* was the command ad nauseum. He must have parroted it as many times as his *Semper Fi* alter-ego shouted *"Dress Right"* and "Present Arms!" in Boot Camp. We had to sit like West Point plebes with our butts tucked against the back of our chairs and our vertebrae like a plumb line. At the time I thought his strictures were unduly harsh and punitive. Years later I was thankful for his strictness because I understood the importance of proper posture for good health. We were taught never to put a whole piece of bread on the palm of our hand and slap butter on it with a house-painting technique. Bread had to be broken into quarters or bite-sized pieces, each being buttered just before it was eaten.

Spiritual spokes of food, drink, conversation, mutuality, and tradition radiated from the center of the family altar. The dining room was an all-purpose room that anchored the family in the morning and evening and in between. Much more than eating took place there. Sarah Breathnach observed in Simple Abundance that it was there that newspapers were read, mail sorted, conversations started, homework completed, cakes iced, income tax computed, flowers arranged, games played, and friends gathered. "Here, at this replica of the Greek goddess Hestia's round earth, rites of passage are commemorated, holidays are celebrated, daily grace is offered, minds, bodies and spirits are nourished." Indeed, during numerous holidays (from the Old English "holy day") generations of families are linked as china, crystal, and silver that had been passed from parents to children, is lovingly removed from open-shelved cupboards and placed on the table as a comforting reenactment of a timeless ritual of hospitality and homecoming.

Not until our parents gave permission could we be excused from the table. Seldom was this granted until everyone had finished. I would often plead with my siblings by means of facial expressions and body language, urging them to hurry up and finish so that I could escape the orbit of Father's omniscient vision.

There was nothing unusual about this 1930s table tableau. Nor was it deemed archaic. Most Pipestone families, whatever their social level, considered the dining room table to be their home's altar. Table protocol might have been stiff and uncomfortable, but it served as an incubator for social capital. It was not only a time to eat but a time to show respect. While ideals travel upward, my parents believed manners travel downward. Heaven help us if we picked our nose, tore our fingernails, belched, or managed our silverware and food without the decorum appropriate to our age. Eating together, like family vacations and volunteer work, was the mortar of the Benjamin bond.

Our table was an arena for instruction beyond table etiquette. In addition, our parents cultivated the virtues of respect, manners, self control, social interaction, morality, and bonding. Every generation faces a barbarian threat from its own children who need to be civilized. This is the perennial challenge: to teach the young the conditions of being human, of civility, of managing life's tasks in a world that is (and must remain) forever imperfect. The Benjamin board was a nursery of civility—the sum of the many sacrifices we are called upon to make for the sake of living together. The refusal to come to terms with this reality in the home and around the table is the heart of the radical impulse and accounts for much of the destructiveness of our era. Fortunately, my parents believed our family to be the theater for our lessons concerning the grandeur and tragedy of the human enterprise.

The coarsening of American manners is a much-bruited complaint today, often illustrated by adolescents who seem constitutionally incapable of removing their baseball caps, who cannot sit up straight in a chair, or who walk the shopping malls stuffing pizza into their mouths. Fault is routinely ascribed to mass advertising, to television, or to the movies. Nevertheless, the acceptance of convention—conventional graces, conventional duties—is not something one is born with. It has to be implanted and cultivated in wild, young children by their patient elders.

Father would have agreed with Thomas Wolfe that there "is no spectacle on earth more appealing than that of a beautiful woman in the act of cooking dinner for those she loves." Ours was not an ethos of haste and waste. Adults sipped their coffee at home, not at Starbucks. School administrators would have been appalled at the duty to serve government food to children at breakfast. The microwave oven, instant cookery, the disposable plastic dish, and the din of television and stereo had not yet arrived to erode life's most fundamental ritual. Nor had McDonalds, Magic Chef, and pizza-a-go-go yet appeared to barter time for quality and efficiency for conversation. During the Depression no product or service was available by means of a drive-through.

A culture of centuries has been killed stone dead in the last 40 years. What was preciously guarded and meticulously passed on from mother to daughter has been casually and treacherously thrown away. Cooking—and not just cooking but knowledge about food, where it comes from, how to choose it, and even how to eat it properly—is taught neither in school nor in the kitchen. If just one generation fails to do its duty, then the chain is broken, the food culture is lost, and society becomes uncivilized. Some of the radical feminists bear heavy responsibility for prejudicing girls and their mothers against this knowledge; for them it is axiomatic that working in a factory or being a lawyer is a higher calling than the knowledge and practice of food preparation. Theoretically it is possible that cook books and TV cooking shows can transmit this knowledge. In truth, such learning takes years and requires an apprentice relationship as well as a fair number of humbling and repetitive tasks. A well-disciplined home can impose them. Television cookery cannot.

Now the family meal is in extremis. George Bernard Shaw's aphorism—"home life is no more natural to us than a cage is natural to a cockatoo"—reflects today's cynicism toward the Victorian family and hatred of the institution that Martin Luther held was the nursery of character. Father would have agreed with Samuel Johnson, however, that a "man is in general better pleased when he has a good dinner upon his table than when his wife speaks Greek." Today, shopping malls, fast-food chains, and takeouts cover our land like an English fog. Our approach to eating and drinking involves ever-less ritual and ceremony. No wonder, then, that a cheese sandwich tasted great on a family picnic, but a lonely, cold cheese sandwich grabbed from a vending machine has all the appeal of cardboard.

The granddaughters of Depression women who piled turkey and dressing and several pies and jars of homemade gooseberry preserves on the tables of the church pot-luck suppers now come with pie-mix pies, third-rate hot dishes laced with Hamburger Helper and ersatz Chinese noodles, and artificially flavored gelatin salads. Women then prized the quality of their recipe boxes, their well-thumbed cook books, and the kudos they received for the gastronomic wonders that issued from their kitchens. We are light-years away from Brillat-Savarin's adage that the "discovery of a new dish does more for human happiness than the discovery of a new star."

Teenagers of the 1930s did not have cars that allowed escape from the family altar. Like it or not, we were at home more. Today dining is often hermit-like and strictly functional: we eat and drink on the run. Our post World War II kitchens with their snack bars and stools, reveal us as a people on the move who want to eat quickly, with a bare minimum of interaction. The omnipresent T.V. has led to a drying of family conversation, and the computer culture has increased the isolation of family togetherness. Many of today's young people have become machine-like on the inside. Their social exchange too often lacks authentic expressiveness and affiliation. We have forfeited a familial shrine, a place of meeting and conversation, that was a central element in my upbringing.

Ralph Waldo Emerson once called Paris the "social center of the world," indicating that its cardinal merit lay in its being the "city of conversation and cafes." While Emerson loved his solitude, he also prized the great benefits of sociability that come from breaking bread with "superior persons." Emerson knew that eating alone fosters egotism, isolation, and the avoidance of paying "little polite attentions." Table conversation, however, accompanied by good food and a proper ambiance, can provide benefits ranging from romance to our civic well-being.

Perhaps we can look to chimpanzee behavior for clues to human psychology. Anthropologists record that a chimp will sit alone and nibble sweet things like berries. But if meat is the entree, chimps share. In like fashion, a person might be happy munching a candy bar alone, but eating alone in a restaurant feels wrong—it exudes a body language of unease. From the interchange at family meals, I began to learn a profound lesson: taking responsibility for others, and thereby leading more vulnerable lives separated my parents from their childless peers. Having offspring does not in itself make one an adult, but not having them—as many in our current generation seem intent on proving—is an invitation to remain a child.

I doubt that the time that is no longer spent in social interaction at the family table is put to comparable worthwhile use elsewhere. Legions of children are now raised without the civility and decorum that parental authority enforced at our Depression-era tables. The fare may have been spartan, but the lessons in social graces were of incalculable value.

We need to rediscover the social—and socializing—aspects of giving and receiving nourishment throughout the life cycle, from the newborn's clamorous demands for its mother's breast to the dying man's grateful acceptance of his last cooling drink. We can recapture this spirit without becoming crass Epicureans. Currently, however, it's only on ceremonial occasions—Christmas, Thanksgiving, Easter, birthdays—that we reach down into the innermost depths of our memory bank and attempt to resurrect it. Then we summon up turkeys and pies, roasts and casseroles, to recapture something we know has been missing in our family and national life. On such occasions, like all religions and cultures, we should bond food with blessing, and give thanks to God for farmers, sun, rain, soil, even life itself. Perhaps I am an antiquarian, but I believe that food is meant to be sacramental and good—or at least it can be, if one takes the time to prepare, present, and enjoy it properly. And family is good. The fact that we insist on uniting food with family on a handful of holidays we treasure is a clear sign that we know we have lost something from a bygone era that was precious.

A swimming lesson at Kee Nee Moo Sha Resort, Woman Lake.

21. Going to the Lake

The most anticipated event of every summer was our two-week vacation at the lake. Ninety-five percent of the lakes in Minnesota's "Land of 10,000 Lakes" are in the northern third of the state. That being the case, "going to the lake" was a part of most conversations of small town prairie dwellers during the summers of the Great Depression. A family could rent a cabin for $15 a week. It was one of the few luxuries affordable on a Depression-era budget.

We were creatures of habit and always returned to a resort of 11 brownish-red cabins named Kee Nee Moo Sha (Chippewa for "Sweetheart of the Maples") on the north side of Woman Lake in Cass county. My parents had stumbled upon the site during a camping trip in the early '20s.

Preparations for our trek started days in advance. It was a trip of 300 miles, and we took most of our groceries with us. The back seat of the Oldsmobile was filled within two-and-a-half feet of the roof with dozens of jars of food, a tent, potatoes, jackets, raincoats, fishing gear and the like. Blankets were placed on top so that we children could lie down. A washtub that contained food on the way up would, we hoped, be full of iced fish on the homeward drive. Sometimes Father would hire a *locum tenens* physician to fill in for him—and thus prevent his patients from straying to a rival medical fold while he was away.

I dug enormous quantities of worms from our garden and placed them in large buckets in the shade on the north side of the house. Every day Grandad Bedell would dump them out to aerate and loosen the soil and we'd pull them apart because they would be all clumped together like a squishy softball at the bottom of the pail. Sometimes we mixed in coffee grounds to improve the quality of the soil and oatmeal to give the worms something to eat. Properly cared for, the bait would last through the entire vacation. We purchased minnows only if we were unsuccessful in seining for shiners in the lake.

On occasion we Benjamins were joined by the Trebon, Knudtson, and Hickman families. We usually got underway at about 11 P.M., after Father had finished his evening hospital rounds. Each car in the procession had a dishtowel tied to the spare tire to help us see one another and stay in formation (spares then were carried outside the car, strapped to the trunk lid). Usually one or two cars had tire trouble along the way, and we would all stop to help. We were fortified with thermos bottles of hot coffee and chocolate, sandwiches, apples, and cookies. Stopping at a cafe was not only profligate, it posed the risk that one of us might pick up a disease from an unclean, wanton waitress.

As our family increased in size, we started using a small trailer to transport our belongings—and our dog! Skippy, a Chesapeake Bay retriever, was too large to ride in the car, so Father nailed a box on the tongue of the trailer and Skippy rode unhappily in that. We were commanded to "keep our eyes peeled on her." Once she jumped out while we were going 60 miles an hour. Fortunately, the clothesline rope that tied her collar to the box had broken. Instead of her mangled carcass we found her running in the ditch with only a small cut on her ear. Too big or not, she rode in the car after that.

To temper the boredom during long trips families often played "ZIP" while traveling. Numbers were attached to a half-dozen objects we might see: the rarer the item, the higher the number. A red-haired woman might be 25 points, a white horse 20, a pheasant 15, a dog 10, a cat 5 and so forth. But given our short attention span and in spite of Mother's plea to "keep our eyes peeled," the game only temporarily diverted the five of us from our normal routine of teasing, arguing, pinching, face-making, and all-around uncivil and anti-social behavior. Cars did not have air conditioning then, and being cooped-up in the back seat was not unlike being confined in a coffin. Mother said we often behaved like a bunch of "feisty cockerels."

The object of the game was to provide extra-vehicular distraction. In reality it often was just another means of exacerbating sibling rivalry. *"I saw that white horse and said 'ZIP' before you did, Martha,"* I would scream. *"No, you didn't!"* was the rejoinder. *"You're in my way, I can't see,"* might be the retort of Roger, as he threw an elbow into someone's rib cage. *"You don't have 35 points, Neb,"* Bob would claim. *"You are supposed to add, not multiply your points."* And so it went. Games meant to foster sibling harmony often ended up stimulating factionalism. Mother had to accept the role of umpire, but her vision as to what was happening in the back seat was extremely limited. When the face-making, hitting, and scratching reached an intolerable level, Father would take his foot off the gas pedal and put it on the brake. He promised to stop the car and cuff us around if we didn't stop. That threat was usually quite effective and it reduced the five denizens of the back seat to a sullen form of silence.

As we neared camp the roads turned to gravel and then to a fine sand that left a cloud of dust billowing up behind us as we urged Father to go faster. Our back seat chorus usually had been singing a Johnny-one-note—*"Aren't we there yet?"*—since shortly after leaving home.

Once we arrived, the car was hardly stopped before I tore off my clothes, jumped into my swimming suit, and plunged into the fresh blue water. For me Woman Lake was a great crystal set in the navel of my earth. Not even a Southern Baptist immersion could compare with the refreshment that its waters brought to my spirit. Sky-blue water! I saw Woman Lake like a Catholic miracle-seeker and penitent views the waters of Lourdes. It was a perfect forest mirror, set 'round with stones—mysterious, threatening, beautiful, enticing, potent, foreboding. It was my only connection to the awe and reverence others experienced 1500 miles both east and west, upon encountering the power and majesty of the oceans. For a small boy from the arid prairies of south-western Minnesota, Woman Lake was a summer Shangri La.

Depression-era vacation cabins were small by today's standards offering perhaps a couple hundred square feet of space. There were no environmental restrictions, and many stood within 10 or 15 feet of the shoreline. Most were made with shiplap siding and crammed one or two bedrooms into their tiny confines. They were set on large stones and had to be shimmed back to level each spring to counteract the effects of frost heave during the winter's freeze-thaw cycles.

To gain privacy for sleeping, we pulled drapes across a wire. Wall studs and rafters were bare, and it was captivating to hear the rain beat against the roof as we lay in bed. Windows were hinged at the top and pulled up on the outside by means of a rope and pulley arrangement. We usually fell asleep listening to the music of the waves gently lapping at the shore.

Grandad Bedell taught us how to predict the weather—"red-sky at night, sailors delight; red-sky in the morning, sailors take warning." A deep scarlet sky tonight meant tomorrow would be another perfect day. We discovered a lot of truth in another ditty Grandad taught us:

When the wind is in the *East,* fishing is at its very *least,*
When the wind is in the *South,* it blows the bait into the fishes' *mouth.*
When the wind is in the *North,* wary fishermen fare not *forth,*
But when the wind is in the *West,* fishing is at its very *best.*

Since there was no electricity, Otto Christianson, the manager, would come by each day with a wheelbarrow filled with large chunks of ice for our ice box. (The ice had been cut with large crosscut saws during the winter and hauled to the ice house where it was covered with sawdust and stored.) A pump at the camp's well was our source of water and a kerosene stove and lamp cooked our food and provided lighting. Dishwater was simply flung out the door onto the grass. We sometimes cleaned pots and pans in the lake, using sand as an abrasive. We also bathed in the lake, scrubbing ourselves with a cake of soap and a wash cloth and employing them discreetly as needed under our bathing suits.

Thirty feet behind each cabin stood a two-hole outhouse. I never quite understood why two holes were needed. The Benjamins I knew did not particularly want company while "going number two." At least I didn't. In fact, I always counted the members of my family to see if they were all present before heading for the privy. Perhaps two-holers were there in case an emergency, like diarrhea, should strike the entire family.

Despite the relatively primitive conditions, it never entered my mind that what for me was a wondrous two-week experience might be viewed as a burden by Mother, who had to give up all the conveniences of her modern home.

One summer Mike, a street-wise lad from Minneapolis, introduced me and some of his younger disciples in camp to "pissing contests." We followed him into the woods where there was a large stump. He'd climb up on this 19th century remnant of the followers of Paul Bunyan and see how far he could project his urine. I began to see that math had some practical value, because the contest involved calculations in geometry as well as physiology. Each of us then mounted the stump in turn. There would be grunts and screams—"Hey, look at that...10 feet!...I beat you!"—as we squeezed down on our tender little bladders and tried to get the angle just right. We were cocky rascals: even the kid who came in last was better than a girl because boys had penises. In the nomenclature of English hunting dogs, girls were "setters" and boys were "pointers."

Vacations during the Great Depression also had a serious side. It was an era before the "catch-and-release" credo of today. Fishing then provided both sport and food for the family larder. We were "meat" fishermen and spent a lot of time on the lake with lines in the water. My uncles were especially hard on my cousins if they misplayed a fish and lost it. "Why did you give him slack?" Charge and counter-charge followed:

"I didn't give him slack."

"You didn't set the hook then."

"Yes I did."

"Your line is probably rotten. Did you dry it yesterday?"

"Of course I did."

Aunt Bessie took this photo in 1935. Left to right: Bob, Walter, Martha, Roger.

"How many times do I have to tell you to keep your thumb on the reel?"

"My hand is tired."

"If you had eaten your breakfast you would have the strength to catch the fish you hook."

"The oatmeal was lumpy."

"Check your minnow!"

"I did just a minute ago; besides, if you're such a good fisherman, why aren't you catching more fish?"

"Now, don't get smart with me or when we go in you won't go swimming today."

And so it went.

(My frugal uncles believed that a good-sized fish would take the place of five pounds of potatoes or an expensive Sunday roast.) The query, "Did you have a good vacation?" would be answered in the affirmative by members of the Tribe only if we were able to bring back a washtub or copper boiler full of fish preserved with hunks of lake ice and stiff as boards.

Besides trying to catch our limit of fish to take home, we wanted a fish dinner every day of our vacation. Fish were always scaled but never filleted. Mother said they tasted better with the skin on, but I suspect that the goal was to preserve as much of the flesh as possible. Mother had the reputation of cooking the best fish in camp. Her secret was using plenty of bacon grease for flavor. The terror of cholesterol, nitrates, and other supposed poisons that today interfere with gastronomic pleasure was as yet unknown. We ate as an expression of the joy of living, not to emulate Methuselah.

Fortunately, because of the lack of angling pressure on Woman Lake, it was not hard to catch a limit of walleyes and northern pike most days. A family photo shows us proudly holding a morning's catch of a dozen walleyes and northerns, each weighing between 5 and 10 pounds, with the caption: "Enough For Breakfast?" Sometimes we didn't even bother to string pan fish such as bluegills and sunfish, but instead just threw them into a gunny sack. There were no electronic fishing aids; we located sand bars by probing with bamboo poles.

I looked with contempt upon those who fished for bullheads, and we used a racist term for that kind of fishing. It didn't take any skill to put a wad of night crawlers on a hook, drop it to the bottom, and reel it up with a bullhead. Compared to other fish they were ugly creatures, and there were scary stories that their horns had poison in them. Bullheads and mosquitoes always bit in concert as the sun went down in Lantern Bay.

This 1940 1/2 horsepower Evinrude "Mate" weighed 10 pounds with a full tank of gas. During World War II the United States government officials ordered a freeze on the production of all nonessential civilian items in favor of military goods. Consequently, regular outboard manufacturing ceased. (Shipyard Museum)

The famous 17 pound, 1.7 horsepower Neptune "Mighty-Mite" was a huge success prior to World War II. Running against moderate waves, however, I discovered it could scarcely move the boat forward. My Grandparents babied their "Mite" like a fine piece of Dresden china. Decades later I used this motor to spare me the drudgery of paddling my canoe across large Canadian lakes. It seemed to run forever on a pint of gasoline.

When we weren't fishing we were swimming. I was in and out of my swimming suit seven times on some days. Many of us learned to swim at the lake. I began as a diaper-clad wader. (It never took long for my diaper to become saturated with sand and water and gravitate down to my knees.) Later I graduated to jumping to Father from the dock, then to swimming out to the raft. Father's Spartan philosophy—"There will be no sissies in the Benjamin Tribe"—dictated a morning dip; whatever the weather, we were required, along with most of the guests under our roof, to take one before breakfast. The other campers thought we Benjamins were insane. They didn't know my Father.

Grandad and Grandma Bedell wore old-fashioned gray wool suits with black horizontal stripes that covered them from shoulder to mid-thigh. They looked funny, but they were no pikers when it came to swimming. They would swim long distances almost effortlessly doing the side-stroke.

Our tackle boxes were small and our choice of artificial baits was limited. My favorites were Hedon lures, the Prescott Spinner, the Pikey Minnow, and the Daredevil. Bob and I tried making our own redhead lures out of plugs of wood, but they turned out to be rather sorry affairs. My first reel, an Our Own Hardware special, cost 98 cents; the rod was 49 cents. When I was 11 I caught a 17-pound leopard muskie with it. Bob and I were casting in some sunfish weeds when the lunker hit. He was twice as long as the net we had, so we leaned way over on one side of the boat until the gunwale was barely an inch above the water and scooped him in. After being photographed, he was put on ice. I had experienced the truth of John Buchan's aphorism: "The charm of fishing is that it is the pursuit of what is elusive but attainable, a perpetual series of occasions for hope."

Father imperiously decided that my handsome muskie would make a nice gift to the Pipestone hospital nurses. I've often wondered whether they ate him.

After each outing on the lake, we strung our lines between trees to dry so that they would not rot. It was a time before "better living through chemistry" had come about, and fishing line was made from a combination of cotton and rayon rather than monofilament.

Our boats were made of wood, usually fir strips. Like most natives, Otto Christianson made a new boat each winter. With narrow three-foot tran-soms, they were easily rowed by one person. At least once a week several families would meet out on the middle of the lake, tie their boats together and have a picnic. We would leave our lines in the water as we passed cold chicken, potato salad, pickles, and sandwiches from boat to boat. The mid-

Bob is play-acting at starting the motor while Father and I look on. Kee Nee Moo Sha Resort, Woman Lake. 1929.

lake rendezvous enabled us to escape the mosquitoes and provided a wonderful vantage point from which to watch the gorgeous sunset.

Running an outboard motor was a significant summer rite of passage for a youngster. I was 10 when Father first allowed me to take out our 2.5 horsepower, 1935 Johnson Sea Horse. It had a dark-red engine cover with the white letters of the logo on either side. The motor started with a pull cord. Grasp the handle. Put your foot on the transom. Brace. Pull. Brace. Pull. Fiddle with the choke. Brace. Pull. Fiddle with the choke some more. Repeat the operation until exhausted or in motion. There was never rhyme nor reason for why it started or didn't. Outboards do not adhere to the general laws of mechanics. But I knew what the outboard was before I touched it: it was flat-out freedom.

I spent hours making figure eights and racing other kids in front of camp. In spite of fiddling endlessly with the lean-rich mixture, my speed maxed out at about 12 M.P.H. Father suggested caution, but I found there were only two speeds: stopped and full.

The shear pin was the serpent in paradise, a treacherous device that promised protection but delivered disaster. You had extra shear pins taped to the handle because of the absolute certainty that you were going to screw up. A shear pin is a soft metal dowel inserted in a hole in the drive shaft. Its two ends protrude to fit slots in the propeller hub to keep the prop from slipping when the shaft turns. If the prop hits something hard, like the rocks off Stony Point or Green Isle, the soft metal pin shears off, and the shaft spins freely to prevent damage to the propeller, gears, or shaft.

Once I hit a rock in Broadwater Bay. ZZZZZZAAAAANNNNNN-GGGGGG went the drive shaft as it spun wildly. I cut the motor in a panic and pulled it up. It was then I realized that the man who wrote the shear-pin instructions was doing it on dry land. With the motor tilted, the prop was three feet away, at the very end of my stretch. A cleat on the transom dug into my belly as I leaned over to reach the cotter pin that held the prop hub. Every time a wave passed, the prop dipped under the water. I was terrified of dropping the pliers—it was a long row back to Kee Nee Moo Sha.

But not everyone used an outboard. Every morning for years Grandad rowed two miles out to his favorite bluegill spot on the other side of Horseshoe Island then rowed back after he'd caught his fish. Later he got a little 1.7 horsepower Neptune "Mighty-Mite," but most motors were from four to eight horsepower. Running around the lake in a 120 horsepower boat, a Jet Ski, or some other "personal watercraft," as many do today, would have been thought a sin.

One can still find quiet at the lake today, but it is becoming more difficult. Vacationers in that era had no mercury-vapor yard lights, spray cans, fiberglass boats, Weber kettles, gas grills, boom-boxes, dirt bikes, recreational vehicles, or any of the other technological toys to which today's consumerist generation is addicted.

Now lakes are ringed with docks, electric lifts, and boathouses. Then, we had to wrestle our boat up a latticework of two-by-fours, which became very slippery when covered with algae and fish eggs. The best one could expect from a fall was a badly skinned shin; the worst, one could break a leg.

At night we would join our friends to eat popcorn, play cards, shoot caroms, and tell "Do you remember when?" stories. After the war electricity came to camp, and Father would show home movies of earlier outings at the lake. A 1929 photo, probably taken by Aunt Bessie, reveals the captivating and emotional aura of the lake. In the picture I am two years old and am sitting cross-legged on the weatherbeaten boards of the dock. Bob is in the boat pretending to start the motor. We both are barefoot and in one-piece coveralls. Father sits protectively behind me, one hand on my knee, an arm around my shoulder. It is a moment frozen in time—a moment of bonding amid the water, sun and sand.

Now, almost 7 decades later, I still go to the lake. What used to be barely a path through the woods north of Brainerd has become a four-lane highway. Now my grandchildren recapitulate in their own ways the memories and magic of my boyhood experience, though I doubt that theirs is necessarily enhanced or deepened by the plethora of the material accessories that surround them.

In 2000 the Ojibway Tribe of the Leech Lake reservation built a new 15 million dollar casino a few miles north of Woman Lake. Hundreds of cars bearing license plates from states as far away as Ohio, Indiana, Illinois, and Nebraska crowd the parking lot. Buses of seniors are also trucked in from Brainerd and other northern Minnesota cities. It is a mystery to me why thousands of tourists would want to spend their precious vacation hours in a dark and jangling cave of a gambling den instead of enjoying the beauty of the flora and fauna of the Land of Ten Thousand Lakes. To be sure, the casino is the largest employer in Cass county and provides good wages and benefits. Its defenders indicate it has lifted many Native Americans out of endemic poverty. Nevertheless, I am not convinced that the benefits of gambling outweigh its burdens, since the social pathologies of the Tribe continue at high levels. I consider this casino (and the consequent evils that follow in its wake as well as the industry in general) to have profaned something pristine and holy that is unique to Minnesota. That this parasitic enterprise has taken place under the sovereignty of the Indian, whose supposed reverence for nature is legendary, is especially distressing.

Today, the mom-and-pop family resorts are almost gone. The large lodges have all the amenities of home and more. Land is expensive and small resorts have been divided up and sold as individual cabins. People demand creature comforts and luxuries that as a child I never knew— electric heat and dishwashers, golf courses, jet skis, tennis courts, and swimming pools, "one armed bandits" and blackjack, supper clubs and hot tubs. Vacation time now simply continues an everyday life style, only in a different setting, with a lake outside the picture window. Few try to reach back and cope with life as it was lived in a simpler, more primitive age, if even for only a couple of weeks.

Even now when I return to the lake, the memories of childhood summers lap the shores like waves. Modernity, thankfully, has not silenced the loons. Fortunately, the wolves and the black bears may be returning. I watch my grandchildren through misty eyes as they repeat, hopefully, my exploration of wonder—marveling at the mallards, wood ducks, and bald eagles; baiting hooks with shiners and nightcrawlers; studying heavenly constellations and cloud formations; catching salamanders, frogs, garter snakes, and clams; hearing the cry of the hoot owl; getting a glimpse of the camp's masked-raider raccoon and the white-tail flag of a deer taking flight.

Will they see nature as I did years ago, as God's sanctuary? Will they, like Emerson, see the sky as the "Daily bread of the eyes"? Will they garner and husband precious memories, as do I, that in a future time of trouble might give them solace and healing? Will they heed the advice of Francis Bacon that "Nature is a labyrinth in which the very haste you move with will make you lose your way"? Will they in time learn, as did I, the wisdom of the Hebrew sage: "A generation goes, and a generation comes, but the earth remains forever."

I am ambivalent about the changes I have witnessed over a lifetime of "going to the lake." But I am grateful that nothing can ever change or erase the timeless joy of a child gazing at the speckled and glittering fish rising into view.

22. The Churches—Sanctifying the Profane

I do not love the Sabbath
    The soapsuds and the starch,
The troops of solemn people
    Who to Salvation march

The Boy Out of Church, Robert Graves

The story of a saint is always a love story. It is a story of a God who loves, and of the beloved who learns how to reciprocate and share that "harsh and dreadful love." It is a story that includes misunderstanding, deception, betrayal, concealment, reversal, and revelation of character. It is, if the saints are to be trusted, our story. But to be a saint is not to be a solitary lover. It is to enter into deeper community with everyone and everything that exists.

Making Saints, Kenneth L. Woodward

The polling data tell us that Americans are a religious people, the large majority of whom attend church, believe in God, and pray daily. During the Great Depression a form of residual, 19th century Sabbatarianism was still evident in Pipestone. The majority of our citizens would have agreed with the Massachusetts Legislature which, as Alexis de Tocqueville noted, enacted in 1792 a law to enforce Sunday observance "inasmuch as it produced a useful suspension of labor leading men to reflect upon the duties of life and errors to which humanity is subject." To these religious folk, as the law stated, the observation of Sunday is in the "public interest."

The nineteenth century, however, had seen a struggle between conservatives who wanted to keep Sunday as the Lord's day—as a day of Christian worship—and liberal Protestants who wanted to turn it into a day of cultural uplift. Even Grant and Coolidge got into the act, siding with those who favored keeping the Sabbath safe for religious worship. The great Sabbath debate may even have foreshadowed the culture wars of our own time.

For the religious liberals, Sunday would still be a special day, but it would not necessarily be spent entirely in church. It would be spent at the library or the art museum or the World's Fair. It would not be a day of "rest" but a day of cultured "leisure"—a day in which Americans would expand their minds, refine their tastes and elevate their very souls. Father held that Sunday was "unique," and a day "set apart" for the strengthening of Benjamin family ties; one that should be for worship, rest and renewal. We eschewed Sunday commerce and travel whenever possible. If necessary, we filled our automobile gas tanks on Saturday. "If enough people choose not to shop on Sunday," he often said, "businesses will close out of necessity and everyone will have time to deepen their family ties."

Father was unhappy that the conservatives lost the great "holy day v. holiday" conflict. By 1900, when he was seven years old, half the nation's libraries were open on Sunday, as were many of its museums. And the secularization of the American Sunday did not stop there. "Progress" has a way of marching ever forward. In 1892 baseball's National League sanctioned Sunday games, and a few decades later professional football games were being played on Sunday (The NFL officially sanctioned Sunday games in 1949). By World War I, only six states still prohibited the opening of movie houses on Sunday. By the mid-1960s state bans on entertainment, sports, and commerce—the so called "blue laws"—were in terminal demise and are now all but dead.

The liberal reformers of the 19th century rarely defended commercial recreation on Sunday. They desired the spread of culture to the working man. Alas, what they got was "shop-'til-you drop" Sunday! They were defenders of high culture, not "culture" in all its many varieties, without distinctions between that which is degrading and "low" and that which is ennobling and "high."

In the end, entertainment trumped culture and attention to the affairs of the spirit. Americans have gone from viewing Sunday as a holy day of rest, to a day of cultural enlightenment, to one of mindless consumption and amusement. We have gone from our Founder's view of thinking of Sunday in terms of broad public purposes, to goofing off or finding the best bargain. Nowadays on the typical Sunday the malls are hopping, the movie theaters are packed, and the roads are clogged with cars and bikers. The elders I knew in my youth would have been angry and depressed at the transformation.

We were a church-going family in a community that had churches in abundance. Including all the sects, cults, and "holy roller types," there were 14 religious congregations in our town of 5,000 citizens. Such fragmentation more than provided for the freedom of every religious expression. Sociologically, it was deleterious to community harmony. While football and basketball contests united us, Sunday was a time of fragmentation and division. As Christians we knew there was one universe, one world, one humanity, one America, one Minnesota, one Pipestone; we professed "One God and Father of us all." Sadly and sinfully, as a community we could not embody our theological principles.

Most of the Protestant churches—those that drew their religious origins from the genius of Luther, Calvin, Knox, or Wesley—were at the center of town and within a few blocks of each other. Most had been created on land provided gratis by the village founders. In spite of their theological common heritage, however, a spirit of religious laissez faire made it devilishly hard for them to work together. A "root hog or die" form of Social Darwinism was apparent, itself a pale copy of the economic conflict waged by the robber barons of American industry a few decades earlier. The town was static in terms of growth and, since the village's small atheist, "don't give a damn about religion" contingent was resistant to all entreaties regarding membership, about the only way a congregation could increase its number was to proselytize.

A pastor who could lure a family away from a competing house of God enjoyed the same inner satisfaction that the Ford dealer, Tracey Hicks, received when he induced a Chevy owner to change his loyalties. It was a time of brawny denominational competition. A future ecumenical spirit was still in embryonic form; separation of the seamless robe of Christ was not seen as sinful. One was not guilted for pointing out the theological flaws and moral trespasses within a neighbor's flock. Four churches—Episcopal, Congregational, Presbyterian, and Methodist— did hold common services on Good Friday and Thanksgiving, but their cooperation owed more to weakness than strength: separate services were too much work for the sparse attendance they'd attract. I suspect our medical doctors had more collegiality within their guild than did our physicians of the soul.

The Catholics existed both physically and ecclesiastically in regal isolation. They were "in" but not "of" the Puritan ethos of the town. Their impressive brown brick edifice with two massive towers occupied the hill immediately to the East of the Court House. Like the military, the Catholics always sought the high ground. Symbolically, this was important. Since God was "up there" and the sky represented eternity, it was important for the Mother of all churches to have the highest edifice in town to indicate it was the closest to heaven. The cynics and Catholic bashers said "the Romans" built on hills because "that's about as close to God as most of their members would ever get." Both physically and symbolically, therefore, Catholics looked down on Protestants. We were better than pagans, of course, but terms like "false believers" and "schismatics" would apply. Liberal priests might use a modern and milder term, "separated brethren," but we noted whether they emphasized the first or second word, which indicated their real attitude. As the only true expression of Christ's presence on earth, they had little to do with false believers. For the most part Catholic priests ignored the Protestants, much like Father disregarded chiropractors. Catholics did not advertise, hold revivals, proselytize, or hold fellowship with other Christians. And why should they? Things were going their way; all trends were positive. It seemed but a matter of time.

While not of the economic or social elite, Catholics seemed somehow religiously superior and yet a bit un-American. They possessed all of Christianity. As a Methodist, I had only a part. They had seven sacraments, we but two. It was harder to be a Catholic. They had to eat fish on Friday, go to mass on Sunday, and follow a lot of nit-picky rules. My friends on the basketball team who were Catholic always crossed themselves before shooting a free throw. It didn't seem to help them much.

But Catholics did seem to have more fun than Protestants. They had large families, could drink, gamble and play bingo. Going to mass seemed to give them a blank check for the rest of the week. And did they drink. Not that I had a lot of personal evidence, only the stories we liked to tell of Catholic drunks weaving their way across the street to attend mass. We also told tales of nuns and priests fornicating in convents, and about Eleanor Roosevelt and the Pope. We criticized Catholics for assuming faith was identical to church dogma and for their unquestioning obedience to whatever their priest told them. They, we thought, were religious aborigines, forever suckling the spiritual fare of babes in the faith. We Protestants, on the other hand, feasted on theological "solid food" because we had a mature degree of Christian consciousness and could weigh and choose what to believe. Under the surface it was clear that we feared Catholics and preferred our fables to honest information. Catholics, it seemed, got their pleasure from John Barleycorn while our laughs came by telling stories about Catholics.

Pipestone Catholics felt our subtle—and sometimes not-so-subtle—Protestant antipathy. In larger communities they created many parallel institutions—Catholic Boy Scout troops, the Catholic Youth Organization, Knights of Columbus, women's guilds, etc., to protect the innocent. Our Catholic church, however, was unique in that it did not have a parochial school, unlike most towns our size. We were happy that priest after priest came and went, either ignoring or unable to fulfill their bishop's orders in this regard. I was never sure whether the priests were just lazy, poor at finance, didn't want the added administrative responsibility that a parochial school would entail, or had made their peace with the common school. I accepted the pervasive rumor that the parochial school was part of the Vatican's plan to subvert our cherished American Way and turn America into a country like Italy or, worse, Ireland. As Protestants, we came to America first and made this country what it was. Plymouth Rock Pilgrims and Irish potato-famine Catholics were separated by over 200 years! Catholics were late-comers, interlopers whose manners, culture, and attitudes weren't quite 100 percent American. While we could tolerate a Pope's platoon in Pipestone, we didn't want his army there.

The anti-Catholicism of popular culture permeated our home. Father bought a dozen copies of Paul Blanshard's *American Freedom and Catholic Power* and gave us each one. I knew enough not to date a Catholic girl and may well have been disowned had I married one. As a member of an all-Protestant school board, Father was always on guard lest this hallowed American institution be undermined by Catholics. It was widely believed that, like Marxists, they might "bore from within." While the board allowed Superintendent Knudtson to hire a few token Catholic teachers, there was an unwritten law not to have one as a coach.

"Coaches get terribly close to their boys," confided one board member, "And we don't want them messing with the beliefs of our kids."

We called Catholics "mackerel snappers" and nuns, "penguins," even though most of us had never even spoken to a Catholic sister. I'm not sure the Catholics had a name for us. They didn't have to. We were going to Hell and they had an ironclad lease on Heaven.

Father had a lot of loyal Catholic patients who kept him well informed as to what plans the Vatican's lieutenant had for our bucolic town. Occasionally, a priest might suggest that they should consider changing to a Catholic physician. Father was usually incensed with such gratuitous advice but inwardly pleased that most of his patients ignored it. Father's suspicion of Catholics was a bit extreme. Most priests seemed like jolly convivial types who enjoyed their weekly cigars, liquor, and poker sessions with Protestant and Catholics alike. Father did admire the nuns who ran Catholic hospitals (he had interacted with them at St. Mary's hospital in Rochester) because they ran things in a "ship-shape manner." He detested, however, Catholic medical ethics. Once, Father and a Catholic physician agreed that a therapeutic abortion had to be performed.

"Then we operate at eight A.M.," Father concluded.

"I'm sorry," I can't help you," answered the Catholic physician.

"But you agreed that she will die without the surgery," Father responded strongly.

"Yes, I know," said Father's colleague sadly, "But I can't be there to help you." Father operated alone.

The most significant conflict Father had with the Catholic church arose out of a bussing issue. Returning from a house call early one Sunday, he saw a school bus bringing Indian children to the Catholic church. Subsequently he wrote to the Department of the Interior asking whether the practice was in violation of our policy of the separation of church and state. A clumsy bureaucrat (my parents considered a "competent bureaucrat" to be an oxymoron) violated Father's privacy by returning the letter to the priest, requesting that he solve the dilemma. The priest, seeing an opportunity to strike at a Protestant Goliath in the camp of the Philistines, ended a Sunday homily:

> There is a physician in the community who hates Catholics. He wishes
> to prevent precious Indian children from attending mass and receiving
> a Christian education. I will not give his name from the pulpit, but if
> you would like to know who he is, please see me after the service.

Father was incensed but pleased that his Catholic patients kept him informed.

This continuing *kulture-kamp* between Catholics and Protestants was deeply tragic. As the circumference of my world widened, I developed a deep and enduring respect for the Catholic Church and not a few nuns and priests became my good friends. Their vows of celibacy, obedience, and poverty were moral Everests compared to the mole hills I had climbed to follow our common Lord. Moreover, I discovered that Protestant Robber Barons had used legions of Catholic newcomers as the raw material to build everything from railroads to steel mills and that many WASPs had paid Irish immigrants $90 to take their place in the draft during the Civil War. I began to realize that Catholic immigrants often made the most loyal of citizens, some ferociously so. Tragically, anti-Catholicism was the anti-Semitism of the liberal and elite classes, whose members might affirm Native Americans, homosexuals and others, but revealed an irrational animus toward Catholicism. Their hateful zealotry caused them to ignore the log in their own eye as they focused on the speck in that of their non-Anglo Saxon neighbors.

The three major Lutheran denominations had fine churches and were unashamed of their ethnic heritage; they were known as the "German," "Swedish," and "Norwegian" Lutheran churches. When I was young the German Lutherans still demanded a pastor who could preach the early service in German to please the older members. Later on, as acculturation progressed and they needed to reach beyond those who were blond and blue-eyed for membership, they attempted to hide their old-world origins by identifying themselves as the "Missouri Synod," the "Lutheran Church in America," and the "American Lutheran Church."

I assumed that the 14 churches of Pipestone were separated by major theological and moral differences. I believed that centuries ago their division had occurred over whether we were to be dipped, sprinkled, or immersed for a valid baptism. I accepted without question that life and death hung in the balance on issues such as:

- wine vs. grape juice, wafer vs. bread
- salvation by faith vs. good works
- crucifix vs. an empty cross
- Eucharist vs. sermon as the focus of worship
- clerical collar vs. business suit
- kneeling vs. sitting for the Lord's Supper
- pastor, minister, or reverend vs. father
- bingo vs. morally "pure" fun
- free will vs. predestination
- the real vs. symbolic presence in the sacrament
- fundamentalism vs. liberalism
- local autonomy vs. hierarchic polity
- Christ's return before vs. after restoration of the earth

I did not know then that much of the religious divisiveness I saw was rooted more in sociology than in theology. That is, Christians of whatever vintage were too much "in the world," and their cultural loyalties had caused fragmentation. A theological veneer provided a thin disguise for old world and ethnic animosities that continued almost unabated in the new world. Hidden from my childhood were the racial, geographic, social and class factors that dismembered Christ's body. These were the origins of the "manyness" of the Christian denominations and the broken and antagonistic witness for Christ. Lamentably, the divisiveness of culture had transformed the Church, rather than the reverse.

Catholics and Lutherans dominated the religious market by supervising two-thirds of the souls in Pipestone. Methodists, along with the Baptists, Presbyterians, Congregationalists, Episcopalians and the "here today, gone tomorrow" sects, had to scramble for the rest.

Competitiveness clearly was not limited to car dealers; pastors and governing boards kept a close eye on their rivals' possible future building plans. Wise shepherds, however, did not rush pell-mell into assuming the large debt that a new addition inevitably imposed; they knew from bitter experience that members weak in the faith and non-tithers would often bail out of a church at the first scent of a building campaign. Their excuse—"I just don't think Pastor Holy Socks is preaching the Gospel anymore"—was a dodge and everyone knew it.

Our major denominations shifted into neutral during the summer. Families were on vacation, there was no air conditioning, and religious spirits conformed to the torpid quality of the heat and humidity. Soloists replaced choirs, Sunday schools took a three-month sabbatical, and most preachers shortened their sermons. A funeral parlor donated paper fans imprinted with mawkishly portrayed Biblical scenes or a picture of the Dionne quintuplets. As if they were listening to a silent metronome, members beat them back and forth as they turned their sweating, expectant faces upwards to receive their weekly spiritual fare. Summer church was sticky hot and a trial. Most men wore the same suit they did in the winter.

For the Baptists, Pentecostal, and other go-it-alone churches, however, the summer was revival time. Most could be classed as sects and had names—Bible Christian Church, True Gospel, Holiness in God— that suggested they had a corner on the Gospel. These groups seemed to find an affinity between hellfire and hot weather; their souls heated up when the temperature rose into the 90s. September through May was a desert of spiritual ennui; but come warmer temperatures, itinerant preachers from the South came to breathe a new Pentecost into their moribund flocks. Billboards, handbills, and ads in The *Pipestone Star* heralded each evangelists's arrival and testified to the foreign mission work he'd conducted or inspired, the prodigious number of souls saved, his homiletic skill, and his vast Biblical knowledge, according to which the Second Coming was near at hand. Apparently the itinerant preacher alone was privy to the true meaning of Daniel and Revelation. Our resident pastors either couldn't discern the "time and the season" of the Second Coming, or they were "hirelings and false prophets."

During July of 1942 Evangelist Carl Sundin, "the Voice of Prophecy," came to town and put up a tent on the corner of 2nd street and 4th avenue. In his promotional photo, Sundin, the sin buster, seemed to combine the boxing stance of heavyweight champ Joe Louis with that of a Greek javelin thrower—only in this case the Bible took the place of the spear. If you liked "the old-time religion with the bark still on it," as an old timer said, Sundin was your kind of preacher.

It took an outsider to know where Lucifer, in a thousand different guises, stalked the streets of Pipestone. Like most evangelists, Sundin accepted Daniel Defoe's certitude:

> Wherever God erects a house of prayer,
> The Devil always builds a chapel there,
> And 'twill be found, upon examination,
> The latter has the largest congregation.

Our town was plastered with fliers announcing his nightly sermon topics during the two weeks he was duking it out with Satan under the Pipestone big top. Among Sundin's titles were: "The March of Dictators—Where Will It End?" "Why Doesn't God Kill the Devil?" "Four Ways You Will Know Your Friends in Heaven," "God's Blitzkrieg V. The Devil's Blackout." I was especially intrigued with the title "Hell Discovered 15 Miles From Pipestone." Maybe he knew something about our county that I didn't. I wanted to find out where this Pipestone purgatory was and secretly go there with my buddies.

One night I attended Sundin's revival with one of my Baptist buddies even though my parents did not encourage me to go. (I went not to be saved, but out of curiosity. I had already accepted Jesus Christ as my Lord and Savior in a less public and more subdued setting.) I didn't tell Rev. Tuck, because he would have considered my attendance a sign of disloyalty—much like one of Father's patients going to another doctor.

The terrible hymns were depressingly pessimistic—"That Awful Day Will Surely Come," "One More Day's Work For Jesus, One Less of Life For Me," "When This Poor, Lisping, Stammering Tongue Lies Silent in the Grave,"—while the fiery sermon was filled with the wrath of God. Sundin sat on the podium looking pious, with a saintly "I've just-seen-Jesus look" on his face. But he was a spell-binder and good with one-liners: "More preachers should put *more fire* in their sermons or put more of their *sermons in the fire!*" When he got wound up an was egged on by a crowd of people bellowing *"Amen"* and *"Preach It Brother,"* he was full of spiritual fire—"I'm going to wham the yellow piss out of the devil and keep on his tail so that he will finally slink all the way back to hell!" Another memorable tirade: "Too many Pipestone shepherds are hirelings! Their boneless sermons are stewed in cream. People need to have hellfire flashed in their faces or they will not move!" Sundin didn't have much faith in what he called the "hardtop churches"—they just keep your money and keep you in the dark about the "real Jesus."

I found it distasteful that, as an outsider, he would criticize his fellow members of the cloth. A few of our shepherds were a sorry lot, but they were doing the best they could. Moreover the anti-intellectualism of the fundamentalists bothered me. I had been taught that God gave us a mind as well as a heart and he wanted us to use them both. John Wesley, himself an Oxford don, had said, "Let us unite the two so long divided—the intellect and vital piety." But Sundin quoted Billy Sunday (a high school dropout and former professional baseball player): "Thousands of college graduates are going as fast as they can straight to hell. If I had a million dollars, I'd give $999,999 to the church and $1 to education."

On the other hand, some intellectuals could be just as narrow-minded. H. L. Mencken was hardly fair when he called fundamentalists "anthropoid rabble," "morons," "one-horse Popes," and "amateur Messiahs." Indeed, some liberal Protestants did great and lasting damage to ecumenical rapport when they stereotyped literalists as "barbarians" and "extremists," and accused them of "militant ignorance." Modernist pastors believed zealots like Sundin barricaded the road of progress, "put out the eyes of intelligence, mutilated learning, and nailed reason to the cross."

It didn't take much to put on a revival meeting. Revivalist Sundin, like most evangelists, had a supportive wife and children who sang and played the guitar or marimba. Like an itinerant salesman, he got a guarantee plus a percentage of the offering. A horse tank below the lectern served as a baptismal pool for immersion of the saved. For the sake of decorum those being baptized used white robes in place of bathing suits. (Methodists didn't believe in immersion. Our pastor said you "could go down a *dry sinner* and come up a *wet sinner*.")

Father was angry that one or two of his patients might temporarily lose their confidence in him after attending a healing service. He took it personally viewing it as a lack of trust in him and in scientific medicine: "Mrs. Baker said she could walk 20 feet without her crutches after evangelist Harding laid hands on her. Nonsense! It's all a temporary manifestation of religious hypnotism. I'll take her back if she will apologize and admit she's been hood-winked." Christ could heal a broken spirit, but Father called the shots when it came to broken bones, cells, and blood.

Most Methodists had given up going to revivals. Although our Wesleyan forebears held them, by the twentieth century we had bootstrapped our way into a middle class respectability that frowned on letting emotions get out of hand. It took almost two generations for our religious ardor to cool. Now and then our minister might close a service by asking whether anyone wanted to come down to the altar to kneel. I don't remember anyone doing so; it would have been considered bad form. An altar call revealed the pastor's anxiety more than ours. We believed in religious nurture, not in getting shocked into salvation by the Holy Spirit in some orgiastic rite. I guess that's why we colored leaves and planted seeds in paper cups in Sunday school.

In the *Adventures of Tom Sawyer,* I remember Mark Twain writing that "there had been a 'revival' and everyone had 'got religion,' not only the adults but even the boys and girls." Yet by the next day, Tom had "suffered a relapse" and Huck Finn was "up an alley, eating a stolen melon." Perhaps the promises made under the duress of passion are especially hard to keep.

By the end of August, our itinerating Elmer Gantrys had returned to the Bible Belt. On taking count, our clergy were relieved to find that few of their flock had gone astray. We Methodists geared up for Rally Day in early September. Pipestone seemed pretty much the same in spite of the Southern invasion and all the shouting. Those who had answered the call to hit the sawdust trail would probably go forward again the following summer.

The Pipestone Methodist Episcopal Church, 1940

The church was a central part of our family life. Morning worship, Sunday School, and evening youth fellowship filled each Sunday. We dared not question this routine. Father determined that our attendance should be as regular as the phases of the moon.

The church was sold to another denomination when a new building was constructed at the edge of town in 1956. Today there is an empty lot where our church used to stand.

23. OUR WESLEYAN HERITAGE

The Miracles of the Church seem to me to rest not so much upon faces or voices or healing power coming suddenly near to us from afar off, but upon our perceptions being made finer, so that for a moment our eyes can see and our ears can hear what is there about us always.

Death Comes for the Archbishop, Willa Cather

The American, when you come to religion, is not a theorizer, an Oriental dreamer or a philosophical speculator. He has little use for a religion which is sedate, or ornate, or ceremonial. He needs a religion that does something for him and in him, and provides something for him to do in the way of helping others. And it must be simple—something that he understands and can catch on to as he passes by, so to speak. Push, go, hustle, is the spirit of the country.

Evangeline Booth, The Salvation Army, England

The symbol of the Cross in the church points to the God who was crucified not between two candles on an altar, but between two thieves in the place of the skull, where the outcasts belong, outside the gates of the city. It does not invite thought but a change of mind. It is a symbol which therefore leads out of the church and out of religious longing into the fellowship of the oppressed and abandoned. On the other hand, it is a symbol which calls the oppressed and godless into the church and through the church into the fellowship of the crucified God.

Jurgen Moltmann, *The Crucified God*

During Father's youth Methodism was a young, aggressive, and growing giant, a veritable rags-to-riches ecclesiastical success story. Methodism had a mediating theology, which saved the gospel from being wrecked between the Scylla of Calvinist predestination and the Charybdis of Unitarian rationalism and Universalist sentimentality. Its catholicity of spirit and doctrines of free grace, free will, and sanctification harmonized easily with the American ethos. Methodist itinerant preachers spoke in the idiom of the rural small village heartland, unburdened by the robes, jargon, and theological intricacies of other denominations. Wesleyans had a fierce and unashamed loyalty to their tradition. Their unity lay not in the jot and tittle or in the fine print of prayer books but in a "strange warming of the heart" that was common to all, albeit variously expressed.

As a youth I sang Rev. Alfred J. Hough's boastful hymn, which was an answer to freethinker Robert G. Ingersoll's prediction of a funeral of the Christian church. Methodist bravado answered that it was building *two new churches every day:*

> The infidels, a motley band,
>   In council met and said:
> "The Churches die all through the land,
>   The last will soon be dead."
> When suddenly a message came,
>   It filled them with dismay:
> "All hail the power of Jesus' name!
>   *WE'RE BUILDING TWO A DAY!"*

By the time of the Great Depression, however, Methodist growth had moderated, acculturation had been completed, and the zeal for saving new souls had abated.

In its Latin root, the word religion is linked to the words ligature and ligament, words having both negative and positive connotations and offering both bondage and freedom. For me, religion was the ligament that connected me to my family tree and to both the positive and negative aspects of the Christian tradition. My church and my family told me neither to reject nor accept wholesale anything to do with religion. Therefore, I neither settled for the rote and easy answers of fundamentalism nor the over-intellectualized banalities of a conventionally liberal faith.

Our Methodist church was the architect of my spirituality, providing the shape, touch and feel of what I was supposed to become. In addition to home and school, it was an important third pedagogue of character formation. It consumed a lot of time—Sunday services, Sunday School and Epworth League, Wednesday choir practice, and vacation Bible school. My version of a sacred grove or a magic stone was the pew five rows back on the left, the balcony, the aging golden-brown stairs, the choir loft, the pastor's study and some other places I was not supposed to enter. The people there also seemed sacred or larger-than-life, like the Sunday school superintendent, the hunch-backed janitor, the choir director, my Methodist Youth Fellowship leaders. Father was always a power on the church board and Mother a member of the choir committee. The rhythmic flow of Sunday mornings was even then strange and dreamlike; now it is a world I can neither leave nor reclaim.

Our church was eight blocks northeast of our home. I walked to Sunday school if it wasn't raining, stayed for church, and rode home with my parents. The church was a modest gray-stucco and brown-brick edifice inside which two offset aisles led to a raised central pulpit. Behind the pulpit rose a loft in which the 12 to 14 choir members sat in full view of the congregation. (Sometimes the choir was more interesting than the preacher, for any singer who yawned, picked his nose, flirted, looked bored, or went to sleep was visible to the entire assembly.) Above the choir loft 24 large organ pipes spread out like an open fan.

Our church's atmosphere always captivated me—its glossy varnished woodwork, the old hymnals, the warm, haunting smell of flowers mixed with wax, coal-gas, dust, and rubber floor mats. The chancel faced east so the stained-glass windows on the south wall filtered the morning light that streamed through them. When I was a child, the beautiful windows were visual aids that unveiled to me the mysteries of the sacred. Like the peasants of the Middle Ages, I was then more stirred by seeing and feeling than by thinking and hearing. I could understand little of the liturgy and sermon, but the enchanting angels, saints, and colors stimulated my imagination and hinted at realms beyond the physical, here-and-now, world. The congregation, usually numbering about 150, was exceedingly territorial. Everyone had his or her own pew. The ushers knew where to escort our family. I could tell at a glance who was absent, sick, home from college, or had a new girlfriend or boyfriend. The church was full of the poor and members of the Depression-era struggling middle class, the very people who kept appearing in the Gospels.

Our world was one, united by a hallowed narrative at once ancient and contemporary. Our theology was restorationist, which meant that the stories of the Acts of the Apostles were sufficient history for us. Each week Pastor Reineke would marshal the evidence for God's goodness and omniscience lest some personal or public event, in Pipestone or on the other side of the globe, cause his flock to forget or doubt these eternal verities. He would sort through both biblical and recent events, moments in his own life, things people had told him, and make up a religious mosaic without loose ends. And when he spoke of God's power, his voice would deepen, his gestures widen, and his eyes would light up.

Reverend Reineke's sermons were one seamless whole, a collage of verses that all pointed to the single theme of salvation by grace alone, a message that had to be continuously repeated but which could be found in any and every Biblical passage. Without Reineke's weekly spiritual inoculations, the ravages of life in Pipestone, with its suffering, pain, enigmas, and death, could have caused untold anguish among his members. Life in general, especially during the Depression, was full of hunger, fear, and loss imposed by invisible forces that could not be controlled or predicted. Therefore, the pastor's mission was quite simple yet profound—to remind his band of Christian pilgrims of that "Old, Old Story" and that *"Cause* of all *causes."*

Reineke's task was to remind, retell, reinforce in the minds of his flock that the sacred canopy of Pipestone was intact—that God and His legions of angels, His sacrificed Son, His ever-watchful and mysterious Providence, His ultimate mercy and His eternal Heaven, however hard to picture but for which our hearts so unmistakably yearned, were ultimate realities, however problematical they might be to the eyes of sight and empirical experience. Hence, the texture of the Bible was flattened into an interwoven textuality in which every verse pointed to another verse and every word proclaimed the work of the cross and the glory of the resurrection.

Sunday school was scattered throughout the church, with classes in the balcony, pastor's study, kitchen, large closets, and in corners of the sanctuary. I liked the balcony best because I could look down and see what was happening in the church. Most classes were in the basement, separated by canvas drapes supported on wires. Five minutes before closing time the superintendent would ring a bell and we would all troop into the sanctuary for reports on attendance, collection, announcements, a prayer, and a closing hymn. I envied my friends who had read the comics before Sunday School. At our house we could read the comics only after going to church, eating dinner, and writing a letter to a favorite aunt or uncle. By that time, our enthusiasm for the comics had waned.

Sunday school was usually a bore except during senior high when the pastor persuaded one of our coaches to teach us. We were usually successful in getting him to talk about Friday's football game or the chances for success next week. But whether interesting or boring, I went because I was not free not to go. My parents believed that character was the sum of good habits and that good influences would rub off on me in Sunday School. Because I was a dutiful son, I grudgingly gave them the benefit of the doubt. They must have been right; I never got into any serious trouble during the time I lived under their roof.

The teachers, usually homemakers, were often more willing than able to help children understand the ways of God. Once, as a third grader, I asked my teacher why God had allowed a beautiful classmate, a girl with lovely long yellow curls, to die.

"God evidently wanted Sally in heaven and to be an angel," she responded. I knew something was wrong with that answer but was too shy to probe further. (It was my first enquiry into theodicy—the reconciliation of cosmic justice to God's existence. The existence of evil, such as pain and death, in a universe whose Creater is both benevolent and omnipotent has always been a problematic issue for an orthodox Christian.) I didn't have a better response, but I wondered why God's wishes took priority over those of Sally's parents. I decided to classify the issue as a mystery, a category that would become larger as I grew older.

Decades before the civil rights movement engulfed America, thousands of churches were planting the seeds of racial harmony. In the basement of our church was a picture of a white Jesus with a golden nimbus around his head. The face of Christ radiated love. Three children—Black, Indian and Chinese—sat on his lap with others gathered at his feet. Jesus was touching the children with loving, open hands. We often sang about it in Sunday School:

Red and yellow, black and white,
All are precious in His sight,
Jesus loves the little children of the world.

The cardinal sociological virtue of our church was that it ameliorated the elitism and class consciousness of the wider community. We were a middle-class congregation in which no one felt out of place. Pipestone Methodism was analogous to a religious town meeting, where all members had a voice in affairs both trivial and momentous. Dozens of committees ran the church and decided issues ranging from the pastor's salary to the color of a new carpet, from the kind of shrubs to be planted around the church to how much of the budget was allocated to missions. Rich and poor, educated and illiterate, the gentry and the landless, all were in our church. While inequality might reign in their lives and vocations from Monday through Saturday, Methodists sang, listened, prayed, and knelt as equals on Sunday.

Our church was an expression of *Gemeinschaft,* that is, a rooted, organic, extended-family type of community. Too many twentieth century organizations were and are Gesellschafts, artificial, mechanistic, and impersonal collections of people usually forced together out of fear or economic necessity by the state or corporations. In our church, I-Thou relationships were prized and were not over-ridden by the I-It, functional relationships. People were precious because of their being, not because of their doing. As children of God they had an inherent dignity against which no one should trespass. Our church softened the harshness of the world of nature and fate that too often brought poverty, death, drought, and disease.

An example was the treatment of a gnome-like custodian, Mr. Harris, who was horribly disfigured by a severe curvature of the spine. He could hardly lift his head up enough to look you in the eye. Upon seeing him I always thought of *The Hunchback of Notre Dame,* even though I had not read Victor Hugo's classic. I doubt that he had held a job of significance in the community. But in our church he was an honored custodian. The church was always warm and clean, the bell rang on time, the walks were shoveled and sanded in the winter. My parents, like all parishioners, greeted him kindly every week. I experienced the truth of the Swedish proverb: "In a small house God has His corner, in a big house He has to stand in the hall."

My childhood recollection of our church is an amalgam of warmth, boredom, grace, wonder, legalism, guilt, acceptance, and fascination. I remember that before each service began, the empty air seemed to vibrate slightly with the suppressed fidgets of kids. But precisely at 11 o'clock, all whispering ceased as funereally suited Pastor Ernest Reineke emerged from his study with Bible, hymnal, sermon, and serious visage, and mounted the pulpit. His mood and bearing made it clear that he considered his vocation as the moral and spiritual mentor of his flock to be a heavy yoke. It was as if the Puritan sage, Jonathan Edwards, was alive again in Pipestone.

Wonder is the basis of worship and is the beginning of the experience of the Holy, the *mysterium tremendum.* At 11:00 A.M. Pipestone Methodists made a shift from an ordinary to an extra-ordinary mode of knowledge. I intuitively knew that Reineke and his flock had assembled to confront, not evade, the realities of human existence; that issues of life and death, freedom and bondage, salvation and damnation, being found or being lost, were matters of ultimate concern. In front of the dark oak altar rail, babies were baptized, teenagers were confirmed, marriages were solemnized, and the dead were eulogized. I began to understand that the task of religion was to sanctify what Shakespeare called the seven stages of man. Since we experience these rites of passage only once, it was the church's mission to hallow and deepen their significance. The realism of a quatrain on a wall plaque near the front of the church impressed me:

I came in the morning—it was Spring and I smiled.
I walked out at noon—it was Summer and I was glad,
I sat me down at even—it was Autumn and I was sad.
I laid me down at night—it was Winter and I slept.

Over a half-century later, I can still pull up out of my memory bank such phrases as "We blossom and flourish as leaves on a tree / And wither, and perish, but naught changeth Thee."

I began to understand that the world is both a beautiful and a fearsome place; that life is a drama between the forces of good and of evil, and that I had to choose between these two kingdoms. I saw suffering, disease, and death all around me. If and when fate struck me, would I be prepared? I memorized verses to fortify me: "Only he who can bear the cross, can wear the crown." In sports I tried to toughen my body to be victorious in basketball and track and to win medals and ribbons. The church promised to give us the armor of Christ to toughen our souls so that we could be faithful in a future time of testing. Christianity could reform my wayward mind and keep me from from falling into a wayward life. It began to dawn on me that my spiritual trial would be far more difficult than any physical test I had endured.

I began to realize that man is incurably and naturally religious. I needed religion to help me confront the grave, deep, doubts, the primal questioning that comes from thinking about the great mysteries and my own moral limitations. I began to realize that although religion's understanding of the external world might be scientifically limited (Father, of course, had no trouble accommodating the theory of evolution with the Gospel), its view of our inner world—the world of value and personality, of sin, corruption, evil, temptation, and the like—was exceedingly persuasive. Humanistic liberalism was not convincing to me, for I knew that simply improving man's social condition or "putting a chicken into every pot," would not remedy the essential flaw of the human condition. Unlike Benjamin Franklin, who eliminated entirely from his *Autobiography* the word "sin" and borrowed a term from the print shop, "erratum," I knew that hubris, idolatry, and the ego-centric predicament were not eradicable. "People always refuse to see beyond the individual fault," George Bernanos once reflected. "But after all, the transgression itself is only the eruption." I knew my soul, like that of Everyman, was in turmoil and a battleground between desire and duty.

Irreligion or rationalism, on the other hand, saw the soul as unconflicted and serene. According to liberalism, man was essentially good and infinitely perfectible because he was rational. During my childhood

I was still under the bland influence of the idea of progress, the idea that because of the advances of science and education, everything was moving in the right direction.

In time I would have to be on guard against having an easy conscience and a smug, hermetically sealed optimism. In my late adolescence I began to see the symbolic meaning of the Great Depression and the storm clouds of war in Europe and in Asia. Evil was at the core of human nature. The demonic could not be exorcised either by science or by new educational trends. Only a mature faith could prepare me for spiritual trial and give me the inner resources of courage and persistence. It would help give a sharp edge to that essence, my character, by which all men are judged. There were plenty of moralisms—"The things ye do, one by one, ye pay for two by two." In later years I found that for the most part they were true.

My favorite hymns were a spiritual parallel to the rousing John Sousa marches I played in the school band. They celebrated the Church militant and the armies of God, the soldiers of Christ, heroism, blood, and courage. A skeptic would have had a belly laugh had he compared our motley, raggedy band, the spiritually halt and lame, of Pipestone Methodism with the words we sang:

> Soldiers of Christ, arise,
>   And put your armor on,
> Strong in the strength which God supplies
>   Through His Eternal Son.
>
> From strength to strength go on;
>   Wrestle, and fight, and pray;
> Tread all the powers of darkness down,
>   And win the well-fought day.

I loved to sing about crosses and blood, pilgrims and martyrs, diadems and seraphims. As a child I didn't know very much of what it meant. But I felt good doing it. It took me out of myself. Long before I was acquainted with St. Augustine, I followed his admonition to sing not because I wanted a life of leisure but to lighten my burden. "You should sing as wayfarers do—sing, but continue your journey," he recommended. "Do not be lazy, but sing to make your journey more enjoyable. Sing, but keep going."

Moreover, stories of David and Goliath, Saul and Samuel, Martha and Mary, Cain and Abel, Jesus and Judas, Wesley and Asbury, Livingston and Judson, and more, dramatized the endless line of splendor that had preceded me. If I studied them enough, could part of their heroic character be mine? My interest in history may have begun here in a desire to know more about those who had left an indelible imprint upon our world.

Such an imprint was left on my memory by the Christmas eve and Good Friday services that I attended as a child. Upon entering the church everyone was given a small unlit candle; at the conclusion of the service, the lights were turned off. For several minutes we sat in silence and in darkness and I often sought my Father's hand for comfort. The symbolism was clear if elemental—the void indicated one's spiritual death, lostness, and depravity without the light, love, and direction of Jesus. (The connection was an easy one for me to make because I remembered how fearful I was at night at YMCA camp without my flashlight.) Finally the pastor lit one candle and used it to light a worshipper's candle. Then, member by member, row by row, everyone passed the light on to the person next to him or her until the entire church was ablaze with candle light. Only then would I drop Father's hand. My parents warned me to hold my candle straight so as not to drip wax and to be careful not to catch my hair on fire.

This simple exercise taught me some profound moral lessons by stimulating my fascination with fire and light, wonder and beauty, the individual and community. All authentic religion, I realized later, begins in teaching children about the wonder and mystery of God, the precious fragility of life and the necessity of community for individuals to flourish. Then, after singing a hymn, we extinguished our candles and left the church in silence and did not speak until we reached home.

I didn't know then that some of the hymns I loved were abominable as measured by the canons of musicology. They dripped of pious Victorian sentimentality. A verse in "I Come to the Garden Alone" was typical:

> I come to the garden alone,
> While the dew is still on the roses,
> And the voice I hear falling on my ear
> The Son of God discloses.
> And He walks with me and He talks with me,
> And He tells me I am His own.

When I was little, the church was music to me and singing was a good catharsis. I was a lusty vocalist. It took me out of myself and the veil of my inferiority complex collapsed while I belted out the words of the hymns. In my love of singing, I was a true son of the Wesleys because it came before theology. I loved to repeat the bit of doggerel I had heard about how the various denominations deal with evil:

The Roman Catholics *genuflect* the Devil out,
The Baptists *drown* the Devil out,
The Presbyterians *freeze* the Devil out,
The Episcopalians *cross* the Devil out,
The Congregationalists *argue* the Devil out, **but**
THE METHODISTS SING THE DEVIL OUT!

The church was a refuge since before I could remember. It was an anchor in a chaotic sea. I intuitively knew that the test of an institution was its ability to endure and perpetuate itself through time. If so, the church had met the test of time. The hymns told me that the traditional values, in spite of the chaos of the Depression, were true and that I was not a fool for abiding by them.

In *The Future of an Illusion,* written in 1927 when I was a year old, Sigmund Freud held that religion was a psychological crutch that held together weak individuals who could not face reality. God, Freud argued, was but an illusion created by infantile'adults who refused to "grow up" and admit they existed in a cold impersonal universe. His theories quickly became the rage for "modern" intellectuals (pseudo and otherwise) and gave them an excuse to denigrate self-control, wholesomeness, and anything "Victorian" or "Puritan." Within a single page he called religion a "neurosis," an "illusion," a "poison," and an "intoxicant," and pontificated: "But surely infantilism is destined to be surmounted. Men cannot remain children forever; they must in the end go out into 'hostile life.' We may call this 'education to *reality.'*"

I wondered where Freud went for his data. Did his theories tell us more about him and his childhood, hatreds, animosities, and unresolved conflicts than it did about the universe? I wondered why so many intellectuals had such an intense hatred for the endurance of faith and the church. Unlike Freud, I encountered strong, not weak, people in church. They were empowered, not weakened, by the Gospel. Fortunately, Freud was corrected by a later disciple, Eric Erickson, the neo-Freudian psychologist, who knew what I knew emotionally as a child. That is, that mature religion gives children a sense of trust, acceptance and love; that the universe can be affirmed and that one's personal existence matters. In time I saw that no one is so competent a witness to the substance of Christianity as the *sinner;* no one, except, perhaps, the *saint.*

Moreover, the focus on grace, that we are "accepted in spite of our unacceptability," helped tenderize my rigid superego. I received the message of Thomas a`Kempis, "Be not angry that you cannot make others as you wish them to be, since you cannot make yourself as you wish to be," long before I read his classic, *The Imitation of Christ*. I began to understand that if Jesus had wanted a Church free of human frailties, he would have turned it over to angels. Experientially, my church was a place which softened the harshness and cynicism of the world. "We have this truth in earthen vessels." The Pipestone vessels were very earthen, but even in my childhood, I intuitively knew the Gospel helped the members of my church to confront rather than avoid their fate.

Looking back from the vantage point of over a half century, I realize my unconscious mind was being filled with a reservoir of images that I later drew upon during difficult times. The hymns I sang as a youth were a treasure that I could mine again and again. Even now, I can recall the first stanzas of dozens of songs. "Jesus Savior, Pilot Me," for example was especially apt in the Land of 10,000 Lakes:

Jesus, Savior, pilot me, Over life's tempestuous sea;
Unknown waves before me roll, Hiding rocks & treach'rous shoal;
Chart & compass come from Thee, Jesus Savior, pilot me!

When at last I near the shore, And the fearful breakers roar,
'Twixt me & the peaceful rest, Then while leaning on thy breast,
May I hear Thee say to me, 'Fear not, I will pilot thee!

When I turned 14, I was asked to join the tenor section in the adult choir. We practiced Wednesday nights and if you skipped practice, you weren't supposed to sing on Sunday. The director, Grace Bailey, had volunteered her talent in that capacity for as long as I could remember. She was a stolid little 70-year-old woman whose long gray hair was always coiled on top of her head in braids. But Bailey had a beatific spirit as well as a good ear. When I was off key she always corrected me in a most kindly manner. She was symbolic of the millions of volunteers that enliven a free church in a land without an established church.

My presence was more important to the choir than my voice. Art Stillwell, a bank vice president and tenor, usually sang solos or duets with Grace. He could take any lyric and make it ooze with sentiment. He was the favorite funeral soloist in town. Father thought Art was close to the caliber of Enrico Caruso but I thought he sang off key. He had grown a nice beer belly (without ingesting John Barleycorn) and therein, I felt, lay the secret of the timbre of his voice.

Our choir normally averaged around 18 members, approximately two-thirds of whom were female. That left three basses and three tenors (of which I was one) to hold the lyrical fort for the men. Because of death and sickness, sometimes our choir was reduced to under a dozen. Then our pastor would issue a "Macedonian Call" and ask for volunteers. "You don't have to have a professional voice," he implored. "Your presence will be as important as your ability to harmonize and stay on key." After one such entreaty, Father heard a couple of elderly ladies who had occupied the pew ahead of him remark, *"I certainly hope that Dr. Benjamin doesn't volunteer. Did you hear his awful squawking behind us? Land sakes, he sounded like a Hereford calf who had lost its mother!"*

It was true. Father had one of the worst singing voices in town. He tried to compensate for his inability to stay on key by increasing the volume. It was a good catharsis for him. He could joke about those "old biddies" and accept their criticism about his appalling voice, whereas he would absolutely repudiate any skepticism about his medical competency. Although a devout Methodist, Father violated one of John Wesley's directions for singing: *"Sing modestly. Do not bawl,* so as to be heard above or distinct from the rest of the congregation, that you destroy the harmony. Strive to unite your voice so as to make one clear melodious sound." Sometimes when I held the hymnal with him and sang, I could scarcely keep from breaking out in a loud belly laugh.

When I was a freshman at Hamline, I took voice lessons paid for by the GI Bill. My instructor was a clone of Grace Bailey who generously gave me a B. She urged me to sing a solo when I was home on vacation but the very thought terrified me. She died over Christmas break— although not from my vocal dissonance, as my roommate charged. A generously constructed creature replaced her in spring term but neither her beauty nor the voice lessons could compete with my interest in tennis practice. I skipped so many lessons that I flunked. I have always been proud of that F.

I took the Christian faith seriously because my parents and all the adults I knew took it seriously. Father never deviated from our breakfast ritual: one of us would read a few verses from Scripture, then he would read the lesson from *The Upper Room* devotional and say a table grace. I was amazed that Father always put a check for $10.00 in the collection plate, an enormous sum in the Depression. From 1930 to 1935 there was a 38 percent decrease in giving in Methodism. In dollar equivalents of the time, contributions to missions declined from $1.95 per capita to 85 cents. With a side-long glance I could see that other families were putting in dimes and quarters. Father also gave large sums anonymously to missions and other worthy causes. He worried that his high level of stewardship might cause others to shirk their responsibility. The Methodist church hierarchy was disturbed by his practice of the Sermon on the Mount mandate—"let not your right hand know what your left hand doeth"—because our church and district would not get credit for his largess.

On Sunday I never asked whether we were going to Sunday school or church. Was the sun going to come up in the morning? Even on vacation or traveling we would look up the local Methodist church or, failing that, find a close equivalent. Father believed and lived the Old Testament proverb, "Train up a youth in the way he should go, and when he becomes a man, he will not depart therefrom." The virtuous life was a compendium of good habits. I began to give up my sophomoric criticisms of the New Testament because I realized it criticized me!

Methodism's message during my childhood, unlike today, focused more strongly on responsibility and obligation than on liberty and freedom. The tension between communal service and self-service tended to be resolved in favor of the former. Duty was an important word then. I was taught that there was no true liberty, or complete liberty, without God. It was superficial to associate authentic religion with restrictions on freedom, with compulsion and conformity to rules. Pipestone was secure and attractive because its citizens, for the most part, lived in awe of God rather than in awe of the police. Like everyone else, I needed to be in awe of something or somebody because I was a flawed creature. Our pastors called it original sin; psychologists, the ego-centric predicament.

My flaw, like that of every Adam's son, could be corrected or held in check by criminal law, by the police, the courts, and the prisons. But to the extent that I feared God and therefore restrained my passions, I was less in need of restraints and punishments of the state, and so more free. I began to understand what St. Paul meant in his Epistle to the Romans when he referred to "the freedom which men find in Christ." By disciplining myself, by holding my appetites and ego in check by voluntary restraints, I could attain a kind of freedom over my passions which is the most valuable freedom of all. This was a freedom no constitution or statute could create.

My microcosm of Christian servitude and freedom, if multiplied millions of times, made for a tranquil and law-abiding Republic. I began to see how desperately our government needed authentic and vibrant churches. In truth, they were the nurseries of self-restraint necessary to states of self-governing men and women.

But there was a down side. However doctrinally orthodox Pipestone Methodism might have been, it somehow combined with my strict and paternalistic home and school to reinforce my feeling that I had to be perfect in order for other people and God to love me. God, I thought, loves only those who are winners, get 100 percent on tests, are on the honor society, are the stars in a basketball game, never lie, don't make excuses, and the like. I believed that if I ever did something really wrong, God and my parent's love would be withdrawn. I may have heard in church that "The law killeth but the Spirit giveth life," but somehow in my gut the law loomed larger than grace. I know that legions of kids my age heard this message and, as a result, were inwardly as damaged as was I. In time I would understand Meister Eckhart's wisdom, that if you wish to discipline the flesh and "make it a thousand times more subject, then place on it the bridle of love. Whoever has accepted this sweet burden of the bridle of love will attain more than all the penitential practices and mortifications that all the people of the world acting together could ever carry out." Gradually, my understanding of the Gospel deepened.

I saw that Christianity urged me to seek a Kingdom that is not of this world and to prepare for its advent by refusing to be conformed to this world. Only by aiming above the world could I master the world. Only by aspiring to eternal life could I give meaning to my temporal life. To be free in the world, I had to remember that I *was not of the world.* "Be assured of this, that you must live a dying life," Thomas à Kempis had written in *The Imitation of Christ,* "And the more completely a man dies to self, the more he begins to live to God." Authentic faith and worship should increase the dissonance worldly culture and not be co-opted by it. Paradoxically, I could never obtain the important things in life by aiming at them directly. I would find happiness and peace as the by-product of an activity that had love as its object. Christ did not say: Seek ye first peace or security, or happiness, but rather "Seek ye first the Kingdom of God and His righteousness" and these things (peace, security, happiness) shall be added unto you.

As a child of God, I learned from my parents and the Church that I always had to be prudent. I could not simply walk around this world as if nothing and no one could harm me. I was terribly vulnerable. The same passions that made me love God could also be used by the powers of evil. Moreover, I became aware of the all too often spiritual and moral drift down through the generations as evidenced by the aphorism: "The grandfather believes, the son doubts, and the grandson denies."

It took me a long time to get over the concept that God was some kind of totalitarian dictator who demanded perfection from a very imperfect kid. My relationship with God was not like getting clobbered in a spell-down where I always lost. Nor was faith identical with piety and putting on a long face. Forgiveness was free, gratis, for the asking. But there was no such thing as cheap grace. My wholeness and forgiveness had come *sola gratia* at the price of the sacrifice of Jesus Christ. Fame and wealth, fortune and honor, were false gods, for the supreme happiness of life is the conviction that one is loved. "Grace is indeed required to turn a man into a saint," observed Pascal, "and he who doubts this does not know what either a man or a saint is."

24. METHODIST PASTORAL SHEPHERDS

Love all of God's creation, the whole and every grain of and in it. Love every leaf, every ray of God's light. Love the animals, love the plants, love everything. If you love everything, you will perceive the divine mystery in things. Once you perceive it, you will begin to comprehend it better every day and you will come at last to love the whole world with an all-embracing love.

The Brothers Karamazov, Fyodor Dostoyevsky

The only difference between the saint and the sinner is
that every saint has a past and every sinner has a future.

Oscar Wilde

The Pipestone Methodist Church was known as a good charge because each of the pastorates of our ministers such as Ernest Reineke, Albert Tuck, "Red" Klaus, and Clifford Wittstruck, approximated a decade in length, well over double the average Methodist tenure. Wesleyan bishops didn't want their ministers to stay too long in a parish lest familiarity moderate their prophetic fire against the liquor dealers, gamblers, and other demonic agents that afflicted American culture. Benjamin Franklin believed itinerant preachers had an advantage over their stationary brethren because "they could improve their delivery of a sermon by many rehearsals." Moreover, our pastors were not men who sidled into the ministry as a path of least resistance, boys looking for the nearest way off the farm or up from the factory floor.

The pulpit has always attracted a certain percentage of child-men, pathetic shepherds who gravitated to the ministry because they preferred the company of women and children to that of men. Such effeminate clergymen seemed to eschew the secular rough-and-tumble and, in the words of William Gilbert, "were fond of uttering platitudes in stained-class attitudes." The French cliché, however, "there are three sexes—men, women, and clergymen"—did not fit any of our clergy. Moreover, our pastors had internalized St. Jerome's warning, "A fat paunch never breeds fine thoughts"; none was obese. Father approved, for a condition that he might have tolerated among his patients was anathema with respect to our pastors. Father believed that they should set an example in following St. Paul's admonishment that "your body is the temple of the Holy Spirit," and that obesity was a condition brought on by boredom and disappointment.

Pipestone was fortunate in being served by men of considerable intellectual and personal endowment who answered God's call out of a reservoir of strength and not of weakness. They fulfilled Pascal's dictum that the strength of a "man's virtue should not be measured by his special exertions, but by his habitual acts." If one definition of character is "choosing what is right when nobody is looking," then our pastors ranked high on any scale of integrity. They were "inner-directed" men who listened to the interior promptings of duty, conscience, and the law of Scripture and their heavenly Father. They were not "outer-directed," chameleon-types who took their cue from the majority or compromised with the moral drift of our culture.

Some ministers seem to undergo the vocal equivalent of puberty when they step into the pulpit—their voices drop an octave and they become sonorous. (I sometimes wonder, do they think that is how God speaks, or are they just trying to impress their audience?) But I liked the voices of our ministers. They spoke with reason and authority and, unlike some, did not seem to be simultaneously begging and bossing.

Ernest Reineke, a true Puritan Gothic, was the first pastor I can recall. Perhaps due to my tender years, he also seemed the most foreboding of them all. Reineke could have been typecast for one of the more humane clergy in Hawthorne's *The Scarlet Letter.* Reineke knew that, cut off from the worship of the divine, leisure became laziness and work inhuman. Hearing that a lapsed spiritual son of Wesley had moved to town to work at the Piggly Wiggly grocery, he strode into the store and thundered, "I hear you have a Methodist who has moved to town. Where and who might he be?" In five minutes the newcomer was signed up as a church member.

Reineke stood high in Father's estimation, for he was always principled, grave, thoughtful, and thrifty, and his sermons were well constructed. I never heard him tell a joke from the pulpit.

Reineke's calling was not an easy one: he was bound to witness to God's Word in Pipestone, to teach his flock that life is a short pilgrimage during which each soul must redeem the time allotted to him. We were all caught in a spiritual and moral crossfire between duty and desire, God and Satan, love and hate, humility and pride, heroism and cowardice. Neither Reineke nor God would countenance the alibis provided by later generations suckled on social science-spawned excuses that negated individual responsibility. Life invariably victimized everyone, and self-pity was the most loathsome of all sentiments. No class, gender, race or ethnic group could claim the privileged status to be more abused than any other.

All churches purchased bargains then—two employees for the price of one. Pastor's wives were homemakers who did not seek financial employment outside the home. They were to be a model mother, spouse, and help implement the church program. Mrs. Reineke did yeoman work with the Ladies' Aid, Sunday school, and choir, and she entertained church members. More than a few pastors were asked to move, not because they lacked personal or spiritual gifts, but because their wives had lost enthusiasm for their joint calling. The career of many a clergy "comer" was ruined by a suspicion that his wife did not entirely share the dedication of her husband. Conversely a "go-getter" pastoral spouse could sometimes save the career of a husband who had but mediocre gifts.

Quite a number of missionaries to China rotated through our church and our home during their sabbaticals in the States. Because Father contributed liberally to foreign missions, Philippine and Chinese bishops often stayed at our house. They described in glowing terms how Methodism was winning tens of thousands of converts from Confucianism and animism. Feudalistic Chinese, they reported, were being enlightened, taught English, treated by Western medicine, given scholarships, and converted to the Gospel. Generalissimo and Madam Chiang Kai-shek were revered for having brought Christian enlightenment to China. Perhaps the motto of a previous generation's Christian Volunteer Movement—"THE WORLD FOR CHRIST IN ONE GENERATION"—could still be realized. If that happened there would be a dominant global Christian political power in the world. I didn't realize until years later that our missionary compounds were in fact frightfully small and impotent and that China had a revered history, culture, and religion of its own. It was a time of ecclesiastical triumphalism over other world religions, not dialogue.

Depression-era pastors suffered heroically and quietly. The father of my high school friend Don Paauw was the Christian Reformed pastor in Holland, Minnesota. His church had only 60 families and worshipped in a pathetic, box-like building in the village of but 187 souls. "We are going to have to tighten our belts even more," Don heard his father tell his mother one day. "There were only 25 dollars in the collection plate last month." Like everyone else they had extensive gardens and when their farm members butchered, sometimes they were given portions of the meat. But the Paauws had eight children, which made things especially fearful.

One of Don's chores was to go the creamery every other day and get two buckets of buttermilk. The milk soured quickly and tasted so awful it nauseated Don, who would often gag as he tried to swallow the stuff. His protests were rendered futile, however, by the universal mantra of parents everywhere: "It's good for you!" I felt both guilty and blessed that our affluence allowed us to drink Golden Guernsey milk. Delivered to our doorstep in quart glass bottles, it was topped by five inches of yellow-gold cream that Mother often made into whipped cream.

The wife of one pastor helped supplement his meager income by cooking a dozen chickens each week. She made them into chicken pot pies and sold them to workers downtown for 30 cents apiece. Usually three workers shared one pie. When her husband was pressured by the district superintendent to urge his parishioners to increase their giving in order to pay down the church mortgage, the normally mild-mannered shepherd resisted. "Superintendent, they can't do it. I can't accede to your request," he remonstrated. "They can barely put food on their tables the way it is." The following year he was punished by being sent to an even poorer charge.

During my high school years Albert Tuck, an Australian, was our minister. I liked him immensely, not only because he had charisma but because he had a beautiful, statuesque, raven-haired daughter, Jane, whom I secretly admired. In Father's eyes, however, Tuck undermined his own effectiveness by obliquely attacking capitalism once a month with comments like, "The only reason why man hasn't gone to the stars is that no businessman has discovered a way to make money up there." Father would fume on the way home:

Who does he think he is? Is he jealous of people who have money? I thought pastors went into the ministry because they focused more on things of the spirit than the material. What does he know about business? Doesn't he realize that the whole church enterprise and his salary is paid by Christian business people? He has never met a payroll. I'll bet he couldn't run a popcorn stand without going broke.

One night Father came home from a church board meeting at which he and Tuck had had a confrontation. "I will continue to attend and financially support the church," he had said to Tuck, "but I will never set foot in the parsonage again." Father wasn't going to let an economically naive pastor ruin his faith. As for me, I didn't care what the fuss was about; I just wanted Tuck to stay in Pipestone so that my eyes could continue to feast on Jane's loveliness.

Tuck was our most academic, intelligent, and prophetic minister. He taught me that if I had a strong faith, I could indulge in the luxury of scepticism.

He was also one of our most fearlessly exacting ministers; he refused to let our small-town conservatism and Republican values soften his interpretations of some irritating aspects of the Social Gospel. "We *stone* our prophets *twice*," he said. "We cast stones to kill them, then build monuments over their tombs when they are dead." Again, "Jesus was a heretic, for he disagreed with the established ways of thinking. Remember, minorities, not majorities, change the world." He even quoted the Indian philosopher Radhakrishnan: "We may turn the waters of the sea into milk and honey, we can take the wings of the morning and seek the uttermost parts of the earth. We cannot by these means escape the misery of the aching heart, the discontent of the divided mind."

Tuck worried that American affluence might corrupt our moral character, and he often dipped back into ancient history in search of parallels to our times. I remember two lines from Savinus, written during the fifth century after the Goths had reached Rome and the Vandals were in Carthage: "The Roman Empire is filled with misery, but it is luxurious. It is dying, but it laughs."

Tuck showed me that exploring Christianity can be a profound experience *with or without intellectual reference.* As an example of "without," he cited the works of the largely uneducated John Bunyan, who wrote one of the greatest of Christian classics, *Pilgrim's Progress.* George Bernard Shaw once said that this masterpiece was "better than Shakespeare." Soren Kierkegaard's and C.S.Lewis' works Tuck said, are an example of Christian literature with intellectual underpinnings. (I have come to suspect that Tuck may have been just a bit too bright and eloquent for our flock.)

Curiously,the minister who meant the most to me, the one who influenced my life more than any other, was LeRoy "Red" Klaus. Red's intellectual gifts were modest, his pulpit abilities unimpressive, and he was never a power in the Conference. But more than anyone else, he epitomized the Christian faith for me. He was at the right place at the right time. His presence and his being were more important than his words.

He was a rawboned farm boy who had earned nine varsity letters playing football, basketball, and baseball at Hamline University. He had attended seminary during the 1930s and had been influenced by the resurgence of pacifism and of liberal guilt following World War I. Red agreed with the ethos of the era that held that the churches had been suckered into participating in the "War To Make The World Safe For Democracy," the "War To End All War." The munitions makers had cajoled Christians into supporting a holy crusade and had come away with obscene profits. The churches had put Christ in khaki and had been co-opted by the merchants of death. Henceforth, Christians should eschew all coercion. About once a month his sermon contained a poem he had written concerning peace. Most of his poems reflected a perspective similar to that of Grantland Rice's *Two Sides of War:*

All wars are planned by old men
    In council rooms apart,
Who plan for greater armament
    And map the battle chart.

But where their sightless eyes stare out
    Beyond life's vanished joys,
I've noticed nearly all the dead
    Were hardly more than boys.

However unlike some pacifists, he was not imperialistic with his ideology, nor did he try to make me feel guilty when I went into the Navy Air Corps.

Although Klaus left seminary as a pacifist, he had the ramrod-straight bearing of a Marine. He gave the lie to the suggestion that the Christian life and ministry was the refuge for the sissified, effeminate, "Caspar Milquetoast" type. He could beat us at any athletic contest we chose. Years later, I was a student at Hamline and considering the ministry when, repelled by the half-men who attended Bible study in the dorm, I thought of Red. When the sanctimonious, pious, "saved" students asserted that one had to choose between Christ and healthy, positive, worldly activity, I thought of Red. He was the antithesis of saccharine religiosity. Red embodied Samuel Johnson's truism, "Example is always more efficacious than precept." He was a John Wayne, macho type of Christian: externally hard, inwardly tender. The life of Christ was hauntingly attractive to me, but the lifestyles of some of His true believers were a stench to my nostrils. Red had come into my life and had become my mentor at exactly the right time.

In 1956 working in concert with Father, who was head of the building committee, Red brought to successful completion the construction of a beautiful new stone and brick church at the southeast edge of town. During construction, Red had assisted the workmen by driving a tractor, operating a backhoe, and pouring cement. Nevertheless, he insisted that without Father, the church never could have been built. In a way, he was right. When the bishop attempted to promote Red to the district superintendency during the building campaign, Father spent an hour on the phone to countermand the directive.

"Doctor, there are no indispensable people," pontificated the bishop.

"There is an indispensable person on this project, bishop, and his name is Klaus," Father insisted.

The bishop backed down, and Red stayed. Father knew that Red was an excellent physician of the soul and that the goal of his ministry was to "comfort the distressed and to distress the comfortable." Unlike many pastors today, Red Klaus never negotiated his salary. He accepted whatever he was paid, trusting that equity would be done.

Father's politicking was not limited to church affairs. As a member of the village elite he often worked behind the scenes in an attempt to improve the culture of the town. When the Old City Hall was given to the County Historical Society for one dollar, Father went to Vern Long, a Methodist loyalist, successful farmer, county commissioner, and later state Senator. The Society needed a grant from the county of two mills in tax funds, equal to $22,000, for its annual budget. Father persuaded Long to submit to the board an outrageous request for four mills ($44,000). As Father had anticipated, the board granted 50 percent of the request, and the Historical Society had adequate funding.

Red considered Father the most supportive layperson in his entire ministry. In his homily at Father's funeral in 1985, Red reflected: "We worshipped together, we ministered to the same clientele, we counseled together, we ate together around the Benjamin table, we visited parishioners and patients together, walked the woods together, planted and grew evergreen trees together," and more. In 1965, with Mother and Dolly Klaus, they visited 16 foreign countries in Africa, the Middle East, and Europe under the sponsorship of The Methodist Board of Missions.

When I was teaching at Morningside College, I was honored that Red asked me to consider becoming senior minister at Hamline University church where he was an associate. I believe we would have made a fine team, but I was happy in my teaching and declined.

25. SUMMER REVIVALS AND RITUALS

Tradition means giving votes to the most obscure of all classes—our ancestors. It is the democracy of the dead. Tradition refuses to submit to the small and arrogant oligarchy of those who merely happen to be walking around.

G.K. Chesterton

There is truth in Goethe's observation that as "students of nature we are pantheists, as poets polytheists, as moral beings monotheists." But however we Pipestone youngsters of the Great Depression might have viewed and experienced the Eternal, confirmation was a rite of passage that coincided with puberty and the adult assumption of moral authority. In it I affirmed what my parents had professed on my behalf at baptism and accepted the responsibilities of church membership. I thought it fortunate that Methodists, born out of John Wesley's heart "being strangely warmed," were more emotionally and less doctrinally focused than other churches. Thus, my confirmation training lasted only a year whereas Les Kallsen, my good friend and a Missouri Synod Lutheran, had to go three full years.

No church had a corner on virtue: Methodists, however, tended to emphasize virtue as the absence of sin. Disappointed that the Kingdom of God was not immediately ushered in with the freeing of the slaves at the conclusion of the Civil War, and seeking another form of wickedness to eradicate, they turned on John Barleycorn as the incarnation of evil (this may also have been part of a subtle nativist tactic of attacking the habits of the immigrant Catholics, arising out of Protestant fears of their growing strength in American life.) There was a strong contingent of the Women's Christian Temperance Union in Pipestone, and Temperance Sunday was an important occasion in our liturgical year. During my adolescence I heard hundreds of stories in which every personal and institutional tragedy was attributed to "drink." Of course, Methodists interpreted temperance not in its classic Greek sense of "moderation" or "in nothing too much," but rather as "total abstinence."

Shortly before I was confirmed, everyone in the class was asked to fill out a card forswearing alcoholic beverage for life. In a rare manifestation of rebellion, I left my card blank. I felt the procedure too coercive. And maybe I didn't want to foreclose any future options. I had heard so much about booze that the message was beginning to be counter-productive. Too much prohibition made the prospects of my future sipping of the nectar of the gods even more alluring.

On Palm Sunday 1938, my Confirmation Day, I dressed up in black trousers, white shirt and tie (my parents felt it was foolish to spend money for a suit or sport coat as long as I was still growing) and stood with 15 others in the chancel to answer questions pastor Reineke put to us. I was frightened and was reminded to speak loudly so that everyone could hear. But Mother had drilled the answers into me and I came through without a mistake.

Toward the end of the ceremony my parents stood behind me as I knelt at the altar and Reverend Reineke placed his hands on my head and received me into the church. A 4,000-year-old ritual—the laying-on-of-hands begun by Abraham when he blessed Isaac—connected me to a mysterious and spiritual lineage. Superficially I worried that Reineke's heavy hands might mess up my hair, but in a deeper sense, I wondered whether something real but invisible was passing through those powerful hands. Was an invisible force, inspiration, revelation, holiness, or goodness quietly invading my being? Was this a sign that I was marked for a great mission in life? Could I be another David, Elijah, Stephen, or Timothy? Would I be protected from injury and an early death? I did not know. But as my imagination ran riot, the choir deepened the moment by quietly singing:

Just As I am, thou wilt receive,
Wilt welcome, Pardon, cleanse, relieve;
Because thy promise I believe,
O Lamb of God, I come, I come.

I only dimly perceived the importance of the ritual: I was accepted by the congregation symbolically as a *man,* a new church member. At the age of 12 I "counted" in the church long before I was taken seriously in society. I had to pledge to the budget, "measure up," and give and take responsibility. Henceforth, as the Bible stated, I had to "put away childish things." The church, therefore, filled the physiological and psychological transitions, the "breaking points" of life, with depth and significance.

I began to see that without mysticism man becomes a monster; that religion begins at the point where reason and knowledge are powerless and forever fail. And then I began to sense the mystery of my harboring both good and evil, of my suffering and destiny as a soul in search of God. In time I would learn the distinction between wisdom and knowledge: knowledge, however beneficial, is seldom more than making careful measurements, while wisdom, which includes knowledge, also includes human mystery.

But traditional ritual today is but a shadow of custom nearly vanished. We no longer invest deep meaning in the transition from adolescence to adulthood. Almost gone is the ecstasy, emotion, role assumption and identity that accompanied those changes. With the shredding of the sacred canopy, secular equivalents—rock music, drugs, sexual conquest, gangs, tattoos, and guns—are often the tragic substitutes as modern young people seek depth and community in their lives.

As I grew older my love of liturgy increased. Methodist ritual incorporated much of *The Book of Common Prayer* from our alma mater, the Church of England. Together with the King James Version of the Bible, the cadence of the ponderous and stately Elizabethan phrases made a deep impression on me. Liturgy helped me see that I was not alone amid my difficulties. My problems were set within the sweep of history; an endless line of splendor upheld by Infinite and Loving Hands, had gone before me. I began to memorize significant passages of our liturgy and, in times of aridity and difficulty, they were like a draught of fresh water to my parched spirit.

> Make them to be numbered with thy Saints, in glory everlasting....Afflicted, or distressed, in mind, body, or estate....To do my duty in that state of life unto which it shall please God to call me....In the midst of life we are in death....Give to all nations unity, peace, and concord....Renounce the devil and all his works...Deliver us, we beseech thee, in our several callings, from the service of mammon, that we may do the work which thou givest us to do, in truth, in beauty, and in righteousness, with singleness of heart, as thy servants, and to the benefit of our fellow men.

I spent Sunday evenings at the church attending Epworth League, later known as the Methodist Youth Fellowship. We would have a light supper, worship, program, and recreation. Our church was not large enough to have separate organizations for junior and senior high school students and, as a junior, I felt intimidated by the seniors. The juniors sat in the back row and let the seniors run the show. We learned skills of dialogue, compromise, planning, and facilitating long before corporations charged exotic fees for teaching these skills.

Our annual project was to raise money so that everyone could spend a week at Camp Frontenac, the newly purchased Methodist camp on the Mississippi River near Red Wing, Minnesota. We washed cars, had rummage and bake sales, sold Christmas cards and fruit cakes and a lot of other stuff people didn't want but bought because they were good sports and wanted to help us out. The seniors made it tough on us if we didn't meet our quota.

Our trip to Frontenac by bus took an entire day and often was interrupted by flat tires. At the camp, girls slept on mattresses in cottages and boys filled straw ticks and slept in Benjamin Lodge, a barn named in honor of Father, who had given money to refurbish it. We swam in Lake Pepin, studied the Bible, played volleyball, hiked, enjoyed campfires, paired off in couples, listened to missionaries, teachers, and professors, and made life-long friends. Years later many of us would meet again at Hamline University.

One night I had a frightening experience. Bud Korfhage, a good friend and p.k.("preacher's kid") from Fairmont, had arranged a before-breakfast tennis date for us with a gorgeous pair of identical twins. After curfew, we suddenly realized we had not set a specific time. Dressed in our pajamas, we ran across the dark camp to the cabin we thought the girls were in. "Are the Olson twins in there?" we whispered as we scratched on the screens. Giggles and more giggles was the only response. We moved from window to window with the same entreaty.

Suddenly, around the corner came the cabin's house mother, shining her flashlight beam full upon us. I felt almost naked in my pajamas. I shivered and wondered whether my fly was open. The girls' laughter went fortissimo. "Come with me to see the dean of the camp," commanded the rotund, house-coated, protector of virgin virtue. There was exultation in her voice. She gloried in performing her duty of protecting the chastity of her charges.

It was almost 1:00 A.M. when a sleepy dean held an impromptu court. "I caught these two taking off the screens," she claimed, "and trying to climb into the cabin. I think they were about to *attack my girls!*" At that time I had not heard of Sigmund Freud, so I didn't know that the outrageous charge revealed more about the house mother's repressed libido than it did about Bud and me. I couldn't speak. I hoped I was dreaming. If not, I had sullied the Benjamin good name. How could I ever go home? Then I saw the dean wink at Bud. Praise God! He was a clerical colleague of Bud's father. He knew we were of good stock, of pure intentions, and that the charges were undoubtedly false. We were safe. He thanked the housemother and told her to go back to her brood. We laughed and joked with the dean before going back to bed. My family's name would remain immaculate and intact!

During those early years we were naive and impressionable. A Hamline student returned home with fearsome tales of the academic horrors awaiting us at college. He told of being subjected to a three-hour essay examination, during which his hand "seized:"

> My hand was paralyzed. It was like a stone. I could not make my fingers move. In desperation I bit my fingers, hit them against the chair, and sat on them. Nothing worked. I handed in my test only half done and told the professor, "I always do better on true/false tests." I went back to my room and thought, "Maybe college is not for me. With each passing day, life looked better on the farm."

Once we had a sharp confrontation in the church with pastor Reineke. Bob had brought a deck of cards from home and, instead of playing shuffleboard or ping-pong after the program, we played a game of hearts. We were nicely into the game when the pastor entered, turned purple, snatched up the cards, and cried, "Don't you know it's a sin to play cards in God's church?"

"I've seen you play Rook in the parsonage," Bob answered, protesting our innocence.

"That's entirely different," Reineke responded.

"I don't see why, cards are cards," someone else said, emboldened by Bob's response.

At that Reineke strode out, taking the unholy contraband with him, and we were left in a state of unease. Had we missed a grave moral trespass? And why had our innocent pastime disturbed the old gentleman so much?

Christmas 1939. Left to right: Walter, Martha, Roger, Robert, Mary.

26. Depression Era Merriment

In addition to our own back yards, during the summers of the Great Depression our city park was the location for a great deal of fun and activity. The park comprised two city blocks at the northwest juncture of US highway 75 and State highway 23 and was easily accessible by bike. At its northern boundary was a platoon of green picnic tables that dressed right between two rows of non-descript ash trees. Their twisted trunks gave evidence of the invisible, enduring, and torturous struggle their roots had made seeking water during the periodic droughts of that era. On the east were three pathetic cement tennis courts. Thanks to depression era belt-tightening, the concrete surface ended just four feet behind the baseline; from there 12 feet of dirt and cinders extended to the back fence—four inches below the level of the court surface. Hardly a day went by in the summer without someone twisting an ankle because of this drop-off. But no one protested the hazard. Everyone agreed that it would have been wasteful to put cement where the ball seldom landed.

Next to the tennis courts was a gravel softball field. Unfortunately, the sacrificial goodness of the volunteer who laid out the diamond over-shadowed his engineering talent—the infield was concave and soaked up rain like a sponge. After a shower the four bases and the pitcher's mound turned into five shallow mud puddles. But the condition of the field, rather than hindering our play, only made our clothes that much dirtier. However filthy I became below the waist, I treated my league's colored T shirt as if it were a cape from Romanoff royalty. I made sure it was always clean and pressed for each game.

My favorite position was the "hot corner"—third base—although occasionally I was allowed to pitch. I had a good arm and could zing the ball over to first base rather well. I loved the infield chatter or "pepper" and contributed my share in an attempt to upset the opposing batter— "He swings like a rusty gate. Blow it by him. Stick in his ear. Oil up his joints or bring out the wheel chair." I was glad we didn't play hardball. The bad bounces off the gravel would have caused a lot of broken noses and busted teeth.

South of the softball field was a hexagonal gazebo that served as a band shell for Saturday night concerts. A swimming pool on the south and two or three horseshoe pits rounded out the facilities the city fathers had provided for their youth. To a sophisticated city slicker, the facilities may have looked pathetic. Seen through my innocent child-eyes, the park was wondrous.

One summer when I was nine, I had a traumatic experience in the pool. A farmer had donated a steel barrel to which the wooden head of a horse was bolted. Kids would put it in the water and, as some pushed, pulled and rolled it around the pool, we'd take turns trying to stay on this water-borne "bucking bronco," a game the horse always won. But on one occasion, as I came up from being "thrown," my gasping mouth caught the barrel's metal rim. My recently acquired two front permanent teeth seemed to be hanging by a bit of gum. I cried as one life guard attempt to staunch the flow of blood by holding a towel to my mouth while the other called Mother. I knew it was serious when Mother came and exclaimed, "Oh Pshaw!"

Upon examining the damage our dentist, Fred Wseth, said he "wouldn't give a nickel" for one tooth, while the other had a "50-50 chance." Hoping for a miracle, Mother told him to leave both teeth alone and I went home to a supper of tomato soup. Soup was my major fare for the next several weeks. But the tooth fairy apparently found me virtuous, for I did not lose either tooth, although they grew back at an angle that made me more buck-toothed than ever. For the rest of the summer, I ate my favorite vegetable, corn on the cob, by cutting the kernels off with a knife.

During the summer of '34 I was traumatized for a week by being forced to attend a YMCA camp on Big Stone Lake. I didn't know anyone there except Bob, and he was assigned to another section of the camp. I fell victim to a strange malaise. Diagnosis: a severe case of homesickness. Symptoms: watery eyes, lips that quiver, low energy level, shallow breathing, head on chest while walking aimlessly and kicking the dirt, listlessness, crying on pillow at night, lump in throat, visions of Skippy and Mother's food. Remedy: time, new friends, or early release. False remedy: kick in the butt by counselor and shouts of "Sissy, Sissy" from cabin mates. Barely eight, I had been thrown in with older boys, most of them extroverts, and a few who were bullies. I counted the hours and days until my release. The *coup de grace* occurred when a cabin mate and I argued over whether a person could eat more by consuming food quickly or slowly. I opted for the latter. "My Father's a doctor," I shouted. "Don't you know by eating slowly, some of the food digests before other mouthfuls arrive at your stomach?" "You're wrong," my counselor pontificated. "By eating quickly, you can eat more because of the time it takes the message to get to the brain that you are full." I was crushed. That was my only camping experience until church camp at Frontenac.

During the summers of the mid '30s, Father, Bob and I played tennis almost every Sunday morning from six to seven o'clock. Bob and I had wooden rackets that cost $4.95 at the local Our Own Hardware store. A can of balls usually lasted all summer. Father had one good shot—a round-house serve produced by an over-the-head, top-spin slice that spun away from us. We compensated for it by over-playing our forehand. I was grateful for these early morning sessions of bonding and training. Their fruition came much later when I was a varsity four-letter winner at Hamline University and captain-coach of the tennis team during my junior and senior years.

After tennis came a communal use of the bathroom, during which Father enforced the Benjamin ritual of the 45-second, cold "Navy shower"—shower on, get wet, shower off, lather up, shower on, rinse off, turn shower off. (Only girls and sissies used the hot water faucet.) Estimated consumption of water per person—two quarts. We dried off using coarse Irish linen towels. They were light brown and covered with tiny nipple-loops and had the texture of steel wool. We rubbed our chests hard as we made Tarzan-like, *"ME, TOUGH-TOUGH, HE-MAN"* grunts. The juices of manhood, testosterone, were beginning to rise. Father looked on approvingly as we scrubbed our chests close to strawberry red. How proud we were of our gorgeous bodies! We envisaged them as replicas of Michangelo's *David*. Any thought of what time and entropy would do to them was as foreign to us as the planet Mars.

Decades later, ecologically sensitive and sexually sophisticated young people urged that economy and bonding could be joined in their motto, "Save Energy, Shower With A Friend." Sadly, we lived in more circumspect times. Father's English genes—Stoicism tinged with sadism—were at work and his motive was Puritan thrift. Perhaps the downside of this boys-on-the-way-to-manhood ritual and the sand-papering of our chests was that it demolished or retarded the growth of our adolescent chest hair.

Beyond the activity at the city park, the Depression forced us to create our own entertainment. We had to plumb our own creativity. There was no Children's Palace with plastic creations near at hand. Store-bought toys were too expensive. We created necklaces out of dandelion stems, made slingshots from stout tree crotches, and carved whistles from twigs. Sometimes I would go to the town dump to scavenge wheels, tin, wire, or lumber to create a go-cart or something. Father encouraged me to use the workbench in the basement as long as I took care of the tools and "put things back where I found them."

Our games were "Pumb-Pumb, Pull-way," "Red Light, Green Light," "Kick the Can," "King of the Hill," and "Capture the Flag." Played for an hour before evening curfew, they involved hiding, running, or stealing a prize. Everyone in the neighborhood could play. My favorites were "Cops and Robbers" and "Cowboys and Indians." Most games, whatever their nomenclature, were repetitions of the eternal "good guys" vs. "bad guys" theme.

At around ten years of age, due to the mysterious promptings of bodily chemistry and socialization, our play became less coed and more gender-specific. Although we sometimes encouraged girls to join us, they usually responded, *"That's dumb!"* and huffed off to do their own activities such as skip rope and hop-scotch.

We played with rubber-guns, pistol and machine gun-shaped weapons hand-fashioned from scrap wood, spring-loaded clothespins, and bands of rubber sliced from old inner tubes; they could fire one or more bands of rubber over 30 feet with sometimes amazing accuracy and speed. My best creation could shoot six rubbers accurately at amazing distances. My parents warned me never to shoot for the head and, surprisingly, no one was ever hurt. "Kills" were rarely "clean" or undisputed. We spent almost as much time arguing the old refrain—"I got you"..."No you didn't"..."You're dead"—as we did stalking each other. Today an OSHA snoop would outlaw the guns as a health hazard.

Mother encouraged me to collect matchbooks and stamps. On the way to and from school, I would often walk in the street, searching the gutter for used matchbooks. If I found any, Mother determined whether they were too dirty to keep. I added to my collection by letting all my friends and relatives know of my hobby. Perhaps because I was a bit curled inward, I collected other innocent things, such as stamps from foreign countries—colored pieces of paper that had the magic ability to transport me around the globe. Mother had a standing order at the post office for four stamps with the serial number of every new issue. I would pour through the back pages of *Popular Mechanics* in search of bargains. I was amazed at the number of used stamps one could buy for 25 cents. The intensity of their colors, the engravings that hinted at worlds where exotic languages were spoken fascinated me and drew me into a safe, small cave. When later interests surfaced—sports, hunting, model airplanes, girls, and the Navy Air Corps—I lost interest in the hobby and my collection mysteriously disappeared.

Making lead soldiers was another childhood pastime. I had a number of molds that I would smoke with a candle, heat (so the lead would not cool prematurely), and clamp, and then carefully pour in the molten lead. The soldiers, marines, sailors and Indians had costumes and uniforms that dated from the American Revolution. After they were painted, I would line them up in formation and have mock battles. Did "playing war" exacerbate my combative tendencies, as some pacifists believe? I seriously doubt it, because I knew it was fantasy. It was a good catharsis and was a ritualized release for tension.

Come spring, scarcely a day passed without a game of marbles—Cat's Eye and Bib Circle. Every kid in town had a couple of quart-sized, brown cotton sacks that contained his precious round beauties. We guarded them like King Midas hoarded his gold. We would draw a circle, shout "who's in?" contribute a marble to the pot, then lag to a line scratched in the dirt. Some boys had agate shooters cut out of stone. Others had "steelies," which were ball bearings (some an inch in diameter) they had scrounged from a garage. I rarely contributed one of my prized glass beauties to the pot. They were "keepers" and had blue and pink swirls in them and if a "steely" hit them dead on, it left a cracked half moon in the glass.

The classic form of shooting, "knuckles down," was hard for me to master. I preferred aiming by grasping the marble between my thumb and forefinger and getting my eye behind my shot. My parents always warned me not to "play for keeps" (they considered it a form of gambling), but had I followed their admonition, I would have always been an onlooker. Only sissies played for "funzies." I never told my parents I played for keeps and they never asked how my marble collection continued to grow. In the winter we played on the living room floor, where two-foot diameter geometrical patterns in the carpet served as the pot.

Crack the Whip was another favorite game, one that has been played by kids since the time of the Puritans of Plymouth Rock. A line of kids would join hands, and the leader (usually a bully and the largest boy on the playground) would start running in one direction, faster and faster and faster, with the line of hand-holding kids trailing along behind like the tail of a kite. Then the leader would turn in a tight circle. The physics of the operation was such that the far end of the line had to cover a lot more territory than the lead end, so the kids on the far end had to run faster and faster and faster to keep up. Soon their feet barely touched the ground. Handholds gave way and the line disintegrated, a kid at a time. Kids catapulted off in all directions, falling, tumbling, tearing clothes, scraping knees and elbows, and sometimes breaking an arm. Don't ask me why we liked the game. The same principle applies in today's sport of water skiing. But water is softer than the packed soil of a playground.

Many childhood games were differentiated by gender. Girls preferred playing jacks and hop-scotch, and skipping rope, to shooting marbles. They jumped rope to a variety of dittys such as: "Charlie Chaplain/Went to France/To see the ladies/Do their dance/First the heel/Then the toe/Then around and around you go." We loved to tease them by shouting the substitute—"WET THEIR PANTS"—in place of to "do their dance."

April was kite-flying month. Pipestone was a kite flyer's paradise because of the strong and steady winds on Buffalo Ridge. Mother would help us make fragile diamond-shaped frames on the kitchen table, outline them with a tight string, and finally stretch and glue colored paper on the flimsy skeleton. Homemade kites seldom worked as well as store-bought kites. The best fliers were box kites that Our Own Hardware sold for 39 cents. Diamond kites always needed tails for stability—the larger the kite, the longer the tail. Some tails were 15 feet long with eight-inch rag "bow ties" interspersed every 16 inches. I liked box kites best because they were more stable and didn't need tails.

One spring Bob built a monstrous contraption, a "kite to end all kites." It was his own box kite design and stood seven feet tall. We shellacked the wide cotton panels, tested the internal braces, and pronounced it ready for a test flight. It was so enormous we could scarcely get it out of the basement. To my child's eye it was as wonderous as the Challenger space vehicle is to children today. We carried the contrivance out to a farmer's field where there wasn't a tree for half a mile. I wondered whether we had enough string—surely this kite was destined to rise far above the clouds. Alas, even with four of us running as fast as we could, it didn't rise more than 20 feet in the air. We may even have tried tying it to a car. Though it was a beautiful creation, there was a design flaw somewhere. I felt as bad as Bob about his failure. It was convincing proof, however, that Benjamin genes weren't coded for engineering of any kind.

Like all my friends, I made dozens of model airplanes. Kits could be purchased for as little as 35 cents. Using a razor blade, glue, and pins, I'd first construct a thin balsa-wood skeleton; the next step was to stretch tissue paper over the frame, dope it, and finally paint the plane. As World War II came closer, more models were replicas of the Allied and Axis air fleets. By the time I entered the Navy Air Corps, I could identify dozens of American, English, Russian, Japanese, and German planes. Most models were powered by rubber bands attached to the propellers although some were large and sophisticated enough to have gasoline engines. Sometimes when I tired of a plane, I would wind it up, set it on fire, and send it on a Kamikaze mission from my bedroom window. Alongside our many airplane posters, Bob and I hung airplanes from the ceiling of our bedroom. (Years later, after Bob and I entered the Navy Air Corps, our room became something of a shrine for Mother. She didn't touch a thing. Her strong love intuitively prompted her to believe that if it was kept "just as it was," we might be kept out of harm's way.)

We had bike races, shot purple grackles with our BB guns, roller skated, and often camped overnight a mile north of town at the shrine park or quarry, later known as the Pipestone National Monument.

One day, Bob, Les Kallsen, and I biked out there to snare gophers and spend an overnight. Minnesota might have been the only state that paid a small bounty for killing its striped mascot. The cute, solitary little rodent rivals the rabbit in its fecundity and is extremely destructive. We got 10 cents a tail from the county authorities.

Gophers usually have three or four openings to their underground dens. Their tunnels were about the circumference of a silver dollar and, counting their lateral shafts, could be over 100 feet in length. We'd stuff rocks or clay in all but one entrance, fashion a noose around the remaining hole, and then pour creek water into it. We worked hard. Sometimes it would take a half dozen pails of water, carried from a couple of blocks away, before a gopher would surface. Then we acted like Tom Mix or the Lonesome Cowboy as we swung the striped little beasts from a 10-foot line of binder twine. Although the gopher was the University of Minnesota football team's mascot, we knew the little golden rats destroyed millions of dollars of grain a year.

Afterwards we put up our pup tents, made a fire, and were lolling around waiting for a can of beans we'd put in the fire to get hot. Suddenly there was an explosion—we had forgotten to punch a hole in the can for the steam to escape. Our tent, clothes, and sleeping bags were ruined by dozens of burn holes from the coals sprayed about by the explosion. We had to pack up and go home; and we couldn't find a single bean to eat.

Because education was "bare-bones," there were no expensive driver education courses. The school board would have considered it a great waste of money to buy cars and hire driving instructors to teach 15-year-olds how to operate a vehicle. By that age most of the adolescents of our agrarian economy had rudimentary knowledge of the mechanics of a car and had operated machinery on a farm.

One Saturday when I was 14, Father said, "Neb, today I am going to teach you how to drive." As is the case today, learning to drive was an important rite of passage. Unlike the current ethos, however, fathers then had not been marginalized and they enjoyed imparting their automotive wisdom and skills to those they had sired. Father drove out to an infrequently traveled gravel road, turned off the ignition of the Ford and set the brake. I moved behind the steering wheel and positioned my bottom on a three-inch hard pillow. Surprisingly, Father seemed unusually relaxed at his new role of riding "shotgun."

"Remember, Ford has shifted the emergency brake from the center of the floor way over on the left, under the dash." he warned. "If you are headed for the ditch or a collision with another car, there isn't a great deal I can do to stop the car." His warnings did not put me at ease. My mouth was dry and my hands betrayed a Parkinsonian-like tremor as I shifted into neutral and turned on the ignition. "Remember," Father declared, "in shifting, think of the letter **H**. Reverse is up and left, first gear is over and back; second is right and up; and third or high gear is right and down. When shifting let up on the gas pedal *while you slowly let the clutch out.*" Automatic, or what then was called "fluid drive," was rare in the 1930s and installed in only the most expensive cars.

Shake…jerk…grind…shake…jerk…grind. The Ford was pivoting back and forth as if it were on a gigantic rocking chair. Or was it like one of those mechanical horses that kids ride to make believe they are in a rodeo? Our heads were bobbing back and forth like they were attached to a metronome. My foot was paralyzed on the clutch that was halfway between fully up and the floorboard. The screech and grinding sound coming from the engine seemed to tell me that if it continued another 10 seconds the engine would explode. I expected the worse from Father for damaging his precious Ford.

Father, thankfully, kept his medically-induced calm. "Neb, you are 'riding the clutch.' It is the worst thing you can do to an engine because it will 'strip the gears'." He reached over and turned off the ignition. Then by using his fingers, he taught me how gears meshed in an engines power train. The next lesson was a dry-run at harmonizing my shifting hand and with my clutch-depressing foot.

For an hour we stopped and started, jerked, lurched, bucked, and skidded down that gravel road. I was grateful that none of my friends witnessed my mechanical ineptitude. Father was amazingly understanding and tolerant of my lack of coordination. As a result, I looked forward to the next Saturday lesson. Soon I had the technique down pat. When I was 15 I was allowed to drive if there was an adult in the car, and I was fully licensed at 16. It wasn't until 30 years later that I was required to take written and driving tests administered by a public bureaucrat. In over 60 years of driving I have never had a serious accident.

Depression-era gasoline stations were very small compared to today's miniature emporiums that serve everything including groceries, snacks and Twinkies. Fuel pumps reminded me of ten-foot totem poles capped with an embossed glass crown that depicted the company logo. By working a large lever back and forth, the attendant would pump gasoline from an underground tank into a large glass cylinder. It would flow through the gas hose by gravity and the lines on the cylinder indicated how many gallons were used. The only gasoline additive was lead, which helped prevent premature ignition or "knocking." Most car owners were happy to get 16 to 18 miles per gallon, and a Sunday drive in the country (an "outing" as Grandmother Bedell called it) was the highlight of the week.

There were no self-serve stations during the 1930s. "Pumping" gasoline, cleaning the windshield, and checking the oil and the radiator were messy jobs. Moreover, help was inexpensive and an "I want to do it myself" ethos would have put legions of men back on welfare. Customers expected good service to be included in the price of their fuel. Getting an oil change was especially primitive, since stations did not have hydraulic lifts. One had to carefully drive over a World War I-like ten by three foot trench. An attendant would climb down some steps to unscrew the bolt on the oil pan. More often than not he would emerge with his hands and his coveralls covered with hot oil.

Cars were not fitted with turn signals. Consequently, we usually drove with the driver's side window down. Sticking your arm straight out meant a left turn. A forearm right-angled upwards signaled a right turn; an arm pointed at the ground indicated that the driver was about to stop. Moreover, since cars were not air-conditioned, travel during a hot summer day was an ordeal. The only way to keep cool was to have all of the windows wide open. After a long trip our faces felt like they had been sand-blasted, and they were close to the color of Mother's American Beauty roses.

I had several hidden retreats, quiet spots where I could turn inward to fantasize and fortify my inner self. Building a tree house was beyond my capability; instead, I carried short boards high up into an old box elder or green ash tree behind the garage and notched them to fit into tree crotches. I would fill my pockets with crackers, cookies, and an apple, then climb 30 or 40 feet into my leafy bower. There, invisible to all, I would dream of great feats of valor. The storm clouds of war were rising all over the world. As they moved ever closer to America, they also penetrated my consciousness. Oftentimes I was a sniper who might, on successive reveries, pick off countless numbers of Italian soldiers in Ethiopia, Germans in Spain, Japanese in China. At other times the danger was closer at hand in the form of Pretty Boy Floyd, Bonnie Parker and Clyde Barrow, John Dillinger, "Baby Face" Nelson, or some other Depression-spawned miscreant. In films such as *"I Am a Fugitive From a Chain Gang"* (1932), Hollywood depicted many such outlaws as wrongly accused Robin Hoods, but I knew they were cold-blooded killers. I did them in with ease, invisibly protected by my leafy sanctuary.

Another magical spot in my childhood was a vacant lot 300 feet behind our house in the middle of some wild plum bushes. It was there that I dug a pit that was used for pole vaulting, high-jumping, and broad-jumping. I fashioned standards from two-by-twos, using finishing nails spaced one inch apart to hold the cross bar, then scavenged thick bamboo poles for vaulting from furniture stores. I'd wrap the poles with tape from Father's medical bag to keep them from splintering. In the high jump I started with the scissor kick and progressed to the Australian roll. I never had any instruction, but during my last two years in high school, it was clear that my time spent jumping and falling in that modest dirt pit had paid off. I was a valued member of the track team, and the pole vault and broad jump were my two best events.

In winter, whenever a foot or so of freshly fallen snow lay on the ground, Bob, Martha, and I would take off our shoes and socks, roll up our pants legs and challenge each other as to how far we could run from the house before turning back. We would squeal with masochistic delight as we ballet-danced through the snow. After running out 200 feet, making a turn, and nearing the house, we would scream, "I'm coming, OPEN THE DOOR!" We would fling ourselves on the rug and feverishly massage our legs to try to halt the pain of a thousands of needle pricks. As feeling returned to our extremities, the debate began: "I went further than you did!...No, you didn't,...Yes, I did...Didn't... Did!" Fortunately, there were no moral crusaders to make us feel guilty about such adolescent macho antics, nor were there any neighborhood snoops looking for child abuse.

The humor I remember from childhood was light, simple, and usually non-erotic. The following stories are typical of the jokes told by my parents and their friends.

"The old-fashioned girl darned her husband's sox. Her daughter sox her darned husband."

When a politician inquired about public sentiment in a rural community, one of the natives replied, "Still going strong—there were 16 cars parked in my lane last night."

The fellow who thinks "evening" means the same thing as "night" should note the effect that it has on a gown.

It's a woman's world. When a man is born, people ask, "How is the mother?" When he marries, they exclaim, "What a lovely bride!" When he dies they inquire, "How much did he leave her?"

The following are typical of the medical jokes Father told:

"I don't like your heart action," the doctor said, applying the stethoscope again. "You have had some trouble with angina pectoris, haven't you?" "You're right in a way, doc," said the young man sheepishly, "only that isn't her name."

Another: "Do you think I shall live until I'm 90, doctor?" "How old are you now?" "Forty." "Do you drink, gamble, smoke, chase women, or have any vices of any kind?" "No. I don't do any of those terrible things. I don't have any vices." "Well, wot-tin-'ell do you want to live another 50 years for?"

27. CHRISTMAS AND NATIONAL HOLIDAYS

Within him, as he hurled himself forward, was born a love, a despairing fondness for this flag which was near him. It was a creation of beauty and invulnerability.

The Red Badge of Courage, Stephen Crane

During the Depression, work was both longer, harder, and more physical than later in the twentieth century when technology had made such enormous progress. The leisure industry was in its infancy. There was no television. Nor was there any doubt about American virtue. National holidays, therefore, held an expectancy and had a depth they do not have today. For me, the time between those holidays moved with a glacial slowness; it seemed that the next holiday would never come. Christmas was my favorite. We always had three lighted trees: two outside, on either side of the brick steps, and one inside. Our Christmas stockings were chosen from the ones we wore every day. They were brown cotton hose that rolled up to the crotch over our long winter underwear and were pinned to a tab at the waist. I always stretched mine, to increase its capacity for more candy. (On Christmas morning I was quite often disappointed to find that three-fourths of the stocking held apples, oranges, and animal crackers.)

We always opened our gifts on December 25th, Christmas morning, because there never was a time during which at least one of my brothers or sisters did not believe in Santa. To the dismay of our parents, we usually were up at 4 A.M. My parents never overspent. Each child received one major present such as a gun, bike, or sled, and a number of smaller ones. Many of the latter were clothes and books.

Christmas vacation always brought one or two of my Father's spinster sisters to our home. We deeply loved his oldest sister, our Aunt Bessie who at times seemed to give us more love and acceptance than did our parents. As an eighth-grade-math teacher from South Saint Paul, she had a vast reservoir of wisdom gained from years of pedagogical experience. "You should thank God, Mabel," she would tell Mother, "that you don't have any little geniuses as children. In my classes they are the misfits and troublemakers and won't be happy in life. Give me solid B students anytime." Years later I would be inwardly warmed and comforted as I remembered her sage commentary.

Bessie had been the first of the seven children in Father's family to have a paying job, and she loaned money to her five brothers and one sister so they could complete college. She lived most of her life in a one-room apartment. Each morning she made a brown-bread sandwich that she ate at her desk at school. She organized a camera club and a bird identification group at the school, and she taught a large Sunday School class for 35 years. She never went on strike and would have continued to teach school even if her salary had been cut in half. Lewis Shepley (Hamline '42) remembered Bessie giving up her lunch period to tutor him in math. "I had been inappropriately promoted through the grades," he reflected. "We cried together over my half-witted attempts in the subject." Bessie was a Methodist nun without a habit or a cloister. At the birth of her nephews and nieces, 24 in all, she gave each $25 to begin a savings account. Of all my relatives, she owns the greatest claim to sainthood.

I once saw Bessie brush her five feet of hair that she rolled up in a bun and wore at the back of her head. She was a dead ringer for the farmer's wife in Grant Wood's "American Gothic" masterpiece, except that she wore a more kindly, Mona Lisa type of face. Mother, never given to superlatives, always said of Aunt Bessie that "she was no trouble." In fact, she fit into our family routine beautifully. She helped get the meals and wash the dishes, read to us endlessly and was lavish in her praise.

Bessie also took excellent black-and-white photos. She gave each of her nephews and nieces a hand-crafted montage of colored advertisements and pictures culled from magazines. Many had a Norman Rockwell quality about them. Mine was inscribed, "A Merry Christmas to Nebbie from Aunt Bessie, 1932." Corporate logos and advertisements for products such as Cream of Wheat or Campbell Soup had been cut away so that our imaginations could run rampant as we devoured each detail in the farm, hunting, mountain, fishing, or winter scenes.

Each picture bespoke a thousand words and deeply stimulated my imagination. The corners of my album's pages became dog-eared from hundreds of turnings. One picture shows a miserable 4th-grade boy in a spell-down before his teacher and a bright female classmate, face aglow, with her hand in the air. The teacher is stern, classmates disdainful as the boy hangs his head. I stood in his shoes dozens of times! Now, 65 years later, I can recall every detail of that picture. Another drawing showed a boy writing *"I Was Tardy"* on the blackboard 100 times in front of a teasing female peer. So much for the feminist charge that traditional education "puts down" girls! A fishing scene shows the astonishment of two fishermen who are eating their lunch when a seven-pound large-mouth bass attacks their unattended lure. The subjects were universal—swimming, farm life, animals in the wild, Indians, airplanes, sports of all kinds, kite flying, selling lemonade, gardening, playing marbles and the like. Always the teacher, Aunt Bessie's Christmas and birthday presents were well chosen children's classics. She never gave a toy.

But times have changed. Modern man, it seems, no longer trusts aunts and grandmothers. Like old furniture, they have become the outfit of museums and geriatric communities.

Great Aunt Myrtle, on the other hand, the youngest sister of Father's Mother, was a trial to my parents. She was an eccentric spinster who taught Indians on a reservation near Lake of the Woods. Her refrain ad nauseum was, "Now don't go to any trouble, Mabel." But her actions belied her words. Myrtle acted like royalty and didn't fit into the clocklike precision of our daily regimen. She never arose before 10 A.M., needed a special breakfast, "didn't lift a finger around the house," had special medical demands, and wanted to be listened to while the other members of the household were doing their chores. Although my parents were kind enough not to say anything to us children, I could sense the relief they felt when she left to return to her charges on the Minnesota tundra.

Father's cousin, Aunt Myrtle McBroom from Chicago, was an independently wealthy city snob who occasionally deigned to grace her hick relatives with a visit. We children thought she was a pain who always overstayed her welcome and we were glad her visits were rare. Once I wired her prized Packard with a harmless firecracker device that went off with a loud explosion when she turned on the ignition. She screamed and ran into our house indicating that I had ruined her car. I got a perfunctory bawling out by my parents but I could tell they thought it was a good joke and were happy that I had taken her down a notch. Mother believed that, with the exception of Aunt Bessie, people who had never had children often manifested aberrant behavior and held strange ideas.

One New Years Day a near-tragedy was etched in my memory. We had left Uncle Arthur's house in Hutchinson and were driving to Uncle Ben's when we were struck broadside and spun around by a car that had run a stop sign. "Papa's hurt," Mother screamed and I saw blood running into Bob's eye from a cut on his forehead. Grandad was severely shaken up and had to be carried into the house. I was five years old and sitting on my Grandmother's lap. I had been late getting into the car and had held up our departure by a few minutes. Months afterward, I would lie awake at night and ponder whether my tardiness had been a crucial factor in that awesome impact. "Why couldn't I have been on time," I asked myself, "or, even later still? A split second either way would have prevented the crash." Unknowingly, I raised questions of existentialism, the absurd, fatalism, freedom, and determinism—issues that I would wrestle with professionally decades later.

I approached May Day with some apprehension. We would make little May baskets filled with candy and nuts, leave them on the steps of our friends, ring the bell and run away. Since I was shy, I was afraid a girl might catch me and kiss me. They never did, but there was always the possibility that I might fall. Boys were only supposed to tag you.

Memorial Day was permeated with both familial and patriotic associations. Because the unity of the Tribe of Benjamin meant a great deal to Father, we would have a reunion in Hutchinson with those who shared our genetic inheritance. At 5 A.M. we were in the garden cutting spirea, honeysuckle, tulips, and other late spring flowers to cram into the trunk of our car. They would be used to dress the graves of my brother, Dickie, and Father's parents. Although they had died before I was born, I surmised that they were great and good people because their brown marble gravestones were large and impressive.

Before we left home I would unfurl the American flag, making sure that it did not touch the ground, and carefully insert the shaft from which it flew in a metal tube buried in our front lawn. I was scrupulous about bringing the flag inside before darkness came, and I always washed my hands before handling it.

I repeated this ritual every Flag Day, July 4, Labor Day, and Armistice Day; I was habitually and spontaneously patriotic. The flag symbolized all the goodness that had come into my life, gifts such as security, love, protection, health and freedom that came gratis. The flag was more than mere cloth. It opened up an interior world and reality not communicated by words or pictures. It was an icon with encrustations of American history. Its mysterious potency made me feel less frail. In battle, I had learned, the staff was carried aloft and provided a rallying point all soldiers could see. It was a portable version of the trees under which many societies had gathered in council for worship. By showing it respect, I intuitively gave thanks. I attached meaning to its colors: *blue* meant that all Americans were of royal birth or "blue-bloods;" *red* indicated the blood that had been shed by patriots for my freedom and the courage I wanted to acquire; *white* stood for the purity of life that I wanted to achieve. In the Benjamin and Bedell experience, the American flag symbolized the bounty, freedom, and success with which they had been blessed. Our family trees replicated the Horatio Alger stories. Dreams had come true. America's sacred texts and hymns—The Declaration of Independence, The Pledge of Allegiance, The Star Spangled Banner—both illuminated and were incarnated in our experience.

Our saga was foreign to that recorded in *The Grapes of Wrath, Uncle Tom's Cabin,* and the histories of the many proletarians for whom the dream was partial, unfulfilled, or demonic. For us the themes of freedom, optimism, and security overpowered the dissonance of cynicism, hopelessness, and despair. I came to believe that children need to be raised with a modicum of trust in the American Way and the essential rightness of things as they are if they are to have a positive and creative attitude toward life. Cynical teachers and parents often find their clones in cynical and unhappy students and children.

During the Depression, Memorial Day used to be more about honoring those who had served in the military than about grilling burgers or driving to the lake to "open up the cabin." Both in Pipestone and Hutchinson, there would be a week of preparation. Flower beds, gardens, and lawns were meticulously weeded and mowed. Loved ones often would arrange displays with flowered crosses on their lawns and at a warrior's grave. Then, on Memorial Day morning, the uniformed public school band would gather on main street and march to the cemetery. People got out of their cars and houses and sat at the curbside. While the children were festive and frolicked, parents reflected a somber mood. Usually the Boy Scouts were assigned the early morning duty of fastening red paper poppies on every veteran's grave.

There were speeches and prayers about the suffering and sacrifice of old and recent wars. As a small boy I was always impressed when a dozen veterans would raise their rifles and, upon command, fire off several rounds of blanks. Then taps would sound and, as soon as the soldiers broke formation, I would join a lot of other kids and fight over the shell casings.

Now Memorial Day has been converted into a family day. Our house is one of only two of the 28 on our *cul-de-sac* that displays the flag on that weekend. Today the colossal conflicts that defined American history are almost forgotten. Memorial Day passes with barely a whisper as to its purpose--honoring the soldier for his sacrifice, suffering, and death, that our country might live in freedom and peace.

After visiting the family graves, we would eat dinner at Uncle Arthur's home, since his was the largest house of the Hutchinson clan. Tables were set up in four rooms. We easily represented Shakespeare's seven stages of man. There were babes in arms as well as octogenarians for whom this would be their last reunion. The racket was deafening! A genetic marker of our tribe destined us to shout loudly rather than listen quietly.

The children automatically paired off with the cousins who were in their age and sex group. Platters of ham, turkey, beef, and chicken vanished as we competed with one another as to how many times we went back for seconds, thirds, and fourths. After everyone had been sated; after laments that "I just can't eat any more" had ended; after reaching, mumbling, gobbling, and swilling of milk and Kool Aid had ceased; after everyone who needed a trip to the bathroom had been there; then, and only then would we collapse on the living room couches and floor to "let the food settle." But before our inflated bellies could even begin their slow process of retraction, Aunt Bessie called for "picture time." The gathering of the Tribe had to be captured on film. In her best schoolmarm manner, she divided us by families, age, sex, and height, to record this slice of time for the Benjamin photo archives.

Bob and I often followed John Gus, Uncle Arthur's oldest boy, up into the attic, where we were invariably overcome by the signs of our cousin's brilliance. John was precocious beyond imagining. As a 10th grader he had a darkroom and several cameras, and he had taken photos of automobile accidents and sold them to insurance companies. Gasoline-powered model planes were in abundance, some with six-foot wing spreads. An extensive chemistry set occupied one corner of the attic, while another corner was filled with a maze of model railroad tracks. I felt depressed and inferior, like an intellectual pigmy standing before an adolescent Benjamin version of Einstein. Although I didn't know the term at the time, I desperately hoped I might be a late bloomer. I also began to realize why it might not be good to have cousins living in close proximity to one another. Our relatives didn't have to make comparisons. We did it ourselves.

July 4th was a glorious delight—a day of noise, color, and explosions. Fireworks were legal, and we bought as many as our allowances would allow. While riding our bikes we would throw cherry bombs under the wheels of our friends. They looked like silver gumballs and would explode on impact like little hand grenades. We'd light powerful cannon firecrackers and throw them into a pond to create an underwater explosion that replicated a miniature depth charge. Any youngster who held one too long risked losing a finger or an eye. We blasted tin cans 30 feet in the air, blew sand out of the sand box, blasted loose bark off of trees, destroyed ant hills and carefully constructed sand castles. Sometimes we'd tie a cannon cracker to the belly of a model airplane, wind up its rubber-band powered propeller and send it off into a balsa and tissue-paper Valhalla.

Father would buy sparklers, pinwheels, Roman candles, and sky rockets and we would help him set them off in our back yard. Our impatience usually forced him to begin the show at twilight, before darkness arrived to provide the maximum effect. For Skippy, our Chesapeake Bay retriever, it was 24 hours of sheer hell; she retreated to her lair under the porch for the duration.

There was always a parade down Main Street and a band concert in the city park on July 4th. Because of our straightened times, the floats were a sorry lot, but any individual or organization could have a place in the short, five-block, civic processional. Our two banks, the Our Own Hardware store, the creamery, the Chevy and Ford dealers, and the grain elevators always paid a few dollars for streamers, bunting, and signs to adorn their own cars or trucks. They must have felt the advertising was worth it.

At least 25 American Legion Post members, on horseback and on foot, led the event. There were a few Spanish-American War veterans limping along, but the majority of the marchers had seen service in the First World War. A few vets carried rifles and flags. They tried to maintain the military bearing and rectitude of a time dimly remembered, but their visible presence was a mere shadow of its former character. Most had steel in their eyes but lard on their bellies. Now gray-haired and forty pounds heavier than when they fought under Pershing in France, I imagined them sitting in the American Legion hall, picking at the scabs on old wounds as they reinvented the war and themselves. They probably missed the intensity more than the danger and came together mutually to remember.

Some of these potbellied patriots had tattoos—the icons of their military servitude and sacrifice—on their arms or forearms. Originally they had been bright red, green, yellow, and blue but time had erased the sharpness of the images and the distinctiveness of the colors. The lines of the tattoos now were washed out and everything seemed to be a light sapphire. The eagle was the predominant image, although an assortment of roses, crests, flags, service or division symbols, and wolf heads, were also in evidence. The tattooed mottoes ran from the heroic— "Death Before Dishonor," and "Semper Fi"—to the intimate and personal—"Mother" and "Sally, My True Love." I thought of how painful it must have been to have hundreds of needle sticks injecting dye into the skin. Was it, I pondered, a form of military baptism, where a physical symbol attested to an inward bond?

It was clear from the set of their collective jaws that the Legionnaires were symbolically replicating a crucial time in their lives. In spite of their exertion and serious mien, the aging warriors' red, sweat-drenched faces and protruding, belt-overlapping guts made the procession seem comical to some of my friends. To be sure, there was an immense discontinuity between the Legionnaire's debilitated physical presence and their attempt to recapture an image of soldiering long past. Still, the taunts of my friends seemed cruel if childish: "Have you ever shot that gun?" "Get in shape!" "Pull in that gut!" "Get in step!" "You couldn't beat your way out of a paper bag!" "I'll race you to the water tower and back!" "I don't see any medals!"

The social pressure from my friends to join in their ridicule was strong. Somehow I found the strength not to participate. The somber faces of the Legionnaires gave me pause. Intuitively, I perceived that they knew something about suffering, sacrifice, death and love of country that I had not gained in my 13 years of life. Sometime later, during a bike ride to the Indian quarries, I took a detour and stopped at the cemetery. I saw small American flags and the bronze Legion symbol at some of the graves. Some of the markers had quatrains that deeply impressed me and I committed them to memory. It was appropriate that I had to get on my knees to read them:

> In fame's eternal camping ground,
>   Their silent tents are spread,
> And glory guards with solemn round,
>   The bivouac of the dead.

> Rest on embalmed and sainted dead,
>   Dear as the blood ye gave.
> No impious footstep here shall tread
>   The herbage of your grave

> Your own proud land's heroic soil
>   Must be your fitter grave;
> She claims from war his richest spoil,
>   The Ashes of the brave

Our Halloween had none of the school and community programs that are diversionary tactics to prevent juvenile delinquency. After we outgrew the excitement of trick-or-treating and soaping windows, we did some rather nasty things. Some of my friends would set an outhouse back several feet from the hole of a farm kid they didn't like, hoping he would fall into the pit. Rotten squash and pumpkins were ideal weapons to throw at your enemies' homes or cars. One of my more daring friends would "take a dump" in a paper sack, set it on fire on a doorstep, ring the bell and run. He hoped that whoever answered the door would stamp out the fire in a panic and end up with very smelly shoes!

The piety of the guardians of Pipestone morals would not tolerate a high school "dance band." We had to label our ensemble a "swing band." Here I stand at the upper right corner next to my fellow cornet players, Neal Knudtson and Les Kallsen.

28. Close Friends

Our youth today love luxury. They have bad manners, contempt for authority, disrespect for older people. Children nowadays are tyrants. They contradict their parents, gobble their food and tyrannize their teachers.

Socrates, *circa* 425 B.C.

One of the advantages of a small town was the common school. All students from kindergarten through twelfth grade walked to the three-story, brown brick and quartzite stone building in the center of the town. Only the farm kids were bussed. Each class had around 100 students.

My parents undoubtedly were aware of the subtle class distinctions in the social fabric of our village but, in my sight, all my friends and their parents were equal. There were no private country estates, no golf or dining clubs, no parochial or private schools, not even any suburbs. Not one family had a backyard swimming pool, kept show horses, drove fancy cars, or wintered in a plush Florida estate. We were all "middle Americans," and the middle was very elastic. The homes of my friends were exceedingly modest. Two-story frame houses had three bedrooms; one-story homes, only two. No one felt uncomfortable in anyone else's home.

A close friend was Neal Knudtson, the oldest son of the superintendent of schools. Father served on the school board and got to know Neal's father, "Oat" Knudtson, very well. The Knudtsons, along with the Hickmans, Lamberts, and Trebons, were families with whom we often went picnicking, vacationing, and tobogganing. Neal was Norwegian, a close replica of a Viking. At six years of age, I took perverse delight in informing him of the nonexistence of Santa Claus. Neal did not give in graciously or easily. It took over two weeks to convince him. He claimed to have seen ashes on the carpet, heard noises of hoofs on the roof and, most convincingly, knew Santa had eaten the cookies left out for him— "I saw the crumbs on the kitchen floor!" Neal got back at me by extolling the gastronomic delights of Norwegian Yuletide cooking, such as lefsa and lutefisk, foods unavailable to me because they were unknown in Mother's culinary repertoire. Only in later years did I discover I hadn't missed a thing.

Another grade school friend was Paul Trebon, the adopted son of Ed Trebon, the owner of *The Pipestone Star.* Trebon's booster enthusiasm had persuaded Father to locate in Pipestone. Tall and spindly, with a mop of black hair, Paul was a constant tease. He never quite measured up, however, to the boy/man his father had envisioned. I overheard discussions on the relative importance of nature vs. nurture, genes vs. environment, that Ed Trebon would have with Father regarding Paul. Ed was troubled that for all of his guidance, Paul was neither the student nor dutiful son he had hoped he would become. "Surely Doc," Ed would lament, "there must be some mediocre genes in his background. I certainly would like to have known his father and mother."

Shortly after a four-week trip to the East coast that we took with the Trebons in 1937, they moved to California. I was heartbroken at losing such a good sixth-grade friend. Trebon had purchased *The Santa Maria Courier* and, forever the Babbit-like booster, began to extol the virtues of California in hopes of getting Father to locate there. "You've got to come, Doc. California has everything—flowers, climate, medical opportunity, growth—everything except Minnesota mosquitoes and ice." Trebon could have marketed Death Valley as Camelot. Father was interested enough to take and pass the California state medical examination. But we didn't go. He never told us why. He may have feared the effect of a rootless and sensual culture upon his family.

Forty years passed before I saw Paul again. He stopped by to see me in the 1970s for a few days on his way to a national airplane convention in Oshkosh, Wisconsin. He had gone to work for a California gas company after high school rather than going to college. I approached our meeting with apprehension; as I feared, there was no turning back from our separate pilgrimages, no matter how close our bond had been as children. In conversation, interests, and culture, we had passed like ships in the night. His was an existence of surf and sand, chrome and carburetors, freeways, fun and frisbees. He wanted to see Hamline University and my study. Paul insisted and, under pressure, I agreed. Upon seeing the walls lined with books, he asked, "What are all these books for?" I tried to explain, but I doubt that he really understood. We inhabited different worlds, and no amount of nostalgia and reflection on our common childhood could bring us back together. We play-acted at comradeship, but each of us was relieved when the time came to say good-bye. The three days together had seemed like three weeks.

Les Kallsen was another close friend. Some called him "Sleepy Les" because his eyelids were usually half closed. Les was the son of August C. Kallsen, who had left farming near Jasper to become the county Auditor of Pipestone County, and lived directly behind us. Although he was six months younger and a grade behind me, he was bigger than I was. His mother had died giving birth to his younger brother, and he called his step-mother by her first name, "Ada," a familiarity I always considered strange. He was a German Lutheran (now Missouri Synod) whose church "laid down the law." The German Lutherans were known as the "Roman Catholic wing" of Protestantism. We wishy-washy Methodists thought that Lutheran theological teachings had been reduced to rote memorization—religious mathematical tables that some said were regurgitated without much understanding. We believed that the "Missouri's" knew the "what" but not the "why" of faith. In good fun I teased Les that his confirmation training took three full years and mine but one. Only later did I realize that the more conservative branches of Protestantism held on to their members and grew much faster than did the liberal wing.

The Kallsens had a garage that Les had turned into a miniature zoo and filled with a menagerie of animals. He kept rabbits and a great variety of pigeons, some of them "pouters." They could force air into bags in their necks and distend them until it seemed as if their breasts would burst. (I was too naive to know it was a sexual come-on to attract females, although later on when I started lifting weights, my intentions were the same as those of the pigeons.) We would release homing pigeons miles out into the country, and usually they would beat us back to the garage. Les also kept chickens, white rats and ducks, but the most impressive animal he owned was a spotted or Indian pony. When the wind blew from the West, it was clear to us that Les didn't clean up after his animals any better than I had done with my chickens. (Zoning laws were lax if not nonexistent, although I suspect the city fathers would have drawn the line at keeping hogs in your back yard.)

Les and I participated in the marching, concert, and "Swing" bands, in football, and in basketball. The "Swing" band was actually a group of 12 of us that played for dances, but the school administration felt it would ruffle the feathers of some pious citizens if we were known as a "dance" band. There was healthy competition between Neal, Les, and me. Due in part to his size, Les made the first team on the football team during his junior year, while I was relegated to the scrubs. However, because of my agility and coordination, I forged ahead in basketball. I also was first-chair trumpet player in all three bands, while Neal and Les were second and third, respectively. The "Johnson Rag" was the theme song of our "Swing Band," but our melodic sound had little renown beyond the confines of our gym floor. Nevertheless, besides fun, membership in the band provided a seedbed for future success in that it demanded discipline, cooperation, civility, good grooming, and punctuality. Years later Neal enjoyed a noteworthy career with Bell Telephone. Les, after achieving a sterling career in the Navy Air Corps—he rose to the rank of a full commander—returned to the land, his first love, and bought a farm near Ihlen, Minnesota.

One afternoon after band practice, a man in a double-breasted suit with slicked-down greasy hair stopped me. Charlie Sparks (I knew him only by name) complimented me on my playing and asked if I wanted to play for him at the Playmore Club, just outside the city limits. I had never had any occasion to enter its premises, but I remembered that Father always made some nasty comments about it when we passed by. "One of my trumpet players joined the army and I hear you are the best around," he said. "I'll pay you $5.00 every Saturday for playing from 9:00 P.M. to 1:00 A.M."

I was ecstatic. Five dollars for four hours—it was an immense sum! Friends who were lucky enough to have jobs after school at department stores were paid 25 cents an hour. I never realized there might be good money in tooting a horn, that there might be a payoff from the long hours of practice. "I'm on my way," I mused. "The world outside school has heard of me. I'm going to be a success after all."

But my enthusiasm was short-lived. Father exploded and almost lost control when I told him. He never gave me a good reason other than "it wasn't a fit place for a Benjamin." "Have you ever had a meal there on a Saturday night?" I asked, feigning a certain amount of innocence. "No, I haven't," he countered. "Some things you don't have to experience to know that they are wrong." "But the money . . . ," I stammered, "I could save it for college." "If it takes their filthy money to go to college, he said, cutting me off, "maybe you shouldn't even go. Sometime you will realize that the road to hell is paved with gold." The intensity of Father's objection precluded my pressing him on the issue.

Later, a classmate told me he had heard that when people got "all liquored up" (Father's phrase) at the Playmore, women sometimes took off their clothes and danced naked on top of the tables. The place seemed aptly named. Shortly afterwards, the man with the greasy hair asked Les to play. I was surprised that his parents reacted in the same insensitive manner as had mine. So much for my stereotype of the Missouri Synod Lutherans as having a tight theology but flexible morals. Sparks finally found some Pipestone pagan to fill the position. I told Les sometimes there were disadvantages to being a morally strict Methodist.

It was a strange world. Father's prohibitions made the delights of the Playmore world even more enticing. But I didn't dare suggest to him that the music would have been difficult and I would have had to keep my eyes on the musical score rather than on the wanton women tap-dancing on the tables.

I proudly sit for my first grade picture.

My grade report for higher algebra in the 11th grade. I barely passed with a 76 (below 75 is an F). Mrs. Colby wrote the two 73s in red ink. Although a friend of my parents she was a "straight shooter" when it came to grading. I was depressed on the days I had to take my grades home, but my parents always signed on the reverse side without negative comment. The As and Bs I received in choir did little to relieve my agony.

29. A Sluggish Scholar

If the days grow dark, if care and pain
Press close and sharp on heart and brain,
Then lovely pictures still shall bloom
Upon the walls of memory's room.

My Burdens, Charles Dickinson

Kindergarten through senior high school was housed in a three-story brick and stone building that covered a block and a half, four blocks from home. I walked the route four times a day and knew the occupants of every house on both sides of the street.

The somber appearance of my grade school correlated with the curriculum. Life was serious. Education meant mastering the three Rs, not "life adjustment." My classroom was "Depression generic." The floors were scuffed, dark wood and the bare windows had neither curtains nor drapes. Desks with flip-up tops and seats and ink wells were bolted in tidy rows to the wooden floors. On one side of the classroom was the cloak hall where miscreants might be excommunicated for a time for hitting, note passing, spitting, biting, chewing gum, whispering, or general rowdiness.

Stuck under the desktops and seats were wads of gum that several generations of students had left. Territorial-type markings, about as decipherable as Neanderthal pictograms, also littered the desks. The scribbling recorded a broken history of crushes, studs, wimps, and teacher's pets. There were carvings of horses, hearts, footballs, guns and airplanes. I was fascinated by the crude drawings of those portions of human anatomy that had to do with reproduction. The creativity of the unknown artists amazed me. I wondered whether such gigantic depiction of sexual organs correlated with reality. If so, I had another area, this one truly serious, to feel inferior about. Later scribes sometimes added the name of some unpopular teacher or student to the drawing.

George Washington, in a regal English powdered wig but with flat stern lips that hid his wooden teeth, stared down at us from the wall in front. The Father of our Country didn't seem very American to me. Our teacher told us his wooden teeth hurt and that we had better brush ours after every meal or we might get to look like that some day. Abraham Lincoln also monitored us with his melancholy mien, and I wondered why he had never had that ugly mole taken off his face. My Father could have burned it off in 30 seconds with his electric needle.

Slate blackboards adorned the walls on three sides of the room. Above them were twelve-inch examples of the letters of the alphabet depicting the Palmer penmanship method. The perfectly formed characters and numbers were our models for writing. "Make a little house with your fist," said my teacher, "keep your wrist on the desk and make your hand go up and down and round and round, as you make your letters. It will become automatic in time." It never did for me. It was a form of torture and seemed so unnatural. The basics were tough and memorization was hard for me. There was no time for or interest in teaching about "social problems," such as the troubles our colored people and those in Africa, Asia, and India were having. Teachers didn't waste their time arranging displays of chickens, squirrels, flowers, and leaves. We saw the real thing every day. I stood in awe of teachers. I did not want them as a buddy, friend, or pal. An immense chasm of power, intellect, and maturity separated us.

Education is different now. A boy growing up today gets confusing signals. A lot of teachers try to be cool and clever in a way not markedly different from their students; they do not slow down or speak from a distance. Classwork has become largely an affair of peer education, the class divided into groups to "pool their resources," that is, "to share" their opinions and to dig up random facts before being called together to present an audiovisual product. Depression-era teachers told me "That's wrong," rather than "Well now, that's an interesting contribution. Thank you for sharing." Teachers now seem to be licensed amusers whose knowledge base is thin, social workers for whom instilling knowledge is less important than instilling positive feelings in their charges. I grew up before the growth of an easy-going tolerance resulted in a leveling of manners, a reluctance to blame or praise heroically or to decide hard cases.

Reticence and decorum were and are close neighbors. When I was seven, the father of a friend, giving me a lesson in manners, told me cooly to address him as "Mr." or "Sir" and never as just "you." It was an unpleasant moment and I thought him an unpleasant man, but the lesson was learned. Interestingly, my childhood felt freer knowing that grown-ups were different from my friends.

When I reached grade school, the McGuffy Reader era of the 1890s had ended. Yet its legacy of spirituality and morality still lingered in the school room. My teachers reinforced the codes of responsibility, restraint, and renunciation I had heard at home. Unlike authorities today who are in their 30s and 40s, my teachers had no trouble saying "no." In third grade I created a little booklet of 20 proverbs covered in purple tissue. Among them:

> Happiness is a perfume you cannot pour on others without getting a
> few drops on yourself.
> A single sunbeam will drive away my shadows.
> There is nothing as kingly as kindness nor so royal as truth.
> He who plants trees loves others besides himself.
> One cannot always be a hero but one can always be a man.
> All that I am or ever hope to be I owe to my angel mother.
> I am not bound to win but I am bound to be true.
> Be sure you are right, then go ahead.

I envy people who can remember details of each grade and the names of their teachers. I mostly draw a blank. Perhaps it means I drifted through grade school in a fog or was unhappy most of the time. The teachers' names on my report cards—Myrtle Peterson, L.M. Pankhurst, and others—evoke no corresponding images. I can dredge few memories of those formative years from my unconscious.

I was one of the youngest in my class, having begun kindergarten when I was four. My kindergarten teacher checked "average" for "effort," "reasoning," "leadership," and "self-control" but ranked me "poor" in "language expression." In first grade I improved to "good" or "average" in most subjects/behaviors, but next to language & expression was written, "good but talks too low—*speech defect*." If my parents were worried, they had the wisdom not to tell me.

Thankfully, my future remained open because teachers' colleges had not yet begun to turn out counselors, testers, and other forecasters of student potential. There were no tests that would pigeon-hole me and mortgage my future. If there had been, my teachers may have said: "Too bad about Nebbie Benjamin. He will be an embarrassment to his parents. But then, the world needs more people to work with their hands."

Looking back, I wish my parents had held me back a year. Most of my classmates were both physically larger and older than I. But even waiting a year might not have helped. I was a miserable speller, a condition Mother blamed on a first-grade teacher who neglected phonics. At the time I didn't quite know what phonics were, but I was angry at being cheated out of something that was rightfully mine. All through my grade school years, Mother and I observed a ritual: on the day before my weekly spelling test, she would drill me repeatedly on the word list. On the Friday morning of the test, I would get a final briefing. It was to no avail. I would miss half of the words and usually get an "F." A "C" would put me in heaven for a week.

From that time to the present, whenever I write, a dictionary must be close at hand. I continue to look up words I have looked up hundreds of times down through the years. I've consoled myself by knowing that many great men, including President John Kennedy, were poor at spelling. Math, too, has always been a weakness; I preferred the concrete and was always good in geography and history.

A traumatic event occurred in fourth grade when I was changed from the "red bird" to the "blue bird" reading group. I wasn't so dumb that I didn't know that as a "blue bird" I was in the group for slow readers. I wept inwardly for days.

Fortunately, there were ways to partially escape the angst of childhood. I was usually home by 4:30 P.M. in time to listen to five or six 15-minute heroic-type radio programs. The cereal companies knew how to hook young boys. "Jack Armstrong, the All American Boy," "The Lone Ranger," and "Buck Rogers and the 25th Century" were my favorites. I would lie on the floor with my head against our large radio-victrola, shut my eyes, and be transported into another realm. Within moments my fears were dissolved in a make-believe masculine world where righteousness, honor, and bravery were always victorious.

Critics of such programs see them as a seedbed for the unhealthy dualism between maleness and femaleness; as a part of the etiology of macho perversion. I have no such recollection. I only hungered for a vision of hope, accomplishment, and moral models to help me through the complexity of physical and psychological growth. My heroes did not stand for the exercise of raw power, the subjection of women, or the genocide of the lesser breeds. Like the protagonists of Louis Lamour's novels of the American West, the prowess of the radio hero was constrained by honor and moral integrity. Looking back, I am happy that television did not control my childhood imagination. Because I was limited to audio, my world of fantasy had greater release.

Each program urged listeners to "SEND THOSE BOXTOPS IN!" in order to earn a special prize that would be mailed to us. I had a tough time securing the proper boxtops because Father decreed that the Benjamin breakfast had to be hot—oatmeal, Malt-O-Meal, or rye—liberally laced with raisins that had been soaked overnight. I begged Mother to buy the proper cold cereals on the sly so that I could get the prizes. Invariably, when the gim-crack came—a ring with a secret compartment, code book, whistle, pedometer—I was disappointed. Never dismayed, however, by the time I received one trinket, I was already saving for a future one.

It may be that the richness of my dreams and my perennial sleepwalking came from listening to those radio programs. My earliest remembered dream involved being grabbed by a grizzly bear that lunged over my headboard. Because I had fallen asleep with my head against the top of my bed, I simply put cause and effect together. For years I was careful not to sleep with my head touching the headboard.

My sleepwalking embarrassed me greatly. My parents would often find me in various parts of the house or yard, presumably doing purposeful activity but consciously unaware. Once, under Father's questioning, I awoke in the front closet putting on leather coats and hats to protect myself from the wild dogs that were attacking me. Another time Mother rescued two coed Hamline choir members who were staying with us when the choir was in town from having to converse with me when I wandered into their room as they were going to bed. They didn't even know I was asleep.

The most serious of my nocturnal ramblings occurred at a Redwood Falls motel when we were returning home after seeing Dr. Pike, my Minneapolis orthodontist. Mother, Grandma, and I had seen "Blood and Sand," a movie depicting a Mexican bullfight. At midnight, I charged out of the room like a matador in full flight. It was a hot summer night, and only the screen door was hooked. I hit the door so hard the hook was straightened out. Mother and Grandma, with their nightgowns billowing, followed in hot pursuit and caught me 10 feet in front of a cliff above the Minnesota River. The story was recounted so often it became part of the Benjamin saga. I would laugh as my antics of the night were retold. But inwardly I felt helpless and I wondered, if the habit persisted, whether it would keep me out of the Navy Air Corps.

30. PUBERTY AND PIMPLES

Let not young souls be smothered out before
    They do quaint deeds and fully flaunt their pride.
It is the world's one crime its babes grow dull,
    Its poor are ox-like, limp and leaden-eyed.

Not that they starve, but starve so dreamlessly,
    Not that they sow, but that they seldom reap,
Not that they serve, but have no gods to serve,
    Not that they die, but that they die like sheep.

The Leaden-Eyed, Vachel Lindsay

Because of poverty, drought, and the "black rollers," many called the fourth decade of the 20th century, the "Dirty '30s." I felt sorry for students a few years ahead of me when Byrma Jones, the dean of students called the seniors of 1932 together and said it was too expensive to wear graduation caps and gowns and that a sport coat or dress would be all right. Until then, everyone got by on "hand-me-downs" and "made-overs." May Wilson (class of 1933) didn't have a "store-bought" dress until commencement day, when her dad sold two pigs for $3.00 and then went to Penneys and bought her a dress. Art Tonsfeldt (class of 1932) was one of the few to purchase a $6.70 class ring, a transaction that was possible because his father had sold a truck load of barley. Someone suggested to Ida Mae Oldemeyer (class of 1934) that she should visit the beauty parlor in honor of commencement and have her hair done. "I remember the darkness of the whole town and how the beauty parlor was lit up like it was night," she remembered. "So much dust had been blown into my hair that the beauty operator had to change the water several times—it was like mud." By the time Ida Mae came out of the parlor, the wind had died down and she made it to the graduation ceremonies quite nicely. The "Dirty '30s" were appropriately named. Graduates resumed wearing caps and gowns in 1938 when the economy began to improve.

Promotion to junior high was a deliverance for me because I had a locker, different teachers for each subject, and I changed classrooms every hour. However, my grades testify that Pipestone was not a bit like Lake Wobegon, "where all the children are above average." Except for history and geography, in which I got A's, most of my grades were C's. Every six weeks I would bring my report card home for a parental signature. It was signed perfuctorily without any "guilting" or lectures from my parents. They knew they had a one-talented son on their hands. Mysteriously, 13 years earlier at the conception of their second-born, the genes must have misfired.

One side of the card listed "Habits" such as "Effort," "Cooperation," "Working up to his level of ability," for which my teacher's options were, "Above average," "Satisfactory," "Unsatisfactory." Like a broken record, the report card showed a repetitious string of checks next to "Satisfactory." Only once did Father question my effort when there was a wayward check in the "Unsatisfactory" box for "Not Working up to His Level of Ability." Obviously, the teacher's new bifocals had caused her to check the wrong slot. It was clear my intellectual engine was running smoothly. It just didn't have enough horse power.

Music was force-fed to me during those years. The cornet was highly digestible, but with the piano I was a bulimic. I had begun taking piano lessons as early as the third grade from an old campfire friend of Mothers, "Aunt" Rachel Hickman, who lived a block away. My parents wanted to give me all the advantages that had been denied to them. Father was forever saying, "We don't have a single member of Kiwanis to play for our singing. *We have to have a WOMAN come in!* Neb, you are going to learn to play the piano!" Father's logic was tortured but, of course, I submitted.

My progress was glacial. "Aunt" Rachel's talents as a teacher were commensurate with mine as a performer. Her playing was mediocre too. She blamed it on her arthritis, an excuse denied to me. She and "Uncle" Charlie lived in modest circumstances and it may have been that my parents wanted to add to their income, knowing that my limited talent could not have been ruined in any case. I had to practice a half-hour a day. Mother had the patience of Job. Practice sessions with her often degenerated into a power struggle, with my arguing "I AM hitting the RIGHT notes" when I was striking wrong ones. After 15 minutes I would cry out, "Is it TIME yet?" After each exercise or piece, I would check the kitchen clock and wonder why it moved so slowly.

In the seventh grade, in a final attempt to unearth some hidden talent, Mother imported a fat little man from Sioux Falls, South Dakota.

He reminded me of a penguin as he marched around our living and dining room on his short stubby legs, crying in 4/4 time: "One, Two, Three, Four; Please, Keep, In, Time; Hit, The, Notes, Firm; One, Two, Three, Four." He was a mobile human metronome. After six weeks, he gave up. My body was on the piano bench but my spirit inhabited the athletic field. According to Thomas Carlyle "Music is well said to be the speech of angels," but under my fingers, it had the scream of the furies.

Like legions of other children, I fell by the musical wasteland because of the individual approach to instruction. If I had taken group instruction with my peers, I might have flourished. Today, decades after all the tears, tension, mangled recitals, and hundreds of dollars expended on hours of bench imprisonment, the results are pathetic. I have only *Largo* and a few simple hymns and carols in my repertoire.

That I had better success on the cornet was entirely due to an outstanding bandsman, Walter "Andy" Anderson. He was a tireless teacher who gave lessons before and after school. I started taking lessons in the sixth grade, once a week at 7:00 A.M. in his office. Anderson followed the newly published, Prescott Technique System developed by Professor Gerald R. Prescott, the Director of the University of Minnesota Bands. A graduate of Upper Iowa University, Prescott had such remarkable success with the Mason City, Iowa, bands that he was invited to Minnesota at the age of 29. He structured exercises using the Arban's musical text to increase students' proficiency in performing runs, slurring, double and triple-tonguing, staccato and the like. Under Anderson's guidance, I developed rapidly.

Little did I know that years later Gerald Prescott would be my father-in-law. After marrying his daughter, Marjorie, I told the joke ad nauseum, "While in school, I had USED the Prescott Technique System. Once in college, his daughter had USED it on me!"

Once a month Anderson took some of his brass pupils to Windom to have lessons with Judge Linky. Linky, who was badly crippled but had played solo cornet in John Phillip Sousa's Band, was a no-nonsense type of teacher. If someone lacked talent, had uncorrectable problems, or lacked motivation, he told Anderson not to bring him back. Fortunately, I wasn't so categorized and must have had 15 lessons from Linky. In fact, it was through Linky that Mother bought me my prized Olds cornet. Much of my ability could be traced to this instrument, because it had such a beautiful tone.

Anderson was a great publicist for his band. At 12, I was playing solos, duets, and trios with Neal Knudtson and Les Kallsen at Pipestone service, church, and social clubs. At first I was terrified. My knees would shake and I thought the vibrations would show through my pant legs. When I was in eighth grade, Anderson entered me in the southern Minnesota regional music contest at Worthington against senior high soloists. I received the only "A" given for trumpet soloists. I had played a simple piece exceptionally well, while those four or five years older than I, had done poorly in attempting scores beyond their ability. I taped the blue ribbon on my mirror where it stayed until graduation. I couldn't have been more than four-and-a-half feet tall at the time. I repressed the suspicion that the judges might have favored me because of my size.

A few years later, a new "enlightened" educational ideology deemed "musical fairs," and the pure "fun of playing" to be preferable to "competition" with its onus of "grading." Previous to then, if 17 soloists or bands competed, they were ranked in excellence from 1 to 17. Those conductors whose performers or bands who consistently failed to make it into the top five became disappointed, if not angry, and changed the system. Merit, ranking, and evaluation lost out to "sharing," "fun," and "cooperation." Standards declined. Nonetheless, I have always been grateful to Anderson. When I was at a tender age, he forced me to perform before crowds so that I could conquer my fear.

Because of Anderson's hard work, the excellence of our concert band was known throughout the region. Our practice times varied from before school or athletic practice to the evenings. I was grateful for the opportunities of a small town school, for I was able to participate in band, choir, *and* athletics. Our band and choir were a microcosm of our school. Athletes were distributed throughout all programs, and no activity was stereotyped as effeminate or unmanly.

I loved playing the marches of John Phillip Sousa. Their verve, brilliance, and martial spirit encapsulated the American experience and my exuberance for life. Anderson would open a concert by having us stand and play "The Star-Spangled Banner." Then we would play several marches before performing a major opus. Sousa's marches were a great playground for the brass section, and I loved strutting my stuff. We would run through "Semper Fidelis," "Mars and Venus," "The Liberty Bell," "The Thunderer," selections from *The Pirate of Penzance,* and others. My favorite was "El Capitan" because it allowed me to show off my ability in double and triple-tonguing. During the brass flourishes, Neal Knudtson, Les Kallsen and I would stand up, make a left-oblique pivot to face the audience, and blast away. It was heady stuff for a timid lad. I told Neal and Les to pay attention to the small stuff—our capes had to hang just so and our horns had to be exactly parallel to the floor. Like 90 percent of the audience, I kept time tapping the toe of my left shoe.

It has been said that music is a sweet nectar for the human soul. However ideologically and divisive other concerns of life might polarize a community, music is a great leveler across class, ethnicity, caste, and race. I was proud to play a small part of being a celebrant in bringing joy and optimism to my school and community through music.

Nonetheless, there were moments of humor. Our school's star half-back, Steve Hicks, was an angular 6'7" tall and an extraordinary sight when he stood up and played the piccolo flourish in *Stars and Stripes Forever.* His hands reminded me of those of Dutch farmers who milked a dozen cows twice a day. The piccolo looked like a soda straw caught between a couple of small hams. No one dared tease him about it though. Twenty feet behind Hicks a small kid with at most 120 pounds on his 5'5" frame was dwarfed behind his monstrous tuba. Once during marching-band practice he tripped and was imprisoned by the metal monster until we lifted if off his body. Anderson never seemed to notice the incongruity of his charges' choice of instruments.

Anderson was a perfectionist. We did a lot of sight reading, and months before the district contest we would start working on a difficult and long musical score. One year we played the *William Tell* overture and received rave notices and As at the district, regional, and state contests.

Unlike our playing, our uniforms were quite modest by today's standards. Band members dressed in their own black pants or skirts, white tops, and dark ties. The school provided red and black capes from a time before our colors had been changed to white and green. The capes' origins probably went back to the era of the Spanish-American War; having been handed down by several generations of students, many gave off an extraordinary odor. It seemed to come from a combination of sweat, dirt, brass polish, catsup, snot, valve oil, and Brylcreem hair oil. Clearly, they had never been dry cleaned. They were Depression-era chic and had served a half a dozen purposes beside draping musicians' shoulders during concerts. Many were moth-eaten as well. A few even had some suspicious-looking yellow stains; the sophomores had to take those.

During one band trip we added to the capes' inventory of odors. One of our drummers had some Limburger cheese left over from a wedding at which he had playfully spread on the exhaust manifold of the newlyweds' car engine. He went up and down the aisle of the bus, dipping his finger in the cheese and wiping it on us. We used our capes to snap at him, hide under, and, if he got us, as towels to wipe off the Limburger.

Despite all of this, Les, Neal, and I always took great care to arrange our capes on our shoulders at just the right rakish angle. No matter how bad they smelled, for us the capes symbolized achievement and our bond of friendship and musical fraternity.

But our bond went beyond moth-holed, smelly capes. Returning from concerts late at night someone on the bus would start singing "Moonlight Bay." Soon everyone would join in and, to my untrained ear, it sounded like a heavenly choir on the ramparts of paradise. "The Old Apple Tree," "Someone Watch Over Me," "Don't Fence Me In," "That's An Irish Lullaby," "Indian Love Call" and "Stouthearted Men," and other nostalgic tunes followed. Rivers of blood were running thousands of miles to the east and west of my secluded Heartland, but I drifted off to sleep without a care.

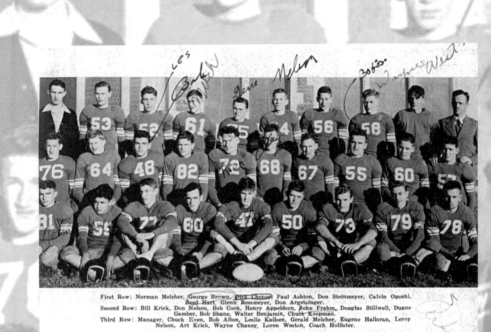

First Row: Norman Melcher, George Brown, Dick Cheney, Paul Ashton, Don Steinmeyer, Calvin Opsahl, Reed Hart, Glenn Ressmeyer, Don Argetsinger.
Second Row: Bill Krick, Don Nelson, Bob Cook, Henry Appeldorn, John Frahm, Douglas Stillwell, Duane Gamber, Bob Shane, Walter Benjamin, Chuck Koopman.
Third Row: Manager, Chuck Even, Bob Alton, Leslie Kallsen, Gerald Melcher, Eugene Halloran, Leroy Nelson, Art Krick, Wayne Chaney, Loren Weston, Coach Hollister.

Football - 1943

We won the district championship in 1943, my senior year. But at 130 pounds, I was a "scrub" and didn't play a great deal. When I did, I took a real beating. I'm number 60 in the second row.

31. Athletics—Passages to Manhood

> Habit is thus the enormous fly-wheel of society, its most precious conservative agent. It alone is what keeps us all within the bounds of ordinance. There is no more miserable human being than one in whom nothing is habitual but indecision.
>
> *Psychology,* William James

As a classic late bloomer in the area of intellectual achievement, I found consolation in athletics during my final years in school. Piano practice and studying received short shrift. Years later I would understand the wholesome psychological and ritualized meaning underlying competition and sport. At the time I was barely aware that I was being tested, shaping an identity, being incorporated into a community, and, as a result, being firmed in courage and character. Athletics were a civilized, albeit pale, substitute for rites of passage that tribal societies forced their young men to perform. One hundred years earlier, from the same turf that nourished me, an adolescent of the Sioux Empire would have taken a forced sojourn in the wilderness. Warrior status was not a right, it had to be earned. An adolescent would have to survive alone for a month and return home with game. Like that of the potential warrior, my acceptance within my high school community was conditional upon my exploits of prowess on the field. In place of scalps, game, and ceremonial cuttings of the flesh, I proudly displayed my ribbons, medals, letter sweater and jacket. I, along with others, even took pleasure in bruises, lacerations, and splints.

Because each class numbered around 100, everyone except some of the farm kids who had to go home to do chores could make at least one of our teams. Moreover, sporting events were occasions of cultural cohesion. *The Pipestone Star* recorded every game with excessive detail and recognition. Whenever my name was mentioned in the newspaper's copy, the clipping found its way to my dresser mirror. After a victory, a walk down Main Street or a stroll after church on Sunday was sure to be met with such greetings as, "Neb, that was a darn fine game you played last Friday. Congratulations." Pipestone was not an impersonal megalopolis. Critics of our village heartland see only the heavy hand of social censure and not the support and nurture given to insecure adolescents.

To be sure, there were the old biddies who marked their calendars when a couple was to be married to see whether a baby came "too early." There also were party line telephones, where your business became *everyone's* business. Certainly one lived under an all-seeing collective eye. But that communal eye, however stern it might appear from the outside, wanted those within its view to succeed. No adult that I knew was jealous of any success I had. They rejoiced with me in my achievements, whether large or small, and they suffered with me when failure came.

My first public athletic performance was as a peewee tumbler at half-time during basketball season. John Davis, a social studies teacher, invited me to participate when I was in the third grade. We had colored T-shirts and shorts and, because I had the smallest pair, I had to use safety pins to keep them from falling off. We would drag pads onto the floor and do somersaults off a springboard, pyramids, flips, round-offs and a lot of other stuff. It was an excellent way to develop body coordination. Davis would start the program by doing a series of body flips from one end of the gymnasium to the other and end it by walking on hand stilts eight feet high.

In the fifth grade I joined a basketball team that played during half-time at the varsity games. We would hardly work up a sweat before it was time to quit. Each March we entered a round-robin tournament hosted by the YMCA in Sioux Falls. I especially wanted to win the year I was in eighth grade. We had won the traveling trophy twice, and with a third win we could keep it and have our names inscribed. Think of it! It would be in a glass cage in the school foyer where generations of future students would look upon it with awe.

That year, after two wins we were in the finals and were drinking malts the afternoon before the final game. In came Butch, a second-team scrub, with tears in his eyes. "Guess what," he stammered; "We're disqualified. An official checked our stats and two of our guys are too old." With that he broke down sobbing. The Sioux Falls School for the Deaf, our opponent, had checked the birthdays from the previous year against our present lineup and had found discrepancies. We had a good cry and left our malts unfinished. It was the greatest disappointment of my young life. Our coach, Marlin Sieg, had wanted to win even more than we did but several members of the team *were* over the age limit. Was it an honest mistake? We never knew, only that Sieg moved on after another year. We wanted that trophy more than anything else in the world. It was a long and silent ride back to Pipestone; the 60 miles seemed like 600.

The antics of my athletic peers were the high-school equivalent of a chapter out of John Belushi's *Animal House.* Whereas the innate modesty of girls necessitated that they have individual shower stalls with curtains, our showers and dressing rooms were entirely open and communal. Skylarking after practice or a game was usually at a fever pitch. Although we neither knew the meaning of, nor could spell the term, *testosterone,* our "can-you-top-this" and "whoop-de-do" machismo and razzmatazz was driven by its rising juices. There was considerable boasting of afternoon deeds, the flexing of muscles, and the snapping of towels at a teammates buttocks. When someone dropped the soap and leaned over to pick it up, there were loud squeals over his motives and his possible sexual orientation. Now and then some wise-acre would tuck his genitalia between his legs, cup his hands under his nipples, and squeal in a high falsetto: *"Here I am guys! Which one of you lucky fellas is going to take me out tonight?"* There were claims and counter-claims over who made the key play that won the game reverberating off the walls. If we lost there was considerable finger-pointing over the jerk who was the "Jonah" responsible for the defeat.

Like the judges calculating the contours of a 4-H Club member's yearling calf at the Pipestone County Fair, we cast critical eyes at the naked bodies of our teammates. The size of our genital "equipage" was on open display. The elect of our dressing room were those lads whose testosterone had kicked in early. Their libidos seemed to be coursing through their bodies like the incoming tide at the Bay of Fundy. The evidence of their masculinity was all too apparent: lots of pubic hair, daily shaving, deep voice, well-defined pectoral and deltoid muscles and, especially, in well-developed genitalia. All of our adolescent horniness under pressure produced a lot of silliness. Those who were "well-endowed" gloried in their superiority and strutted around like prize peacocks fluffing their fan of feathers on the manor lawn of an English lord. Once, a second string guard, Jim Little, came out of the shower with a long white shoe string tied around his penis. He tippy-toed around the dressing room, holding the string delicately between his fingers, telling everyone in a fairy-like voice, "I'm juss takin' the *dawg* out for a walk."

Alas, the more academically oriented athletes could not display their high I.Q. or G.P.A. with the élan and cockiness that others could do with their "private parts." There were claims and counter-claims as to whose "manhood" was most "manly." There were boasts of wild sensual escapades of who was "getting some" and which girls were "easy lays."

Andy claimed to know the most about a wide array of aphrodisiacs—his favorite was "The Bosom Caresser"—that were guaranteed to "heat-up" the girls. I gradually came to realize that most of the stories were fictitious and to suspect that those who did the most talking were in actuality the most timid with the opposite sex.

Nevertheless, many of us had enough hubris that we considered our own bodies to be the replication of Michangelo's *David*. Everyone seemed to be sorry for the poor guys whose genitalia were small. Alas, they had little control over their latent maturation. They were not unlike a farmer who had a field of late-germinating corn. In due time they too "would reap!" It seemed to me they usually dressed with their backs to their fellow jocks and usually were the first to exit the locker room.

Years later the truism of Arthur Miller's *Death of a Salesman* dawned on me; that is, those who give undue attention to the body beautiful, including the groin, and believe they can live off past athletic success, usually are deficient in developing the most important organ of all—the one that resides on the top of their shoulders.

Unlike today, the majority of boys during the Depression were not circumcised. Father felt the surgery was unnecessary and relegated it to the category of a religious rite. Moreover, he knew that medicine was not immune to cultural affectation and faddism, and he wanted to spare his patients a $15 bill for the procedure. Circumcision was not necessary if the rules of genital cleanliness were followed. It was a necessity that he impressed upon mothers and boys. During the Second World War there were countless occasions, in actual events and in novels, where male European Jews paid with their lives for being "sons of the covenant." When in doubt over whether a man was a Gentile or Jew, the Nazis simply made him drop his pants.

SUCCESS ON THE HARDWOOD

He sought the old scenes with eager feet—
The scenes he had known as a boy;
"Oh! for a draught of those fountains sweet,
And a taste of that vanished joy."
He roamed the fields, he mused by the streams,
He threaded the paths and lanes;
On the hills he sought his youthful dreams,
In the woods to forget his pains.
Oh, sad, sad hills; oh, cold, cold hearth!
In sorrow he learned the truth—

One may go back to the place of his birth—
He cannot go back to his youth

The Return, John Burroughs

By the time I had reached my senior year in high school, the memory of that crushing disappointment had faded. I still played basketball, but in the fall I devoted myself to football.

Although I could not articulate the experience then, in athletics I existentially felt the paradoxical truth of the Biblical phrase, "In whose service is perfect freedom." That is, I willingly accepted a difficult regimen, a form of dietary and physical servitude, as freely fulfilling the deepest urges of my nature. To follow the will and rule of my coach was my deepest joy. I had read that Napoleon boasted that he could make his soldiers face death for a piece of red ribbon. Like the warrior and the police officer, I, too, was willing to risk my physical integrity for a

Built in 1919 of Indiana limestone, Sioux quartzite, and brick, the Pipestone High School covered more than a city block. After being voted down twice, a 21 million dollar bond issue for a new school was passed in 1999. Many fear that this beautiful building may subsequently be demolished. An adolescent American culture seemingly does not prize its architectural artifacts as do more traditional European societies.

First Row: Walter Benjamin, Don Argetsinger, Dick Cheney, Don Steinmeyer, Willy Van Nieuwenhuyzen.
Second Row: Coach Moilanen, Art Krick, Don Earhart, Jack Sturdevant, Les Kallsen, Merton Dale, Manager.

Basketball

Basketball was my favorite sport because my speed and quickness made up for my lack of height. Like most athletes, we had a close and enduring bond. First row, left to right: Benjamin, Argetsinger, Chenney, Steinmeyer, VanNieuwenhuyzen. Second row, left to right: Coach Moilanen, Krick, Earhart, Sturdevant, Kallsen, Manager Dale.

snippet of colored fabric or a cheap piece of brass metal. I never missed a practice. My coach demanded that we rest before each game, abstain from smoking or drinking (a nonissue in my home), eat certain foods, drink a lot of water, and get nine hours of sleep at night. I obeyed him religiously.

In the Fall of 1943, our Pipestone Arrows football team was the conference champion. Our 8-1 record was the best since 1917. I was number 60, the second-string left end. There were 25 players on the team and, at that time, most of the starting team played both offense and defense. Even in shoulder pads, at 130 pounds I looked like a Lilliputian among giants in the team picture. Although I took a real beating in practice, I was never hurt. Many of the sophomores and juniors were larger than I; I was "on" but not "of" the team.

I usually got to play for a few minutes late in the third or fourth quarter when we were comfortably ahead. Once, against Flandreau, I caught a pass for a 30-yard gain and would have made a touchdown had I not slipped. My exploit was noted in *The Pipestone Star,* one of the few times it mentioned my name in football. I was happy when the winter snows brought basketball, for I was more at home on the hardwood than the gridiron.

On the afternoons before games I would rush home, lie down with my feet elevated, and attempt, always unsuccessfully, to get an hour's sleep. At exactly the proper time—two hours before the game—Mother would prepare two poached eggs on toast and hot tea. I would then go up to my room for a period of quiet time before walking to the gym. In the lingo of a later generation of athletes, I was "psyching myself up." I never apologized for my devotion to athletics. In a world history class, I came across the Duke of Wellington's famous assertion that "The battle of Waterloo was won on the playing fields of Eton."

My tumbling apprenticeship paid off handsomely in basketball. I was at home with my body and could feint, dribble and shoot well. As a forward on the varsity team, the Pipestone Arrows, I was always a starter during my junior and senior years. I compensated for my small stature (5'7", 130 pounds) with quickness and deception. I averaged 12 points a game. On the day of a game, we all strutted about school in our letter sweaters like male peacocks in full plumage. Some of my teammates gave their sweaters to their girlfriends. I was too bashful and feared being turned down. Besides, I wanted to wear it myself.

Don Argetsinger, at forward, was one of the other four starters. Argetsinger was always good for eight points. Don was a lean, greyhound-type athlete who moved with an easy fluidity. He was also an avid pheasant and duck hunter, who followed his father's career and became a Marine Corps "lifer." After 20 years in the Corps, he became a member of the Secret Service detail that guarded retired President Truman in Independence, Missouri. Don died of a heart attack in his 50s.

Our center, Don "Baldy" Steinmeyer, was our class president and the most popular male in our class. He was so normal, no one would have known he was the German Lutheran preacher's kid. "Baldy" had an "aw shucks" type of attitude and an infectious smile that curved up one side of his face. He was usually high point man. After a career in the FBI, Baldy joined the management of Coastal Oil Company.

Dick "Goose Neck" Cheney was one of the guards and a talented but often erratic, showboat-type of player who blew hot and cold. He was well named. His neck was twice the length of mine and came off his shoulders at a 30 degree angle. I lost track of "Goose Neck" after graduation, but I'm sure that his career fit the norm of our class and that he was very successful in his chosen field.

A Dutch kid, "Willy Van" Nieuwenhuyzen, who was a grade behind the rest of us, played the other guard spot. He had flexible knees that enabled him to feint and drive well; like "Crazy Legs" Hirsch, the famous *Wisconsin* halfback, his legs would signal to an opponent that he was headed one way when he actually went the other direction. He was the only player on the team who wore knee pads, considered an effeminate affectation in those days, and he took a lot of kidding about it. He also was the team's scapegoat, partly because in tight games he often would tried impossible "Hail Mary" shots from 40 feet out. Once he forgot his shorts and ran out on the court with only a jockstrap on. He had an unruly blond cowlick that he doctored with hair oil. We'd often have to yell, "Come on, the other team's already on the floor!" and drag him out of the bathroom where he was fussing with his hair.

We rotated captains for each game. Our coach would give the ball to the person chosen, who would dribble out of the locker room first and lead our team onto the floor. When I was chosen and the band played our school song as the crowd rose, screamed, and applauded, I had fire in my belly and felt like Paul Bunyan dribbling my way into heaven.

Our coach, Fred Moilanen, doubled as my social studies teacher. He was understanding and supportive but didn't know much about basketball. He taught us a few plays and before games he'd diagram some of them on the blackboard, but invariably, about 30 seconds into the game we had completely forgotten his instructions. Our game plan was simple: get open, screen, use the fast break whenever possible, never miss a lay-up, control the boards, hit the open man, accept with good grace the ref's bad calls, don't "hog" the ball, make the free throws. The index finger of Moilanen's right hand was off at the first joint, and we used to mimic him by gesticulating with a collapsed digit. That was before the extended middle finger became a popular sign of contempt.

Basketball in the 1940s was significantly different from today's game. Due to gas rationing, we played only 16 games, and our traveling team numbered only nine or ten players. Quarters were only eight minutes long, so the winning team rarely scored more than 35 points. The most popular outside shot was the two-handed set shot. The accepted form for free throws was underhand, lofting the ball with two hands starting from between the knees. Our fast break plays were effective, but driving the lane was a rare occurrence. Moilanen didn't tolerate any hot-doggers. I never saw Moilanen scream at the referee nor did any of us ever get a technical foul. But we celebrated our victories and suffered our defeats every bit as much as players do today.

Our uniforms were our school colors's, white and green. The tight-fitting tops and shorts, made of rayon and laundered and pressed by Mother after each game, were entirely different from today's baggy outfits with their bloomer trunks whose crotch resides at about knee-cap level. Every game began with an intense if secular prayer—all players joining hands in front of our bench—that ended, *"LET'S GO GET 'EM!"* I had great hopes for my senior year. We had a winning season and the Saturday-morning quarterbacks were picking us to go to the state tournament. Each weekend *The Star* had a 30-to 40-inch write-up of the previous Friday's game that was usually a great ego-booster for me. The report of our 43-33 victory over Worthington on March 10, 1944 is typical: "Pipestone, on the strength of Neb Benjamin's return to form after a lapse which had seen him go nearly scoreless the past two games, stepped into a big lead in the first quarter and was never headed. Benjamin got four buckets in the opening period and, though closely guarded thereafter, picked up two more and a free throw for second high honors of the evening."

Unfortunately, in the district tournament we lost to Luverne, 27-24 in the first round. Somebody had goofed, because it was a mistake to have the district's two strongest teams meet in the opener. But Cheney and Argetsinger were stone cold, having "choked" under the pressure of the tournament. *The Star* was right: "Benjamin and Steinmeyer were the only Arrows having much success in the scoring department, the former getting 10 points, the latter getting 8." I consoled myself that I had done my part. I tried to remember the comforting words of Grantland Rice: "When the One Great Scorer comes/to write against your name, /He marks not that you won or lost, /but how you played the game." It didn't help much.

Later, at the closing ceremonies, dressed in my letter sweater, I waited with a racing pulse. I hoped to salvage something in defeat by being named to the all-district team.

But because we were eliminated early, Pipestone had only one selection and it quite rightly went to Steinmeyer, our high-scoring center. Through misty eyes I congratulated Baldy, knowing that an important chapter of my life had ended and, on the way home, I committed myself to compensate for it in track.

SPIKES AND CINDERS

Track was my second most successful sport but, because of its individual character, did not foster the comradeship of basketball or football. There weren't even cheerleaders to spur me on. I competed in both track and field—the 440-yard dash and the broad jump (now the "long" jump), the pole vault, and the high jump. I came close to 15 feet in the broad jump but, because I had been practicing for years in my home-made dirt pit, the pole vault was my best event. I gave up my taped bamboo pole for the school's aluminum pole. It was rigid, unlike the flexible fiberglass poles that give such a tremendous advantage and height to today's vaulters. Eleven feet was an excellent vault then.

In those days, pole vaulters landed in sawdust or sand, not on foam cushions. Once in tenth grade while practicing alone in the evening, I landed with my instep on the edge of one of the boards that surrounded the sawdust pit. The pain was nearly unbearable and, because nobody was around, I had to crawl over a mile through the darkness to get home. I had torn ligaments and muscles up to my knee, and my leg was black and blue for two months.

Track was at a low ebb during my senior year. The school board, in a patriotic but ill-considered gesture, promised a high school diploma to anyone who enlisted in the Armed Services. As a result, many of my friends exchanged their gray sweats for Army khaki or Navy blue. Others broke training. Once we lost a key match with Worthington because our star sprinter ate half a dozen green bananas (they were hard to get in wartime) and vomited all over the track just before his first race.

To compensate for poor training regimens, we constantly experimented with fast-energy tonics made up of combinations of chocolate,

Karo syrup, honey, black-strap molasses and patent medicine elixirs. We carefully guarded our individual one-quart glass containers, which we'd periodically shake vigorously before taking a belt. For true believers, the more vile and nauseous the concoction, the more potency it had. After awhile I began to suspect that the strange concoctions were only placebos, because I never experienced the sudden burst of energy that my teammates testified their special brews gave them. I was told the secret was to drink it exactly at the right time, not too early and not too late, so that the stuff kicked into your system when you were running. But my "energy cells" never exploded during a race. My friends said I never had my timing right.

On a Saturday morning in May 1944, we squeezed into three cars and drove to the prestigious Carleton Relays in Northfield for my final track meet. Even though our team had been decimated by patriotic drop-outs, Coach Moilanen thought we would do well. He thought I would place in both the pole vault and broad jump. I was looking forward to getting a couple of medals to add to the ribbons above my dresser. It was a prelude to the more serious contest against the "Japs" and "Krauts" that I would undertake in a few months. As we drove onto the Carleton campus everything was strangely quiet. The place should have been teeming with athletes from all over southern Minnesota. The parking lot was empty and the doors to the gym were locked. Did someone goof? I began to feel faint and a heavy force pushed my body down into the car seat. I didn't have any tonic to cure what I felt.

Moilanen finally dug out the letter of invitation and discovered we had come ONE WEEK TOO EARLY! We got back into the cars and drove home in silence. Because of gas rationing, we couldn't return the following week. I had completed my final track meet a week earlier without realizing it. Our season had ended with a whimper rather than a bang, and I had been deprived of the sense of closure regarding another important chapter in my life. I felt cheated. Moilanen tried to make it up to us by buying us malts on the way home. Anger had all but closed off my stomach and I could only drink half of mine. Some of my teammates could have emptied their glasses but left them unfinished as a protest against the coach's stupidity. We didn't talk to him or to one another. It was a time-honored gesture with which the powerless strike back at the powerful. Pridefully, we wore our anger on our sleeves.

First Row: Luella Flynn, Daisy Wakefield, Frances Givens, Gladys Evans, Laura Chapman.
Second Row: Helen Engebretson, Florence K. Sacks ,Emma Mattill, Dorothy Wark, Elvera Meyer.
Third Row: Ruth A. Studt, Russell Hall, James Gladhill, Marjorie Bassett, Mildred Bertram.

First Row: Marion Colby, Byrma Jones, O. E. Knudtson, John Davis, Muriel Plowman.
Second Row: Milton Hollister, Margaret Lowe, Marie Kraus, Myrtle Holteen, Marian Schmit, Fred Moilanen.
Third Row: Noah I. Nelsen, Fred Walz, R. J. Knutson.

The Pipestone High School faculty, 1943-44. Upper Picture: Miss Daisy Wakefield (history) and Miss Gladys Evans (geography) are second and fourth from the left in the front row. Lower picture: Left to right, front row: Mrs. Colby (algebra), Miss Byrma Jones (Dean of Students), O.E. Knudtson (Superintendent), John Davis (Principal). Several teachers, including Mr. Robert Owens and Mr. James Figgy are absent.

While intellectual capabilities of our faculty were modest, their focus on academic fundamentals, rigorous standards and grading, and the enforcement of discipline was the seedbed for the future success of their students.

32. Memorable Pipestone Pedagogues

A teacher who can arouse a feeling for one single good action, for one single good poem, accomplishes more than he who fills our memory with rows on rows of natural objects, classified with name and form.

Elective Affinities, Johann Wolfang Von Goethe

By no stretch of the imagination could any of our teachers be classed as intellectuals. We held them in high regard, nevertheless, because of their vocation, their calling. It was their "being" more than their "doing" that impressed us. Moreover, paternalism and hierarchy were unquestioned paradigms in the Pipestone social cosmos. It never occurred to me to question the quality of their teaching. Because they were there they must have earned their status, and I had a duty to obey. No teacher's union brokered their interests, nor was their modest compensation out of harmony with their limited intellectual attainments. During the early 30s, high school teachers were paid $90 a month. As the Depression deepened, their salary was cut to $75. Along with clergymen they joined physicians and lawyers to form the four classical professions. But unlike the latter two groups, teachers did not especially "do well by doing good."

My teachers, nonetheless, had a sense of dedication and duty that many of their guild today seem to have lost. For the most part they did not deliver brillant lectures, yet they were good role models. They seemed not to mind that their private lives had to conform to the moral norm of the community. Contracts were simple and did not spell out minute legalistic "work to rule" details. I never knew a teacher who left school before 5 P.M. No one I knew moonlighted at a department store, although most sought summer employment. I never knew a teacher who felt abused or victimized by low compensation. To strike or threaten to strike was held to be beneath the dignity of the profession.

Most female instructors were either single or widowed and thus unencumbered by loyalties to husbands or children. They were secular nuns whose convent or priory was the school. When additional work was needed, they picked up the slack without additional compensation or complaint. They were visible in such community activities as church gatherings, service clubs, and athletic contests. Most continued in their profession because they enjoyed their subject matter and loved young people.

The school was prized because of community ownership. Real estate taxes, not state and federal monies, fueled the enterprise. State-mandated regulations were minimal. Roots were important, so everyone had to have courses in American and Minnesota history. Today's iron triangle of self-interested parties—state politicians, teacher's unions, and the state bureau of education—did not exist. Our school was a truly public, not a state institution. The school board, P.T.A. and local citizenry had built the facilities and controlled the ethos.

A focused and traditional curriculum based on the Western canon was in place. The pressures to turn the school into a service center that tried to correct all social pathology were minimal. Absent from my transcript were courses in "human relations," "physics for poets," "driver's education," "sex education," "peace studies," "learning about others," and "knowing yourself." We read Wordsworth and Shakespeare rather than pop novels; history rather than "touchy-feely" psychology. We were offered Latin, German, Spanish and solid offerings in physics, chemistry and advanced math. A common curriculum enhanced the roots of community at our school.

Teachers never asked me, "Neb, what do you *feel* about Franklin Delano Roosevelt, the Civil War, Bismarck, the French Revolution, or the Public Works Administration?" What right did I have to feelings about subjects of which I knew almost nothing? Our classes were made up of lectures that imparted information, not the pooling of ignorance through group dynamics. We had to learn the names of the presidents from Washington to FDR and know their major accomplishments and failures. We were indebted to an endless line of splendor that had gone before and we had to know that national and worldly genealogy. The stability of our world was reflected in a core curriculum. The center held firm. I was spared a fragmented education without coherence or substance. The nihilistic, existentialist, absurdist world view created by the Second World War and Vietnam did not yet exist.

There were few frills. When our school was damaged by a fire in l939, we met in lodge halls, the court house, and churches for a year until a bond issue provided funds to repair the old edifice. We did without guidance counselors, a media center, a hot-lunch program, police in the hallways, a swimming pool, photocopying machines, psychologists,

truant officers, metal detectors, blood and urine tests, courses for pregnant girls or nurseries for their babies.

Excluding the superintendent, principal, and dean of girls, 30 teachers covered our entire junior and senior high. Except for four Carleton
graduates and one each from Macalester, Gustavus Adolphus, and St.
Olaf, most of the faculty had bachelor of education degrees from the
state teachers' colleges in Mankato, St. Cloud, and Winona. Moreover,
the faculty was primarily matriarchal. Only 8 of the 30 were men, of
whom three were also coaches. The other five male teachers were in
chemistry, music, physics, industrial arts, and agriculture. They were
better than their academic pedigrees would have led one to believe.

I remember several teachers with a combination of fear, fascination,
and respect. Gladys Evans, the junior high principal who taught geography, was a heavy-bosomed, no-nonsense matron who strode the corri-
dors with the bearing of a monarch. Her demeanor combined the impe-
rious hauteur of a Queen Victoria with the gimlet-eyed severity of "big
nurse" in Ken Kesey's *One Flew Over the Cuckoo's Nest*. After a split second of looking into her eyes, you found yourself staring at your shoes.
She duplicated as well as any female could the war face of General
George S. Patton. Or was she an amalgam of a convent mother superior
and my Aunt Bessie? No matter. Her somber dress and gravel-like bari-
tone voice were so intimidating to any potential miscreant that she had
few discipline problems within her realm. She followed Joubert's maxim
that "Education should be gentle and stern, not cold and lax." Strangely
enough, I did not fear her and flourished under her high standards.
State and national capitals, rivers, forests, oceans, mountains, valleys,
plains, boundary lines, coal and iron fields, and more were labeled on a
map and then transferred to an indelible impression in my mind. I loved
geography.

After a few weeks I could draw a freehand outline of the United
States, with the state divisions, capitals and major cities. In time, the
same was true of the globe. Geographical count-downs, unlike spelling
bees, usually found me at the head of the class, and I inwardly gloated
over the long list of gold stars by my name on the chart at the front of
the classroom. Miss Evans planted the seed that in later years flowered
into my love of travel. I longed to visit the thousands of places I had
studied. This was reinforced by *The National Geographic*. Mother faithfully kept every back copy and on rainy weekends I would spend hours
poring through them. My fascination for "far-away places with strange
sounding names" began with Miss Evans.

But my most impressive junior high teacher was Daisy Wakefield. She was a hunched-over "maiden lady," 50ish, stringy-haired; a female version of Ichabod Crane. She had nothing in common with today's all too familiar, Kotter-type, jokester teacher whose superficial knowledge of subject matter is rationalized away by a *"I just love kids"* mantra. Sometimes during her excitement in lecturing she "misted" any pupil within five feet of her. Once after John Frahm got sprayed, he had the temerity to ask, "Miss Wakefield, do you furnish towels?" Surprisingly, she took it in good grace.

Miss Wakefield knew her American history like a 4-H Club member knows his prize heifer. I memorized the places, names, battles, arms, strategies, forts, and forces of the Revolutionary War to perfection. History was high drama. Like Ezekiel's desert of dry bones taking on flesh, under Miss Wakefield's instruction Jacques Cartier, Samuel de Champlain, Marquise de Montcalm, James Wolfe, and the French voyageurs came alive. She described in vivid detail Burgoyne invasion from Canada, Benedict Arnold's duplicity, Washington's crossing the Delaware on Christmas eve to route the Hessians, the final victory at Yorktown, and much more. Miss Wakefield put maps on the wall depicting the French and English struggles in Canada, the Revolutionary War, Westering pioneers, the Civil War, the Minnesota Territory, and the Oregon Trail. Her pointer traced with strokes of a bright red crayon the rivers, mountains, and deserts that our heroes of the American Experiment had traversed. Her glowing spirit, enthusiasm and determination were a microcosmic reflection of the energy that had shaped these momentous events. She gave me the facts, strategy, and set the historical stage. I added the wonder.

Miss Wakefield had a large store of moralisms that she dispensed as regularly as my parents gave me my weekly allowance. She trotted them forth with all the solemnity of the Vicar of Rome releasing a papal encyclical: "Order is everything." "Perfection is golden." "Keep chaos at bay." "Think before you speak,." "Speak only in sentences." "If something is worth doing, it is worth doing well." Long before Professor Kingsfield warned in *The Paper Chase,* "You come here with a skull full of mush, and, if you survive, you will leave thinking like lawyers," Miss Wakefield told us that "an untrained mind is like oatmeal. If you want to be successful you must read great literature and write with precision."

Miss Wakefield's narrative of our collective past was establishment history. To question the idealism and heroism of our Founding Fathers was unthinkable. Their patriotic genealogy was respectfully traced through the War of 1812, the Mexican, Civil, Spanish-American, and First

World Wars. We did not poke holes in the robes of the American royalty. We did not look for fleas on the coats of our nobility. We committed to memory passages from the texts of our Civil Religion—the Pilgrim's "Mayflower Compact," "The Declaration of Independence," Washington's "Farewell to his Troops," Lincoln's "Gettysburg Address" and "Second Inaugural," and selected passages from the addresses of Teddy Roosevelt and Woodrow Wilson. The more I read and pondered, the more our American Experiment took on the character of a holy pilgrimage.

Little was said about the holocaust involving the Native American, his disappeance under the avalanche of immigrants rolling westward seeking homesteads. There simply hadn't been time for a "primitive" people and those of European ways to adjust to each other. Nor did we see the underside of Manifest Destiny, repent of our complicity in slavery, or study how an urban proletariat often became the raw material exploited by a laissez-faire industrialism. The historical dark side of our beloved nation's rise to greatness was passed over. Our captains of industry were *Builder* Barons not *Robber* Barons. Our lessons saw the sunshine and not the shadows. Three decades later the national shame resulting from our behavior in Southeast Asia, the Watergate scandal, racial conflict and other national traumas would produce throngs of revisionist historians who took delight in seeing the somber side of our national past. Could there ever be a balance?

To be sure, the intricacies of historiography and philosophies of history were beyond Daisy Wakefield. The anti-establishment, revisionist historians, and psychohistorians had not yet appeared in the graduate schools to produce a generation of teachers cynical about our national inheritance. Bizarre and titillating episodes in the lives of the founders were happily discovered, and their genius of character and contributions were minimized. "Tradition," the *living* faith of the dead, became portrayed as "Traditionalism," the *dead faith* of the living. Peccadilloes such as George Washington's padding his expense account, Benjamin Franklin's womanizing in Paris, and Thomas Jefferson's supposed fathering of a child via a mulatto maid were uncovered gleefully. The marginal became center-stage. The angle of vision determined what one saw. National legends and ideals were dying, but there were precious few principles to take their place.

I came to see that it is dangerous to destroy traditional values and role models in the minds of adolescents. Not only may they not rally to the defense of the American Experiment in a time of crisis, but I believe such children may harbor attitudes of distrust and suspicion regarding life, our laws and institutions for the remainder of their lives.

The Daisy Wakefields were legion in the 30s and 40s. With marriage and children not an option, they sublimated their energy into nurturing the minds of youth. They held high academic and moral standards. They preferred being respected to being loved. No teacher I knew wanted to be a buddy or pal to his students. Once in shop class, Mr. Russell Hall shouted at a student and turned a drafting table into kindling with a blow from his fist. He wanted discipline, not emotional bonding with his students. He wanted to turn out craftsmen who respected his tools and returned them to their place. He taught me how to create simple but useful objects out of wood and metal.

I never heard a student address a teacher by his or her first name. At class reunions 30 years later, we still greeted them as "Miss Wakefield," "Mrs. Colby," "Miss Jones," "Mr. Owens" etc. My female teachers probably would have laughed at the charge that they were imprisoned by male chauvinists, that it took a feminist movement to release them from their unconscious fetters. They controlled their turf and wrote indelibly on the minds of youth. Others may have had *greater force,* but did anyone else have greater *power?*

It was in math that I really suffered. Mrs. Marion Colby was a prim and conscientious Macalester graduate, under whom I struggled with algebra, geometry and trigonometry. In spite of her competence in the classroom, Mrs. Colby was a divorcée and, therefore, assumed to bear a stain on her character. Only a few educational "insiders" knew this fact. But because of this moral trespass, Mrs. Colby was on probation for six years. I rejoiced in my Cs but often got Ds. She usually was erasing the board—and the answer—while I was still copying down the problem. My grades might have been even lower except that Mother and Mrs. Colby were members of a sisterhood. It must have been an embarrassment for my parents to socialize with some of my teachers. Teachers are often uneasy in the company of parents whose children are dull. I suspect that with Mrs. Colby, the conversation must have been restricted to the war, weather, and the winning football team.

Keith Thorndyke, who sat directly ahead of me, was the mathematical genius I longed to be. Besides, he could whistle and hold a tooth pick in his mouth at the same time. Upon graduation he entered the Army Air Force as a navigator and lost his life aboard a B 26 medium bomber when it took a direct hit over Normandy.

James Figgy, my 12th grade physics teacher, was a baldheaded, perpetually smiley man in his 50s who, because of the war, had been recycled from 20 years of teaching 8th grade general science. He was stuffy, dull, and hopelessly out of date—an incompetent pedagogue, albeit a genial one. He wore conservative vested suits with neckties set firmly against the collar buttons of his primly starched white shirts. His bald pate was always shiny. Under Figgy we continued to do the same dreary experiments of four years earlier. He pumped air out of a tin can under water and we watched it collapse. We lit a candle under a glass globe and watched the flame slowly die out. He had half a dozen scientific commandments he repeated ad nauseum: "Remember students," he'd state, "for combustion to take place, three things are *always* necessary—heat, oxygen, and an organic substance." The fact that some of his graduates went on to major in science in college was due to their Pipestone grit and gumption rather than his tutelage. Perhaps he missed his calling and should have been an undertaker. He always dressed in a black suit, wore a fixed grin, and had gracious manners.

A lifelong bachelor, Mr. Figgy enjoyed squiring the unattached female teachers around in his long black Packard. Once when we were in junior high, Johnny Corcoran found a used condom at the edge of a field where we had played football. At first I didn't know what a "rubber" was, but I soon figured it out as my buddies began to fantasize about which faculty pair might provide the greatest amusement if "discovered in the weeds." Some of my friends made crude jokes about Figgy, how comical it would be to catch him in the back seat of his car with a pretty grade school teacher in a compromising situation. It would never have happened. Pipestone was not a depression-era Payton Place. He was always the gentleman. But he was miscast as a science teacher. I knew something was wrong when I saw him rub snow and ice on the frost-bitten fingers of children.

Robert Owens, from whom I took biology and aeronautics, was one of my favorite teachers. Owens had had a hard life, having lost his right arm in a motorcycle accident as a young man. He wore a wooden prosthesis that ended with a leather glove on it. He told us of the pain and the heavy doses of morphine that had eaten away at the enamel of his teeth. But he knew his subject matter and would tolerate no skylarking in class. He would throw erasers and chalk at those who slept. Once he bounded off the podium, wound up his only good arm and hit Don Argetsinger across the face for sassing him. "How does that feel?" he asked. "Not too bad," an unrepentant Don answered. Owens clobbered him again with twice the force and repeated the question. "That hurt," was the meek response, "and I'm sorry." There were no behavior problems the rest of the term. No one thought of lawsuits in those days. Student miscreants deserved whatever teachers gave them. It was a law of the Pipestone cosmos.

Aeronautics was a new elective because of the war, and it was my most interesting course. The principles of flight and International Morse Code helped me when I entered the Navy Air Corps. Later, Owens left teaching and became the Registrar of Deeds of Pipestone County, married, sired four children, became a pillar of the Methodist Church, and helped found the annual Hiawatha Pageant that brought national notoriety to Pipestone.

Unlike today, high schools in the Depression were not tortured by issues of Church and State. A subtle canopy of Christian morality over-laid our town and school. Baccalaureate services were held in the high school auditorium the day before graduation and all the seniors, their parents, and relatives attended. There were no atheist or agnostic "free spirits" who felt the occasion straight-jacketed their religious autonomy or who desired to use the occasion for a *cause celebre* to sue the school. The Pipestone clergy cooperated in planning the service and participat-ed in turn. At that time no one would have dreamed that this ecumenical celebration might in the future be banned because it violated the Constitution or that it constituted an "establishment of religion."

Moreover, I participated in an active 30-member high school YMCA, or Hi-Y, group that was made up of some of the best students and ath-letes. The advisor was usually the football or basketball coach and the membership was organized into five standing committees. Our 1943 Hi-Y pledge was: "To create, extend, and maintain Christian principles throughout the school and community, which is a very good policy for any organization in this war-torn world. Each member is required to live up to certain standards made in the club which are called the 'Four C's': *Clean Living, Clean Speech, Clean Sports and Clean Scholarship.*"

Each meeting consisted of a few prayers, moral exhortations by some of our favorite teachers, and ended with some "horse play." Our Hi-Y sponsored scrap drives that collected over 2,000 pounds of copper, brass, and bronze. It also planned school dances and parties, and printed basket-ball programs, which we sold to the audience. In 1943 we purchased a service flag for graduates serving in the military. On April 22, 1942 we helped sponsor a conference whose theme was, *"The Role of Christian Youth in War Time."* The Worthington Hi-Y, the Flandreau and Pipestone Indian Schools, the Jasper High School, Girl Reserves and Leagues, and church groups attended. The speaker was Dr. Frank Eversull, President of the North Dakota State Agricultural College at Fargo.

Tragically, the ethos of accommodation between religion and public schools of my adolescence is now over. *"Freedom For"* religion, the philosophy of our Founding Fathers, has of late been interpreted by the Supreme Court as *"Freedom From"* religious expression. In the late 1940s some secularists and anti-Catholic Protestants founded Protestants and Other Americans United for Separation of Church and State (POAU). Now almost 60 years later as we enter the new millennium, religion that was communal and supportive of the common good has been compressed in expression to but hearth and home.

First Row: Henry Appeldorn, Leroy Nelson, Paul Ashton, Art Krick, Leslie Kallsen, Fred Dahl, Don Nelson, Don Earhart.
Second Row: John Pinnell, Glenn Ressmeyer, Lloyd Thorndyke, Bill Krick, Gilmore Tostengard, Gerald Melcher, Reed Hart, Walter Benjamin.
Third Row: Willis Van Nieuwenhuyzen, Bob Cook, John Frahm, Don Steinmeyer, Doug Stillwell, Don Argotsinger, Dick Cheney

The 1943-44 YMCA (HiY) of Pipestone High School. During my youth the zone of cooperation between churches and the school, religious faith and morals and public expression was encouraged. Today radical church-state "separationists" are usually successful in elimination of any semblance of religous expression in the public sphere. The author is on the far right, second row.

Today the hyper-sensitive are zealous over their "rights." Autonomy often takes preference over the celebrative occasions of the majority. During the past 60 years the United States has suffered a subtle de-Christianization, due to a growing state atheism under the guise of pluralism and multiculturalism. Our courts seem to be turning themselves into the enemies of even private religious expression. But avoiding government-coerced belief is far different from suppressing the religious beliefs and practices of students. Alas, the desire to be secular on the part of even one individual student can trump the desire of a thousand to be exposed to religion. This would be a great surprise to George Washington, who endorsed religious belief in his farewell address as an "indispensable support for political prosperity." What has been lost, of course, is the precious communal and cultural center. American public space is increasingly barren of collective expressions of praise, repentance, celebration, and thanksgiving. Our civic sphere has been rendered sterile and sanitized.

How tragic that when someone today stands on "their rights," the end result is a diminishment of freedom for the majority. Holistic and centripetal forces wane while centrifugal movement and anti-clericalism is increasing. We are all sail and no anchor. Diversity now often means division and divisiveness and the ideal of an American "melting pot" is now turning into a "tossed-salad." *Factionalism*—the societal virus our founding fathers knew to be the disease that destroyed democracies—is on the increase. Alas, our national motto—*e pluribis unum* ("out of many, one"), has been inverted to mean a "Nation of Factions." It is not far from the truth that at the local level the Pledge of Allegiance to the flag is about the only bond we share; at the national level, our cardinal celebratory event seems to be the Super Bowl.

Throughout high school I was a middling if indifferent student, resting in the middle of the bell-shaped curve and moving through the educational shadows unheralded and unrecognized. My grades were barely respectable and oscillated between the low 90s in history and social studies and the high 70's and low 80s (75 and below was an F) in math and chemistry. I wondered whether the grades might even have been lower had Father not been a pillar of the community.

Of course, the Depression was a time before our present two-grade system of giving only A's and B's. Teachers ran our school and neither feared nor were intimidated by parents or students. Their grading system conformed to the symmetrical Gaussian curve: the number of A's could not exceed the number of F's. The same was true with B's and D's. The educators' job was to have us master the subject matter, not to improve our self-image or esteem.

English was also a problem for me. A wag would have said I had diarrhea of the mouth and constipation of ideas when my hand held a pen. I would go to my room, pull out the one-and-a-half foot draw-bridge desktop that came out of the rock maple book case, and sit for hours with my head in my hands. Assigned an essay of 400 words, I was a fair representation of the chimpanzee sitting before a typewriter wondering how best to start work on *Hamlet*. I wondered whether a gene was malfunctioning, or if the blood flow was weak to the part of my brain that dealt with creativity in writing. I would type a sentence or two, only to tear it out of the typewriter, crumple it up, and begin again. The wastepaper basket would be full before I completed the first page. Like Midas hovering over his gold coins, I counted my precious words time after time and added conjunctions, articles, and modifiers to get closer to that magical number of 400. Mother, so helpful with my incapacity regarding spelling in grade school, wisely kept her distance and let me suffer alone. Today there's doubtless an esoteric medical term for my condition of writer's block, plus special help and perhaps even a monthly government Supplemental Social Security entitlement check for such a "disability."

Compared to the student exposure to the world today via the Internet, educational horizons during the Depression were very circumscribed. Every ninth grade class, however, looked forward to the spring "field trip" to Sioux Falls. We toured a trinity of wonders—the Morrell Packing Plant, the South Dakota Penitentiary, and the South Dakota School for the Deaf. Although the population of Sioux Falls was only 35,000, through the prism of farm and village adolescents, it seemed to be a gargantuan metropolis. Our visit in 1940 coincided with Republican Wendell Wilkie's presidential campaign visit and some of us were close enough to touch his car as his motorcade drove through town.

Our class looked down on the Morrell slaughtering floor from the second floor. There were no guardians to protect adolescent sensitivity in those days. Cattle were closely wedged together by movable walls, then "cold-cocked" by men wielding sledge hammers, then skinned and cut into quarters. Twenty hogs were "dispatched" for every Hereford. Hogs huddled in a large pen and then were flicked persuasively, a few at a time, into a smaller chamber, where a man fixed a hook to one of their hind legs. Then they rose in the air suspended from the railway of death. Lordy, did they scream. A wise-acre classmate said they were "crying for their mothers and promised not to be bad little piggies any more."

The tackle-man pushed them on their backs over to a brick-floored passage where the "sticker," dressed in a yellow slicker like a Maine lobster-man, gave them the coup de grace. His knife went through the throat as if it were made of butter and suddenly, the full-voiced shriek ended in a sputter as the bottom third of the butcher's slicker turned to scarlet. Other "stickers" waded through the gore in their Wellington boots while squeezing it into underground containers where it would be processed into adhesives, medicines, and paint.

On the way home there was a hilarious incident that helped shorten the ride and added to the collective memory bank of our class. Dick Cheney, a friend and fellow basketball player, had over-indulged with Coke Cola and malted milk. The result? Dick was in agony due to a full bladder but was too embarrassed to ask the driver to stop the bus. Sensitivities were near the surface during that era and Dick may have been afraid of being kidded by his female classmates. Or, perhaps in drought-stricken Dakota, there were not enough bushes to ensure privacy. In any event, some sensitive soul handed him an empty coffee can and Dick took a pee in that.

Up until then the girls had been unaware of Dick's predicament since, like the whites in the South, they sat in the front half of the bus. Dick's urinary capacity was astounding. It seemed like he would never finish. I worried that a female classmate might turn around and scream when she saw what he was doing. Dick reminded me of one of Bert Vander Slice's prize stallions. Finally, he let out a hugh sigh and buttoned his fly. The two quart can was filled right to the brim.

Dick was precariously balancing the can on his lap. We wondered whether he would be able to maintain control if the bus hit a chuck hole As the decibels of our kidding and skylarking rose, it seemed that momentarily our female classmates, too, would discover his amazing feat. With the smell of his urine beginning to waft through the bus, Dick suddenly flung the can out an open window.

Alas, Mr. Figgy's general science class had not taught Dick about the physics of air pressure, partial vacuums, and vectors. Since it was a hot day, all of the windows of the bus were open and at least half of Dick's piss swept back into the bus and sprayed over those in the rear third of the seats. We were doubled-up with laughter all the way back to Pipestone. I tried to bring some solace to those unfortunate enough to have been showered with urine by relaying some of my Father's medical wisdom; that is, normal urine is sterile. That did not help with the aesthetics in this case, since it was before the invention of Hand-i-wipes.

The School Board in 1944. Father is seated, fourth from the left; Superintendent O.E. Knudtson is standing at the left. Our school then was truly public. Local tax revenues supported the enterprise and policies were established by the board. Today, control has pasted to an "iron triangle—teacher's union, the state department of education, and federal and state politicians. Critics call them "state" or "government" schools.

33. Mentoring Under a Dutch Farmer

To lift up the hands in prayer gives God glory, but a man with a dung-fork in his hand, a woman with a slop-pail, give Him glory too. He is so great that all things give Him glory if you mean they should. So then, my brethren, live.

An Address on St. Ignatius, Gerard Manley Hopkins

He sees not that sea of trouble, of labour,
and expense which have been lavished on this farm.
He forgets the fortitude, and the regrets.

J. Hector St. John de Crevecoueur,
Sketches of Eighteenth-Century America

When I turned 13, Father, disappointed with my horticultural labors at home, decided that it would be good experience for me to board, room, and work for a farm family. I think he wanted to relive his adolescent experience through me. He had a romantic image of the rural life that often comes to those whose who idealize the positive aspects of childhood experience but minimize their occasional harshness. Had he looked into my eyes, he would have seen deep apprehension. However stern my home environment was, I had a fierce attachment to it. The very thought of being placed on unknown soil with an anonymous family, with indeterminate obligations and a certainty of homesickness, terrified me.

One evening we drove out to a couple of farms operated by patients of Father. After pleasantries, he asked whether they needed an extra hand. I'm sure they wanted to accommodate their physician but, after looking at my Lilliputian stature, they politely declined. They knew I would be more trouble than I was worth. I would not enhance their bottom line, would be underfoot, perhaps would even be injured or killed. But my reprieve did not last long.

In the early 1930s, Father purchased a 240 acre farm two miles south of Ruthton and 18 miles from Pipestone for $27.50 an acre. He followed

Grandad Bedell's advice: "Land is the best investment. God only made so much of it. It can't burn down, it never needs painting, and it can't be stolen from you. Remember, people always have to eat." He picked a stolid Dutch family by the name of Vander Slice as the new tenants, and they were only too happy to accede to the pleasure of their new landlord. I suspect they knew I wouldn't eat much and could possibly provide a diversion for their two youngest children.

In March, 1926, the year I was born, Bert Vander Slice, along with six other "Hollander" families from Edgerton had taken a celebrated "immigrant train" to Lebanon, South Dakota. Each family had purchased land "sight-unseen" from John Miller, a "shifty" land agent, who "sold the earth by quarters." The train consisted of 12 freight cars with a passenger car and sleeper "so the families could enjoy the modern comforts of the trip." It hauled their entire belongings, including their meager farm equipment and livestock. Four "helpers" along with 20 children accompanied the Dutch couples. "All hope that these pioneers," stated *The Edgerton Enterprise,* "will be happy and prosper in their new home." Everyone looked forward with hope to a rosy future.

Alas, even the world-renowned, agricultural genius of Hollander farmers could not overcome the arid conditions and marginal soil of the South Dakota prairie. Conditions were Spartan. The snow and dust blew through their weather-beaten shacks, and prairie fires were a constant threat to their crops. Without barns the livestock had to be milked outdoors and stabled in "lean-tos" during the winter. Water was secured by means of a shallow well dug by a post auger.

After a sojourn of eight years and only four miserable crops, Bert succumbed to the drought and grasshoppers. Along with 10 other families, he swallowed his pride and returned to his roots in southwestern Minnesota.

Adding to his woes economic laws turned topsy-turvy during the Depression as corn and wheat prices plummeted and interest rates skyrocketed. Legions of farmers were sucked under in the surging waves of land speculation as land ownership rolled and shifted from farmer to insurance company to bank to landlords. Bert had been taught a stern lesson by mother nature and the financial machinations he didn't understand. He was the Minnesota version of the Joads in Steinbeck's *Grapes of Wrath*—an agricultural proletarian who lost his land. Like Pa Joad he wandered, suffered, and endured. His survival was itself a form of triumph.

"For every atom lost to the sea, the prairie pulls another out of the decaying rock," wrote A. Leopold in *Sand Country Almanac.* "The only truth is that its creatures must suck hard, live fast, and die often, lest its losses exceed its gains." Vander Slice had sucked hard as the South Dakota prairie turned to desert. But it wasn't enough and his family was destitute.

Bert looked over our farm and wondered whether he should accept Father's invitation. He discovered that seven farm families were making a living off a section of land a few miles to the north. "If seven families can do that on 640 acres," Wilber Dick, Bert's oldest son remembered him saying, "Certainly I can succeed on 240 acres." But his South Dakota ordeal had left deep wounds—scars that made him both wiser and more timid. "I never want to be on my own again," he said fiercely, "Thank God, your Father came along and saved my family." For 19 years Father and Bert had a wonderful relationship based on common values, the bond ended with Bert's retirement because of ill health.

The term "landlord" in classic as well as contemporary literature is one fraught with negative connotations. Happily, Father was as far from being a slumlord as one could be. "The name Benjamin must never be linked to that which is shoddy or run down," he reminded me. "It's a matter of stewardship." Acting on his credo, he replaced the barn that was in imminent danger of collapsing. A new hog house, and improvements to the farmhouse, silo, granary, fencing, and wind break, quickly followed. Father took an active interest in the construction—again, I believe he was reliving his youth—and he picked out the shrubs, evergreens and deciduous trees for the grove.

The sloughs and potholes on the farm were drained by laying thousands of feet of tile. Tiles were 12-inch, fired-clay cylinders of varying diameter that were laid end-to-end in a gently sloping trench and then buried. A grade of two inches to a rod (16.5 ft.) was enough to carry standing rain water to a dredge ditch. The ancestors of Vander Slice were the world's best soil engineers in their struggle to maximize the productivity of their precious Dutch soil. But it was a mystery to me how the water percolated through the soil and into the tile. Yet, the invisible spider-web lines of tile "drew" the water, dried the soil, and enabled Vander Slice to get into the fields with machinery or horses a day or two after a heavy downpour. Magically, tile produced prosperity—more bushels per acre of a better crop, year after year, wet or dry. Today drainage tiles are long snakes of plastic tubing that require less labor and are easier to install, but are less romantic overall.

When all the improvements were finished, Father had doubled the farm's value. At that point, Father offered to sell it to Bert. But Vander Slice still demurred. He was doing well without much risk.

I felt bad that the Vander Slices probably took me on as a field hand out of gratitude to my Father. My apprehension increased when I compared my small stature and skinny arms and legs with their Charles Atlas-type builds. I regretted not having ordered that weightlifting set from *Popular Mechanics*. I inwardly repented of all the farmer jokes I had told in school. Now I was on their turf. My polyglot "Heinz 57" genetic inheritance put me at a disadvantage compared with what they'd received from their Dutch genes. It would be a gruesome summer. I would be an alien in an unfriendly land and the butt of "city slicker" jokes.

There were legions of "Hollanders" in the county. In fact, the town of Holland was only seven miles northeast of Pipestone. Many of my classmates were "Vander" something-or-other. Along with the Germans, they were blue-ribbon farmers, hard workers, and deeply religious. Their barns were often more impressive and immaculate than their homes. Once a Dutch farmer's wife, in order to get out of a squalid home, moved all the furniture into the barn when her husband was in town. "I'm living here until you promise to house your family as well as you do your hogs and cattle." she demanded when he returned. She had her new home in six months.

The Vander Slices had four children—boy, girl, girl, boy. The gender assignment of work was not rigid. While the daughters usually helped their mother inside the home, they also helped with the milking. If they were needed in the field they helped there, plowing corn, putting up hay, and shocking grain. The house was pre Rural Electrical Association (R.E.A.) that is, without electricity. Water was secured from an outside well and a hand pump in the kitchen sink. A two-hole outhouse was screened by a couple of lilac bushes in back and, ironic as it might seem, the toilet paper came from an old Montgomery Ward catalogue. A screen of non-descript ash, cottonwoods, and box elder trees northwest of the farm buildings served as a modest barrier to winter winds and snow. Groves also served as dump-yards where a farmer's discarded implements were placed to rust away. During the summer you couldn't spot an untidy farmer, but from November through May, without the shelter of leaves, his detritus was there for every passer-by to tut-tut about. Fortunately, the scrap drives of World War II cleaned up most groves.

Fearing the worst, I moved in with the Vander Slice family and slept with Buddy, the youngest son, in an upstairs bedroom. Morning chores began at 5:00 A.M. with Bert's gruff wakeup call to his oldest son, "Wilbur Dick, Wilbur Dick." He didn't have to call twice. We would pull

A 1997 photo of the Ruthton, Vander Slice farm home. "Buddy" and I shared a second floor bedroom and arose each morning at 5:00 A.M. to milk cows. The house was in better condition in the late 1930s.

ourselves out of bed, light kerosene lamps if needed, and drag them and ourselves 200 feet out to the barn. The 25 Guernsey cows would be waiting to be let into the barn, mooing in pain from their distended udders and pleading for relief. The Guernseys came in through the south door, a cow named Sharon always in the lead, and each cow would peal off at its own stanchion with the kind of stateliness of Pipestone Methodists taking their pews. Besides milking their assigned cows, every family member had specific tasks—giving a coffee-can full of supplement to each cow, throwing hay down from the haymow, forking hay to each cow, washing the udders.

The oldest and strongest hands squeezed the most and toughest teats. Wilber Dick and Bert each milked seven cows morning and night. Their Popeye-the-Sailor-man hands and forearms were like iron hams. Even Mrs. Vander Slice and the oldest daughter milked three or four cows apiece. Each cow had a name, knew her own stanchion and was always milked by the same person, who knew her idiosyncratic behavior.

They started me with Ramona, saying she was an "easy milker." After five minutes my arms felt like lead, the bottom of my pail was barely covered, and someone else had to finish her. Squeezing a three inch teat to produce a solid stream of milk was much harder than it looked. I had to learn to make a fist starting with my thumb and forefinger and grind my fingers together, while at the same time pulling down vigorously on the teat. Ramona did not enjoy having a neophyte mess with her private parts. She would turn and look at me, conveying a disturbed message with her brown eyes: "Whatever did I do to deserve this? This guy is playing with a delicate part of my anatomy without relieving my painful udder at all." Ramona retaliated by letting go with a steaming arc of urine or a soft cowpie in the gutter that splashed up on my pants.

My ineptitude provided the Vander Slices with great amusement. I became even more flustered when a neighbor farm kid suggested I should return to Pipestone and practice stroking the breasts of some of my female classmates. Then, when I became proficient, I could transfer my new-found skill back to Ramona. I cursed my Father for my predicament. It was going to be a long summer.

I found it difficult even to assume the proper milking position. I had to sit on an 8-inch high wooden stool supported by a single 4-by-4 inch leg, hold the pail between my legs, and rest my head against Ramona's flank. I lived in constant fear of being stepped on, stung by Ramona's swishing tail, or splashed and spattered by Ramona's piss and dropping cowpies. Wilbur Dick joked that he could tie a brick to the end of Ramona's tail if that would help. I longed for the simple garden and lawn chores back at 808 Third Avenue. But after two weeks my hands toughened up and I could milk Michelle as well as Ramona. Four or five cats would usually gather in the barn during milking, and every once in awhile I would squeeze a stream of milk in their direction. It was amazing how they could keep their mouths open and drink a stream of milk without gagging.

Cows feeding on grass, especially in the spring, tend toward a "looseness of the bowels," to put it politely. The tail of a cow, being located in close proximity to the elimination process, would sometimes get, to put it delicately, a little on the "mucky" side. Having that appendage wrapped around my neck during milking was not an experience that caused me to look favorably on the vocation of dairying. Because old unventilated barns become stuffy and hot during the summer, sometimes a "recalcitrant" cow, such as Amanda, was milked outside while crowded up against a fence in the cow yard.

One of the more humorous experiences of my milking internship occurred when Dutch, a Vander Slice relative, tried to milk "Mandy." But Mandy was a restless critter and kept moving away a step at a time. Dutch was left sitting on a one-legged stool, the pail scissored between his knees, his outstretched hands grabbing empty air. Mandy looked around, took aim, and belched. A greenish-yellow stream squirted from her rear end. Dutch was just leaning over to pick up the milk stool with one hand and had the pail in the other. His bib overalls gapped wide open. Mandy's timing and aim were perfect. Slowly Dutch lowered the milk pail and then the stool. With ever so much care he continued to lean forward as he slowly unbuckled his overalls. *But the trickle was already starting down each pant leg!* He slipped out of them with as much grace as the situation would allow and headed for the horse tank. Only after Bert and Wilber Dick started to laugh did I dare to join in.

An active milking barn has a most exotic, addicting perfume. The warm, moist aroma arising from the cows and horses, combined with whitewash, stale milk, sweet hay, fermenting silage, cow and horse urine, and manure launch a formidable and fascinating assault on virgin nostrils. In time, that unique blend comes to have an almost pleasing bouquet. And though long cobwebs festoon rafters and windows, the sounds of a barn are comforting to the ear. The noises—cows chewing their cud, soft moos, subdued neighing, streams of milk beating a rhythmic tattoo, and even a gush of urine and a periodic plop of manure hitting the trench—suggest that the animals might be communicating with you at some primordial level.

The milk was carried to the separating room where a hand-cranked separator spun off the lighter cream from the milk. The hogs were then "slopped" with the skim milk, and the containers of cream were kept cool in the horse tank until they were picked up by the creamery truck. Sometimes containers of cream, milk, and butter were placed on the cool concrete floor of the house or placed in galvanized buckets and lowered into the well to just above the water level. Woe to him whose knot slipped and spilled everything into the water!

Almost every Minnesota village of 300 or more had a creamery that serviced farms within a radius of three to five miles. The cream was churned in large cylindrical tubs with interior baffles. Through a curved side window, I could see large masses of butter gradually forming on the baffles. When the churning was finished, a dairy attendant would reach into the tub with his bare arms and bring out large gobs of butter and compress them into two-by-three-foot stainless steel trays that were divided into one-pound rectangles. The formed butter was then boxed for sale. Families in straightened circumstances would be allowed to fill their containers with the buttermilk. Otherwise it drained off into the sewer.

A creamery never sold a quarter-pound stick of butter. Diet-wise, the era was B.C., that is, "before cholesterol," and the consumption of fat, largely lard and butter, was immense. (Most people, upon hearing the word *Mazola,* would have guessed it to be the name of a newly discovered planet.) Many families consumed a pound of butter a day. We slathered butter on everything—pancakes, toast, cornbread, mashed potatoes, vegetables, oatmeal. Some farmers even put butter on top of their pie—whose crust was made of lard.

By 7:00 A.M. the milking would be finished and we trudged back to the farmhouse to eat large bowls of oatmeal or cornmeal, pancakes or French toast, bacon or ham, and inch-thick toast made from homemade bread. Because I couldn't stomach coffee, I drank unpasteurized milk. I attempted to turn coffee into hot chocolate by liberally lacing it with cream but it didn't work.

Hollander families in more precarious circumstances than the Vander Slices had a diet that, judged by today's standards, was far from "balanced." Jacob and John Van Bockel in their respective autobiographies, *Hollander Heritage* and *Another Time,* remember meals of *Vet en Stroep*—a delicacy of bread dipped in bacon grease and syrup—that their parents enjoyed because it "gave them energy." In addition Dutch families ate rice cooked in buttermilk and *Ollie Bolla* (dough balls with a bit of apple inside) which were fried in lard. Other staples consisted of boiled potatoes with a gravy of hot lard, beets, red cabbage, Swiss chard, cream, soft boiled eggs, homemade bread and the omnipresent pork, either fresh or canned.

Many German and Dutch families concocted their own varieties of "home brew." Jacob Van Bockel's grandfather had a special formula in which potatoes gave his beer an "additional kick." He cooled and hid his brew in the well or horse tank. "Invariably he would find the bottle missing or empty, for someone in the [threshing] crew was aware of his hiding places. One day Grandpa substituted horse urine and the thievery stopped." Other families made wine from everything including dandelions and a variety of wild berries.

We rarely ate eggs because they were saved to be sold. Egg and milk money were as dependable as the phases of the moon, and the monies they produced paid the mortgage on the farm and kept the family solvent in case a drought or early freeze ruined the crops.

For all of the grinding routine of milking, I discovered that most farmers were addicted to the ritual. Some of Bert's neighbors had pictures of their favorite milkers in their wallets, along with photos of their kids. They bragged about the amount of milk that Violet gave or the high butter fat in the milk of Morning Glory. Their kids often had plain-as-post names such as Betty or John, but their cows had flower names like Primrose or Marigold. After the war when economic trends caused legions of small-town creameries to shut down and farmers gave up their herds, it seemed like the *esprit de corps* left thousands of midwest farm families. An archetypal agricultural ritual, one that opened and closed the daily cycle was now considered archaic. Except for the few crucial days of planting and harvesting, farm families no longer had to arise together and work in communitarian fashion. Centrifugal forces in the family overpowered those of centripetal cohesion. Children slept in or drove off in their own cars, the wife got a job as a clerk in town, and the farmer headed for a cafe or bar to chew the fat with his buddies. Like their urban counterparts, farm children were no longer integrated into the success or failure of their families.

The parlor was used only when Sunday company came to call. It was analogous to the sanctuary of a cathedral—profane peasants with sordid clothes, dirt, and smells were forbidden to enter its immaculate space. It had dark brown blinds and a deep green carpet. On a precious piece of Vander Slice furniture—a gilt-legged marble-topped table—rested a huge family Bible with a deeply tooled cover. There were four straight parlor chairs, one against each of the four walls. On one wall hung three large pictures in gilt frames, each of which held a colored photograph of an old-world Vander Slice relative. They looked very stern, very Calvinistic, and very dead. Another wall contained a red-bordered nee-dle-point that proudly proclaimed: *"CHRIST* is the *HEAD* of this *HOME."* On still another there was a tapestry of Millet's Angelus. I couldn't imagine why family friends wanted to visit in a place that reminded me of a mortuary chamber.

The most important room in the farmhouse, the large kitchen, was the theater of activity of the Vander Slice family from before dawn to bedtime. At center stage was a massive cast-iron stove that cooked the food and heated the house. It was beautifully embossed with blue and white enamel inserts and panels, fueled with corn cobs, and polished until immaculate. Grates in the ceiling allowed heat to flow into the upstairs bedrooms. Each side of the stove had large tanks for heating water. Shelves at various levels in the front allowed food to be kept at the proper temperatures. Mrs. Vander Slice never used a thermometer. She knew the temperature of every part of the stove by feel and sight, or by the reaction of water drops sprinkled on the top.

Now let us praise the heroic farm wife! Mrs. Vander Slice managed the physical and emotional environment of her home. Her stove and table provided the primary glow and nurture of her family. Most family activities such as schoolwork, cooking, baking, canning, sewing, mending, and devotions were performed under her sovereignty. In addition, discussions about the hopes and fears for the future, and most contact with outsiders—neighbors, egg buyers, traveling salesmen—took place within her realm. Dozens of activities were carried out without plumbing or electricity.

Outside the house Mrs. Vander Slice was the general of the large garden, managed the chickens, gathered the eggs and planted the flowers around the house. All this and more with no vacations and little leisure time. While Bert often gained respite from his daily routine by running into town or visiting with a neighbor to talk about the weather or politics, Mrs. Vander Slice was far more isolated. Loneliness and depression were too often the consequence of a mountain of tasks to which there seemingly was no end.

Farm activity was captive to and synchronized with the weather. Because the weather affected everyone pretty much equally, Vander Slice could neither get very much ahead nor fall behind his neighbors. It determined whether we would "make hay," mend harnesses, sharpen implements, clean the barn or hog house, tighten fences, cultivate corn, slaughter an animal, patch the roof, chop Canadian thistles or cockleburs, go to town, or do any number of other chores. But pity the poor farmer whose machinery was not ready to go when bad weather broke and there was a sudden window of opportunity to get into the fields. Ordinarily, before planting time, Bert did a good deal of visiting back and forth with his neighbors. They would sit on their haunches and pick up a handful of dirt and break little clods between their fingers. They would discuss markets and crops, recall years when hay, flax, or corn had done especially well or poorly. Bert's judgment as to when to plant and which seed to use carried great weight.

With adequate rain we could get three crops of alfalfa a summer. Each successive cutting was better, because there were more leaves in proportion to the stalk. To attempt four cuttings was dangerous because it might cause winter kill if the last cutting in September left the alfalfa too close to the ground before frost. A legume imported from Siberia, alfalfa was the only perennial on the farm—the only crop that could endure the tough Minnesota winters. But after four years, alfalfa tends to poison itself and is plowed under. A heavy user of potassium and phosphorus, it generously enhances soil fertility by taking nitrogen from the air and fixes it in the ground in small root nodules by means of a bacteria called rhizobium. Sometimes alfalfa roots penetrate 15 feet into the ground. When alfalfa fields were plowed up and returned to corn, the crops did very well.

Of the various farm activities, I enjoyed haying best. "Make hay while the sun shines" is the fable of the grasshopper and the ant played out in thousands of southern Minnesota farms every summer. Alfalfa was cut by a five-foot sickle bar attached to a power take-off from a tractor. Each morning Bert used a large file or carborundum stone to sharpen the diamond-shaped serrated teeth—which reminded me of large, black shark teeth lined up in a row. Engaged, they gave off a *snick-snicking* like a thousand knives being sharpened. Cut hay was wind-rowed by a side-delivery rake and sun-cured for about a week. A farmer's greatest fear while "making hay" was the weather. A rainy spell when the hay was "down" could be disastrous. It would mildew and not cure properly.

Alfalfa is excellent fodder but was dangerous to cows in early spring. After a long winter diet of desiccated stems with few remaining leaves, sometimes cows would break into a field and gorge themselves on fresh alfalfa shoots. The result: bloat. Bloating occurs when foam in the first stomach (they have four), the rumen, prevents a cow from belching. A cow normally belches 200 gallons of gas a day. Without relief they swell up as if hooked up to an air compressor and lose the ability to breathe. Once I saw a farmer render emergency treatment to Matilda. He took an awl and jabbed it just under the short ribs to release the gas. The sound was not unlike removing the needle valve on a truck tire inflated to 150 pounds per square inch. Matilda was no worse for the wear—her stomach and belly healed up much like a self-sealing tire.

When cured we would drive a team of horses over the windrow of alfalfa, and an elevator would pick up the loose hay and carry it at a 65-degree angle into the hay rack. We would tramp it down, periodically stopping to place two or three rope slings through the alfalfa. Back by the barn, horses pulled the slings by pulleys up to the massive 12-by-16-foot haymow door, where it spun into the dark cavern of the mow and was released. The hay would be leveled with pitchforks and salted down down to prevent a fire by spontaneous combustion. In the winter it would be forked down through an open hole to the cows below.

The haymow was one of the major playgrounds of the farm, albeit a most hazardous one. It was a cavernous space dimly lit by two light-bulbs. Buddy and I would climb the ladder that brought us to the peak, where we would sit on a six-inch board hunched over, with our heads against the inner ridge-pole. Pigeons, bats, and an assortment of birds would flit about through the darkness like vampires seeking our blood. Grabbing a rope anchored to a rafter, Tarzan-like, I would leap out into the void, describe a long arc to the other end of the mow, and drop 20 feet into the hay. I prayed that no one had left an unseen pitch fork in the alfalfa.

In the 1930s farmers like the Vander Slices spread their risks by having a wide variety of crops and animals. Most farmsteads had horses, milking cows, beef cattle, hogs, sheep, and chickens. A few might add ducks, geese, and goats. The generic term, "I have to do chores" encompassed the care and nurture of all of these animals and more. Besides corn and alfalfa, farmers would plant oats, barley, flax and, occasionally, wheat. Monoculture was dangerous because it meant putting all of your eggs in one basket. Besides, without commercial fertilizer, pesticides, and herbicides, it was necessary to rotate crops to control weeds, enhance soil tilth, and improve yields. There were no $150,000 gargantuan combines that could do several procedures in one pass over the field.

Harvesting small grain began in July with oats, followed by wheat and barley and finally, in late August, flax. Power for cutting and tying the grain bundles was supplied by a tractor drawn reaper by means of a power takeoff. Bert dropped them off in bunches every 60 feet. Buddy and I would follow down the rows, grasp a bundle in each hand, butt side down, grain side up, and throw them together to start a shock. Oat bundles were lighter but more slippery than barley. However, barley had beards that would lacerate your forearms if you weren't careful. Depending on their girth, eight to twelve bundles made up a shock. The grain shocks would ripen and were safe from the weather until the threshing ring came to the farm three to six weeks later. Few agricultural tableaus can compare with the beauty of thousands of shocks set in an undulating landscape canopied by an aqua sky. They reminded me of a massive army dressed in golden uniforms, perfectly in step and on parade, moving over the horizon.

Corn silage was not chopped in the field as it is today. Like small grain, it was cut in bundles and shocked, turning the field into what looked like an encampment of Sioux with 1,000 six-foot teepees. Later we would pitch the corn bundles on a wagon and haul them to the base of the silo. A chopper powered by a tractor flywheel would cut stalk, leaf, and ear into one-inch sections. The silage would be blown up a 6 inch tube to the top of the silo and cascade down inside. Each day a farmer would have to climb an inside ladder and throw down enough silage for his cows. Fermented silage has a pungent odor, but we didn't know then that prolonged exposure to silage gas can harm your lungs and brain cells. The cows ate it with gusto, much as I devoured sweet corn.

Ear corn was harvested in late September and October and, since I was in school then, I worked only on weekends. A good crop was 50 bushels an acre, about one third of what is expected today. There were no six, eight, or 12-row combines that could pick and shell 100 acres of corn in a day. Most farmers had only a one or two-row picker, and a few farmers picked by hand. The ear corn was elevated into a slatted crib where it was kept dry. It would gradually be fed out to hogs, cattle, and cows during the year after being put through a hammer mill.

Several times I put on a husking glove and picked small patches, usually nubbins, by hand. With my left hand I would grab the ear, hook it with the prong on the husking glove on my right hand, rotate my

The kitchen stove was the "altar" of the farm home. In addition to cooking food, it served as the furnace of the house and provided warm water for bathing and washing dishes. Women took pride in keeping its chrome and blue inserts polished to high gloss as well as using lamp black on its major surfaces.

wrists, break off the husk, and fling it against the backboard of the wagon. Grasp, hook, wrist-snap, throw. A good picker kept up a metronome of "thud...thud...thud" every second or two as the ears hit the side board. As I moved down the row, I whistled to my team of horses to keep up. It was hard work and in the beginning my arms, would throb with pain after 15 minutes. A good husker could pick several acres a day, and champion pickers had enormous forearms. I began to understand why the hands of farmers looked like hamhocks and their grip was vise-like. Stories of some farmers breaking horseshoes in their hands were believable.

Technologically, power options in the 1930s were a horse or tractor. A small Farmall tractor was used for some operations, but horses for most. Farmers over 50 years old were reluctant to become totally mechanized. Horses were exempt from the common fate of other farm animals. They traded their labor, not their flesh, for their keep, seemed less brutish, and had a status somewhere between the hired hands and rest of the livestock in the barnyard hierarchy. Farmers considered their horses almost to be members of the family. They had names and personal histories, were talked to, curried, grained, brushed, bragged about, and subjected to many forms of endearment. During my summers on the farm, I never saw a farmer abuse a horse. But horses engendered a mixture of fear and fascination in me. I never walked behind one without announcing my presence by talking or touching, because it might kick out of fear. Whenever a large group of farmers gathered, there usually was one who had been crippled by a kick from a horse.

Although I was reluctant to admit it, the life of the farm grew on me. The sights, sounds, and smells are with me still:

Cricket serenades arising from the stubble field.
A billowing ocean of blue when flax is in bloom.
The long arc and buzz of a grasshopper in flight.
Roosters crowing at dawn to hurry up the light.
The grunting contentment of hogs as they lap up the swill.
Aromatic clover clothed in the color of cranberry.
A mother mouse and babies surprised under a shock of grain.
The creak of the windmill turning slowly in the wind.
Freshly baked bread set out to cool.
Whipperwills tolling the end of light.
The teeth-numbing iron taste of cold farm well water.
Flashes of evening heat lightening on the horizon.
A yellow-bibbed Meadow Lark crying for its mate.

The fresh and invigorating ether after a rain storm.
An oasis mirage from heat waves rising from the stubble.
Chickens in frenzied fighting over potato peels.
Lunch of cold chicken in the shade under the hay wagon.
A swaying line of cows wending their way to the barn for
    evening milking.
The race to the barn to beat a thunderstorm.

Probably the most beautiful landscape during the summer was when flax was in bloom. Flax had an ethereal blue hue. When a field of flax was caressed by a gentle breeze, it was easy to imagine you were looking over a rolling sky-blue ocean. But since the Atlantic and Pacific oceans were 1500 miles away, it was the closest imitation most Depression-era farmers would ever get to seeing an ocean.

Since flax lacked a barley-like beard, had a short 18-inch stalk and had light-weight bundles, it was a joy to shock. The seeds were crushed for linseed oil and, for a time, the stalks were used for linen and cigarette paper. The seed husks were pressed into cakes for cattle. During the Depression some cereal companies—"Uncle Sam's Cereal" was a popular brand—mixed flax husks in their product for use as a mild laxative. Some old-timers whose intestinal peristalsis had slowed down swore by it. But flax had a short crop "window" during the 1930s and 40s. Today it is seldom grown in the midwest, and many old-timers miss its beauty and its simplicity as a small grain.

Of course, there were embarrassing moments. I was kidded for my city ways. An awkward moment came when I took my first Saturday night bath in the separator room in the barn. A Dutch farm family wanted to keep as much of the farm from entering their house as possible. In addition, they didn't want to wear it, either, especially to town or church. It was a matter of pride. But the house had no bathroom, and modesty and limited space prevented our bathing in the kitchen. Beginning with the oldest, then, each of us in turn would carry a bucket of cold and hot water to the barn, bathe in a galvanized metal tub, put on fresh clothes, empty and clean the tub, and return to the house. Not knowing the proper formula, I seized the bar of Fels Naptha soap and started work on my feet and only later worked upwards through the nether regions to my neck. By the time I had reached my belly button, a thick gray scum had formed on the cooling water.

When I stepped back into the house after completing this end-of-the-week ritual, all six Vander Slices burst out in laughter. Without a mirror in the barn, I had washed everything from my neck down. My face and hair still revealed a weeks accumulation of grime. They thought I was afraid to bathe in the barn and had put clean clothes on over my filthy body.

After I'd been on the farm for a few weeks, it began to dawn on me that the Vander Slices were engaged in a Herculean but deeply satisfying life. This humble Dutch family believed that *laborare est orare*—to labor is to pray. Noble yet humble, collectively they had a vocation that was truly holy. No apology was needed. Adam, primal man, had been commanded to till the Garden of Eden. Bert and his family were following an endless line of splendor in bringing wealth from Mother Earth. Their lives were in harmony with the rhythmic pattern of nature and Nature's God. I stood in awe of the deep satisfaction of those who drew their sustenance from the bosom of Terra Mater.

What was good about work, according to the Vander Slices' Dutch Calvinist orthodoxy, was that you were allowed to savor and enjoy it and were forgiven, within limits, of the sin of pride. Work was not, as Aristotle had held, "a brutality of the mind." Ecclesiastes' assertion that "The labor of man does not satisfy the soul" was not true for the Vander Slices. The Vatican had made work obligatory for its monks but ruled that only prayer brought them to God. It was the twin pillars of the Protestant Reformation, Luther and Calvin, who created a Golden Age for all forms of labor. All legitimate work elevated the worker and simultaneously served God. In the Vander Slice cosmology, the great split between Christian piety and worldly activity was resolved. Work became a calling, a religious path to salvation. On the Sabbath, however, normal fieldwork was forbidden, although broken harness straps or fences could be repaired and plowed-up stones could be carried from the field.

The differences between Bert Vander Slice, however, and his son, Dick, were the differences between the generation that came out of the Great Depression and the generation of the Future Farmers of America (FFA) that came into prominence after World War II. The FFA had educated Dick in the holy writs of modern farming—the "Commandments," as the county extension agents referred to them. Thou shalt plant rows close together (Bert thought this was greedy and abused the land); Thou shalt tear down fences and enlarge your fields (Bert's small plots would in time become large eighty-acre fields); Thou shalt rely on pesticides as a first line of defense (Bert would probably have thought they poisoned the land); Thou shalt not covet thy neighbor's acreage (Bert seemed content with his 240 acres) and so on. Bert's innate conservatism felt the young and new "scientific" farmer was in "too much of a hurry to get ahead," too prone to worship at the short-term, bushels-per-acre pagan altar. Perhaps it was more than a generational difference. Perhaps Bert was the true environmentalist who was happier with his lot, intuitively sought the long term good, was less impetuous, and was the greater steward of the land. Bert didn't seem to worry, like many modern folk, about what he didn't have. He had what counted, his home and his church. His contact with the soil gave him a life that was centered and rooted.

Our day always closed with devotions. The Vander Slices were Dutch Calvinists and members of the Holland Christian Reformed Church. They were unabashedly public and straightforward with their faith. A chapter from the Bible, followed by a devotional reading and a short prayer from each member of the family, took place about 9 P.M. each evening. Body and spirit acted in concert. Some family members dropped to their knees, clasped their hands together and placed their elbows on the seat of their chairs. Others placed their heads on folded hands on the table, while two or three simply sat quietly. After devotions, some family members drifted off to bed, while others read, sewed, mended clothes, paid bills, played cribbage, or reviewed catalogues.

I began to see that, although the Vander Slice family had neither fame nor fortune, it was secure, rooted, and at peace. Years later I read Tolstoy's small volume, *Confession*. In it, one of Russia's greatest writers described his personal crisis upon achieving success. In spite of becoming world-famous, wealthy, and artistically fulfilled, he nevertheless was thrown into a depression so profound that he had to lock his hunting rifle in his gun cabinet lest he use it on himself. In desperation he sought succor in the classic philosophical authors, only to come up empty. None—not Plato, Aristotle, Descartes, Hegel, nor any others—were of any help at relieving his angst. How could it be that the legions of peasants spread across the Russian steppes possessed a happiness that eluded him? He had everything while they had nothing. He found the answer in their acceptance of the Christian gospel of salvation. It alone was the source of their solace and strength. With this revelation, Tolstoy gained exit from his dark night of the soul. He gave up all his worldly possessions and went to live among the peasants he admired, even adopting their faith.

Some evenings I would step out on the porch before turning in. If I walked a quarter of a mile to the south ridge of the farm, on a clear night I could see not only thousands of stars but the lights of towns 30 miles away. (Today that ridge sprouts wind generators because the wind there averages 16 miles an hour.) Scattered on the horizon, the lights of farmhouses looked like ships at sea. The evening lay before me, and all I had to do was receive it. Long ribbons of clouds floated above the western horizon, and the cornfield on the other side of the road rolled up to meet it. A wash of pale pink seeped upward from the lower margin of the sky and rimmed the clouds with fire. Above them, clear blue shaded to lavender. On some evenings I would watch the northern lights flicker in electric clouds on the horizon, mount, die down, fade and mount again until they filled the whole northern sky with ghostly light in motion. Sometimes I would apply my budding interest in astronomy and marvel at the glittering Pleiades in the east on the shoulder of the Bull. But I would have to turn in before Orion would clear the horizon for his nightly hunting with the big and little Dogs.

On other evenings I would settle into the porch swing and drink in the mysterious rural smells. The lilacs, the barnyard, remnants of supper from the kitchen, newly mown clover, wet tomato vines, camomile and more all contributed their part. I could see lightening bugs and cabbage moths against the dark greenery of the grove. In the distance I heard a quiet sonata of sound—the rattle of hog feeders, croaking bull frogs staking out their territory, the bark of a dog, the sawing of cicadas, the screech of an owl calling to its mate. Sometimes a full moon arose out of a cloud bank and now and then bats would flutter across its light. In Pipestone I had never been so aware of such an entrancing panorama. I wanted to linger, but my exhausted body demanded rest. By 10 P.M. the kerosene lamps were out and everyone was in bed.

Farm life was serious, but here and there a grace note of humor crept in. A neighbor, Joe Carlson, enjoyed telling the following: A little kid comes in late to school. Teacher says, "Why ya late?" Kid says, "Had a take a heifer down—get 'er bred." Teacher says, "Couldn't your ol' man do it?" Kid says, "Sure he could, but *not as good as the bull.*"

A German family a mile away also provided plenty of gossip and a few laughs because of the dictatorial arrogance of the father. Adolph Schmidt had three teen-aged sons and once a month the four men of the household would gather at the kitchen table for a Depression-era family conference. Each would have a glass of wine and Schmidt would cut two cigars in half so the four-some could have a smoke. "Boys, this is the time to let our hair down," Adolph would begin. "What needs to be fixed, how can we improve our operation, what are your complaints?"

"Well," said Karl, 16, "I'm the oldest and doing the most work. I think I need a bit more free time." "I'll take that under advisement," mused his father. "Meanwhile, don't get too smarty-pants with me. It seems you got a mouth full of gimmee and a handful of grab." Karl kicked over the traces the next week-end and went to the Cities. Upon his return Adolph took his dinner plate and cracked it in half over the side of the table. He threw one half in the garbage and placed the other half on the table: "Seems like yo'r one-half playboy and one-half farmer. From now on you'll get one-half a plate of grub." When Eric, the youngest son, was caught chewing tobacco, Adolph held his jaws together until he finally swallowed the acrid mess. That was the end of experimenting with tobacco in the Schmidt family.

Going to town on Saturday night was a weekly family ritual. Everyone pushed a little harder Saturday afternoon with chores, bathing, and supper. A couple of 12-dozen-egg cases were put in the trunk, and a can of sour cream. They would be used for bartering. The heat had gone out of the day, and the family was dressed in clean shirts and cotton dresses. On the way to town the family checked the height and color of the neighbor's corn, the status of weeds in the corn rows, and the size of his spring pigs. Early-birds would get a choice spot to park on Main Street, hopefully near a corner where groceries wouldn't have to be carried very far. After the eggs and cream were disposed of and groceries loaded in the car, the cardinal activity was "people-watching." The Vander Slices knew virtually everyone they saw. Crowds stood around "chewing the fat" about the weather, crops, family illnesses and just old-fashioned gossip. The younger kids would go to the movies, buy some ice cream or run up and down the streets and alleys.

The barber shops were jammed until 11 o'clock or later. Besides a haircut, quite a few men had a shave and "got fixed up for Sunday." Most of the barber clients were "two-toned." Protected by straw hats, the foreheads of men were the color of white bread, while their faces, necks, arms and hands were as bronzed and rugged as those of a Sioux warrior. About 10 o'clock the crowd would begin to thin out and mothers began to call—*"Remember, we have to do chores earlier tomorrow because of Sunday school!"* The family would gather around the car, drive through the cool of the night, and recount the bits of gossip they had learned from their weekly sojourn.

The worst insult Bert could give a fellow farmer was, "That guy, he farms straight out of a book." He enjoyed ridiculing "academic" farmers and city-slickers. "Do you know," said the young student at agricultural college to an old Dutch farmer, "your methods of cultivation are a hundred years behind the time?" Looking around, he remarked, "Why, I'd be surprised if you make a dollar out of the oats in that field." "So would I," smiled the old Dutchman, "it's barley." And another: A farmer was explaining to a city woman what a menace insects are to farm products—how potato bugs ruin potato crops and corn borers destroy corn.

The woman listened attentively, then exclaimed: "And you poor dairy people. How the butterflies must bother you!"

Like his neighbors, Bert Vander Slice accepted the Farmer's Credo:

What is a farmer?
A farmer is a man who feeds the world.
What is a farmer's duty?
To grow more food.
What is a farmer's second duty?
To farm more land.
What are the marks of a godly farmer?
Clean fields, painted buildings, breakfast at six, no debt,
     good machinery and livestock, dutiful children, no standing
     water, tight fences, faithful church attendance.

It is, of course, dangerous to wax too nostalgic about childhood memories. The passage of time tends to leach out the hurtful and enhance the positive reflections of one's youth. Farm life during the Great Depression was vastly harder than it is now. Karl Marx spoke for most urban social theorists when he decried the "imbecility of the life of the peasant." True, the Vander Slices had less leisure and mind culture than did the urbanite. Moreover, without the array of today's household technology, domestic duties took up most of the day and of the week. Relative to today, Mrs. Vander Slice and her two daughters lived crabbed lives, unleavened by the possibility of jobs in town and wider social contacts. There was little reading except for the Bible and the Montgomery Ward and seed catalogues. Life had a boxed-in and fatalistic quality that is unknown today with our television, e-mail, the Internet and the World-Wide Web. Add to this international travel, cultural exchange, medical advances, and creature comforts, and we seem light years away from the agrarian society I experienced as an adolescent.

But could a Depression engendered, chastened fatalism be the better part of wisdom? Did people like Bert understand life's simple joys, the dangers of personal hubris and narcissism, and the basic principles of life more clearly than many do today? Perhaps. One example is suggestive.

In the early 70s, a neighbor of the Vander Slices, Gertrude Olson, then 81, took a Greyhound bus to the Twin Cities. She was "feeling out of sorts" and wanted a medical check-up. The tests completed, a family physician and an oncologist gave her grave news. Her cancer was extensive, the prognosis "guarded." They believed, nevertheless, that they should "treat her." But it would be a tortuous experience of surgery and radiation. There were no promises.

Resisting their powers of persuasion, Gertrude put them off. She seemed to know that specialists sometimes treat themselves (eg. their own sense of helplessness) while ministering to their patients, and that they are unconsciously captive to their narrow disciplines: "if the only tool you have is a *hammer,* everything you see looks like a *nail.*" "Thank you very much," Gertrude responded, "Please call me a taxi so that I can get back to the bus station. I have had a good life and I want to go home."

Six months later Gertrude died, as was said of Abraham, "full of life and full of years," in the bosom of her family. The cycles of nature and nature's God seemed to tell her when enough was enough. She did not want any part of the ravages of medical torture and death in a sterile and alien and impersonal arena.

The classic theological themes—the goodness of creation, the sacredness of work, the family as an Order of Creation, the need to honor thy Mother and Father, the acceptance of God as the Author and End of Life—were all embodied in this pious Dutch family. Like other fathers of his era, Bert Vander Slice did not want his stable world to change; it was the only one he knew. The city could not be controlled like an agrarian womb-nest and therefore it was feared. Secularism and urbanity meant options, freedom, unbelief, immorality, family dissolution, and other foreign ideas and strange ways. "If my kids go to college, they may get high falutin' ideas," he may have thought, "and think they know more than the old man. What's good enough for me, is good enough for them." It was an old pattern—fathers becoming silent and feeling vulnerable as their sons grew into manhood and became educated and increasingly self-confident.

Wilbur Dick left high school after his sophomore year; Buddy, after eighth grade. They were limited, like their sisters who married farmers, to but one vocation—tilling the soil. But the next generation knew the old order was passing away. A family-sized farm had escalated from 100 to 1000 acres and required astronomical amounts of capital to acquire and to bring under cultivation. Wilbur Dick had six children, all of whom went to college. A daughter became a physician, and two sons are engineers. Their world and that of their grandparents are light-years apart.

"Putting up Hay" *was my favorite activity on the farm. Here an elevator con-*
veys alfalfa to the hay rack before it is taken to the barn. The horses are each
wearing a harness with hanging cords which help to keep the flies away.

34. BRINGING IN THE SHEAVES

Half of our misery and weakness derives from the fact that we have broken with the soil and that we have allowed the roots that bound us to the earth to rot. We have become detached from the earth, we have abandoned her. And a man who abandons nature has begun to abandon himself.

That Day Alone, Pierre an Paassen

Harvest is a sensuous time, the most enjoyable experience of the year. It is full of vivid blues, browns and gold, a resurrection before death, a ritual of communalism that brings together neighboring families to reap the harvest. The onset of the autumn drama heralds the reward of six months' work. The emotion at threshing time is still primal, perhaps rooted in the not-too-distant era of subsistence farming, when whole farming villages lived or starved depending on the munificence of the harvest. Caught up in the intoxicating mix of power, sweat, bounty, and exhaustion, everyone wears a happy face. Threshing is a time of completion and rejoicing—"when all is gathered in, ere the winter storms begin"—celebrated by poet and hymnist since time immemorial. In the days of my youth, it was a communal, not individual, event.

Today's farmer is more of a Robinson Crusoe type. He harvests by piloting a $150,000 air-conditioned combine over the fields while listening to stereo, wonderfully cushioned 6 feet above the earth. Periodically he stops to auger the grain into a truck that hauls it to an elevator in town or a bin on the farm. Using this efficient, antiseptic process, he can cover 70 to 100 acres a day.

Because the farmer and his soil have been increasingly separated by a technological wedge, farming is not nearly as earthy as it used to be. Sixty years ago the farmer's great grandfather belonged to a threshing ring composed of four or five farmers who collectively owned a threshing machine. Each farmer had to contribute two bundle teams, each consisting of two men pitching steadily, one on each side of the feeder trough. The rig would be pulled from farm to farm. To do the entire circuit would take over a month.

The separator would be placed in a feed lot where the discarded straw could be used for winter bedding. A stacker would turn up his collar and hunker down under the pale yellow snowstorm and carefully construct a conical pile of straw. It would have to shed the rain and snow melt-off and last until next fall. Through the eyes of a child, the separator looked like a giant grasshopper or praying mantis spouting a torrent of golden bile, or perhaps a metal dinosaur whose proboscis, the slanting feeder, seemed out of proportion to its body. Whatever image one chose, the separator ate up the bundles like some hungry steel dragon. The separator was powered by means of an 80-foot-long belt that stretched between it and the flywheel of a powerful tractor. Hay racks full of bundles of grain were driven parallel with and close to the spinning belt so that the bundles could be pitched evenly into the feeder, the clanking maw of the machine. When all the machinery was operating full tilt, the noise was deafening and sounded like the roaring and groaning and bellowing of some Greek monster god arising from the underworld.

The feeder's crossbars carried the side-by-side bundles into the chopping knives that cut the twine and pushed the grain into the grinding teeth of the cylinders of the separator. As I listened to the pounding, blowing, sifting, shaking, the grinding of gears and rattle of chains and the whine of pulleys and belts, I marveled at how far we had come from Biblical times when the flail or a donkey had to do this kind of work.

From a distance the tableau might have appeared as a peasant drama, perhaps an Oberammergau theatre set. Grandma Moses would have loved recording the scene:

> Spikers high in their racks waiting their time to unload.
> Children running from the house with baskets of lunch.
> A hunkered-down stacker leveling the cascading straw.
> Retired farmer-seers on a duck-squat, picking their teeth.
> A farmer testing the heft of the augered grain as it drizzles
>   into a wagon.
> A field hand dipping deep into a 10-gallon cream can for water.
> A dog chasing a cottontail rabbit across the stubble field.
> The eyes of field hands fixed on a pretty girl in a calico smock.
> Two farmers comparing harnesses and horse flesh.
> Pale shirts turned deep blue where sweat has broken through.

Usually I was in the field as a spiker. That is, I went from wagon to wagon, helping fill. I felt abused because I had to pitch bundles without respite. Those in charge of a hay rack could rest a bit while driving to and from the threshing machine. On the rare occasions that I was trusted with a team, it was exhilarating.

Status within the guild was achieved by seeing who could stack his wagon the highest. "Now there is a load of bundles!" was the compliment every driver hoped to hear as he came up from the field. Sometimes the reins that controlled the horses barely reached the wagon-drivers perch 15 feet above the ground. My horses would belch, slobber foam, and fart as they struggled to keep the swaying rack moving toward the thresher. You were ridiculed if part of your load was lost before you came in; the worst humiliation was a tip-over. When it happened the driver would hang his head in shame—with good reason. The thresher would have to shut down, the other drivers would have to help him right his rig, and precious time would be lost. Happily, it never happened to me.

It was frightening even to think about what might happen if I fell on the belt or, worse yet, into the feeder. Every threshing rig had a well-worn story of a guy who fell into the feeder and ended up as hamburger. Farming and mining were the two most hazardous occupations. But a litigious spirit was unknown then, and there were no OSHA snoops around to make farming less dangerous. Farmers with scars and limps—and without fingers, hands, or arms—were commonplace. Cycle-bars, horses, bulls, belts, pulleys, pitchforks, ropes, farm machinery of every kind, silage gas and more took a frightful toll. During the Depression, a quiet but real war of attrition, one without an armistice, went on in every midwestern farmstead.

My deepest fear was to have a runaway team. Picture two massive Pertcheron-type horses hitched to a hayrack, scared by a loud noise, a snake, or a snarling dog. They "spook" and the driver loses control. In their terror the horses bolt and parts of the wagon, bundles, or whatever else they are carrying begin to disintegrate and fly off in all directions behind them. As they bolt through a gate the wagon catches on a gatepost and there is a massive crash. Once I saw a team run through a barb wire fence that lacerated their shoulders and flanks. When we caught up with them, the horses were bleeding profusely. Their eyes mirrored sheer panic and their nostrils were fully flared. It was a sad sight, dumb animals traumatized, equipment and harness reduced to tatters. They would heal, of course, but the scars would blemish their salability and be seen by an outsider as symbols of having been treated badly. If a horse fell and broke a leg, it would have to be shot. The experience of a runaway would cast gloom over a threshing party for days, not unlike that of lightening striking a barn or a herd of cows.

In contrast, a beautifully functioning team was a delight to the eyes. Each threshing ring had at least one team that was exceptionally well-trained, well-matched, and well-driven that would "lay in there" to move the heaviest load. Like an Olympian-coordinated duet—almost crouching, muscles bulging, dirt flying, nostrils flaring, harness creaking—a great wagon load began to move. When onlookers exclaimed, *"Now there is a team of horses!"* the owner-driver's heart would have a warm glow for days.

The most common accidents involved cornpickers. Whether in the field or coming down the road, their very presence looked menacing. Their large silvery two heads tilted toward the ground at a 45-degree angle gave them the appearance of a species of dinosaur I had studied in grade school. In use, their powerful rollers seized corn stalks and shredded them as other gears tore off the corn ears before they were elevated and dropped into wagons. But cornpickers frequently became clogged with debris or wet stalks. Then a farmer would have to get off his tractor and clear the obstruction by hand. He could save precious time by not shutting down the machinery or disconnecting the power take-off. But the briefest moment of inattentiveness, carelessness, weariness, or hastiness prompted by the need to finish the day's work before an approaching squall line reached the field might result in his arm getting caught in the rollers. Not even the strongest farmer was a match for his mechanical monster. The result: an arm ground to mincemeat. I was warned never to work around machinery in a loose jacket or sleeve.

Of course, along with such frightful tales there were heroic recountings as well. There were tales of brave lads who were able to get to their pocket knife, open it, cut away their arm, make a tourniquet, and walk a quarter of a mile home before collapsing on the porch. Such stories made a deep impression on me. I was saddened by the frightful penalty that a moment of forgetfulness might exact.

For all of its apparent picture-book beauty and quiet simplicity, the typical farmstead was in fact a frightful maiming and killing field.

But the farm was also a place where the most basic acts of creation were taken for granted. One of the most indelible experiences I had during threshing time was the breeding of one of the mares of my team. Marigold was "in heat" and Bart, a neighboring farmer, brought his stallion over to do the "servicing." I helped Bart unhook my lady horse from the rig and we led her behind the bundle wagon so innocent eyes from passerbys on a nearby road would be screened from the "action." The stallion was entirely black, even though he had been given the name Silver, after the famous steed of the Long Ranger. Bart told me that Silver seemed to enjoy these "outings." They gave him a refreshing respite from the drudgery of pulling the plow or a threshing rig. Marigold seemed to have a primordial sense of what was coming. Her ears laid back on her neck and she started a nervous whinny. She must have had the nose of a bloodhound and had a sense of what was about to transpire. We pushed her harness up on her hind quarters so it would not get in the way. I held her bridle and patted her neck in a futile attempt to calm her down. My heart went out to her. With her blinders on, she never even laid eyes on her "stud lover of the moment."

But Silver was approaching from the rear. It was the first time I had seen a horse's penis at full extension and ready for "action." Bart was holding fast to his bridle. Silver's muscular hindquarters were rippling for action. His hooves were carving out great clots of dirt that he kicked out in all directions. Silver's "member" was pink and enormous, perhaps as long as my Louisville "Slugger" baseball bat and two or three times its diameter. Silver needed no lessons in reproduction; an internal genetic program told him what to do. He mounted Marigold in a frenzy. Suddenly his penis was completely out of sight! It was inside the mare. After ten seconds of convulsions it came out—bent, weak, dripping and started to shrivel and retract. Marigold and Silver had had their moment. Gradually they seemed to settle down.

As I readjusted the harness I mused that there had been no preliminaries, foreplay, teasing, or "will you still respect me in the morning?" questions. With animals "it" was mechanical, automatic, genetically-coded, and natural. Maybe animals went at the whole issue of reproduction with a lot less fuss, emoting, and potential damage than do humans. At the end of 12 months, there would be a frisky little colt. Then Silver might once again be called on for another 10 second "peak" experience.

The high point of the day at harvest time was noon-time dinner. The threshing machine was shut down and 20 men and boys were drawn to the house like metal filings to a magnet. We washed up under the grove using tin basins, lathering our faces, neck, and forearms (farmers had enormous, muscular wrists and forearms) and then dried ourselves on a roller-towel that was already wet and gray with dirt. The soapy gray water would be thrown into the weeds.

Everyone had a "farmers tan"—white forehead, tanned face, and upper arms split in half, white and golden brown, by a sharp tan line. But we city kids wouldn't be caught dead with the two-toned, white and brown body of a farmer. In Pipestone I had the leisure to tan much more of my beautiful body at the swimming pool. When I worked on the farm

I took off my shirt as much as possible when alone to get color into my chest, and to blur that despicable symbol of the farmer.

Years later, when I read Thorstein Veblen's, *The Theory of the Leisure Class,* I understood tanning as a status symbol indicating enough affluence to "sun for fun." The "farmer's tan" was only one mark of disdain we held against farmers and their offspring. They wore old fashioned, ankle-top shoes with eyelets, were less coordinated in sports, and had a lingering odor of the barn. How cruel we city kids were! But now the tables were turned and I began to admire them for their practical knowhow, their physical strength, and their ability to accomplish a prodigious amount of work in a day. My muscles, honed on the athletic field, had trouble adapting to the necessities of the farm. We city kids could "talk"; farm kids could "do."

Once in the house we settled around tables weighed down with immense platters of food provided by the wives and daughters of the threshing ring. The meals were truly heroic. Because the farmers and hired hands were constantly coming and going, we dug in and the food went unblessed. The threshers were prodigious trenchermen, capable of polishing off two and even three mounded plates of victuals. I doubt that the court of Henry VIII or the Epicurean gourmets of Greece and Rome ate any better. Beef, pork, chicken, and ham, were the usual meats, all from animals butchered on the farm. They were complemented by mashed potatoes and gravy, sweet potatoes, cabbage salad, squash, parsnips, jello, peas, carrots, pickles, jams, jelly, and several kinds of bread. I was most impressed with the desserts. There were always several different kinds of pies and three or four varieties of cakes. Table talk ranged from the serious to the humorous. Field hands were ridiculed for losing part of a load, breaking an axle, or letting horses get away. Others discussed the quality of the grain, worried about bad weather moving in, and estimated when we would move to the next farm.

The women hovered over us lest any platter show a sign of emptying. Competition existed between them as to who could create the best meat, salad, or dessert dish. It was a mark of distinction to have their particular dish emptied first. Critical eyes inwardly judged the quality of the various dishes, not unlike the home economics judges at the county fair. There always was food left over and, after we staggered out, the women cleaned the tables, socialized, and had their own meal. I marveled at these daily thanksgivings in August and September. And I began to understand why many of the farmers of my acquaintance had such prominent bay "windows."

Outside we men sought a comfortable piece of grass on the shady side of the house on which to lay our bloated bodies. I opened the side buttons on my Oshgosh-By-Gosh bib overalls to get relief. Most of the older farmers pulled out a wooden matchstick and worked at their teeth. The outhouse was in heavy demand, and those who couldn't wait headed into the grove.

At this point some of the younger hands often would start exchanging stories. The yarns were for men only and were more "earthy" than "dirty." The tales invariably began with "Did 'ya hear the one about…?" and then continued with a yarn like the following: "A farmer is working in his barnyard one day when his 10-year-old boy comes rushing up to him, all excited. 'Pa,' said the boy, 'come quick. The hired man and Sis are up in the haymow, and he's a-pulling down his pants and she's a-liftin' up her skirt. Pa, they're gettin' ready to *pee all over our hay.*' 'Son,' said the farmer, 'you've got your facts absolutely right, but you've drawn a completely wrong *conclusion'.*" Other young bucks would recite earthy aphorisms that had been passed down from threshing season to

Saturday night in town was the week's major social event. Trading eggs and cream for flour, yeast, sugar, and other such necessities was the excuse for the trip.

threshing season, such as, "a farting horse will never tire and a farting man is the man to hire."

All too soon, the sound of the tractor starting up recalled us to our racks.

I began to understand why the land has such a hold on the human spirit, the family-sized farm on the American psyche. Our society is often indicted for being individualistic and self serving, but farmers know their solitary life necessitates cooperation and community. Nature rewards those who work together. Moreover, the farmer lives in a community that has an empathetic union with the primal order of reality. Ecclesiastical priests unveil the spiritual through bread and wine. An agricultural priesthood uncovers the divine through symbols of water, soil, sun, and seed. In later years I understood why Stalin had to kill 15 million kulaks in order to collectivize agriculture.

Everyone had a place in the agrarian womb. Young or old, able or handicapped, normal or retarded, had valued contributions to make. Anyone could gather eggs or milk cows. I uncovered a familial interdependency unknown in urban culture. The daily chores proclaimed: "You are precious and needed. If you slack off, someone else has to do more." In the city, parent-child linkages are less organic, and "make-work" chores seem superficial. Children, to be sure, are told they are loved, but I think it's harder to physically demonstrate caring in the city than on a farm. The importance of keeping one's room clean, taking out the garbage, and mowing the lawn, pales in comparison to the duties necessary to keep a farmstead functioning. While a few libertine spirits might experience some personal suffocation because of the cultural limits of agrarian options, I experienced a sense of worth and belonging.

Sexuality, too, was objectively and honestly integrated into human experience. Animals mated, gave birth, suckled, grew old, and died. 4-H Club animals were raised, fed, groomed, won prizes at the county fair, and took a final ride to the packing plant. All the Vander Slice children wept when they had to bid final farewells to their animals, but that was their fate. We butchered chickens, geese, hogs and sheep. Shakespeare's seven stages of man were accepted because we experienced their animal equivalents every day.

35. Mentoring Under a French Sheep Farmer

Where is the man who owes nothing to the land in which he lives?
Whatever that land may be, he owes to it the most precious thing possessed by man, the morality of his actions and the love of virtue.

Emile, or Education, Jean Jacques Rousseau

In addition to occasional weekends, I spent two summers when I
was 15 and 16 working at the Lee DeGriselles farm, an easy bike ride
away, one mile southwest of town. Each morning I arose at six, ate a
hurried breakfast of oatmeal, and enjoyed a leisurely bike ride down a
small gravel road in order to begin work at 7:00 A.M. It was pleasant to
hear the choir of birds on the way: the shiny red-winged blackbirds in
their Geneva robes with red epaulets; the meadowlarks that sang like
water; the wrens whose flute-like song trilled up and down the scale; the
mourning doves who seemed perpetually to be singing at a wake.
Sometimes I stopped to let fly with my slingshot at grackles, whose
harsh sounds caused dissonance in my avian choir. I had a number of
good slingshots carved out of oak Y's and, with store-bought rubbers, I
was quite accurate. I had to find just the right stone—round, slightly
flattened and heavy enough to carry through the air. Unlike some of my
friends, however, I never broke any glass telephone insulators.

DeGriselles, a small, sinewy Frenchman, embodied the rags-to-riches story of the American dream. As a young man, he had managed the
Jack Spratt grocery store. At his death he owned several farms in
Pipestone county. Every morning I biked out to the farm to help with
the day's tasks. DeGriselles' children, a daughter and two sons, were
too small to help. Beva Lee, the daughter, was two years my junior. She
was very pretty, with platinum blonde hair, but had the reputation for
being somewhat cold and distant. I began to discern, however, that we
were soul mates; that is, both of us were very shy. Father could not
escape his eugenic concern for the species and fired several warning
salvos lest I become too interested in her. "Neb," he cautioned, "She has
several allergies. Go easy. Play the field." Rumor had it, probably generated from the envy of other jealous mothers who had less striking
daughters, that she put lemon juice on her hair to make it even whiter.

DeGriselles was a wonderful mentor. He was patient and kind, and never uttered a harsh word to me in two summers. (The pay—$50 a month for June and July, $75 for August—could have been better, however.) Under his guidance, I learned how to plow, cultivate corn, feed, shear and castrate sheep, chop hay and corn silage, and much more. From the moment he first wiped the dew off the tractor seat in the morning, Lee taught me that farming is absorbing, utterly interesting. Like Bert Vander Slice, he longed to stay enfolded within the fabric woven of nature privacy and physical exhaustion.

A corn field is a picture of monochromatic greenness. Corn grows with a mechanical uniformity that seemed a little surrealistic to me. Corn stalks put forth six or eight pennant-shaped leaves that float in smooth jointless, arcing opposite pairs, one above the other. The summers I worked for DeGriselles, by the end of July the plants were large enough to shade out most of the black soil of the field. Ever since I was a child I had heard the hoary tale, "It is so hot you can *hear the corn*

The old-fashioned threshing dinner has been much romanticized. Farm women used to compete with each other as to whose dish was emptied first. Twenty to 25 ravenous men were fed every day for over three weeks—without the help of refrigeration, frozen foods, and running water—during threshing season. This ritual was probably the origin of the enormous stomachs that I saw on many farmers beneath their Osh-Gosh-By-Gosh overalls.

grow." And it was true! On some still days the corn would grow six inches and you could hear the leaves unfolding from the stalk.

With a gentle breeze corn plants rattle like an infinite number of violins being quietly played with but one string. Corn grows as tall as a man in a tiny fraction of a man's lifetime by drawing water from the earth and exhaling it in a vast and deep breath. I mused that a cornfield was a marching army in green uniforms; the leaves always reminded me of shoulders, the tassels of heads. When our silage cutter moved down the field, I thought of myself as a machine gunner,, mowing down thousands of Germans who were going "over the top."

I enjoyed working the corn binder. Green corn stalks were cut at their base, tied into bundles of 15, and stood upright into a tepee-like shock, creating a typically Rockwellian corn-harvest scene. The shocks reminded me of an encampment of Civil War tents in proper alignment. A child might have seen them as soldiers costumed in parade gold, dressing right.

In October we pitched the bundles into wagons and then into a silage-cutter that blew one-inch segments 70 feet up into a silo. As we moved gyroscopically around the field in circles, rats would run from one shock to another. Lee let them escape until there might be over a dozen in the one remaining shock. Then it was a time for killing; Lee's favorite weapon was a baseball bat. Like crows and snakes, rats seemed somehow deeply primitive and fearsome. I wondered whether they might remind us of our primordial origins.

During the war years Pipestone was the foremost county in the state in fattening sheep, and Lee was one of the best. Upon securing a loan, he would purchase several thousand Montana lambs averaging 40 pounds each. After three months on corn and alfalfa, they more than doubled their weight and were sent to market. Most of the meat went overseas to feed our soldiers. In many cases it was the only meat they'd have for months. As a result, when the war ended hundreds of thousands of servicemen never ate mutton again for the rest of their lives.

The lambs came to Pipestone by rail. I would shepherd them several miles to Lee's farm, stopping traffic, trying not to lose too many, and hoping none would be run over. I came to hate the little beasts. The beatific and poetic perception of sheep, like that of most farm animals, increases in direct proportion to the distance of the observer. I came to doubt the paeans of enchantment written by the English Romantic poets over the supernal beauty of white flocks on mountain vistas. I strongly doubt that they had seen sheep at close hand. They certainly didn't have to take care of them.

Sheep are stupid, smelly, brutish critters. They are totally devoid of affection and will smother each other when afraid or during a snow storm. Their wool? Whiter than snow? Don't believe it. Leave that to children's story books. Their wool is oily and filthy. Nursery rhymes—"Mary Had A Little Lamb" and "The Three Little Pigs"—have falsely dignified sheep and maligned the hog. Given an option to live elsewhere than in a dirty puddle, a hog will keep its environment far cleaner than a sheep.

Lee and I would castrate the young rams by the hundreds. We would cut their "nuts" out and squirt kerosene as an antiseptic into the empty scrotum. In France, a farmer would bite down on the empty bag and seal it with his teeth. The first few times I did this primitive surgery, my groin tensed up a bit in a sympathetic reaction to what I was doing to the sheep. But they would bounce up and run off not realizing they had just been deprived of the chance to get their genes into the next generation. The operation accomplished two goals—it pacified the males, and, by ending the production of testosterone it guaranteed that their feed would more efficiently be converted to mutton. There were no animal rights groups around then. They would have thought we were barbarians. We certainly didn't practice informed consent.

Lee said that the French considered sheep testicles a great delicacy. Out West some ranchers prized them as Rocky Mountain oysters. Rumor had it that a diet of testicles would do wonders for sexual prowess. Lee said some men in their declining years would even grind them up and inject the stuff into their veins. Billy goat gonads were supposed to be the best. There were clinics in Switzerland that made millions of dollars from men worried about becoming impotent. (For some Asians, the keys to sexual paradise were discovered in rhinoceros horns and the gall bladders and stones of bear and cattle.) The Depression was a "B.V." era; that is, "before Viagra," and many men sought help however bizarre, for their weak libidos. I marveled at the inventiveness of those who sought the sexual fountain of youth. I would have liked to try Rocky Mountain oysters, but I never got the opportunity. Maybe it was because Mrs. DeGriselles wasn't French. Only later did it dawn on me that perhaps Lee didn't need any help in that area.

Some of Lee's neighbors who also fattened lambs would tell lurid tales of Western sheep herders who engaged in the unspeakable "it" with a special ewe of their herds. "Montana is a state of 10,000 horny sheep farmers and 10 million anxious sheep," was the way the tale was usually framed. The men would laugh, slap their thighs, wink at me and expect some response. "After all," one would add, "it can be mighty lonely out in those mountains. All the women are back in town, in the saloons working the slot machines." More laugher. I would blush but gave little credence to such tales. It was simply beyond my imagining.

These good old boys were full of stories of farmers trying to stay alive, of the earth drying up and blowing away, and of the privation and desperation that was the result. These grizzled old yeomen would gather around the feeding bunks, a tractor, or the silage cutter and spin their yarns as they picked at their teeth with matchsticks. I found their jokes, such as the following, replete with sardonic humor:

> Did you hear of Ole Johnson having his baby? Wal, his misses was a tiny little thing, so the doc urged Ole to take her to the Cities. Ya know, that's where all those high-falu'tin, butter-and-eggs guys live. Waa-ell, Ole was in this fancy hospital, a-pacing back-and-forth, wait'n for the kid to come out when in comes a rich and fat, high-muckety-muck guy, dressed in fancy duds. He, too, was await'in the birth of his baby. Pretty soon, the nurse comes out and says, "Mr. Jensen?" "That's me!" replied the round little drummer. "Congratulations! You are the father of a beautiful nine-pound baby boy!" Jensen jumps up, hugs and kisses the nurse and pulls some cigars out of his pocket and says. "Say, that's great. Here, Mr. farmer-man, have one of my fancy imported cigars... no, have two." Mr. city-slicker was bust'tin his buttons over his healthy new son. A few minutes later the nurse again appears, this time she had a frown on her face, looked a bit worried and asks. "Mr. Johnson?" "That's me," shouted Ole. "You too, have a boy." But the nurse was ac'tin a big strangely, so Mr. Money-Bags, shouted. "Well, how much did his baby weigh?" At first she wasn't going to answer, but finally she whispered, "Oh, about a pound." "Judas H. Priest," shouted the rich drummer, "Lordy, that's too bad. Sorry old man about your tough luck."
>
> Tough!" shouted Ole, beaming from ear to ear. That's not tough. Livin' out where I do in the Dust Bowl, why land sake! We're lucky to git our seed back!"

Lee always warned me not to be too loquacious. "Did you hear about the starving sparrow who gorged itself on horse manure," he once said with a twinkle in his eye. "He was so proud of his banquet he began to chirp at the top of his voice. This attracted a cat who feasted on him." The moral was an earthy farmer's version of Miss Daisy Wakefield's "empty wagons rattle the most": "If you're full of sh.., it's best to keep quiet."

Several times I would help Lee shear some of the sheep that had overly long coats. He would man-handle a sheep and set it on its butt.

After tucking its head under his left arm, he would start shearing at the hocks and peel away the thick wool so the fleece came off in a single piece, like a dirty union suit.

One afternoon I went with Lee over to a neighbor's place to butcher a Hampshire boar. Chester (the hog) was a monstrous thing of over 400 pounds with a pillow-sized scrotum. He lumbered and snorted around his pen, proud as a pasha that he had sired thousands of progeny; he looked like the Puritan's Plymouth Rock on legs. Tim Johnson, Chester's owner, 13 and a 4-H'er, had done well to get third prize at the county fair. But that white ribbon wasn't high enough for his hog to be be purchased by a local bank or cafe for publicity purposes. Now it was Chester's time (Tim had named the pig after a favorite uncle) to pay his final dues for the loving care his master had provided during the past year. Tim had never "stuck" a pig before and, because his father was an invalid, Lee volunteered to mentor Tim regarding this archetypal ritual. Chester was a handsome hog—completely black with the exception of a 10 inch white strip down his forequarters. His breed was named after a shire in England where it was developed. I came along to give Tim moral support and help hold the hog down. Selling or killing your prized animal is a unique agrarian rite of passage, a bar mitzvah for farm kids.

The three of us wrestled Chester onto his side. Lee hogtied his legs together so he couldn't maim us. With Lee's coaching I placed all my 120 pounds on that portion of Chester's anatomy the butcher shop labels "spare ribs," although with Chester's girth, they were anything but spare. Chester's grunting, snorting, and bellowing hurt my ears and I wondered whether he could be heard in downtown Pipestone, two miles away.

Lee handed Tim a stout knife with a five-inch blade. "Feel here, Tim," Lee said as he placed Tim's hand on Chester's neck. "Feel that? That's his jugular. You've got to stick 'em there good to let him bleed out. Nothings so bad as pork that's not 'bled out.' Think you can do it?" "Neb, stay on his back but away from his head so he can't bite you!"

There was a tremor in Tim's hand and terror in his face. His eyes were turning red and watery. He had the look of a 120 pound halfback about to be hit by a 220 pound linebacker. I sympathized with Tim. After all, he was about to give the *coup de grace* to a creature that had become an adopted member of his family. During the past few years he had spent more time with Chester than he had with Mary and Elmer, his sister and brother. He never swore at his hog like he did his siblings.

Tim plunged the knife in and Chester's bellowing doubled in volume and went up an octave. A squirt of blood as thick as my thumb sprayed over Tim's knife, arm, and jeans. Chester was squealing like a power drill on sheet metal. "Twist that knife around, Tim. Cut 'em good! Do all the damage you can in there! Good job! Good job!" But Chester was fighting back. He bounced me off his side, slipped the rope off his hocks, and struggled to his feet. Blood poured down his front and splashed on his hoofs. Lee jumped on his back and tried to ride him down, but a cowboy would have better success riding a saddleless bronco than Lee had with that hog. Lee slid off Chester's back, and then Chester did a couple of pirouettes. Finally, his stout legs seemed to quiver and turn to jello. They splayed out and Chester collapsed, gave a few grunts and died. He lay in a pool of blood that gradually welled over a yard in diameter.

I was riveted in place and couldn't say a word. Lee cried, "Good job, Tim. You stuck him in good shape." He grabbed Tim's bloody hands and shook them as if he were priming a pump. Tim had a strange look on his face, something between seeing a visitation of the Virgin Mary in the nearby grove and the apprehension of a kid who has killed his mother. We pulled Chester over to a tree, hoisted him up with a wagon singletree hooked into his back-leg tendons so he could finish "bleeding out." We found some lye soap and washed up at the horse tank. Later some of Tim's relatives would throw Chester in a tub of scalding water, roll him out on some planks and scrape off his bristles. Someone would probably jest "Shave and a Hair Cut, Two Bits," "Little Piggy Has Gone to Market," or "Chester is About to Get His Last Shave."

A farm is such a carnival of birth and death that there is no wonder it should frighten a youngster. But farmers, like physicians, must indulge in black humor. For without it psychic survival would be difficult. To birth and to kill are the bookends of a farmer's existence. In between, they lovingly nurture animals who often times are anthropomorphized and nearly become members of their extended families.

Most of Chester would be cut up for the freezer, although a few cuts might go to the smokehouse. Every part except his squeal would be used. His brain would be made into head cheese, his feet would be pickled, and his belly would be smoked and renamed bacon. I thought it strange that some ethnic groups preferred the insides of an animal to the outside. Even Chester's shapely snout, ears, and jowls, which helped him win third prize, would be ground up as sausage and stuffed in his intestines or casings. As for aesthetics, I didn't give it a thought.

Tim promised Lee a ham for his fine job of mentoring.

(Butchering a beef was different; no hot water or scalding, but in other respects the same. The steer or heifer, usually weighing 800 pounds, was one of the best in the feed yard. Most farmers kept back a "choice to prime" calf for their own table rather than eat a tough dairy cow. The condemned critter would be driven out of the feedlot, roped and snubbed to a post at the place where the butchering was to take place. A gandy-dancer type lick with a sledge hammer or ax would stun the brute, after which a big gash in the neck would release a tremendous amount of blood in huge gushes. A block and tackle would elevate the rear end of the carcass to assure complete bleeding. The hide was carefully removed by skinning, stripped off and sprinkled with an ample amount of salt. Rolled up and tied with twine, it eventually would be sold to a hide merchant for a few dollars.)

I began to understand what the Hebrew sages meant when they equated blood with the mysterious life force. As the blood gushed out of Chester, he literally died before our eyes. Perhaps the ancients were not far off the mark with they equated life with blood. Henceforth, statements like "Saved By The Blood of Christ" would have deeper meaning. Transfusions of blood both then and now, meant reanimation—life, both physically and symbolically. I surmised that it is unwise to discard a cultural and behavioral pattern simply because, in the light of modernity and sophistication, it might seem inhumane if not barbaric.

Chester's death gave me insight into the ritual offering of animals to the gods. Homemakers today purchase antiseptically packaged chops and roasts in supermarkets. But from the Stone Age until recent times, families knew the conflicting feelings of expectancy and angst, of joy and sadness, in the killing of their animals. Such animals, as members of their extended families, were sometimes given human characteristics. As part of the killing ritual, the best portions of the meat were offered to their gods. How flat, in comparison, is a check to God or the church budget in comparison to the gift of a member of your agricultural family. I inwardly thanked Lee for allowing me to participate in a ritual, which however superficially brutal, was profound at its core. I promised myself in the future to explore time-honored cultural rituals and extract their meanings.

Lee was the opposite of his Dutch peers. While his house had nice appointments inside and out, the farm buildings were a Minnesota version, without the sexual frolicking, coon dogs, and corn liquor, of Erskin Caldwell's *God's Little Acre.* A Dakota "black roller" would have flattened his unpainted barn, sheds, and fences. But he knew the sheep didn't mind. Besides, well-kept buildings, however nice from an aesthetic standpoint, don't add to the bottom line.

In one shed Lee kept a Piper Cub airplane. I went flying with him a few times, once to the Twin Cities. We got lost in a rainstorm, and he circled the water tower of a small village at an altitude of 50 feet to read the name and find out where we were. He was a devil-may-care pilot and took risks with his life that he wouldn't have taken with his precious sheep. He landed in side winds and didn't put a great deal of faith in getting weather forecasts. He was deaf to the pilot's creed—"There are *old* pilots, and their are *bold* pilots, but there are no *old and bold* pilots"— that I often recited to him. Fortunately, I wasn't on board when he had several crack-ups, none of which caused him serious injury.

One Spring I spent the week of Easter vacation cleaning out the feedlot. During the winter thousands of sheep had turned tons of corn, hay, and feed supplement into a two-foot-deep morass of manure. In 1940 there were no front-end loaders on tractors to distance me from animal excreta. The smell was close to being asphyxiating. But to Lee, thinking of the increased corn yields it would bring in the Fall, it smelled like money. I used a coal shovel or closely tined silage fork to shovel his liquid gold. I would fill the manure wagon, pull it out to a field with a little Fordson tractor, turn up my collar, hunch down and draw in my head, turtle-fashion, behind an old leather coat, engage the gears, and drive at break-neck speed.

Ever since that Easter vacation, I always smile when someone uses the phrase, "and the SH.. HIT THE FAN," for I am one of the very few people who truly has an existential knowledge of the meaning of that graphic phrase. The blades at the end of the spreader created a shower, an Old Faithful yellow geyser, 30 feet on each side of the wagon. My coat and hat would be plastered. The routine was repeated 10 times a day. Biking home, I left an invisible 1000 foot stench behind me. I undressed in our detached garage and streaked naked through the house on the way to the shower. I used a lot of soap, fearful that a lingering odor might indicate to my friends how I had spent my vacation. I received $11.50 that week. It wasn't a bad wage for renewing the fertility of Terra Mater.

36. A GANDY DANCER ON THE MILWAUKEE RAILROAD

The malice of sloth lies not merely in the neglect of duty (though that can be a symptom of it) but in the refusal of Joy. It is allied to despair.

The Seven Deadly Sins, Evelyn Waugh

During the summer of 1944 Les Kallsen, Neal Knudtson, and I signed on as "gandy dancers" for the Milwaukee railroad. I was anxiously awaiting my 18th birthday so that I could enter the Navy Air Corps. The railroads were making enormous profits during the war and, because of a shortage of adult labor, the Milwaukee hired 92 high school juniors and seniors for summer jobs improving their running track. Every morning at 5:30 we boarded two school buses for the ride out to the tracks. Starting west of Flandreau, South Dakota, over 40 miles from Pipestone, we laid a foot of fresh gravel, jacked up the tracks, put in new ties and tamped them tight, straightened the rails, and "dressed" the right-of-way by leveling the gravel one inch below the top of the ties.

We had no automatic tampers or machinery of any kind. Our only tools were heavy jacks, level bars, and shovels. It was hard work, often performed under a relentless sun. The railroad ties were beyond counting. The tracks seemed to quiver in the summer heat and stretched forever up and over an endless horizon. Mirages of watery oases beckoned at each end of the track.

The work provided little sense of accomplishment or progress toward a goal. To relieve our boredom Neal Knudtson and I would sometimes see how far we could walk balanced on a rail. When I was "on," I could go for close to 1,000 feet.

Years later I interpreted the summer in terms of the protagonist in Albert Camus' *The Myth of Sisyphus*. As punishment for various sins against classical deities, Sisyphus had been condemned by the gods to an eternity of pushing a rock to the top of a mountain. But each time he neared the goal, the rock always fell back down and had to be rolled up again. Camus, the great French existentialist novelist writing after the Second World War, believed that Sisyphus was everyman. In attempting to wrench meaning from the absurdity of the human condition, Camus held that "We must assume Sisyphus was *happy*" in his nihilistic condition.

Really? That's not how I saw it. My fate was to tamp and dress railroad ties that seemed to stretch out to an endless horizon. That summer was an absurd experience. I was treading water, yes, but that didn't mean life was meaningless; I was waiting for my call from the Navy so that I could hurl my small but nevertheless meaningful weight onto the scale to balance the forces of Evil. Each night I entered a check-mark on my calendar and mused: "Another day closer to the Navy Air Corps."

A July 13, 1994 article in *The Pipestone Star* had two photos of our crew and indicated that "to date over $9,000 in checks had been paid, giving some of them tidy bank accounts." What made the work bearable was the pay ($35.00 a week), working with friends, and the humane qualities of the gandy dancer lifers who were our bosses. Larry O'Brien, the foreman, made a profound impression on me. He had spent his life on the rails, laying and repairing track from coast to coast. Even his home was on the rails—a freight car converted into a bunkhouse. The Milwaukee Railroad was his family. His wife couldn't tolerate the nomadic life of a gandy dancer and left him long ago. He hadn't heard from his children in years. But the harshness and tragedy of his life did not affect his treatment of me. He never asked me to do anything he was unwilling to do. Our conversation often drifted into politics. I parroted Father's Republican faith and the conservative clichés on which I had been suckled—F.D.R. was "ruining the country," setting "class against class," the poor were "lazy, shiftless, and no-goods," W.P.A. was a "make-work, leaf-raking project," "welfare is the great narcotic of men's souls," and "the Democrats were trying to spend us rich."

Everyone I knew told terrible jokes about the WPA. One I remember had a rich woman call the WPA to have her lawn mowed. In a couple of days eight men showed up and began to dig a large hole in her lawn.

"What are you doing?" she remonstrated.
"We are going to mow your grass," the foreman answered.
"Why are you digging that hole?" she screamed.
"We're fixin' to put the outhouse here."
"What in the world for," she demanded, "and what are all those
    other men doing here?"
"Well, ma'am, we're from the WPA. We're gonna have two comin', two
goin', two shittin', and two mowin'."

But my words were only that—words. They were abstract and theoretical, not experiential and concrete. Larry had traversed a pilgrimage straight out of D. H. Lawrence's *Sons and Lovers* and John Steinbeck's,

Grapes of Wrath. He had known, as I had not, fatherlessness, unemployment, poverty, hunger, tragedy, and homelessness. At 17 years of age, I was years away from the wisdom Larry's 50 years had brought him.

"Franklin Roosevelt's enemies call him a cripple," Larry said, "but all I can say is that I would rather have as president a physical cripple with a heart for the working man than a moral cripple like Hoover." I was frightened by his bitterness; he had suffered too much to see life through my rose-colored glasses. Class warfare was a fact, a reality that I, as a member of the middle class, did not want to acknowledge. But the fact that Larry saw a will-to-power between groups did not erode his personal one-to-one kindness.

My carefully tended Puritan values, the idea that any individual could prosper through discipline and drive—an idea exemplified in a few conspicuously public lives, like those of Carnegie, Edison, Hearst and, dare I say it, my Father, was less than the whole truth. To legions of Larrys, trying to get ahead through the old virtues of self-reliance and individual exertion seemed like throwing snowballs at the sun. I feared there were masses of Larrys attesting to the graveyard of American ideals. He told me that the term "scab," for example—once a synonym for a prostitute because of its reference to venereal skin lesions—now came to mean a shameless man who takes a striking worker's job. An ironworker who agreed to toil extra hours in the heat of the blast furnace was called a "hog" or "chaser" or "blackleg" or "boss's pet" or "Jim Grabs" in honor of his indifference to safety and the bargaining power of his comrades.

I had entered another world, foreign but strangely attractive. Chance, fortune, fate, and luck had entered my evolving philosophy of life as the connection between merit and reward increasingly widened. It was becoming harder to believe that an active Providence governs all. I became uneasy with the use of the terms "winners" and "losers"—as if life itself were a game—as synonyms for people's station in life. I was surprised that Larry read a lot and loved to quote the memorable passage from Horace Greeley: "That as things now are, a man possessing the talent of Fulton, the strength of Samson, the uprightness of Job, may perish of want in the streets because no one knows his abilities or chooses to employ him."

The CIO unions were becoming a threat to the bourgeoisie ethos. Larry was proud of the fact that, for the most part, unions did not discriminate against blacks, women or ethnic minorities. But one day he heard John, one of my co-workers, sing a little ditty to the tune of Walt Disney's *Snow White:*

Hiho! Hiho!
Don't join the CIO
And pay your dues to a
    bunch of Jews
Hiho! Hiho!

Larry's face turned crimson as he screamed, "Get out of here!" His throbbing neck veins seemed the size of a garden hose—"You're fired. Don't you dare set foot on my track again!" John picked up his lunch bucket and walked back to the school bus.

Larry was my first contact with a labor proletarian. He was not a Communist, nor had he heard Marx's plea—"The proletarians have nothing to lose but their chains. They have a world to win. *Workers of the world, unite!*" But he had heard Roosevelt say in 1936 that he believed in individualism, up to the point where the individualist starts to operate at the *expense of society.* Larry did not want to overturn the American Experiment, he just wanted a fairer division of its benefits.

True, I had known some agricultural poor people, but farmers, even destitute ones, were more individualistic in their thinking. Farmers were less prone to unionize and support overt coercion as a remedy for injustice. Larry had much more anger and rebellion in him than the poor farmers I had known. His sense of injustice was intensified by the daily sharing of grievances with his comrades as they laid track. Farmers lacked such reinforcing mechanisms, because they were more like Robinson Crusoe solitaries. Depression-era farm proletarians probably suffered as much as their urban counterparts, but they were not elbow to elbow with them in the mine, factory, and mill. As individuals they only had the will to survive. Urban workers, as a collective, were driven by the will to power. The unique characteristics of farm culture—isolated living, the vagaries of nature, the tendency to blame one's self or the fickleness of nature, the strong sense of duty, and the annual rebirth of optimism with every spring and gentle shower—all this and more mitigated against agrarian solidarity.

Bert Vander Slice knew farmers who were members of an oil cooperative who would buy gasoline from a competing company if it was two cents cheaper. Thus, while the O'Briens and Vander Slices may have shared common economic straits, they were worlds apart in their psychological perceptions. As a result, labor organizers were singularly unsuccessful in organizing the rural proletarians during the Depression.

During the early 1930s, Father's youngest brother, Uncle Ben, a Hutchinson trucker, had several confrontations with union militants. A group of farmers had created the Farm Holiday Association and pledged to withhold farm products from the market until they could extract a fair price. The organizers had promised to use Gandhi-like methods, but some farmers armed themselves with pitchforks and clubs and manned roadblocks to make sure no produce could be delivered to the cities. Some threw logs or a "porcupine"(a threshing belt studded with nails) into the path of a truck. The militants dumped milk into ditches, burned wheat, and killed livestock in attempts to secure higher prices. Once Uncle Ben was on the way to the stock yards of South Saint Paul with a load of hogs when labor picketers stopped him and demanded that he turn around. He knocked a militant off his running board by delivering a firm left elbow to his chest, shoved his truck into gear, broke through the barrier, and delivered his livestock. "I took gravel roads back to Hutch," he remembered. "I was afraid they would be laying for me." Some Minneapolis truck drivers, Ben reported, would just as soon crack a cop as drink a beer.

I wondered how many Larrys there were in America. As an individual he was fascinating, but I feared for our country if hundreds of thousands of Larrys were to act in concert on their grievances. Because of Larry O'Brien, my inherited middle class values began to waver. Now I was not so sure that character and property went together. Perhaps members of the middle class are as hardened to the distresses of the poor as surgeons are to their patients' bodily pains. I began to realize that whenever a separation is made between liberty and justice, neither is really safe. The virtues enshrined by my family—no smoking, drinking, swearing, or Sabbath-breaking—seemed rather petty in light of the larger economic and political issues of the 1940s. While I was grateful for the wholesome family values I had been given, I realized that I had been insulated from a brutal world of factories, mills, and mines where millions of Larrys were struggling to improve their marginal condition. My inherited values were ideal in the personal world around hearth and home but I began to doubt that they were the only solution to the national calamities of poverty, racism, and disease.

I began to discover that business and professional classes of Pipestone hated Franklin Roosevelt with pure venom. They detested him for his wit, sagacity, life style, and his brilliant, liberated wife. "There are people whose watch stops at a certain hour," observed Sainte-Beuve, "and who remain permanently at that age." By smoking in public, Roosevelt toyed with middle-class Puritan sensitivities. His ten-inch cigarette holder came up at a 45 degree angle from the corner of his mouth, as if to say "I don't give a fig for your moralistic peccadillos."

His Fireside Chats were excellent political theater. "I can endure Republican censure of myself, my wife, and the members of my family," he would say in mock outrage, "But they have gone too far when they castigate my little Scottie dog, Falla. Have they no shame?"

Roosevelt ended Prohibition, the "Noble Experiment," and that was more than enough for most Baptists and Methodists. I remember Father and Ed Trebon listening to the election returns in 1936. When it was clear that Roosevelt had beaten Alfred Landon in a landslide, they went around in a blue funk for days. Father and Mother voted for a Democrat only twice: for Woodrow Wilson in 1916 because "he had kept us out of war," and for F.D.R. in 1932 because of the Depression. They repented of both mistakes within several months.

Roosevelt had changed the equation of power. He knew we could avoid a revolution, indeed, save capitalism, only by bringing the marginalized classes into the system. But to the Pipestone gentry, he had betrayed his class, and they felt that their power was being curtailed. More than that, he was destroying the myth that they had earned, not inherited, their privileged status. I began to understand the adage that the course of a river is almost always disapproved of by its source. Roosevelt knew that middle class manners, however nice if adopted by the poor, would not correct a fundamental imbalance of power relationships between the classes. Nor was an increase of philanthropy the solution. In later years I could put into words what I began to feel—"Love can only do *more, never less,* than justice." It became increasingly clear to me that love without justice turns into sentimentality; justice without love often is harsh, cold, and impersonal.

The risqué stories about Eleanor! During the Roosevelt re-election run of 1936, the Republican underground unloaded on Eleanor and Franklin. My grade school friends and I would chant in unison the scurrilous piece of doggerel—"You kiss the Niggers...I'll kiss the Jews...We'll stay in the White House...As long as we choose!"—without realizing how shameful and inhumane its message. Eleanor had broken the traditional mold of the First Lady and she was paying a terrible price for her independence. As her views on racial equality became familiar, she became known simply as *"That Woman,"* and for many, she was the world's most hated person. There were dozens of bawdy if not vulgar stories about her. Conservatives made jokes about her buck teeth and her rubbing noses with Eskimos. Dirty little books made the rounds at school. If you thumbed through them quickly, a jerky animation showed Eleanor having sex with a Negro.

Work on the railroad ended at 3:30 in the afternoon. I would hurry home for a quick dinner before being picked up by friends to drive out to the country to search for a grain-shocking job. With many farm boys off to war, there was a lot of grain that was down. Farmers were happy to pay us $5.00 to shock until sundown. I always preferred to shock barley or wheat because, while the beards penetrated my gloves and shirtsleeves, I could literally throw the bundles at each other and they would stick together. Oats and rye, on the other hand, were slippery and difficult to make into a solid, good-looking shock. A good farmer would have clean, tight bundles with neat, flat-cut butts. Gradually I improved my ability to build a shock that kept the weighted heads of grain from tipping over into the soil.

Working from sunrise to sunset put me in good shape for the Navy Air Corps. When I was sworn in, I had 134 pounds of bone, muscle, and sinew on my five-feet nine-inch frame. After four months in the service, I jumped to 165 and stood five feet, eleven inches tall.

37. THE SALOON

The reign of tears is over. Slums will soon be only a memory. We will turn prisons into factories, jails into corn cribs. Men will walk upright; women will smile; children will laugh. Hell will be forever for rent.

> Billy Sunday, upon the passage of Prohibition

Now I'm resolved to try it,
I'll live on a moderate diet,
I'll not drink and will deny it,
And shun each alehouse door,
For that's the place they tell us,
We meet with all jovial good fellows,
But I swear by the poker and bellows,
I'll never get drunk anymore.

A man that fond of boozing,
His cash goes daily oozing,
His character he's losing,
And its loss he will deplore.
His wife is unprotected,
His business is neglected,
Himself is disrespected,
So I'll not get drunk anymore.

> Old Temperance Song

Forty feet west of Father's office was Sammy's, Pipestone's saloon. Father never passed it either by car or on foot without castigating what he considered our community's cardinal symbol of social leprosy. The phrase that John Wesley had used for slavery, "the sum of all villainies," Father transferred to liquor. From his perspective, Sammy's served the elixir of the devil and all those within this house of sinners were robbers, murderers, fornicators, or worse. When I was with Father, I always averted my eyes; I didn't want him to catch me looking within, lest my glance betray a note of interest. The saloon was a vile place, a veritable slippery-slope to Hell for all of those who frequented its premises. "The only time I have been in a saloon," Father boasted, "is when I went in to pull some drunken sinner out." I never asked for further information. I suspected his story was apocryphal, because he was vague on the details. He recounted his Good Samaritan heroism only for its pedagogical purpose.

Father would have agreed with Dorthy Parker's quatrain: "I like to have a Martini/Two at the very most/After three I'm under the table/After four I'm under the host."

Ostensibly, Sammy's single-handedly kept our town mired in ignorance and vice while 14 churches fought valiantly for devotion, temperance, and decency. On the face of it, the battle seemed exceedingly uneven. In spite of this, the smell from Sammy's both enticed and repelled me. It was like nothing my nose had ever before encountered. The aroma's major component seemed to be stale beer, but there were also elements of body odor, rancid grease, sweeping compound that I had smelled in school, old wood and varnish, perhaps even a grace note of the remains of dried vomit.

Even when I was by myself, I had a hard time clearly seeing what Pipestone's den of iniquity really looked like. Huge cardboard posters of bathing girls, blondes with big breasts, slender hips, and waxen faces, in white bathing suits—"See what you get with a Coca-Cola!"—blocked the view through the display windows. Post-card sized signs glossed over with shining mica were taped to the window: "Credit Makes Enemies, Let's Be Friends"; "Ladies May Smoke But Be Careful Where You Lay Your Butts"; "Eat Here and Keep Your Wife For a Pet"; ITY-WYTBAD.

To further obscure the view, the saloon lights were dim, almost as if its denizens did not want those on the street to know of their presence. A rainbow-colored jukebox stood against the wall, and electric tableaux for Hamms and Grain Belt beers hung on thin chains from the ceiling above the back bar. Usually I could make out several foursomes playing cards or checkers. Others were at the pool table or sucking on beer bottles while perched on chrome-legged stools with red seats at the bar.

In our small town, the Anti-Saloon League (ASL) and the Women's Christian Temperance Union (WCTU) had a strong presence. The latter was primarily middle class, and its members were predominately the wives of physicians, lawyers, merchants, and wealthy farmers. They wanted to improve the working class economically, socially, and morally—even against its wishes and inclinations—and replace the hated saloon with a coffee house. The ecumenical ASL was created during the last decade of the 19th century by midwestern evangelical Protestants. Its goal, "the *extermination* of the beverage liquor traffic," perpetuated the use of military metaphors of the Civil War. Roman Catholic groups, notably the Catholic Total Abstinence Union, along with the nationally renowned Archbishop Ireland of St. Paul, also joined the forces aligned against demon rum. Even liberals joined in, not because of any emphasis on personal holiness, but as a means of transforming society for the better.

The WCTU members whom I knew from our Methodist church ran to type—fiftyish or older, heavy of bosom, wearing somber dresses of black and long hair that was rolled in a bun or was of an unkept type that Mother called a "rat's nest." They looked like the kind of Jack Spratt wife illustrated in children's books—ones who "could eat no lean." However victorious they were in fending off the temptations of John Barleycorn, the majority had lost on the battlefield of calories. A few were rubbery, dough-faced types who collapsed into a chair in a form of hereditary fatigue, as if they had recently been boned.

Each year the WCTU sponsored a "Temperance" sermon delivered by a celebrated itinerant booze slayer. Usually the warrior was an elderly "maiden lady." Of course, youth ever grins scornfully at the wreckage of age. The young parishioners might have embraced the message more eagerly if the messenger had been a coach or athletic star. Even Father dozed off during temperance sermons. When I remarked about it, he remonstrated that he was "just resting his eyes." The service invariably closed with the singing of the "Prohibition Battle Hymn:"

> We've played the Good Samaritan
> > But now we'll take a hand
> And clear the road to Jericho
> Of the robbing, thieving band;
> > Distillers and Saloonists
> Shall be driven from the land
> > As we go marching on.

I often wondered whether Reverend Reineke really wanted to give over the pulpit each year to someone so absolutely boring—it made us appreciate him all the more.

Methodism's absolutism on liquor was rooted in the fact that it came from a land, Britain, where in the 18th century pub owners routinely displayed the notice "Drunk for a penny, dead drunk for two-pence" in their windows. Hogarth's "Gin lane" immortalized the degradation of

London's wretched "lumpen proletariat," the urban refuse that the Wesleys knew most intimately.

Temperance sermons violated, however, the normative meaning—"moderation in all things"—of the classic virtue that gave the movement its name. For the Greeks, for example, courage was the proper warrior virtue between the extremes of cowardice and rash, irrational self-sacrifice. But I never heard "in nothing too much" regarding drink. Yet, until the late 19th century Temperance Movement, Christendom and Western culture had held that, "Wine is of the Lord, but drunkenness is of Satan." Temperance sermons were easily predictable—long litanies of poor souls done in by booze who, once on the wagon, found life to be a bowl of cherries. The secret to a happy life was simple—be a teetotaler.

I was bored stiff with this notion, because it was a replay of the broken-record message I received at home. The Biblical text was usually Proverbs 20:1: "Wine is a mocker, strong drink is a brawler; and whoever is led astray by it is not wise." The speaker always quoted Abraham Lincoln's famous aphorism—"Liquor has many defenders but no defense." But I noticed that the temperance lady never dealt with St. Paul's advice to Timothy (5:23): "No longer drink only water *but use a little wine* for the sake of your stomach and your frequent ailments." In spite of this Biblical prescription, I never found any wine in Father's medical bag. At home I read Proverbs 3:18-19:

> Honor the Lord with your substance
>   And with the first fruits of all your produce;
> Then your barns will be filled with plenty,
>   *And your vats will be bursting with wine.*

I was perplexed about my church and my parent's fixation on booze as the sum of all villainy and wondered why virtue so often wore such a sour face.

Later I discovered that Protestant America's fixation on John Barleycorn arose from a double fear. On the one hand, the Pipestone gentry, like WASPs nationwide, was threatened by momentous changes in our nation's character. Immigrant hordes, different in religion, ethnicity, mores, and class flooded our urban areas. For southern and eastern Europeans, liquor—*aqua vitae*, the very stuff of life—was a good creation of God and a part of their culture. They saw WASP Puritanism as a veiled attempt to impugn their integrity and power. Protestants feared that the foundations of their moral and social hegemony were being eroded. Those Americans who were here first, who could claim connection with the colonialists, had a right to define the moral landscape. People with strange-sounding names and antisocial behaviors were invading the heartland.

Our Italian butcher represented just one drop in a wave of immigrants invading our towns, bringing with them strange cultural values that not only tolerated but actually enjoyed liquor. But even my parents admitted that Mr. Tarango sold excellent meat, kept a clean shop, and had a good sense of humor. The gentry in Pipestone seemed more prone to fear in the abstract than in the particular.

A second fear arose out of the disappointment that a Victorian-era utopia had not emerged after the abolition of slavery. All the passion for a new American Eden had not been vented on the battlefields between Fort Sumter and Appomattox; zeal left over from that titanic conflict shifted to a new channel. If the Kingdom of God on earth had not come with emancipation, perhaps a crusade against Demon Rum might succeed in bringing it about.

Sadly enough, my church and my parents allowed moral judgment to overpower their psychological and sociological analysis regarding alcohol. Moralism may have been a cover for an elitism and repugnance toward the new immigrant. "I drink," commented a steel worker, "because it is the cheapest and fastest way out of Pittsburgh on the weekend." Demon Rum was a dirt-cheap anesthetic for the brutalities of life. The Robber Barons of laissez-faire capitalism treated the immigrant as a thing, a commodity who was ground to bits by a 10-12 hour day and a six day week. Liquor for the industrial laborer was an easy and inexpensive escape.

Karl Olson was one of the few citizens that I knew who frequented the saloon with any regularity. Karl was a Pipestone handyman, a rural counterpart of his urban industrial comrades. He was an on-and-off again worker, who occasionally did dirty and odd jobs for my parents. He lived literally and figuratively on the other side of the tracks. Gertrude, his wife, had a voice like that of the fishmonger's wife. Not surprisingly, Karl preferred the saloon to listening to her screaming at home.

For the Pipestone proletariat, indeed the Karls of all America, the saloon provided an escape, a sanctuary from the world of women and the everyday reminders by their betters as to their failures. At Sammy's they celebrated their good fortune or, more often, wept their grief. It was a place where they could relax and not have to go tippy-toe before their superiors. Sammy's was the club of the poor, the church of the dispossessed.

I don't recall whether Karl attended church. Had he done so he may have experienced the heart of a stranger and felt "these are not my people." Moreover, most of the churches were closed during the week. One or two of the finer ones might have felt he would have dirtied the carpet.

The saloon, then, was the only club that would have the Karls of the world. Pipestone's moral monitors never came to its pews. But if they had, they would have found camaraderie, back-slapping, story-telling, and acceptance without finger-pointing. The barkeep gave ear to the Karls of Pipestone without raised eyebrows or censure. Sammy's bartenders didn't have to wear a Roman collar or carry a Bible to give Karl absolution. On the few occasions when Karl was able to buy a round of drinks, it was a mark of his manhood, of the acceptance of his *being* in spite of his *doing*. The saloon had some of the characteristics of a Christian community even though it didn't have a cross on the roof or stained glass for windows. The Karls from distant cities ceased to be strangers the moment they entered Sammy's. I suspect that Jack London, Erskine Caldwell, John Steinbeck, Ernest Hemingway, Jack Kerouac, and especially Jesus would have enjoyed the company of the Karls within. I began to understand Mencken's observation that a "prohibitionist is the sort of man one wouldn't care to drink with—even if he drank." Few things are more unpleasant than a virtuous person with a mean mind.

But not all the citizens of Pipestone held the saloon in low regard. My friends who were Catholics and Missouri Synod Lutherans viewed the fruit of the grape as God's gift. They loved to taunt their Baptist and Methodist buddies, including me, with a bit of doggerel:

There's Henry Ward Beecher
    And Sunday School teachers
    And drink of the sassafras root.
But you bet all the same
    If it had the right name
    It's the juice of the forbidden fruit.

And they would belt out the refrain and do the sailor roll as if they were drunk:

Oh, the juice of the forbidden fruit.

And then with a Bacchanalian scream, they would shout the chorus:

Oh, the juice of the forbidden fruit!
  But you bet all the same
  If it had its right name,
It's the juice of the forbidden fruit!

Our saloon was unlike an English pub, the village social center, frequented by both men and women, where food and ale are served. By making liquor irredeemably evil, prohibitionists drove a wedge between food and spirits. A traditional unity, symbolized by the Lord's Supper of bread and wine, was broken. Tragically, liquor was wrenched from its context with food and was often consumed in isolation, becoming a symbol of rebellion. The consequence—the increase of alcoholism—was, of course, predictable. Evangelical churches like mine had to invent self-serving rationalizations that Jesus drank grape juice, not wine. Yet for centuries, monasteries had breweries and the sugar in their ale was the winter fuel that kept the monastics warm under their layers of cassocks.

Tragically, because of the dominant influence of Evangelical Protestants, Americans have not been able to differentiate between a variety of alcoholic beverages. Unlike wine makers anywhere else in the world, those in the United States have had to contend with the Prohibition factor. Our third President, Thomas Jefferson, for example, held that wine-drinking was an essential part of an agrarian democracy. This was partly because he saw the alternative tipples—spirits, especially the frontiersman's whiskey—as a danger to the civilization he wanted to engender, but also because he thought drinking wine was itself civilized. He consumed it, as proper wine-lovers do today, as part of a meal. For Jefferson, wine was the drink of temperance, of moderation, until the meaning of that word got perverted to mean abstention. Taken at the table as part of a meal, it was a rational source of pleasure, not simply an agent of intoxication. The unhappy side of the story of wine in the United States is that the "temperance" yahoos who finally foisted Prohibition on the country thought of wine as just another kind of booze and persuaded most of the population to do the same.

A riddle that plagued our Pipestone divines for years was the fact that in many towns where a tornado struck, the church was usually the first building to go. Because most saloons invariably survived, like Job, men of the cloth wondered why evil seemed to prosper and the righteous were struck down. A few Christians may have even lost their faith until modern weathermen pointed out that the churches, closed all week, made an ideal target. With windows and doors tightly fastened, the differential air pressure literally caused the houses of worship to explode. There were no divine lessons to be learned. The saloon, with swinging half doors in constant use, was able to withstand.

None of the above is written to absolve or erase the tragic legacy of John Barleycorn. A moral case can still be made that beverage alcohol does far more harm than good and that its absence would—in the long run—be a blessing to the population. "Melancholy," observed Samuel Johnson, "should be diverted by every means but by drinking." There is little doubt that Demon Rum killed and maimed far more men than did the Civil War. The Protestant churches, moreover, were wise to be in the vanguard in the late 19th century in working for women's suffrage. Women and children bore the brunt of the alcoholism of men. Many clerics even postulated that women have a higher spiritual and moral nature than men and that, if given the vote, women would enact legislation for a finer America. Liquor was and remains a unique American curse on the legions of Pipestones across our land.

One need only read Jack London's work, *John Barleycorn,* to discover the tragic results of liquor in one creative life. My parents and my church were right in pointing out that some choices can lead to bondage. Freedom is not simply alternative choice. It is abstaining from behaviors which, if done, diminish and destroy freedom. True freedom is directing life toward God and the Good, to go the direction that human nature was created to go. It was the manner and context of the message I was given by my church and the moral establishment that was wrong, not its content.

For all their good intentions, the prohibition forces were not attractive to me. The pinched-up old biddies of the Temperance Union seemed like self-righteous old crones to me. I suspect that I was not alone, and that my parents also wished that the forces of virtue might have presented a more pleasant face. Moreover, in their attempt to protect me, the warriors of Temperance were guilty of overreaching. I understood George Santayana's observation that it is easier to make a saint out of a libertine than out of a prig. How ironic it was that many of the insights of the saints arose from their experience as burly sinners!

My church had forgotten St. Paul's teaching regarding the law. Its negative and legalistic intensity in opposing Demon Rum simply made liquor more attractive to me. Moreover, many teetotalers were cold of heart and cold of head. The feeble fibers of their egos did not allow them to smoke, drink, swear, or do much of anything else of risk or daring. Their lives were unlovely, restrained, and ghetto-narrow. They were too concerned about keeping their feet dry, conserving their heartbeats and making unlovely life successes of their spirit-mediocrity. I began to understand that more people are flattered into virtue than bullied out of vice. Moreover, I longed for the company of the generous-hearted, not the rabbit-hearted. I would sing this little ditty as a mild ridicule: "I don't drink and I don't smoke and I don't chew, nor do I go with girls who do!"

Salvation originally was a moral change *within the self* that transformed *external* behaviors. As a child of a straight-laced home, I never experienced the angst of being a slave to liquor. I had to be careful not to assume that having the right external habits was itself proof of having a transformed heart.

I gradually came to see that misuse should not forbid use. Otherwise knives, guns, cars and much more would have to be prohibited. Moreover, temperance should refer not only to drink but to all pleasures. It should mean not abstaining but going the right length and no further. Islam, not Christianity, is a teetotal religion. As C.S. Lewis has observed, a mark of a certain type of bad man is that he cannot give up a thing himself without wanting every one else to give it up too. A Christian may see fit to give up all sorts of things for special reasons— fur coats, marriage, meat, dancing, hunting, beer, military service, the theater—but the moment he begins saying such things are bad in themselves, or pontificating against such people as do use them, he has taken the wrong road.

It would have been a great blessing if prohibition had worked. But men are earthen vessels and not angels. State-enforced abstinence in our society or, for that matter, any other society, is asking too much of human nature and would put human freedom in a straight-jacket. No sooner had national prohibition become law than the country seemed to regret it, and a new occupation, bootlegging, sprang up to quench the public thirst. In 10 years the federal government made over half a million arrests and secured over 300,000 convictions for violations of the Volstead Act, but smuggling increased. Bathtub gin, Al Capone, "leaks" at the border, and much more continued until we wised up and "The Noble Experiment" was repealed. Nothing seemed to work, and Will Rogers opined that "prohibition is better than no liquor at all." The adage—"The perfect is the enemy of the good"—had once again proven itself to be true. If law attempts to exterminate every moral taint from society, it turns man's meat into his poison.

But for my parents generation, abstinence may have been the best policy. They would have agreed with Samuel Pepys' observation that "since my leaving drinking of wine, I do find myself better, and do mind my business better, and do spend less money, and less time lost in idle company." They were convinced that social drinking started the slippery slope to divorce, disease, pauperism, degradation, sexual escapade, crime, an earlier death; indeed, a legion of personal and social pathologies. Schopenhauer was right in stating that there is no "more mistaken path to happiness than worldliness, revelry, and high life."

The maggots of intoxication were real even though I had not experienced them. I could not disagree with my parent's logic that I would never become an alcoholic if I never took that first drink.

MARGARET AGNITSCH

*If you need any information about
the Navy—Just ask me.*

Girls' League, 2.

DARLENE ANDERSON

Take it easy—I'm fragile.

Student Council, 1; Girls' League, 2;
Choir, 2, 3; G.A.A., 2, 3, 4; Operetta, 2;
"Hobgoblin House", 3; "Plane Crazy," 4.

MILDRED ANDERSON

She is a quiet girl—at times.

Girls' League, 2; Red Caps, 3; Library
Cadet, 4.

LORRAINE APPELDORN

Where does an alien go to register?

Operetta, 2; Choir, 1, 2, 3, 4; Girls' Glee
Club, 1, 2, 3, 4.
Debate, 1; Girls' Octet, 1, 2, 4; Madrigal,
3; Girls' League 2; National Honor Society,
3, 4; Annual Staff, 4; "Plane Crazy," 4;
Valedictorian, 4; "Hobgoblin House," 3;

DON ARGETSINGER

His bark is worse than his bite.

Debate, 1, 2; School Patrol, 1, 2; Football,
2, 3, 4; Basketball, 3, 4; Track, 3, 4; Hi-Y,
4; "Hobgoblin House," 3; "Plane Crazy,"
4; National Athletic Scholarship Society, 4.

PAUL ASHTON

He will take the "Rapp" any time.

Football, 1, 2, 3, 4; Hi-Y, 3, 4; Boys' Glee
Club, 4; "Plane Crazy," 4.

WILMA BANNICK

Gentlemen prefer Blondes.

WALTER BENJAMIN

Go away, girls—

Football, 3, 4; Basketball, 1, 2, 3, 4;
Track, 3, 4; Hi-Y, 1, 2, 3, 4; Debate, 1, 2;
Band, 1, 2, 3, 4; Brass Ensemble, 1, 2, 3;
Swing Band, 2, 3, 4; Choir, 3, 4; National
Athletic Scholarship Society, 3, 4; "Plane
Crazy," 4.

VELMA BROOKS

"Strawberry Blonde"

Choir, 1; "Plane Crazy," 4.

LES BUTMAN

The perfect specimen.

WAYNE CHANEY

"Drum Boogie"

Football, 4; Band, 1, 2, 3, 4; Swing Band,
2, 3, 4; Operetta, 2; Madrigal, 3; Choir,
2, 3.

DICK CHENEY

He gets along—neck?

Football, 2, 4; Basketball, 1, 2, 3, 4;
Track, 2; Hi Y, 2, 3, 4; Class Vice-Presi-
dent, 3; Debate, 1; School Patrol, 3;
Madrigal, 3; Choir, 3; Boys' Glee Club, 4;
"Hobgoblin House," 3; "Plane Crazy," 4.

*The first page of our 1944 school annual. If my classmates didn't like their
picture, they signed their name across their face. At our 50th reunion in
1994, of our 88 graduates, 14—all men—were deceased.*

38. Girls—The "Forbidden Fruit"

> Really great moral teachers never do introduce new moralities: it is quacks and cranks who do that. As Dr. Johnson said, "People need to be reminded more often than they need to be instructed."
>
> *Mere Christianity,* C.S. Lewis

Under my senior photo in The Pipestone, our 1944 year book, appears the phrase, "Go Away, Girls —." I have often wondered about the source of that enigmatic phrase. Was it, as I hoped, from the pen of a secret female admirer of mine on the staff? One who feared to go public with her affection for me? No, more likely it accurately identified my schizophrenic, ambivalent, love-fear relationship with girls during high school. In the presence of girls I had paralyzing seizures of blushing embarrassment. I was small and skinny, freckled and buck-toothed, and sometimes had a few zits. If a girl smiled at me I automatically blushed and turned away. In grade school, I would cross to the other side of the street to avoid meeting certain girls who were threatening. Girls were a profound enigma for me during adolescence. With their emancipation today's women have lost their mystery.

In junior high, activities usually did not include girls. In senior high, those of us who were terrified and stammered in front of girls, shared a bond cemented by insecurity. Outwardly we were bonded in athletics; inwardly, we found release in fantasy. Together we fabricated stories of sexual wantonness. For most of us, a girl's physical attributes overpowered our analysis of her inner qualities. Our highest accolade was— "she's build like a brick outhouse." The juices were rising and many of us had a bosom-fixation and looked for classmates who could replicate, however inadequately, the magnificent chests of Jane Russell, Betty Grable, and the other Hollywood sweater girls of the era.

No one could top Sam Turner when he started regaling us with tales of supposedly wanton female classmates. Under his picture was the phrase, "I Can Top That!" It fit him perfectly. Sam was our class collector of wanton and dirty stories. He was a slick type of guy—who put gobs of Brylcreem on his hair. I don't think he could have gotten a date with the plainest Jane of our class. He spent a lot of time dreaming about interesting pairs who were copulating. "I wish Alexandra," he said of a generously constructed cheerleader, "would spend as much time on her feet as she does on her back. Can't you see she's getting more bow-legged every day?" He couldn't cut it in athletics, band, classes, or with girls and sought notoriety in creating wild stories. Somewhere a gene or normal socialization had misfired, but at the time, we didn't know enough about Freud's theory to diagnosis his problem. The more he directed terrible stories at others, the more he told us about his own pathetic condition. But he could always command a crowd. He was a pathetic kid, although most of us didn't think so at the time. I think he went into politics.

To be sure, there wasn't much fornication in our high school. Pipestone was a Peyton Place in fantasy, but not in reality. Our moral bedrock was intact.

A social trinity of censure and control—detection, disease, and denunciation—was a strong antidote to "going all the way" or "making out." Stigmas and aphorisms controlled behavior. "Men make the laws, women keep the morals." "A woman good enough to sleep with is a woman good enough to marry." Shot-gun weddings were the result, and most of them worked out rather well. Outside of marriage a girl who got herself pregnant, if not cast into outer darkness, certainly had her character stained. Illegitimacy was not a no-fault behavior. Abortion was not an option. Nor were there entitlement benefits for single mothers of apartments, food stamps, and programs where a pregnant girl could continue her education at home.

Sulfa drugs had not yet been invented. Anecdotal stories concerning venereal disease were frightening. Occasionally Father would see a cripple dragging himself along in a peculiar jerky manner and would comment, "Neb, syphilis has invaded that man's brain." You couldn't be too careful. One of our coaches had a mantra—"girls, keep your legs crossed; boys, keep your fly zipped"—that he repeated regularly. One of my friends advised wearing two athletic supporters so that he would not embarrass himself when "bumpering," that is, dancing close to girls.

Movies that today would be rated "R" and "X" simply didn't exist. You had to imagine what happened when a scene faded after a heavy kiss. Very few of my friends had cars and gas rationing prevented those who had cars from using them as mobile motel rooms. In three years of high school I never knew a girl who got pregnant out of wedlock. If it happened, the code demanded that one make an "honest woman of her." The mottoes under the photos of many senior girls revealed reverie and fantasy, not reality and practice: Vila—"Why Didn't Someone Tell Me This Was Leap Year?'; Jeannette—"She Looks Innocent, But Don't Let That Fool You!"; Lucille—"She's Little But, Oh Boy!"; Cathy—"Katy Did, Katy Didn't." Most of the talk about sexual activity, was just that, talk.

Girls compensated for the shame of having an illegitimate baby by giving it up for adoption or forcing a shotgun wedding. The adage applied by some, "two wrongs don't make it right" did not apply, because most shotgun marriages turned out well. "No fault" divorces were nonexistent and social pressure and state law made it extremely difficult for men to abandon their wives. Ninety-five out of 100 women who couldn't persuade their young men to accompany them to the altar gave their babies up for adoption. Now the percentages are reversed and, if the option of abortion is rejected, both mother and baby often suffer more than when the traditional stigma was in place.

There were a number of girls who fascinated me, but I admired them from afar. Dorothy Moore, a farm girl and our class secretary-treasurer, was the most popular girl in our class. She was attractive and had a great personality. No one dared fabricate any lurid stories about her. She fit the mold of girls being "sugar and spice and everything nice." Dorothy had a fine mind, was charming, and didn't have an enemy in our school. Unfortunately, she was already taken by Don Nelson, our class vice-president, who also was deservedly popular. For a while I was interested in Darlene Anderson, a pale Pipestone clone of Marilyn Monroe. Her logo was "Take It Easy—I'm Fragile." But I was simply too shy to do anything about it.

Although it was decades before the Einsteins of American lingerie technology invented the "wonder" bra, our cheerleaders needed little help in that important area. Indeed, they seemed pleased at the opportunity to display the fullness of their natural endowments as they kicked, bounced, and sashayed on the hardwood in front of their bug-eyed male audience. Like other shy athletes, however, I dared steal but brief sideways glances at their perky-breasted, magnificently constructed facades. If one of them caught me looking too intently, my face took on the appearance of one of Grandad Bedell's Roman beauty tomatoes from our garden. But I marvelled at the generosity of Mother nature, and that such generosity, when contained under a tight sweater, could produce such a mesmerizing effect on adolescent boys. We felt sorry for girls with "fried eggs" as Adam Peltz called them. Because they didn't have to spend a lot of time fending off the predations of those with highly charged libidos, the flat-chested girls usually got better grades. They covered up the paucity of their bosoms by wearing loose sweat shirts or blouses with lots of ruffles.

Sometimes in our locker-room discussions we attempted to prioritize the order of accouterments in female attractiveness. Serious debate ensued over eyes, hair, mouth, buttocks, thighs, and breasts. Some who were on the honor role often appeared to pass themselves off as being high-minded. They disdained the "naughty bits" and proclaimed "I'm an ankle man" or "I'm attracted first to a girl's hair or her eyes." We would shout them down with shouts of "that's a crock" or "you can't be serious!" It seemed that 90 percent of us were "breast men." It seemed unmanly, even unpatriotic, to be anything else.

My only real girl-friend was Ruth Hess. I first got to know her in ninth grade, when we took English and debated together. She broke my stereotype of the farm girl: she was pretty, well groomed, had a nice figure, and had an infectious laugh. My parents thought she was "wholesome" and came from a "substantial farm family." For them, that was their highest accolade. What was more important, I felt at ease in her company. With other girls I experienced the ignominy, the terror of a potential turndown for a date. How I longed to be suave and steely and strong, but when I talked to girls, what usually came out of my mouth was something lame and weak and stupid. Ruthie put me at ease. Moreover, she was smart and a member of the National Honor Society but wasn't showy about it. More than that, she was a good sport. She had lost her two front teeth and had a plate which, after my pleading, she would thrust forward with her tongue so that her teeth would drop down a fourth of an inch. I would laugh and she would blush beautifully.

We had modest parts in the senior class play, "Plane Crazy," and would often have a coke or catch the movie after rehearsal. We were without guile and pretense, as pure and chaste as the fallen snow. Neither of us had dated much before and could laugh at the foibles and ineptitude of our relationship. We were both going through an arrested case of puppy love. Her freshly-pressed cotton dresses and lilac cologne made me light-headed and turned my tongue into sandpaper. Once, in the movies, she said she was wearing a new pair of silk stockings. During the war they were very hard to get. "Let me see," I said, surprising myself with my boldness as I rubbed her leg from her ankle to her knee. "That's not only a fine stocking," I laughed, "but also a very nice leg." "That's not nice," she laughed, "I'm not supposed to let you do that." But I knew she enjoyed it. We were like newborn innocent lambs, gamboling together across a spring pasture of new grass punctuated with fresh buttercups. That spring we went to the senior formal together, although as the yearbook said, "the girls missed the thrill of wearing formals because of the war." Ruth's senior logo, "Lovable And Sweet, So Pretty And So Neat" fit her exactly.

Commencement exercises took place on June 1, 1944. For me it was an occasion of mild depression for I had earned no awards—not a D.A.R. medal, recognition by the American Legion, or even a "citizenship" scholarship. My peers had not picked me to become class officer and I had not come within 10,000 fathoms of being elected to the National Honor Society. I salved my bruised ego by the fact that some sensitive soul had chosen me to play a cornet solo, *The Philistine*. The title was most appropriate! Indeed, I felt like an outsider in the elect company of scholars.

After the graduation dance, I took Ruth home early and joined a dozen of my buddies at a gravel pit 6 miles West of town. The bond forged in athletics proved stronger than that of sexual attraction. Don Argetsinger and several others were to leave by bus the next morning for the Twin Cities to enter the Marine Corps. The moon was full as we performed our last rite of passage. We laughed, punched each other, told stories, but were careful not to hug each other. That would have been bad form and effeminate in our eyes. We sat cross-legged in a circle and passed a couple of jugs of cheap wine around. Our ceremony was a sorry imitation of the Sioux who may have sat in such fashion on that very ground. But symbolically we were saying: *"Move Over World and Let Us In. We Have Come of Age and We're Going to War!"* Outwardly it was all bravado; inwardly we were afraid.

I cannot remember whether there was a "passing of the pipe" ceremony at my graduation. Before the advent of rising ethnic sensitivity, up until 1940 our graduation always included the transference of a Pipestone peace pipe. A large Lakota pipe, festooned with the satin banners of the colors of previous classes, was passed from the president of the senior class to his junior class counterpart. Although I barely grasped the meaning of the service, I was awed by the custom. Years later I understood that in Indian cosmology all space (as represented by the offerings to the cosmic powers) was embodied in the six spatial directions. All physical reality (as symbolized by the grains of tobacco) was contracted within a single point (the bowl or heart of the pipe) so that the pipe *contained or represented the entire universe.*

Because the pipe is the universe, it is also man (or the one who fills it) who establishes his "own center," and he "expands" so that the six directions of space are actually brought within himself. No longer "split" or "fragmented," this "expansion" symbolizes that man has become whole or holy and the illusion of separateness is gone. I began to see that, for the Native American, the sacred pipe was something far deeper than a sign. A stop sign, an exit sign, or the sound of a car horn are examples of signs, that is, conventions that explicitly convey a message or denote some superficial aspect of reality, and whose appearance or even meaning can easily be changed by popular will. A symbol, however, such as a flag, religious icon, or the sacred pipe, has meaning beyond the specific thing it designates. In fact, a symbol by definition conveys more than can be explicitly explained and evokes emotional and physical responses to a wealth of connotative meanings. A symbol is "transparent to" and "participates in" the reality to which it points. Unlike a sign, a symbol opens up levels of existential meaning and angst. Those who are "grasped" by the power of a flag, crucifix, menorah, hammer and sickle, *sacred pipe*, or other such symbols, are inwardly transformed.

While our ceremony of "passing the pipe" was done with solemnity (even though we "palefaces" did not understand its existential meaning), I began to understand why Indian sensitivities might be offended; that is, if their most sacred symbol was handled in a cavalier manner by the descendants of those who had expropriated their land. Nevertheless, I came to see the profound parallels to the Christian Eucharist. Just as the wine and bread are sacramental food that unites the Christian believer to his Lord, so too does the holy smoke of *kinnickinic* (Indian tobacco of sumac, red willow, and arrowwood) taken into the lungs, couple the Indian with the cosmic forces of the universe.

Upon graduation, I hoped for a paean of love from Ruth as I handed her my year book. I envisaged my future in an airman's uniform, leather helmet, and white scarf, shooting down Japanese Zeros. I needed her devotion to sustain me through the dark days ahead. Imagine my depression as I read:

> Hi Neb—It's really grand to know a swell guy like you. Hope I see you this summer. Remember the class play and all the fun we had back stage. Don't ever forget how we tried to learn to dance. Lots of luck to a really super guy! Ruthie

I missed a tender salutation—*darling, lover, sweetie*—before my name and looked in vain for a romantic valediction—*devotedly, warmly, fondly*—before "Ruthie." What I could not express myself, I desperately wanted from Ruth and others. I needed more than this if I were going to go out and die for my country!

We dated during the summer, wrote while I was in the Navy Air Corps, and Ruth sent me boxes of cookies several times. Sometimes they went to several duty stations before they caught up with me, and crumbs drizzled out of the four corners as I opened them. I saw her several times on leave but the intensity of adolescent attraction had cooled. I had the agony of choosing a career and, with my modest high school record, college looked terribly formidable. We both moved on with our lives and did not see each other again until our 30th high school class reunion.

The wedding photo of my Father, July 1, 1922.

39. An Iron John Father

Greatness of name in the father oft-times overwhelms the son; they stand too near one another. The shadow kills the growth; so much, that we see the grandchild come more and oftener to be heir of the first.

Timber, or Discoveries Made Upon Men and Matter, Ben Jonson

My Father held the power in our family constellation and was the center of my universe. There was much in his character that was both beautiful and noble, but he ruled us like a pasha. He saw himself as an integral part of the Scale of Being archetype—a gradation of higher to lower beings both in nature and in society. All life was contained within a pyramidal form. Just as Homo Sapiens was the crown of creation, successive lower levels of beings, from other mammals, birds, insects, slugs, flora, to finally inert matter formed the base. Human society, too, was not egalitarian. There were orders and levels of governance, higher and lower stations of work. In the family, both God and nature had ordained a divine triad—father, mother, child—whose apex was the father. He would have laughed at critics who hold that Holy Scripture and Western tradition are vitiated by patriarchy and the subjection of women.

Father was the professional warrior—strong, decisive, invulnerable, in command—whose judgments I assumed were always right and true. From my earliest recollections his presence brought order, law, and protection. He was my mythic ideal, the monolith, mentor, a powerful home-made god. Medicine had cultivated in him the habit of giving orders, a pattern he carried over to our family. I never heard him say, "I was wrong," or "I made a mistake," or "I am sorry I hurt your feelings." Nor did I ever witness him crying. Only years later did I see that he periodically represented the castrating Father, the wounded authoritarian who played God with his family and who pontificated on all subjects. At times like those, I walked tippy-toe in his presence.

Time was when the father was the son's destiny. The son became what the father was—farmer, shoemaker, knight, duke. That time had passed when I was young. Yet I consider myself fortunate that the recent ethos of marginalizing, emasculating, or demonizing fathers had not occurred. My Father's world was one where he gave his sons a destiny, not today's mobile, open-ended world where men are but a ghost of the fate of those they sire. I was neither a psychic nor a physical waif who, like so many boys today, had to search for my fate, my model, my ideal, my family god. My boyhood generation was fortunate. I had lived before the dreary rearrangement of gender roles and the depressing mantras of "deadbeat dads" and "patriarchy," all of which poison the shaping and identity of future fathers. The family of my adolescence, unlike today's families, had not been rubberized out of shape, left with no definable boundaries.

It was only as I was about to leave home that I began to come to terms with my Father. Like a Polaroid print that gradually comes into focus, it took me a long time to come to an understanding of him and our relationship. As a child I saw only his nimbus. As I grew older his emotional deformities became clearer. As a result I oscillated from pole to pole—from idealization to denigration, from fantasy to denial, from love to hate—in an attempt to achieve a balanced portrait. Personal grieving, reflection, time, and distance have helped. I have had to demythologize an idealized and dreamlike image of him in the childhood mind that still resides within me. I have had to uncover the negative and long-buried memories of frailties that he, like all fathers, possessed.

It was easy to locate the geographic and historic setting of his birth. It was harder to find his ethos and authentic self as a boy of the late 19th and early 20th century. What were the demons with which he struggled? Was his father kind or dictatorial, loving or harsh, compassionate or denunciatory? The emotional burdens and roadblocks that hinder objectively and clinically looking at one's father are exceedingly hard to overcome. Bits and pieces had accumulated over time, but not the whole picture. I had to do some personal archeology, a psychic dig, on my Father. The spade work and sifting, weighing and measuring, have taken a very long time.

I am sure that Father suffered a grievous wound when he lost his father at 13 years of age. There is a photo of the seven children and their mother taken shortly after the funeral. A large framed portrait of his deceased father stands between the two oldest sons, George and my Father. The faces of the children are rock-hard, stoic, jaws set, eyes staring fearfully into what they must have believed was a frightful future. He must have heard dozens of times from well-meaning relatives, "Now *you* and your brother George, *have to be the men of your family.*" Life was serious enough in those days without being catapulted from adolescence to family provider in an instant.

Father, like many men of his generation, was almost destructively inarticulate about his emotions—unable to express his love. Today the embarrassingly sad line in most father-son books is: "My father never hugged me; he never said he loved me." Alas, our family followed this Victorian and Depression-Era pattern. Once, in my thirties, I asked him about his reaction to my brother Dickie's death. It was obvious he was unable to openly grieve; "At his death," he answered, "I *redoubled my effort at work!* That was the only way to deal with it." It was a time when strong men buried rather than ventilated their grief. He must have been mired in misery, never venturing beyond it to accepting pain, where healing begins. Did he blame his father for abandoning him? Where was his support system? Where was his suffering validated and understood? Where was the joy and exuberance of life? In spite of medical bravado, did Father suffer from hidden insecurity? Did his unhealed wounds suppress his joy and cause him to inflict pain on others? Did a wounded soul pass a personal virus onto the five children he sired?

Understanding the psychological antecedents and precedents of harmful behavior patterns still does not excuse those behaviors. Many have suffered deep scars like those my Father incurred during impressionable years and, upon reflection, have become less hard and more sensitive in transcending their wounds. Only a rigid determinist would hold that childhood hurts cause mechanistic conditioned reflexes in later life. Human freedom, albeit finite, is real. Whatever their childhood traumas, all men have the capacity to *"act upon"* the human condition as well as be *"acted on."*

Father and I had a relationship characteristic of the sabra cactus. The sabra is hard and spiny on the outside, soft and sweet on the inside. But Father's gentleness and support was almost never made public. His passion and caring poured out to his children, and later his grandchildren, largely through cards and letters, seldom face to face. Consequently, two dichotomous streams, one healing, the other poisonous, flowed into my life and shaped my attitudes. I was inwardly torn by conflicting emotions. I was to love, honor, and obey my Father, yet his rigidity, stern manner, and Mount Everest expectations made that exceedingly difficult.

How I longed for his approval and praise! I needed it as much as our August burnt-out lawn needed a soaking thundershower. I hungered for his confirmation that I had the potential for a credible future; that I could "make something" of myself and not sully the good

Benjamin name. I longed to be accepted because of *my being* and not just *my doing.*

After lunch one summer day when I was 11, Father asked me to show him the results of the chores I had been assigned. He followed me into the backyard. A cursory look revealed the meager results of my pulling weeds in the rock garden. Suddenly he expostulated about my incompetence and kicked me hard in the rump. His words stung like a hundred needles but the kick was almost unbearable. I felt the terror of sheer helplessness. I was unacceptable in my home, the only security I knew. I did not know how to respond. Where could I flee? I knew no safe harbor. Like a mongrel with its tail between its legs I moped about for days, overcome by shame and failure and fearful of his presence. I wanted desperately to please him but, even if I did my best, I was not assured of a kind or generous word. That kick was an invisible wound I would carry for many months.

"If you strike a child, take care that you strike him in anger," reflected George Bernard Shaw, "even at the risk of maiming him for life. A blow in cold blood neither can nor should be forgiven."

As Shakespeare reminds us, words often wear hard boots. I often longed that Father would have more often worn slippers rather than authoritarian clod-hoppers. In spite of this, my feelings were reflected in Jane Austen's observation that "one does not love a place the less for having suffered in it."

As I grew older and conversations turned to intellectual affairs, I continued to have the heart of a stranger in my home. My two brothers were headed for medicine which, according to Father's bias, was the highest of all vocations. All other callings were second-rate. With conversations turning to drugs, surgery, and patient management, I was out of the family loop. I would never be a priest at the shrine of Aescalepius and thus always something of the prodigal. Even after I became a doctor in the classic sense (*doctrina,* Latin for "teacher") by achieving the Ph.D.(doctor of philosophy) degree, Father never could bring it upon himself to introduce me as "Doctor Walter." Yet, all my associates, professional, medical and otherwise, did so.

Father, now dead to this world, still roams free in my mind. Sometimes he comes tramping through my dreams like some ascetic and rigid Norseman, to remind me of life's expectations and the high demands of those who continue in the Tribe of Benjamin:

"Amount to something."
"Turn those Bs into As."
"Make Something of yourself."
"You have a family name to live up to."
"Don't be like the Templers."
"Genius is 98% hard work."
"No alibis are allowed."
"Those who fail don't have enough 'gumption'."

Father's indoctrination of his children regarding his world view was unrelenting. Aphorisms such as "It's shirt sleeves to shirt sleeves in three generations" he elevated to the status of the Ten Commandments. That is to say, regarding family fortunes "The first generation *builds them,* the second *enjoys them,* and the third *destroys them.*" He would have been unhappy with today's cultural climate. A paternalistic welfare state, he was convinced, is corrosive to our democratic ideals. Toward the end of his practice, he saw the enervating effect of welfare on his patients. He knew that no government social program could ever give to a child what a loving father offers. He knew a life on welfare was not an expression of compassion but of condescension which perpetuates dependency and weakness. He would have viewed "affirmative action" in the same light. Its beneficiaries are taught they can't fend for themselves, thus robbing the officially favored of self-confidence while stirring fierce resentment among those not assigned by bureaucratic fiat to the privileged status of favored victims. Above all, he wanted to spare me from the cloak of self pity, the most wretched of all human affections

There is no deliverance from his demanding psychic stream of challenge. The flagellation of my conscience will continue until I die. My *rational self knows* that I have surpassed him in notoriety and reputation but my *subjective/emotional self* continues to drive me on—*"Now, will you approve of me?"*—in a never ending quest. I have been trained to pass hard, even superhuman judgments, on myself. I was and continue to be a Father-haunted son almost crushed by his Atlas-like, world-bearing expectations. What I wanted was Father's recognition that I, too, had won a few hard truths. That he could look upon my growing record of accomplishments as a worthy contribution to the Tribe and the causes we shared. In moments of grace, I know that he would greatly honor my accomplishments, even though five simple words—*"I Am Proud Of You"*—would be like sand in his mouth.

In spite of his harshness and his super-human expectations, I still miss my Father. He was entwined around the tree of my being, and I around his. Father was vital to my moral and intellectual development, my physical safety and financial security. Father set the spiritual temperature around the house by "walking his talk." I clearly saw that God was important to him and should be to me as well. Moreover, I needed Father to brag about my accomplishments and make him proud of his progeny even if he could not express his pride to me. For children can brag only to their parents. How strange it is that although I had become a father to my own children and indeed a father figure to many of my students, in Father's presence I was still his little boy. Nevertheless, he was incorruptible and the incarnation of duty and rectitude. Nor was he especially "sensitive" by modern measures. And yet he was part of a generation that seemed to have a knack for imparting to us a certain surety, in the simplest way: by making it clear, through countless prosaic acts, that the grown-ups were competent; that they could be depended upon to bear the responsibilities of grown-ups; that children would not have to bear the burden of keeping the family together and acting as therapists.

Father had a Kantian inner spiritual column that supported the immense weight of his medical obligations. His Christian faith protected him from the lure of worldly temptation, the drumfire of flattery, and the inebriating effect of special privilege. Later I discovered that the majority of the great early physicians and scientists were deeply religious: from Hippocrates to Claudius Galen; from Maimonides to William Harvey. Father was part of that spiritual and medical endless line of splendor.

He had no time for sophistry, no patience for equivocation, no room for the shaded areas separating right and wrong. Compassion for his patients was his guide, their health and welfare his sole mission and reward. He lived frugally and honorably and expected those he had sired to do the same. Prudent investments in Iowa farm land provided security for his children and grandchildren even if toward the end of his life he seemed to agree with Thoreau's observation that "property is more easily acquired than gotten rid of." He liked the simple unadorned life without useless goods and affectations. I never heard him tell an off-color joke, and I doubt that he said the word *damn* more than a half dozen times in his life. Father gave me continuity and both roots and wings. He taught me the necessity of setting high expectations, of disciplining myself first, so that I might enjoy the fruits of my labors later on.

As I moved into my early 30s, Father's demanding paternalism moderated. His generosity was boundless. He took me, along with my brothers and brother-in-law, on a once-in-a-lifetime Alaskan big game hunting expedition. It was a time before the deification of Mother nature's furry creatures and each member of our party of five secured a moose, a grizzly, a black or brown bear, a Dall ram, and a caribou. Excursions to Canadian fly-in fishing camps quickly followed as did hunting for mule deer in Montana and elk hunting in Wyoming. Father seemed intent on filling up our memory banks with wondrous events we could recall when he was gone. Time seemed short. Perhaps he knew that a mental incapacity lay ahead.

Father's focus on the Tribe of Benjamin was a bit overbearing at times. Yet, he evinced no interest in seeking geneological research on the Benjamins and MacBrooms in England and Wales. Like Seneca, I knew that he who boasts of his descent praises the deeds of another; that while fate makes our relatives, choice makes our friends. Yet his recitation of the values of the Tribe informed me that I belonged to something greater than myself—to a clan with a history and one with standards of intellectual and moral excellence. And when our own children started coming, he wrote each one tender notes on their birthdays and provided money toward their future college education. Now that I, too, am a father, I understand that separation across a gulf of years and the pathos which always must divide a father from his son.

There are dialectical truths we ought to learn from history: one, that we are not in ourselves superior to our fathers; another, that we are shamefully and monstrously inferior to them if we do not advance beyond them. Alas, many of my accomplishments—outstanding teacher awards, notable research, publication in flagship medical, business, military, and church history books and journals, presentations on medical and business ethics before national and international conferences at American, Canadian, and British universities—didn't come to fruition until I was in my 50s, by which time much of the circuitry in his brain had been blown out in the aftermath of a subdural hematoma.

The night before his surgery he held his pain-wracked head between his hands. "Neb," he lamented, "your Father is now an *old man*." Two years later Mother took him to the University of Minnesota hospital for an evaluation. "Doctor Benjamin," asked a kindly internist, "what is the diagnosis for appendicitis?" His eyes fixed and unresponsive, Father's face was almost as impassive as the Indian stone face of the Pipestone monument. Yet, tears welled up and coursed down his cheeks. He was slipping away from us. Mother, stoically strong on the outside, inwardly and silently suffered her grief. Diagnosis: cerebral atrophy. Father's brain was being deprived of oxygen and was in a self-destructive mode.

Three years later, with my brothers and sisters, I accompanied him to a nursing home, that familiar and final station before eternity. He was compliant. The cells in his brain had been disintegrating for some time. Like an abandoned house on the *Coteau des Pairies,* his body was bereft of his once potent spirit. Father had become like a little child. Had he been lucid he would have thundered: "NO! NO! NO!" at what we were doing. Guilt covered me like a London fog. He now had to be diapered, bathed and fed like a newborn. I had lost my Father! An angst of ontological proportions overcame me. Depressed, I shadow-walked through my duties at Hamline University for weeks.

Father shuffled into the room and stood before an old dresser. Along with a single straight-back chair and the bed, it was the only other piece of furniture in the room. Earlier we had placed some children's toys there to lure him into the room and to make the sterility of the place seem less foreboding. His eyes seemed to brighten a bit. Then, like a two-year old finding a lost bauble, he said, "I wondered where these were."

My eyes misted over. A form of anguish I had never known before surged up from my innermost being. I was in torment from experiencing the diminishment of the once proud man who had sired me.

Sometime later, during the long years of his nursing home confinement, I wheeled Father outside so that he could feel the growing warmth of the April sun. A half dozen English sparrows were playing "king of the hill" at a nearby bird feeder. Something deep within the recesses of his brain made a neural synapse connection with an experience long ago. Deadpan and without feeling or expression, he said, *"barn birds."*

Those were the last two words I heard from my Father.

Father languished in a nursing home for over a decade before mercifully dying at 92 years. During that time I often inwardly lamented his tragic condition. How strange it was that at the death of a parent a man becomes a boy again for a moment—a terrible, poignant moment filled with all the grief of childhood and none of its joy. It was now too late to tell my Father the things—the expressions of affection—the sons of WASPs find so hard to utter. Sadly I recalled the words of Herodotus, "Call no man happy till you know the nature of his death." Why this scourge that had no villain? He had missed his death. The purpose and goal *(telos)* of his life had been accomplished but his temporal end *(finis)* had not come. The condition feared by the Stoic emperor-philosopher, Marcus Aurelius—"It is shameful in a life where the body does not fail you that the mind should fail you first"—had happened to him. Medical intervention that had proven so beneficial in the lives of legions of patients had failed him. It had violated the law of nature and the advice of Aurelius—"Graciously depart like a ripened olive might fall, praising the earth that produced it." Our family had witnessed the truism of Virgil—"Age carries all things, even the mind, away."

Had Father been struck down a decade or two earlier while wearing his white coat, the Pipestone community would have shut down and gathered to mourn and celebrate his passing. For he had joyfully participated in ushering legions of their offspring into the light. And he was present in their grief when their venerable ones crossed over into darkness. Pipestone would have paid homage to the one who, for half a century and by common consent, had earned his title, "The Doctor." What a shame that he never experienced Cicero's truism—"The harvest of old age is the recollection and abundance of blessings previously secured."

But by then he was beyond the world of ambition, success, prizes, and vanity and I had crossed important finish lines too late for his approval.

During those nearly 11 years in the nursing home he died by inches. His spirit gradually vanished without hearing my words of gratitude and closure. In my travels in Europe I had discovered that medieval canvases fell into three categories—dramatic war scenes, portraits of royalty, and dramatic death-bed episodes. In the latter the dying protagonist was center-stage, with sunlight on his face and his hand extended, bestowing a blessing. Around the bed in proper order stood the wife, daughters, sons, relatives, and close friends. After last rites and ministrations, the priest and physician retreated to the shadows. Having witnessed such scenes before, the dying person was socialized to bestow final words to each—words of acceptance, forgiveness, advice, and closure. Most of them, I suspect, brought it off with verve—this their last act in the theatre of life. Such *kairos* events, indelibly engraved upon the minds of the witnesses, became part of the prized oral tradition of the family.

But for Father there were never any "last days" of closure where, in spite of all the scars, I could tell him how much I loved, cherished, and respected him. Alas, the magical cycle by which the child becomes the parent and the parent the child had not occurred. His brain was beyond my reach before I realized Father had been born again—born to me. I never stroked his forehead and told him how much I loved him. I was never able to thank him for teaching me right from wrong, for giving me a moral heritage beyond price. There were moments when I confronted the void—convinced that I could not live without my Father.

Together with Mother, he had given me a genetic endowment that was rugged and without physical impairment. Even his harshness had a silver lining, for I experientially knew there were no perfect families, fathers, or sons. He taught me to play fair and to "play the man"—to take whatever life throws at you and be an unbending Christian Stoic. From him I learned that the rule of joy and the law of duty were one. "When one has not had a good father," Nietzsche believed, "one must create one." Hence, the rise of totalitarianism. As I grew to manhood, I realized how graced I had been to have an honorable Father, whatever his faults, and realized that being a good father or a good mother was the most demanding, sacrificial, and heroic of all callings.

Nonetheless, as a Depression-reared youngster, I discovered that the hunger for success, to seek to soar into a Father-induced stratosphere, can be bred so deeply that one often is powerless to stop chasing the goal long after it has been achieved. Dylan Thomas evokes the forbidding distance, the "sad height," of both our bond and our separation:

> And you, my Father, there on that sad height,
> Curse, bless me now with your fierce tears, I pray.

The hunger for approval was a motor that ran my ambition but I had lost the key to turn it off. There were always more papers, research, and presentations to give in the never-ending quest for approval. "I am sure your ancestors are always with you," General George Patton once remarked. "They are watching. They expect a hell of a lot out of you." Alas, the demands of our parental mentors are carried with us long after we have taken their coffins to the graveyard.

I have written about my Father and myself because when my own children leap beyond me into their futures, I want them to find something of me there, waiting for them as a memory, as an unmistakable declaration, as an articulate embrace of grace and love.

Merry Christmas 1941

Our family on the day, December 7, 1941, we heard of the Japanese attack on Pearl Habor. The somber picture indicates our fear for the future.

40. THE THUNDER OF WAR

Disarmament is a prescription for war. Perpetual peace is a futile dream conjured up by internationally minded pacifists, the jellyfish of the world. They wish to change Armistice day into disarmament day. I regard with horror a state of affairs which would make our country unwilling to defend its honor. A permanent fire department is better than a volunteer one.

Memorial Day Speech, 1932, General George Patton

Who is this man [Adolf Hitler]? Half plebeian. Half God! Actually Christ, or only John the Baptist? This man has everything to be a king. The born tribune of the people. The coming dictator. How I love him!

Joseph Goebbels, *Diary* October 1925

"History admires the wise, but it elevates the brave."
Edmund Morris

As the clouds of war began to build over Eastern Europe and Asia in the late 1930s, a sense of foreboding began to permeate my spirit. On the surface nothing changed, but from the tone of the radio, newspapers, and my parent's conversations, I knew that distant events were threatening the innocence and stability of my world. Violence and social chaos were on the march. The profound malaise, the cultural pessimism, the fear of the decline and decay of western civilization represented by the rise of Hitler's Naziism deeply affected my adolescent mood. The cult of violence, a Darwinian struggle for existence, the exalting of the strong at the expense of the weak and innocent seemed to ring down liberal hopes for progress and our middle class family values.

I was only eight when Japan invaded China and our gunboat, The Panay, was bombed on the Yangtze River; I was 10 when one million people were killed in the Spanish Civil War, 11 during Mussolini's slaughter of Ethiopians, 12 during Hitler's Anschluss of Austria. The thunder was growing louder, the lightening strikes coming closer. In my dreams I saw a cyclone on the horizon with the vortex spinning ever faster and wider.

In sixth grade I had chosen "The Gettysburg Address" to memorize and recite before the class. Although poor at memorization, Lincoln's classic speech was easy for me. I reveled in the beauty of his sparse, carefully crafted words. I linked his description of what happened during those first three days of July 1863 in a village in Pennsylvania to a time of testing that was certainly coming. "Four score and seven years ago…" I can still recite it without missing a word. Its images of birth, suffering, blood, death, and rebirth, became engraved in my memory.

Two years later, in eighth grade English class, each of us had to memorize some poetry and recite it before the class. Some mysterious force, perhaps my love of history, drew me to verse born of the heroism of World War I, and I settled on "In Flanders Fields." The author, Lieutenant Colonel John McCrae, was killed in France early in 1918 after four years of service on the Western Front. The irony in the beauty of blood red poppies growing out of the gory fields on which men died put me in a melancholy mood.

> In Flanders fields the poppies grow
> Between the crosses, row on row,
>   That mark our place; and in the sky
>   The larks, still bravely singing, fly
> Scarce heard amid the guns below.
>
> We are the Dead. Short days ago
> We lived, felt dawn, saw sunset glow,
> Loved and were loved, and now we lie
>   In Flanders fields.
>
> Take up our quarrel with the foe;
> To you from failing hands we throw
>   The torch; be yours to hold it high.
>   If ye break faith with us who die
> We shall not sleep, though poppies grow
>   In Flanders fields.

I delivered it without a pause and received the applause of my classmates. It remained indelibly in my mind, almost as a foreshadowing of future seasons of poppies growing among the crosses of American dead. In times of quiet I would catch myself reciting it and I can do so to this day.

There was no protective adult screen to filter out the real from the imaginary. It was difficult to fall asleep on our front porch during the hot summer of 1939. The grave voices of William L. Shirer in Berlin and Edward R. Murrow in London floated from the living room to the porch as they spoke of mobilization and ultimatums, hurried conferences of ministers, more mobilization, and the movements of troops. A demonic virus was breaking out and efforts at containment were failing. The radio brought a Dionysian counterpoint to the singing crickets and cooing mourning doves that attempted to lull me to sleep.

In English class a young teacher whose name I have forgotten told us of her interest in T.S. Eliot. I turned to *The Waste Land,* written in 1922, and read, "What are the roots that clutch, what branches grow, out of this stony rubbish?" and became apprehensive to think of what he might have meant by the image of "stony rubbish."

Classic photos from those days are etched in my memory.

An orphaned, wounded baby crying on a Shanghai railroad track.
Ethiopian tribesmen throwing spears at an Italian airplane that is strafing them.
A Spanish loyalist soldier caught in mid-air in instant death as a bullet crashes into his skull.
An Austrian man crying unashamedly as German tanks rumbled through his beloved Vienna.
Neville Chamberlain in black stovepipe hat, umbrella, and Edwardian suit, holding a paper at the airport, and pontificating, "We have peace in our time."
Goose-stepping Storm Troopers passing like robots before Adolf Hitler and chanting "Sig Heil."
The heart of Rotterdam converted to rubble by Stukka dive bombers.
Japanese troops administering the coup de grace to the heads of Chinese soldiers as they knelt in the streets of Shanghai.
Ukrainian farms, villages, and wheat ablaze to the horizon as Germans apply their scorched earth policy.
Masses of British soldiers in the water and on the beaches of Dunkirk, waiting rescue in small boats.
Churchill walking amid London rubble, holding a cigar in one hand and giving the "V" sign with the other.
Droves of children leaving London by rail prior to the Battle of Britain.

As time went on I lost more of my innocence. During my freshman year I read Jan Valtin's book, *Out of the Night,* a frightful account of the brutal ideological warfare between the German Marxists and the Nazis. Valtin's interrogation and torture at the hands of the Gestapo and the SS were so grisly as to almost defy human comprehension. Because of these traumatic adolescent memories, I have never assumed the goodness of human nature or been enamored of utopian dreams. Any perceived improvement in human nature is illusionary. In any event, we must begin where man *is*, not where we *wish* him to be. Man can hope and dream of worlds he can never create. History is progressive but not redemptive. Taken individually, man is rather noble; en mass, he too often is brutish. Thus, I have never tolerated romantic or pacifist fools gladly.

Yet my Victorian romanticism regarding war did not die. I yearned for valor. The vision of martial splendor was entrancing. Printing presses were turning out legions of inexpensive copies of "Buddy Smith Goes to West Point" or "Andy Doe Enters Annapolis." I devoured them. The pacifism of the 1930s maddened me, for I was reading Kipling, not Hemmingway; Rupert Brooke and *Gone With the Wind,* not Stephen Crane and *The Red Badge of Courage.*

My spirit resonated to the lines of Shakespeare spoken by King Henry V before the Battle of Agincourt: *"And Gentlemen in England now a'bed / Shall think themselves accursed they were not here."* Like a football scrub who hopes that the coach will put him in the big game, I feared having to sit on the sidelines during the momentous events of our time. I dipped into Rudyard Kipling and loved his stories of English soldiers, of their grit, sacrifice, and heroism for the Empire. Kipling's poems, written in rough Cockney dialect, had the common touch, and his ballads celebrated a camaraderie of military service that was far deeper than that which I had experienced in athletics. Kipling understood the hunger for an existential community and the lot of the private soldier as he criticized the pompous indifference of the stay-at-home and detached civilian:

> For it's Tommy this, an' Tommy that, an' 'Chuck him out, the brute!"
> *But it's 'Saviour of 'is country' when the guns begin to shoot:*
> An' it's Tommy this, an' Tommy that, an' anything you please;
> An' Tommy ain't a bloomin' fool—you bet that Tommy sees!

The desire to join the service was uncontrollable, the mystique and power of the uniform overpowering. I had already experienced the addictive nature of the bonds of sport; intuitively I knew the covenant between warriors was infinitely more cohesive. Moreover, during my senior year in English, Miss Schmidt had required us to read one of Shakespeare's tragedies. I had resonated to the martial speech of Henry V and tried to commit it to memory:

Whoever does not have the stomach for this fight, let him depart. Give him money to speed his departure since we wish not to die in that man's company. Whoever lives past today and comes home safely will rouse himself every year on this day, show his neighbor his scars, and tell embellished stories of all their great feats of battle. These stories he will teach his son and from this day until the end of the world we shall be remembered. We few, we happy few, we band of brothers; for whoever has shed his blood with me shall be my brother. And those men afraid to go will think themselves lesser men as they hear of how we fought and died together.

But I held a secret that filled me with a dread of being found "4-F," that is, mentally or physically unfit for service. That label signified a form of social leprosy, an inner scarlet letter, that could not be exorcised. Neither God nor Father's medical ministrations would be able to remove that mark of the beast.

I worried constantly that my secret "thorn in the flesh" might keep me out of the service. No one knew about the limited range of motion of my right knee, for it was a secret I had not even told Father or my best friends. I could not do the squats or the duck-walk, much less the Cossack dance. No matter how hard I tried, a gap of six inches remained between my right heel and buttock. It was a congenital limitation I worked hard to ameliorate. At night I would put hot cloths or a heat pad on my knee. Several times I tied a rope around my thigh and ankle, pulling it tight, and slept all night under this form of torture.

From 1939 through 1941, I craved news of wartime events in Europe, Asia and Africa as intensely as an addict coveted his opium. Nazi spearheads were knifing here and there. Every day I read the news releases and worried as the black virus of Naziism spread from Norway to within miles of Cairo; from the Channel Islands to the banks of the Volga River. The values of Western Civilization—the freedom of religion, liberty, democracy, individual rights, and more—were tottering. But through the deepening darkness, one voice, that of Winston Churchill, kept hope alive and proffered a vision of ultimate victory:

I have nothing to offer but blood, toil, tears and sweat...Never in the field of human conflict was so much owed by so many to so few. ...We shall fight on the beaches...landing grounds...in the fields...in the streets and hills; we shall never surrender. ...We would rather see London laid in ruins and ashes than that it should be tamely and abjectly enslaved... If the British Empire lasts for a thousand years, men will still say, 'This was their finest hour.'

That was the beginning of my becoming an Anglophile, and my love of all things associated with Britain joined my genes which had long ago come from that Sceptred Isle.

Much later Peter, a friend from a neighboring town, joined the Navy Air Corps with me. He came from a Mennonite family and his father boasted that no one in their family tree had ever been tainted by military violence. Peter had been suckled on the pacifist mantra—*"Any peace* is better than *any war."* An agricultural womb had protected him from the twentieth century genocide that was sweeping the earth. It was hard to hear the screams and imagine the terror of those in the death camps while surrounded by beatific fields, clean air, pure rain, and the lowing of cattle. When Peter told his father of his intentions to join the Navy, Mr. Van Dyke was outraged and shouted, "I can't believe you are my son!" "Father, my contribution to the war will be far less than yours," Peter answered. "Your hands are not clean. The thousands of turkeys you market every year feed our troops." The day Peter entered the service, he was disowned by his father.

I was later attracted to the Christian Gospel not because of theological dogmas one had to take on faith but because, in my experience, the Christian analysis of man rang true. Original sin is the only empirical doctrine the Church can put forward. Theological doctrines related to hubris, original sin, idolatry, and will to power, notions that 19th century savants had thrown into the wastebasket as unworthy of such a noble being as Homo Sapiens, came crashing back into the 20th century with a vengeance. Classic theologians were not clerical crepe hangers but mysteriously brilliant regarding human nature. Christianity was something more than pious moralism. Human nature was vitiated at its core. Rescue was needed. Man could not be the initiator of his own redemption; he could not be "lifted" and "lifter" at the same time.

It was hard to give up on liberal sentiment, future visions, and the tender longings of the heart. But it is not the classical Christian theologians who have misread human nature. Rather, romantic poets like Frederick Lawrence Knowles—"When navies are forgotten/And fleets are useless things/When the dove shall warm her bosom/Beneath the eagle's wings"—are tragically mistaken if they think their transworldly mental images can be realized in human history.

The authors I was to study—St. Paul, St. Augustine, Martin Luther, John Calvin, Blaise Pascal, Jonathan Edwards, Kierkegaard, Karl Barth, Paul Tillich, Reinhold Niebuhr—were more on track than such moderns as B.F. Skinner, Bertrand Russell, J.B. Watson, and William James, all of whom felt human nature could be improved through social engineering. The former taught that knowledge of our moral dilemmas was no more important than finding—outside ourselves—the power to overcome them. Man knows better than he does. Humans are more likely to know what's morally right than to act in accordance with that knowledge. I did not see moral evolution in human history. Neither science nor technology, psychology nor progressive education, could save us. Indeed, they had not only struck out but had complicity in turning the 20th century into an abattoir.

Later I came to see that World War II was an unnecessary war. The supreme irony is that pacifism helped create that war, and its conclusion was brought about by the most destructive weapon in history—the atomic bomb—produced from the research of a pacifist, Albert Einstein.

There have been two very different visions of war and peace that have coexisted in the Western world for at least two centuries. One vision sees peace as being accomplished and maintained through disarmament and the compromise of international differences. This position, which has long been held by much of the Western intelligentsia and liberal churches and is symbolized by Neville Chamberlain, says, *"Speak softly and carry a very small military stick."* Long-forgotten international conferences based on this view, held at Geneva, Locarno, and Lausanne during the 1920s, generated pious agreements and the illusory hope that peace is preserved by high-sounding words and impressive signatures on parchment.

The opposite vision sees peace as being primarily a result of successfully deterring war. The Romans recognized that *"no peace keeps itself."* John Jay wrote in *The Federalist,* "Nations will make war whenever they have a prospect of getting anything by it." The first vision dominated our statecraft between the two world wars. The result? We became one of the most completely disarmed great nations of history. The total number of American military personnel on active duty fell below a quarter of a million in the early 1930s—and kept falling. The army's budget was sliced in half in 1934 to help finance New Deal social programs. The American army was smaller than the armies of 15 other nations, including Greece and Portugal. Some American troops still trained with wooden guns and mock-ups of tanks and cannon as late as 1941.

If pacifism prevented war, there would never have been a Pearl Harbor.

We should never forget how close the Western democracies came to being defeated—or what a horror it would have been for the entire world if they had lost. We should never forget the policies and illusions that brought the Western nations to the brink of catastrophe. Those illusions, which today are often mixed with a barely concealed hostility to Western civilization, have spawned an extensive coterie of revisionist historians. This new breed tends not only to overlook the historic achievement that saved our civilization, but is intent on denigrating the West in general and excoriating the United States in particular. Symbolic of this mind-set have been the annual pilgrimages to Hiroshima and Nagasaki to denounce the dropping of the atomic bomb.

Every generation at some point has the utopian dream that somehow the god of war, Ares, will finally be enchained. In 1944 when a clergyman, a "visiting fireman of great eminence" told General George S. Patton that World War II would be the last war ever fought, Patton responded heatedly, *"Such statements since 2600 B.C. have signed the death warrant of millions of young men. My God! Will they never learn?"*

Tragically, utopian dreams are more captivating and intoxicating than is the harsh reality of military sufficiency. Had the allies responded with force in 1936 (the same summer in which at 10 years of age, I caught the 9-pound Walleye that adorns the cover of this book!) when Hitler marched into the Rhineland and began rebuilding the Wehrmacht, the Nazi incubus would have been stillborn. In 1928, when I was two years old, 64 nations signed the infamous Kellogg-Briand Peace Pact. The signatories promised to *"Abolish War As An Instrument of National Conflict!"* Glory Be! Newspaper headlines around the world screamed. *"War Is Outlawed!" "Peace Now and Forever More!" "Everlasting Peace in Our time!" "No More Guns, Only Butter!" "The War to End All War Was Not Fought in Vain!"* Church bells tolled the joyous news throughout the West. The lion and the lamb would feed together. The great powers began to sink their warships and melt down their tanks and artillery. The Biblical dream would become reality—we would turn "swords into plowshares and spears into pruning hooks." The locus of war was not in the heart of man but in its horrid armaments.

We had forgotten the words of Lenin who spoke the universal sentiment of the tyrant: *"Treaties promising peace are like pie crust. They are meant to be broken."*

The great misfortune in the 1920s and 1930s was that both France and England lacked leaders wise enough to move against the pacifist current. The Conservative prime minister, Stanley Baldwin, was a kindly, patient, and genuinely virtuous man who hated anything that smacked of confrontation. His favorite mood, according to a biographer, was "one of a sunset calm and nostalgia, in which the British nation, like an old couple in retirement enjoying the peaceful ending of the day, contemplated some sweep of English landscape and harkened to the distant church bells." Plagued by the memory of what it had endured in World War I, Britain wanted to hang on to what it had without fighting. Left or Right, everyone was for the quiet life.

Yet, in the pre-Victorian era, Britain's leaders had been ruthless strategists—tough, skeptical, and suspicious, ready to fight with swords, pistols or fists. The hard, not the soft virtues, had created "Rule Britannia." For over 200 years Britain had lived by the truism written by one of its own, Thomas Hobbes—*"Covenants without swords are but words."* But in the 1930s, the steely British backbone had turned to pasta. Blinded by its own virtues—gentleness, breeding, manners, compromise, compassion, idealism—Britain was soft and ripe. A wag opined that her approach to diplomacy was rather like the English approach to sex—"Romantically remote from the distressing biological crudities."

Later I was to learn that appeasement can only be effective when applied from a position of strength, when it is a freely taken action meant to allay a grievance and create goodwill. It is a dangerous device when it is resorted to out of fear or necessity, for then it does not reduce resentment but shows weakness and instills contempt. Later when American soldiers went to war, Christian congregations made sure that "their boys" were well supplied with New Testaments. A loving people back home in God's country issued them with heartfelt blessings and sent them off to fight the Germans and the Japanese. Tragically, their pacifist, "head-in-the-sand" sentiments often introduced them to combat with outmoded World War I equipment. "Christians," reported one cynical warrior, "are such charming people."

The rising fever of a malignant German cancer was evident very early for those who had eyes to see. William Shirer and others repeatedly warned the West of the effect Hitler's megalomania and egomania had on millions of Germans. He observed them at a Nuremberg rally in 1933 as "little men with big bodies and bulging necks and cropped hair and pouched bellies and brown uniforms and heavy boots. Little men of clay in his fine hands leap to their feet like automatons with their right arms upstretched in the Nazi salute and screaming *'HEIL!'"* Shirer was mesmerized as to the intoxicating effect Hitler's two to three-hour tirades had on his audience:

> *They spring, yelling and crying, to their feet. The audience in the galleries does the same, all except a few diplomats and about fifty of us correspondents. Their hands are raised in slavish salute, their faces now controlled with hysteria, their mouths wide open, shout-*

ing, shouting, their eyes, burning with fanaticism, glued on the new god, the Messiah. The Messiah plays his role superbly.

Years later when I was a professor at Morningside College, Iowa, I had the privilege of taking Mr. Shirer to lunch before introducing him at a convocation. Shirer told me that during his long career as a journalist in Germany, he had never heard a more captivating yet demonic speaker than Adolph Hitler.

In 1936, the year Aunt Bessie took the cover photo of Bob and me with our large fish, Hitler sent his troops into the demilitarized Rhineland, an action that violated the Versailles Treaty, and thumbed his nose at the League of Nations. *Many historians believe that if France had countered with but one division, Hitler's bluff would have been called and World War II might have been avoided.* That event symbolized for him that Western democracies were spineless and weak. His megalomania was without bounds and Hitler was swallowed up in boundless adoration of his volk. His overweening arrogance caused his rhetoric to take on the messianic allusions from the New Testament:

How deeply we feel once more in this hour the miracle that has brought us he is with us, and now we are Germany. . . THAT YOU HAVE FOUND ME...AMONG SO MANY MILLIONS IS THE MIRACLE OF OUR TIME! AND THAT; I HAVE FOUND YOU, THAT IS GERMANY'S FORTUNE!

Alas, our statesmen were blind to the fact that such megalomania, if not promptly checked by military force, would lead to the abyss. Hailed as a man of peace, Neville Chamberlain followed a policy of appeasement that was applied from a position of cravenness, not strength. *He was the all too-familiar peacemaker who encourages war!* Motivated by the highest ideals, he nonetheless lacked the will to realize them. "In spite of the hardness and ruthlessness I thought I saw in Hitler's face," he wrote his sister after Munich, *"I got the impression that here was a man who could be relied on when he had given his word."* After his monstrous error in judgment and his subsequent heartfelt invocation—"I believe it is peace in our time!"—the delighted crowds outside 10 Downing Street sang, "For he's a jolly good fellow." Britain had slipped into a collective and extensive denial.

Chamberlain had violated the first principle of prudent statecraft: *"He trusted the protestations and promises of an enemy rather than their military capability!"* Alas, he fell back on the idealism of the Gospels and romantic poets rather than reading Machivelli and *Mein Kampf.* He had regarded Hitler and Mussolini as rational men like himself, with limited goals, who could be dealt with by flexibility and reasoned discussion. Chamberlain was the kind of man Theodore Roosevelt had in mind when he referred to William Howard Taft as one "who means well feebly."

Winston Churchill, in contrast, had the character and judgment Chamberlain lacked: indeed, the sagacity to understand the nature of the Nazi threat, and the gumption to oppose it tooth and claw. Churchill knew that you can't tame or appease a rabid dog. You shoot it.

As Churchill himself put it before the House of Commons in 1938, the British people had before them the choice of shame or war. He feared that they would choose shame—and have war nevertheless. He was right.

The French, too, were senseless beyond comprehension. Like the British, they had learned nothing from losing an entire generation of men in the flower of their youth a few years earlier. France relied on the Maginot Line, a perfect emblem of Gaelic military fatuousness. Neither France nor England deployed a credible offensive force. Western leaders examined their situation sentimentally and hopefully rather than objectively and realistically. They were moved by the horror of war, the fear of its reappearance, and the blind hope that a refusal to contemplate war and prepare for it would somehow keep the peace.

Later I was to read Albert Camus' *The Plague* (His many-faceted metaphor that introduces Chapter 14 *can apply to war as well as disease, even original sin born by each individual)* and saw in it a warning against pacifist complacency. His greatest novel ends with an admonition. A pestilence that gripped Oran has finally run its course and the rats bearing their plague bacillus have retreated to their underground bunkers. But a final victory "against terror and its relentless onslaughts" is not to be. Rieux, the heroic if absurdist existentialist physician, listens to the shouts of joy: "He knew what those jubilant crowds did not know but could have learned from books...*The plague...bides its time...and that the day would come when, for the bane and enlightening of men, it would rouse up its rats again and send them forth to die.*"

Modern antibiotics can easily exterminate pestilences spread by bacteria. Camus, a French freedom fighter against the Fascist bacillus, did not intend us to take literally his figure of speech. His warning is clear: scourges and terrors mutate and recycle in hideous shapes and forms throughout history. In spite of the passing of the Cold War era, the world is more and more a tangle of scourges. Tribal, ethnic, and ideological enmities are exploding across the continents like the naval salvos off the Normandy beaches during D Day. The notion that peace is natural and war an aberration has led to a failure in peacetime to consider the possibilities of another war. Creating pacifist "peace studies" institutes, and sanitizing the Bible and hymns of images of war has nothing to do with creating a statescraft that maintains world order. We must never forget the military proverb that the enemies within a city's walls, well meaning though they be, are ten times more dangerous than armies in the field and on the move.

Refusing to allow little boys to play cops and robbers or have G.I. Joe playthings as an antidote to aggression and war is fatuous and dim-witted. The origins of war are not to be found in the sandboxes of children, but in places where the power of predatory collectives is unchecked by vigorous and corresponding constraint. In the 1940s it took 300,000 dead and one million American wounded to learn that lesson. Today it is estimated that 1500 World War II veterans die every week. With their passing, we may be in danger of forgetting that important lesson.

Like these Minneapolis children donating aluminum for defense, I eagerly scoured our home neighborhood, farm yards and dumps for metal that would increase America's defense.

41. "TO ARMS" AT PIPESTONE

I want (my son) to see for himself upon the scale of the universe that God, the soul, are not simple matters...that the problem of good and evil is not more simple than the immensity of worlds. I want him to understand that evil is not something that can be condescended to, waved aside, or smiled away, for it is not merely an invited guest, but lies *in foro interno* at home with good within ourselves. Evil can only be fought.

Witness, Wittaker Chambers

To the end of history, the peace of the world, as Augustine observed, must be gained by strife. It will therefore not be a perfect peace. But it can be more perfect than it is. If the mind and spirit of man does not attempt the impossible, if it does not seek to conquer or eliminate nature, but tries only to make the forces of nature the servants of the human spirit and the instruments of the moral ideal, a progressively higher justice and more stable peace can be achieved.

Reinhold Niebuhr, *Moral Man and Immoral Society*

For the Benjamin household, December 7, 1941 began quietly as we went through our fixed Sabbath routine: table devotions, breakfast, Sunday School, church, and a dinner of roast chicken. It was a cold and crisp day that indicated our Indian Summer had come to an end. We had not changed out of our Sunday clothes because Father told us he had invited a man from Sogn's studio to take some family pictures. About 2:30 P.M. the photographer entered the house and said, "Have you heard what has happened in Hawaii?" From that moment on successive images were imbedded in my mind like those on stereopticon slides. We turned on the radio and went to the globe to find Pearl Harbor. As I knelt in front of my parents with my brothers, sisters, and Skippy for our portrait, the radio gave us fragmentary accounts of the tragedy. It was hard to smile. I feared that "dastardly act," to use President Roosevelt's term, might ultimately destroy our family. I wondered whether future portraits might be different because of it.

The next morning classes were canceled, and we gathered in the school auditorium to hear President Roosevelt's speech. He began: "Yesterday December 7, 1941, a day which will live in infamy, the United States of America was suddenly and deliberately attacked by naval and air forces of the Empire of Japan." The address was fewer than five hundred words. We sat like automatons—no one dared move. All the normal skylarking was gone. The president's speech was a "call to arms"—an American parallel of Churchill's oration after Dunkirk—but it had none of Churchill's soaring prose, patriotic summons, or bugle calls to action. Roosevelt simply and directly recited the facts, and then concluded: "I ask that the Congress declare that since the unprovoked and dastardly attack…a state of war exists…With confidence in our armed forces—with the unbounded determination of our people—we will gain the inevitable triumph—so help us God." From that day until Hiroshima, the Japanese would be called "Japs," for they had violated Bismarck's assertion that "even in a declaration of war, one observes the rules of politeness." We left the auditorium in a daze and, robot-like, went through the motions of attending our classes for the rest of the day.

On the evening of December 7 college students on a thousand different campuses were on the march, churning about, moving without a destination, a mass of nervous energy seeking release. Their initial impulse came from what the French call *rage militaire*—a patriotic furor that swept across the land. They sang "Over There" and "The Star-Spangled Banner" and shouted "On to Tokyo!" At Yale they sang "Bright College Years," thinking it was the song of their alma mater when actually the tune came from Germany's World War I anthem, *"Die Wacht am Rhein."*

> Bright college years, with pleasure rife,
> The shortest, gladdest years of life;
> How swiftly are ye gliding by!
> Oh, why doth time so swiftly fly?

The next day the lines at recruiting stations were blocks long. Legions of young men were consumed with visions of honor, manhood, duty, adventure, and glory. Samuel Johnson's barb, "Patriotism, Sir, is the last refuge of the scoundrel," was put on the shelf for the duration of the war. Scoundrels and saints, and all those in between, were jingoists now. Later there would be anguish enough for all as the words of Herodotus came true—"In peace, sons bury their fathers; in war, fathers bury their sons." Student enthusiasm was contagious, ambiguity, gone. Like their fathers in World War I, the sons marched into the recruiting stations and later onto the battle fields with the words of Horace ringing in their ears: *Dulce et Decorum est Pro Patria Mori!* ("How sweet and noble it is to die for your country".) Tragically, most of their fathers had not told them about the horrors of trench warfare, poison gas and the machine-gun slaughter that made even the bravest soldier wonder what he was fighting for. The contrast between glorious expectation and ugly reality led to the suspicion of authority, doubt about absolutes, irony and cynicism, that came to define modernity in life and in art. War can make cynics; it can make a "lost generation." Or perhaps like life itself, war merely makes cynics of cynics—and saints of saints. Like their fathers the men who fought in World War II would learn too late the reality of war as seen in the quatrain of Wilfred Owen, the English poet, who died a few days before Armistice Day in 1918:

> My friend, you would not tell with such high zest
> To children ardent for some desperate glory
> The old lie *Dulce et decorum est*
> *Pro Patria Mori*

My student generation had no idea of the hardships and sufferings that lay ahead of us, of the names and faces that would become but dim memories of lost comrades forever young, or of the thin margin that at times would separate America and its allies from defeat. In our surge of patriotism, we could hardly imagine that we would be seeing certain friends for the last time. All that was for the future; for now it was defiance, laughing, cheering, and, for only a few of us, tears. The strident debates about whether to help Britain were over. An unsought war was on our hands, and America took its metaphor of resolve and unity from the lock-step patriotism of marching students.

Much later we learned that many facts had been kept from us. Our entire Pacific fleet, less the aircraft carriers, had been sunk, and it was feared the Japanese would invade the West Coast. Within months, defeat followed defeat and those "faraway places with strange sounding names" entered our lexicon and became commonplace—Bataan, Clark Field, Corregidor, Malaya, Singapore, Java, Solomon Islands, New Guinea, Coral Sea, Guadalcanal. (War, I discovered, is a great stimulus as a teacher of world geography.) Admirals and generals would be sacked for incompetence. The rays of the Japanese sun, it seemed, incinerated everything they touched, and the armies of little yellow men seemed unconquerable.

Foolish speeches were made. Senator Gerald P. Nye of North Dakota, a bitter Anglophobe, said that Roosevelt had wanted "to pick a war with Japan." When the reports came in about the Pearl Harbor disaster he refused to believe them for a time, saying "it sounds terribly fishy to me." Isolationist Senator Borah of Idaho, who had voted against universal military conscription and every defense appropriation, shouted from the Senate well, "Now let's go out and whip the little yellow bastards in the next seven weeks." It reminded me of his parody two years earlier after Hitler crushed Poland and started World War II—"Lord, if only I could have talked with Hitler, all this might have been avoided!" I knew that his isolationist and pacifist stance had helped create our national debacle.

Our leaders had forgotten the truism of Flavius Vegetius, the Roman military philosopher, "If you *want peace, prepare for war.*" They had ignored the lesson of history that defeat—and sometimes annihilation— is the penalty of blindness and apathy. Our isolationists pontificated that George Washington told us to steer clear of foreign entanglements. But they ignored the warning in his First Annual Address (1790) to Congress: "To be prepared for war is one of the most effectual means of preserving peace."

I realized how vacuous and wrong Christian "sunshine-and-blue-sky" liberalism had been. Modernism's optimism, idealism, and hope for the Kingdom of God on earth were gone. In a single sentence, H. Richard Niebuhr uncovered the tragedy of liberalism: *"A God without wrath brought men without sin into a kingdom without judgment through the ministrations of a Christ without a cross!"* For the rest of the 20th century the church would attempt to find out where it took the wrong turn. It would rummage through the theological wastebaskets of the 19th century and attempt to recover the classic Christian doctrines it had discarded.

How quickly Pipestone changed because of the war! We were a microcosm of the nation. The war revived our flagging enterprise culture and gave us focus and unity. Hundreds left for Sioux Falls, the Twin Cities, the West Coast and other industrial centers to help create the infinite panoply of weaponry—Liberty Ships, jeeps, tanks, uniforms, machine guns, trucks, battleships, radios, etc.—demanded by Mars, the god of war. A tidal wave of millions of civilians was on the move across the land in answer to the plea, "Give Our Boys the Tools and Let Them Finish the Job." For millions still living on handouts, good jobs at high wages were now available. Like our nation, Pipestone would never be the same.

My favorite periodical, *Life Magazine,* changed significantly as the number of articles and photos of war increased. Even advertisements for products and services as mundane as Vaseline hair tonic, Florida grapefruit juice, and Jarman shoes for men, invariably included pictures of soldiers, sailors or marines. *The Pipestone County Star* and *The Pipestone Leader* broke out of their agrarian repertorial cocoon, and every issue carried photos and short articles on the USSR and Germany, defense production, and our men in training. A new *column—WHERE OUR BOYS ARE IN TRAINING: WRITE TO THEM!*—began with 75 names and addresses. By the end of 1942 the names covered an entire page and the addresses were dropped because of lack of space.

On July 10, 1942 a Pearl Harbor "car riddled by 18 Jap bullets" was exhibited on Main Street. The paper regularly listed the men who'd been taken to fulfill our town's selective service quota. The war, it seemed, was sucking men off farms and factories in ever-increasing numbers. Nevertheless, under a "food for defense" program, our county was asked to assume a 10 percent increase in its quota of milk and eggs.

Since Rev. Steinmeyer, the Missouri Synod Lutheran pastor, was the chairman of the county selective service board, no one questioned the fairness of the draft. By February 1942, the county stopped publicizing the names and numbers of those inducted to prevent the enemy from estimating the size of our military forces. During the same month Pipestone went on "war time," and we set our clocks an hour ahead. A mild protest by farmers—"cows go by the sun, not the clock"—said it would cut milk production. A wag in town joined their lament, complaining that the extra hour of sun would "burn out his lawn!"

A Defense Council was formed and there were drives to collect aluminum, household fat (glycerin was needed for explosives), copper, brass, rubber, tin foil, paper, and scrap iron. We collected unneeded winter clothing to help the Russians get through their Siberian winters. The alliterative cry went out—*"LET'S JOLT THE JAPS WITH JUNK FROM PIPESTONE!"* An article published on September 16, 1942, complete with drawings, indicated that an old shovel could make four hand grenades, one tire made the rubber for 12 gas masks, and a discarded disc provided the steel for 210 semi-automatic light carbines. Scarcely an edition passed without a cartoon that held up Hitler, Tojo, or Mussolini to ridicule. When rationing forms for sugar, fat, gasoline, red meat, and shoes were filled out, we learned that the 1,032 persons who had hoarded sugar would not be given ration books until their supplies were exhausted. Coffee rationing began in November 1942—each person was allowed one pound every five weeks or "slightly more than a cup a day per person."

My "War Ration Book Two #363815 EC" was issued by a certain "Blanche Parker" in 1942 and used by Mother when she went to market. The reverse side carried this information and warning:

> Rationing is a vital part of your country's war effort. This book is your Government's guarantee of your fair share of goods made scarce by war, to which the stamps contained therein will be assigned as the need arises. Any attempt to violate the rules is an effort to deny someone his share and will create hardship and discontent. Such action, like treason, helps the enemy. Give your whole support to rationing and thereby conserve our vital goods.
> Be guided by the rule: "If you don't need it, DON'T BUY IT."

In February 1943 the second county-wide blackout test was deemed a "100 percent success" by officials." Air Raid Wardens had been rehearsing for six months and lights were out for 18 minutes. Vicarious participation with our loved ones in battle came through the movies such as "Crash Dive" (Tyrone Power) and "Keeper of the Flame" (Spencer Tracy, Katherine Hepburn). The screenplay was beautifully romantic and the violence was nuanced.

Our county regularly met and then exceeded its quota of four successive War Bond initiatives. The 1943 drive raised $408,301. The propaganda to buy bonds was powerful: "They GIVE their lives; you LEND your money!" Again, "MEN ARE DYING...ARE YOU BUYING?" It did not matter that the interest was a puny 2.5 percent. Nor did anyone worry about the use of emotional appeals to coerce children to purchase savings stamps: "They write their names on a Roll of Honor of Americans who are doing their part to show the dictators that a United America will never flinch to preserve her sacred liberty."

With a scarcity of consumer goods, these successive appeals took money out of circulation and reduced the threat of inflation. In September 1943 our school proudly flew a "Schools at War" flag because 94.1% of our teachers and students had bought bonds.

In the winter of 1944, like many other 17- and 18-year-old boys, I joined the Rifle Club. Financed by the Jaycees, members of the Woodstock Rifle Club gave us instruction every Monday and Wednesday in the basement of the Model Grocery. I learned the four positions for shooting—prone, sitting, standing and kneeling—the way to compensate for windage, the use of the leather carrying strap to steady one's aim, and much more. It was a labor of love by these men who wanted to give us pre-service training to improve our chances for survival. At the same time, our athletic coaches created a "toughening program" replete with rope climbing, an obstacle course, calisthenics and the like "to develop less-frequently used muscles" to prepare us for the rigorous training in the military.

A few notes of discord interrupted the positive harmony of our war effort. In early 1942 a run-away Indian boy was "taken for a 'Jap' by an Iowa farmer" and captured. There were reports from Nebraska that some Jehovah's Witnesses had asked for protection from some thugs who claimed they had not shown "proper respect" for the flag. A year after Pearl Harbor our German painter, Fritz Seidel, who had so decoratively painted our dining and living rooms with old-world elegance, was "in jail for failing to register as an 'enemy alien.'" He had come to America in 1923 and had never bothered about citizenship or to register as an alien. In June 1943 five "speed violators" had to give up their gas ration books for three to six months. In the same month, in a burst of misguided jingoism—"many counties have already contributed *similar relics*"—our 4,789 pound Civil War cannon in front the court house was hauled off for scrap. As if expecting criticism, an unnamed official opined that "kids were getting hurt on that old relic. It was good to get rid of it."

After the war, the 80-year gap between the 1860s and the Second World War was erased when a Sherman tank took the place where our unique Civil War muzzle-loader used to stand. Thirty feet behind the tank a Union soldier at parade rest seems to peer somewhat quizzically over the scene, perhaps reflecting, *"Where did my artillery go?"* The limestone statue is unique and has a quiet classical dignity. But the particularity of our war monument is now gone, since tens of thousands of such tanks now grace American parks.

Surprisingly, it was not until November 1943 when *The Pipestone Star* reported "Wilfred Weiss is Probably the First Man From This County to be Killed in Action (Italy)" that the reality of war came home to us. The 11th gold star had been added to neighboring Murray county's service flag that same month. The reprieve was only temporary. Soon the death curve of our county would turn exponential.

Because it had to last for the duration of the war, every family treated their car like a piece of heirloom Dresden china. On February 10, 1942, small ceremonies were held in car plants as the last chassis came down the line. Then the machinery was ripped out and new tools installed to begin the mass-production of military vehicles. During the next four years Detroit would build millions of army trucks, Jeeps, and tanks. (In 1941 Detroit produced over three and a half million automobiles. During the war, production dropped to the extraordinary figure of just 139 cars.)

Pipestone county was allowed only 16 new passenger car tires from March through May, 1942. In place of selling Fords, Hicks Motor Company won a $5000 war contract to make a "war item"; the part and the number made weren't specified because of wartime secrecy.

Civilian goods were in scarce supply, and it was a real status symbol if a father or brother had sent you a military cap, insignia, scarf, watch, or jacket that you could wear to school.

The Sunday comics changed. Buck Rogers, Dick Tracy, and the Lone Ranger gave way to the heroic exploits of our army, navy, and marine personnel. Even Popeye cited the advantages of putting on the bluejacket: "In the Navy you get free uniforms, free food, and no doctor's or dentist's bills. In the Navy your pay is gravy." In one strip he pointed to a sailor with a pretty girl on his arm. The subliminal message? You could have it all in the Navy.

The traditional symbols of evil, Indians and bank robbers, were replaced by sadistic German and Japanese soldiers. Hitler was shown in countless cartoons and posters as a scavenging animal—a hyena, a rat, a vulture—or a primitive ape-like creature; his followers became vermin. Popular magazines portrayed "yellow Jap" soldiers with fang-type teeth feasting on the flesh and blood of our dead marines. I was too innocent to realize that for one to maintain psychological balance in war, the enemy had to be transformed into either a superhuman devil or a subhuman beast.

My doodling changed from pheasants, deer, and the female figure to sketches of tanks, ships, and airplanes in combat. German and Japanese planes always trailed smoke as they spiraled down to their doom. I quickly learned to identify all the airplanes of friend and foe. I could draw the P-47, P-37, P-39, B-17, B-24, PBY, PBM, P-51 the Airacobra, and many others by heart. I could also sketch Japanese Zeros and Bettys and German Stukkas, Heinkles, and Messerschmidts.

Many of our male teachers accepted commissions in the service. As a result, the faculty became feminized with retreaded homemakers. Andy Anderson, our band director, became a military instructor in radio; our coaches, physics, and math teachers also left for the armed service. Some male instructors had been exempted from military service because of physical disability. Anderson's replacement, Arnold Woesterhoff, was well meaning but incompetent. We didn't respect him as a musician, director, or teacher and discipline became lax. Once he kicked Neal Knudtson in the butt for acting up in marching band. Noah Nelson, a genial teacher of unpretentious talent, continued on in chemistry, and continued his moonlighting at the post office. My social studies teacher and former tumbling coach, Mr. Davis, became senior high principal and adopted autocratic tendencies.

Once in study hall he caught me returning a spitball to its former owner. He ordered me into his office and showed me a piece of paper. "Do you know what this is," he asked rhetorically. "It's a recommendation form for college, and, just maybe, you will need me to write one for you one of these days. What do you think I should say?" Like an obsequious monk before his abbot, I outwardly toadied to him. Or was I like a cynical old chimpanzee who goes through the motions for the sake of the bananas? No matter. I would never need his accolades. College was beyond my comprehension. Within months I would be on some unknown battlefield upholding my nation's honor while he was pushing poor kids around. I wondered what had become of the gracious man who had been my tumbling coach.

The war changed the school curriculum as well as the faculty make-up. Mr. Owens, the biology teacher, developed an excellent class in aeronautics that dealt with thrust, pressure, lift, weather formations, navigation, and principles of engine combustion. A unit of International Morse Code was the most valuable, and even today, I can remember the "dit dahs," the short and longs, for many letters and numbers. Industrial arts students were given a quota of 50 wooden model planes to build (the Navy wanted 500,000 overall), sand, and paint. Later, when I was in the Navy Air Corps, I used such replicas of both friendly and enemy planes, built on a scale of 1 to 72, to learn airplane recognition.

Our generation was well-suited to fight in World War II. The Great Depression had been a struggle for survival and habituated us to hard work on the farms and in the foundries and warehouses of America. Whatever complaints even the lower classes might have had about how life had treated them, their love of country had not turned sour. We were self-reliant yet accustomed to taking orders. Through sports or hunting or both, we had gained a sense of self-worth and self-confidence. Of course, we would have preferred to throw baseballs instead of grenades, shoot a .22 rifle instead of an M-l. But having been caught up in a "just war," we viewed military service as a positive experience.

We were not afraid to get our hands dirty during a time when skills had value. Most of us were clever with tools and machinery and had repaired old cars and tractors. We had created scooters and "go-carts" from refuse salvaged at the city dump. Almost every boy I knew had built model airplanes, fiddled with a chemistry set, or made a crystal radio. Moreover, "youth culture" as we know it today did not exist. The military promised a novel, almost exotic vista.

Unlike the Vietnam generation, we were in this together. Unlike the legions of Bill Clintons who pulled strings 25 years later to escape the draft, I knew no one who was reluctant to be a citizen soldier. The four Roosevelt brothers were in uniform. The sons of Harry Hopkins, Roosevelt's closest adviser, and Leverett Saltonstall, one of the most powerful Republicans in the Senate, served in the Marine Corps as enlisted men and were killed in action.

Occasionally friends who had graduated in '42 and '43 would return from the service with lurid tales. Unqualified for one of the regular branches of the military because he had lost a kidney subsequent to an injury in a football game, Clark Hickman had joined the United States Merchant Marine. Clark entertained us with stories of convoys during "Battle of the Atlantic." "German U-boats picked off our ships like birds in a state fair shooting gallery," he said. He spoke of exploding tankers and sinking lifeboats, of depth charges, heroism and cowardice. Most often death came quickly, but there was also the slow, agonizing starvation in lifeboats. "One frigid night a number of us were ordered into a lifeboat to look for the survivors after the torpedoing of a tanker," Clark remembered. "When we found a floating body we had to be careful not to hit it against the side of the boat or the body would shatter like a piece of china dropped on the floor." Our eyes went wide as we wondered whether Clark had embellished his reflections.

I marched in lockstep with our nation as it shifted to a total war effort. To sacrifice, suffer, and limit our needs would deepen our bond with our fighting men. Our gardens, now designated "Victory Gardens," grew more bountiful so that more food could be diverted abroad. During the summer of 1943 the city plowed and prepared seven acres of vacant land for apartment dwellers who wanted Victory Gardens. I became a member of the "clean plate" club because it was unpatriotic to waste food. Once, on a streetcar in Minneapolis, I joined other riders in staring at a man in his early 20s with a suspicious eye that said, "You look strong and healthy enough. Why aren't you in the service? Do you have a yellow streak down your back? Has political pull gotten you a deferment?" It was every young man's fear that a hidden physical condition might keep him out of the service. Cruelly, we stereotyped 4-F's as lepers even though they had no control over their physical and mental limitation.

Unlike men, women were not conscripted. But the haunting photographic image of the 1930s, the Madonna of the Depression, gave way to the propagandistic ideal of war-working womanhood, "Rosie the Riveter." (Though given the changes in work practices, "Wanda the

Welder" might have been more appropriate.) Women who volunteered for military service became nurses, did commissariat and secretarial work, drove trucks and jeeps, ferried aircraft, and did other bureaucratic, "behind the line," types of work so that more men could enter active combat. The acronyms WAC (Army) and WAVE (Navy) became the butt of many jokes regarding the sexual habits of women in the military. In some quarters the feeling ran deep that virtuous women should have nothing to do with a hard-fighting and hard-drinking military. Those who subscribed to that view saw uniformed women not as patriots, but as sexually promiscuous females. Obviously a great injustice was done here. Women, like men, were prompted to join the military by motives of patriotism and a desire to break away from family and cultural suffocation.

I eagerly hunted jackrabbits and sold their pelts for $1.25 so that they could be made into parkas for our pilots. We recycled not for the sake of ecology but to add material to the national war effort. I took Mother's fat drippings to the butcher store so they could be made into gunpowder. I washed tin cans, removed their labels, cut out the bottoms, tucked their covers inside and pounded them flat with a hammer. Distressed because our newspaper collection grew so slowly, I often tucked cardboard into the pile to fatten it up. I reconnoitered dumps, farm groves, and alleys for scrap iron that could be made into grenades or battleships. I walked home from school in the street gutter looking for discarded cigarette and gum wrappers that could be salvaged; my ball of tin foil was almost eight inches in diameter before I turned it in. I collected canned food and old clothes for the children of Britain. Homemakers by the hundreds sewed and knitted apparel for the troops overseas. New shoes were unavailable. If ours got wet, we received a lecture from Father and had to stuff newspaper inside them to soak up the moisture and help them keep their shape. By the end of the war some of our shoes had been half-soled two and three times.

Even the appearance of women's legs suffered during the war. Legions of women heeded the plea to turn in their silk and nylon stockings so that they could be fashioned into powder bags and parachutes. Bare legs or unsightly and unshapely cotton hose with baggy knees were symbols of patriotism that endured for the duration. Six months after the war, on February 6, 1946, over 13,000 women—and a considerable number of their cooperative husbands—packed the streets around the downtown Minneapolis Dayton's department store standing in line for several hours for a two-pair allotment of nylon hose. War-weary women were eager to finally unbare their public-spirited legs.

My efforts and those of millions like me contributed only marginally to the war effort. But civilian activism was a psycho-social means of identifying with those who were risking their lives. How I wished I could do more!

As a high school senior, to gain perspective on the war I dipped back into my first love, history, and did a special study on the Civil War. I memorized the names of the major generals, tactics, defeats and victories of both sides in the crucial battles. From the nation's total population of 25 million, the North and South had, collectively, lost over 600,000 men during that titanic struggle. Thomas Jefferson had said that "the tree of liberty must be refreshed from time to time with the blood of patriots and tyrants—it is its natural manure." (I wondered what price we would have to pay before Germany and Japan were destroyed.) One source I reviewed dealt with poetic memorials to those who had fallen at Vicksburg. I ended my essay with them:

> The neighing troop, the flashing blade,
>   The bugles stirring blast
> The charge, the dreadful cannonade,
>   The din and shout are past
>
> The muffled drums and roll has beat
>   The soldiers' last tattoo
> No more on life's parade shall meet
>   That brave and fallen few
>
> No rumor of the foe's advance
>   Now sweeps upon the wind
> No troubled thought at midnight haunts
>   Of loved ones left behind

Indeed, I wondered when I would go and thought of my "loved ones left behind."

Later, I was pleased to be able to join the Navy Air Corps, even though I knew the adage, "heroes in wartime, dogs in peacetime." I thanked God that our "just war" had not ended before I joined, and that I had not been classified 4-F. I began to sense the addictive character of a military uniform and walked all over town so that people could see me. At church in my dress blues, I sat ramrod straight. I knew I represented the mystic sense of what America meant to millions. Afterwards, I tried to act humble as the congregation gathered around and told me how proud they were of me.   On leave during the Spring of 1945, I

1. Alex Newcomer
2. Hannah Walseth
3. Don Radi
4. Clark Hickman
5. John Hallahan
6. Chubby Wahlstrom
7. Hilda Johannson
8. Marvin DeVries
9. Tommy Nelson
10. Arlene Pfantz
11. Gordy Bowman
12. John Knuth
13. Buckley McMahon
14. Curtis Sabie
15. Marvin Swenson
The staff wanted
more snaps but
couldn't get them.

The 1944 high school annual had several pages of photos of former students who were now serving in the military. Their letters and photos, together with the patriotism of the era, caused many of us to hope that the war would not end before we came of age. Students who left during their senior year were granted their diploma upon completing their military service. The son of our high school custodian, Marvin DeVries, # 8 (upper center) was killed in action in the Pacific theater.

entered the court house and saw my name inscribed on a large plaque as one of "OUR PIPESTONE BOYS WHO ARE FIGHTING FOR FREEDOM . . . THEY HAVE PLEDGED THEIR SACRED HONOR AND PRECIOUS BLOOD, THAT WE MIGHT LIVE IN SECURITY AND PEACE . . . OF WHOM WE ARE VERY PROUD!" By the end of 1945 the Memorial Honor Roll contained 611 names from the First World War and 1500 from World War II; 100 had gold stars by their name. I bowed my head and remembered the words of Eisenhower: "Humility must always be the portion of any man who receives acclaim earned in the blood of his followers and the sacrifices of his friends."

Gas rationing greatly reduced teen-age cruising. We would pool our gas stamps and five or six of us would pile into a car in the afternoon after basketball practice. Someone would usually bring a dog-eared copy of *Esquire* magazine along and we would gaze at the Petty Girl drawings with their full bosoms and elongated legs. Everyone would confess to prickly sensations, but those drawings were as racy as anything got in Pipestone county. We would shoot a few squirrels and rabbits, perhaps restless that we weren't in the military going after some really evil critters. Once someone in the back seat had a .22 pistol that accidentally misfired and put a hole in the roof of Don Nelson's car. We put some mud over the hole to hide it from his father until Don could get it repaired.

Father held a "C" gas rationing card because he was a physician. He could have as much gas as he needed. His sense of rectitude would never allow him, however, to use the Ford for recreation. Mother's Olds, however, had an "A" card and was restricted to three gallons a week. Because there were no new tires, we had to get by on retreads, and the speed limit was dropped to 35 MPH. Tracey Hicks, the Ford dealer, strongly protested the stupidity of the law: "Henry Ford would roll over in his grave at such nonsense. Fords will self-destruct if driven at such asinine slow speeds." Throughout the war he was arrested again and again by the highway patrol for speeding. To the charge that semi-trailer trucks broke up the highways, he answered, "The greatest pressure in pounds per square inch that is placed on our streets is the high heel spike of a woman's shoe!" Father had moral rather than technological complaints about rationing: "Why is it milk trucks can't get tires but I've never seen a beer truck without good rubber?"

We never had to pull in our belts thanks to our garden bounty and Mother's canning. A national campaign promoted saving so that scarce civilian goods would stretch farther and inflation would be curtailed. I saved every penny I could to buy stamps to fill up my War Bond books.

When it was full of stamps and worth $18.75, I would rush down to the post office and get a bond. The interest paid was modest—in ten years it could be cashed in for $25.00—but at that time inflation was non existent.

Families with a son or daughter in the service proudly displayed an 8-by-10-inch white and blue flag with a red star in the front window. Some homes had three and four stars. When a home lost a son, the star turned to gold. When we passed the home of a gold star mother on the way to school, our voices always became soft and our skylarking stopped.

In December of my senior year, an Army Air Force recruiter spoke to our aeronautics class. If I would sign up now (I had just turned 17) with my parents permission, I could enter flight training immediately upon graduation. I ran home with the application. It meant I could enter the service four months before my 18th birthday, the earliest time the Navy would take me. My greatest fear was that the war would be over before I could volunteer.

I was angry that Father refused to sign. "What about your plan to join Bob in the Navy Air Corps?" he said. "But this is just as good...I'll be flying, that's what I've always wanted to do," I pleaded. "Besides, if I wait until I'm 18, the war will be over and I'll be looked upon as a coward and a 4-F. I'll never be able to hold my head up."

I was struck by Father's honest realism in his rebuttal: "People get very excited during wartime but they have short memories," he said sadly. "After this war is over, they will quickly forget who served and who didn't. Democracies like our country hold the soldier in honor only in wartime. During times of peace, they consider the warrior a barbarian. It shouldn't be that way, but I'm afraid that's the way it is." In trying to protect me by dampening my patriotic fervor, he had revealed a profound truth. (Unknown to me, however, he had tried to volunteer for the Army Medical Corps. Time had evidently erased the trauma of his Mexican Border experience. But because of the physician shortage in Pipesone county, he was not accepted. Father was always patriotic and grateful for the opportunities America had given him.)

Years later an event proved the truth of Father's words. I had been entranced by the romanticized view of war that runs like a red streak though our literature. But he was wise enough to see the other side of the dialectic—bodies, blood, and destruction—even though he had not experienced combat. In 1954, while working on my doctorate at Duke University, in Durham, North Carolina, I opened our apartment door and was confronted by a somewhat shabbily-dressed, desperate-seeming man who had metal pinchers for a right hand. He was selling magazine subscriptions and begged me for a sale. Confessing to graduate-school poverty, I began to close the door when he exploded: "I didn't ask for that frick'en Korean war, or to lose my arm, or to go hat-in-hand selling magazines. And now I'm trying to support myself and nobody gives a damn!" Guilt-stricken, I remembered Father's words, and my heart felt very heavy.

My graduation photo at 17. I appear "tender and innocent." But after a summer spent as a "gandy dancer" on the Milwaukee Railroad, I eagerly looked forward to military service and contact with a larger world.

My parents are reading one of the many letters I wrote home.

I carried these two photos of my grandparents and parents around in a small leather frame during my service in the Navy Air Corps, 1944-46.

42. PIPESTONE: THE ETERNAL AND MYTHIC VILLAGE

There are all those early memories; one cannot get another set; one
has only those.

Shadows on the Rock, Willa Cather

"No man is an island, entire of itself, every man is a piece of the continent, a part of the main; if a clod be washed away by the sea, Europe is
the less, as well as if a promontory were, as well as a manor of thy
friends or thine own were; any man's death dimishes me, because I am
involved in mankind; and therefore never send to know for whom the
bell tolls; it tolls for thee."

Meditation XVII, John Donne (1572-1631)

At mid-life I began to reflect upon my origins. Almost the first feeling I could remember was the joy of being myself instead of somebody
else—one of those millions and millions unfortunate enough to have
been born somebody other than Walter William Benjamin at 808 Third
Avenue, Pipestone, Minnesota. And I speculated why and how a boy of
but modest gifts had evolved into a competent teacher, writer, and schol-
ar. I'd been the recipient of careful nurturing in a loving if disciplined
and demanding home, but I wondered if there was something else perhaps more illusive. It began to dawn on me that my small town origins
deserved significant credit. I discovered that there were many little
"Our Town" Pipestones across our land. Places like Boise, Saint Johns,
Mission, Westminster, Shirkieville, Floresville, and Clio had something
in common. The riddle deepens by adding Laurinburg, Walters,
Rumford, Mitchell, Everett, Doland, and Pocantico Hills. The common
connection becomes apparent when five more small-town names are
added to the list: Plains, Grand Rapids, Russell, Dixon, and Hope. These
are the contemporary "Can anything good come out of Nazareth?"
places; the "god-forsaken" spots where people say, "I would not be
caught dead here," Or, "This is God's country because only God would
want to live here."

But such isolated little hamlets are the birthplaces or home towns of 19 past or current presidents or aspirants to that high office. Their names, paralleling the towns listed above, are: Church, Udall, Bentsen, Shriver, Bayh, Connally, Wallace, Sanford, Harris, Muskie, McGovern, Jackson, Humphrey, Rockefeller, Carter, Ford, Dole, Reagan, and Clinton.

Many times when I thought of Pipestone, Thomas Gray's *Elegy in a Country Churchyard* came to mind. Gray wrote movingly of unrecognized greatness—"full many a flower is born to blush unseen"—of those living in small towns:

Full many a gem of purest ray serene
The dark unfathom'd caves of ocean bear:
Full many a flower is born to blush unseen,
And waste its sweetness on the desert air.

Some village Hampden, that with dauntless breast
The little tyrant of his fields withstood,
Some mute inglorious Milton here may rest,
Some Cromwell guiltless of his country's blood.

Here rests his head upon the lap of earth,
A youth to fortune and to fame unknown.
Fair Science frown'd not on his humble birth,
And Melancholy mark'd him for her own.

No farther seek his merits to disclose,
Or draw his frailties from their dread abode,
(There they alike in trembling hope repose),
The bosom of his Father and his God.

Life is more manageable in smaller places. "The mobs of great cities add just so much to the support of pure government," wrote Thomas Jefferson, "as sores do to the strength of the human body." Immense cities often overwhelm people, discouraging them before they reach the age of leadership. The Pipestones of America nourish hope, confidence, and the ability to cope. I had a better grip on myself and on the world because of my nurture in a tribal village. I had a warm environment where families stayed close and landmarks endured.

Had I committed transgressions in Pipestone, I would not have been able to hide them as easily as would my counterpart in the urban multitudes. Peer pressure was effectively brought to bear against unruly neighbors in Pipestone because people there feel the sting of being singled out and held up for public censure. Such informal community punishment is far cheaper than police and jails, and far more efficacious. Well-targeted, well-justified gossip directed at miscreants through the church, school, barber shop and coffee shop was a form of therapeutic tough love. Such barbs, frowns, and finger-wagging, however lampooned by the urban media, produced better results, by and large, than the banging of a judge's gavel or the clang of a jail-cell door in a large, impersonal city.

The lack of anonymity in Pipestone also produced a fundamental social benefit. It required me to acknowledge my neighbors as individuals, not merely as indistinguishable faces in a crowd. The amiable example of small-town advantage is still seen in the way country folk wave to each other, often to complete strangers, as they pass—even from behind the steel-and-glass armor of a motor vehicle. It is considered impolite not to recognize the individual humanity of a person you encounter along the way—after all, he is most likely one of your neighbors.

I was fortunate to have been reared in an egalitarian community with little sense of class consciousness. George Bernard Shaw's cynical aphorism about England—"Ladies and gentlemen are permitted to have friends in the kennel but not in the kitchen"—did not apply to Pipestone.

I lived, therefore, within the arms of family, neighborhood, school, church, and flag that bred into me a strong strain of Calvinism. It was composed of equal parts of missionary zeal to help others and fierce self-interest. Industry, integrity, civic-mindedness, self-denial, and duty were the pole stars by which to steer, come what may. Free of the corrosive cynicism of our present age, I accepted the moral canon, "Do good and you will do well," as a law of the universe.

On October 10, 1944, my 18th birthday, I left Pipestone to enter the United States Navy Air Corps. A month earlier I had passed the demanding mental and physical examination required to become a Naval pilot and had sworn that "I will bear truth faith and allegiance to the United States of America; that I will serve them honestly and faithfully against all their enemies whomsoever, and that I will obey the orders of the President of the United States, and the orders of the officers appointed over me, according to the Rules and Articles for the Government of the Army, Navy, and Marine Corps of the United States." In short I had put my life on the line and against our barbarous enemies. I was dimly aware of the fact that war was a brutal, deadly game. But after all, don't men love games? I also knew that if I came back whole, I would bring with me the knowledge that I had explored regions of my soul that in most men will always remain uncharted. As I rode the bus to the Twin Cities, the thought crossed my mind that I might never again see the spot that, in shaping me, was so cherished. Yet, I felt an intoxicating sense of being free for the first time in my life. Adventure! Flight! Freedom! Now at last all were going to be mine.

But I was inwardly warmed by something that had occurred a few hours earlier. At breakfast devotions, a singular event had transpired—Father broke down and could not continue. As usual he was sitting at the head of the table dressed in his white shirt and conservative tie. He wore a gray cardigan that he would later exchange for his suit coat. Mother was at the other end of the table, her dress well covered by a serviceable apron. I had finished the Bible reading, his cue to begin the lesson of the day from *The Upper Room* devotional that ended in a table grace. But after speaking one sentence, there was silence.

We sat in utter stillness as the minutes ticked by. The oatmeal no longer gave off steam. The toast grew cold. I peeked under my eye-brows at Martha, Mary, and Roger, my sisters and brother, for a clue as to what was happening. But their faces were frozen and impassive and seemed set in stone. I sensed their impatience at the delay that might mean they would be late for school. I could not meet Father's eyes for they were on his plate. A side-long glance at Mother at the foot of the table found her helpless, Buddha-like, without a wisp of a smile. The silence was awesome and even a bit frightening. No one moved, know-ing that they were witnessing a truly singular, never-before-experienced event. How was it possible that the one who was the master of every sit-uation, the one who knew all the answers to all life's enigmas, of issues of life and death, was suddenly voiceless.

The tick of the cuckoo clock, normally unheard, reverberated in my ears. Then the bobwhite tolled eight oclock. Periodically, Father tried to continue reading the lesson but could not. Because his head was down I could not see if there were tears in his eyes. I detected soft whimpers and sniffles. Occasionally he blew his nose and tried to continue. He was humiliated to be out of control. I was embarrassed for him but did not know what to do.

Finally, he picked up his spoon and began to eat. It was our clue that the lesson would not be completed. My last meal at home went unblessed. Yet, in a deeper sense, that quietness was sacramental, a holy moment, that betokened the compassion that would follow me into the service. It was a silent talisman of his love, however inarticulate, for me.

I am sure my parents always knew that Bob would have to serve. Inwardly they had continued to hope that the conflict would be over before I came of age. Father's innate stoicism prevented him from being verbally affectionate and warmly expressive with me. I never once experienced a father-son bear hug that is so in vogue today. Like most men of his era, Father felt more than he was able to express. His letters were fairly effusive, but his words were constrained. For him deeds were more important.

In my innocence I could not speculate about what lay ahead for me. My parents may have magnified the moral, spiritual, and physical perils that awaited, but I looked forward to high adventure, eager to follow my friends into a time of testing against the adversary. I wanted release. The Pipestone womb, so supportive and protective in early years, was now suffocating me. My time of gestation was over, I was full term, and looked forward to my deliverance. But Father's trauma that morning, the only time I had experienced him out of control, has always been the lodestar of his love for me.

Later that morning Mother drove me to the Calumet Hotel to catch the Greyhound bus that would take me to Minneapolis. Although Father's office was only a block away, he did not come to see me off. Perhaps he did not want to risk losing control again. I fit the Norman Rockwell portrait of the apprehensive yet expectant new inductee. In my hand was a small cardboard suitcase containing a few clothes. Like a newly robed postulant who discards his profane garb upon taking holy orders, so too did I dump my clothes in an ash can once I was in uniform. Like the monk I, too, cherished receiving a new habit for my new incarnation.

I had brought along two or three books to read on the way to Minneapolis. At the time I had little appreciation of poetry, but in my haste I had inadvertently pulled a book of verse from a shelf at home. Before we had reached Holland, it fell open to a few lines from A.E. Houseman's "To an Athlete Dying Young:"

> To-day, the road all runners come,
> Shoulder-high we bring you home,
> And set you at your threshold down,
> Townsman of a stiller town…
> And round that early-laurelled head
> Will flock to gaze the strengthless dead…

With a start I awoke from a state of dreaming innocence with the realization that, in my attempt at escape from the Pipestone womb, I might return "strengthless dead" in a coffin "shoulder high." But in English class Miss Schmidt had quoted Oliver Wendell Holmes, Jr. that "life is action and passion." Therefore, it was required of me that I should share the passion and action of my time or be judged in peril not to have lived.

So like millions of other American boys, I went forth to war. Fortunately, the vast majority of us were neither maimed nor killed. Most of us could not articulate what we felt in terms of patriotism and duty, challenge and sacrifice. For many, the military was a bit romantic, for the myth of war and combat is deeply imbedded in the male psyche. But I had discovered my exemplar four years earlier during the Battle of Britain, where a few hundred pilots had saved England and Western Civilization. Eighty percent of the British Eagles who flew the Hurricanes and Spitfires had lost their lives in turning back the almost endless *Luftwaffe* squadrons. *"Never in the field of human conflict,"* Churchill truly stated, *"has so much been owed by so many to so few."*

I never knew Bill Millington, a British airman who left the hospital to rejoin his squadron and to die in the ether over the undulating Kentish downs. Millington still carried splinters in his thigh from a prior engagement in which he had been shot down by a Messerchsmitt 109. Like many warriors on the eve of battle, Milliongton wrote a final letter, sealed it, and left it with a nurse. Posthumously, it was delivered to his parents. It speaks of the noble and universal impulse that will forever prompt free men to sacrifice their lives to that which is just, true, and good. With only a change of national loyalty, Millington duplicated my conviction upon entering the Navy Air Corps:

> My dear Parents:
> I have asked Miss Macdonald of the Isles, who has been a particularly good friend to me to forward this short note...the possibility of a hasty departure from this life is ever present...I go forth into battle light of heart and determined to do my bit for the noble cause for which my country is fighting. Having studied the subject from all angles I am certain that freedom and democracy will eventually prove victorious.
>
> For any sorrow or suffering I may have caused I sincerely apologize.
>
> Being British I am proud of my country and its peoples, proud to serve under the Union Jack and regard it as an Englishman's privilege to fight for all those things that make life worth living—freedom, honour, and fair play. But please do not grieve over my passing... Flying has meant more than a means of livelihood...the companionship of men and boys with similar interest, the intoxication of speed, the rush of air, and the pulsating beat of the motor awakes some answering cord deep down, which is indescribable.
>
> Farewell, Your loving son, Bill

Only after leaving Pipestone was I able to see that the world had passed it by. What had been my axis munde, the center of my universe, now seemed to have become greatly diminished, even Lilliputian, in size.

After the war I periodically came back with Marjorie Prescott, first as my girlfriend, then as my fiancee, and finally as my wife, to recapture the nostalgia of my past. But I had changed. Within a few years of leaving, I had witnessed the whoring, boozing, and high rates of venereal disease of my squadron. I had been in 43 of the 48 states, hitch-hiked through war-ravaged Europe and had experienced life "warts and all." I had seen man not perfumed and prettied up for a portrait but caught unawares as in a candid camera shot.

In my visits home I could see that Pipestone also had changed. My childhood universe that seemed so spacious now seemed incredibly reduced. What had happened to a place so wondrous? Over time had my mind romanticized the good events but erased the hurtful experiences? Perhaps we both had changed. I was no longer a child and had lost the wondrous prism through which I viewed my spiritual commune.

Each street and building that contained the vivid transparencies of my past looked strangely different to me. Now I had an odd sense of emptiness and saw peeling paint, closed businesses, and experienced a deathly air. I once had been able to name every family and the children who lived in each house in my walks around Pipestone. But death and mobility had scrambled the deck and made the certainty of my memories suspect. The world of enchantment known only to a child-adolescent was gone. Time and travel, experience and suffering, had given me the cataracts of detachment. The Pipestone of my childhood was no longer my only world.

The Pipestone National Bank had been torn down and was now a parking lot. One of our largest employers, Alton's "Pan-0-Gold" Bakery had moved to Sioux Falls. The creamery was locked and other businesses on Main Street had crudely lettered "For Sale" signs in their windows. Our towns premiere men's clothing store, Wilsons, was about to go under. The Ashton Memorial Hospital that had seemed so impressive when I had accompanied Father on his rounds had been turned into a nursing home. It was diminutive compared to the urban hospitals I knew. The movie theater had but one word—CLOSED—on the marquee. Like an octogenarian who has lost some teeth, Main Street had empty spaces where once there were buildings. When the monthly government checks arrive, an old friend mused, "you'd think that whole world was on Social Security."

Alas, the ubiquitous McDonalds, Pizza Hut, and Subway had taken root in Pipestone, but I hoped that Gannon's, Lange's, and the other truly Ma and Pa cafes would survive so that the seniors could enjoy their gossip over nourishing home cooked food.

During my youth on Saturday nights Main Street seemed like a cross between a village Mardi Gras and a church basket social. Farm families came by the hundreds to shop, relax, and socialize. Now it looked a bit more like a Colorado mountain town after the silver lode had played out. Three of the four railroads had abandoned their rights of way, and pulled up their rails, and weeds were luxuriating between the ties. The Rock Island depot had been partly restored by some preservationists but now sat locked and empty, waiting a further transfusion of funds. The other depots were gone and existed only as pen-and-ink drawings on the office walls of railway buffs. The electronic age had turned many small-town banks into branches of their urban counterparts. The cracks in the streets seemed wider, the trees smaller, the homes more weatherbeaten, and the citizens more antiquarian. Sad images came to mind. An old mare about to be put down; the pendulum on a long case clock about to stop, a basket of overly ripe fruit showing decay and rot.

To see your village in extremis has some parallel in viewing a loved one sinking towards death.

Alas, Pipestone was at the center of a triangle of cities—Marshall, Luverne, and Worthington—that were sucking it dry. They had, respectively, a state university, a hog kill, and a junior college. Their commercial, octopus-like tentacles were growing while those of Pipestone were withering. They, not Pipestone, seemed to be the survivors of an agrarian Social Darwinism. Fifty miles to the southwest, Sioux Falls' population had exploded to over 125,000 and *Money Magazine* had designated it in 1991 as *"the number ONE American city in terms of total livability."* City Bank of New York had transferred its credit card operations there and thousands of jobs had followed. Like prairie dogs, millions of urbanites were hunkering down in the savannas of the heartland to escape the decay, drugs, gangs, and crime of the city. Subdivisions and office parks now occupied land where I had once hunted pheasants and jack rabbits.

"Rural Minnesota has been 'malled-to-death,'" groused a local physician. "Folks are taking their shopping and their illnesses to the K-marts and multi-specialty clinics in Sioux Falls and the Cities." The citizens of Pipestone had "played by the rules," commented an old-timer, "but still were getting screwed." In the early 90s over a dozen casinos had, like

Canadian thistles, sprouted up on the fertile soil of Indian reservations. Flandreau, South Dakota, and Redwood Falls had them. They sucked up the seniors with the same zeal that a winter Alberta clipper sent them scurrying pell-mell to Arizona.

"I call it 'the revenge of the Redskins'," remarked an old-timer. "They're getting even with us for stealing their land." Alas, the casinos preyed on our weakness, not our strength. Sadly, our Pipestone Indians had only a cottage industry of selling Pipestone artifacts and beadwork at the national monument. And even they were threatened by their radical urban brothers, who want to prevent "pale-faces" from owning the sacred blood-red stone.

To be sure, in the 60s the Feds had built an eight-story high-rise for the elderly poor in Pipestone. Funds generated by Lady Bird Johnson had turned three blocks of Main Street into a pathetic serpentine of bricks, flower pots, benches and green ash. But could government antibiotics or beautification keep my beloved old dowager alive? She was losing at both ends of the demographic curve—the young headed pell-mell for the Twin Cities, while the middle class elderly were pulling their fifth wheels to the Sun Belt. Only the unenterprising, lethargic, and the elderly poor seemed to be left.

Still, the boosterism decried by Sinclair Lewis was alive and well in my home town. Pipestone may yet prove to have the staying power of the persistent cockleburs that Lee DeGriselles and I had to hoe every week. For there were good people and fine organizations who were giving life support to my dear, old dowager. The Chamber of Commerce guide book was hyping our history—Indian Peacepipes, our National Monument, the Historic Buildings District, "romantic packages" at the historic Calumet hotel, and the venerable Hiawatha Pageant. A new Performing Arts Theater, Civil War Days Battle Re-enactment, and Festival of Trees were up and running. Moreover, the guide book touted side trips to the Jasper Quarry Festival, Split Rock Creek State Park, and Lake Benton's old Opera House and its new Buffalo Ridge "wind farms." Through it all, I sensed a note of anxiety and worry: "Even if our marketing goes well, will 'they come,' or are we too far off tourism's beaten path?"

A sign in a local cafe-bar revealed the ironic humor of its owner: "Sadly, our village can no longer afford the luxury of a full-time town drunk, so we have agreed to take turns. When it's your turn, *Be Here!*" When I left in 1944, the sign coming into town read, "PIPESTONE, Population 6,240." Some say this is too high. At my 50th year class reunion it read "4,554."

Without a dedicated dozen new and small industries, the future looks bleak. At present the largest employer, U.S. Marine Bayliner, on highway #23 southeast of town, is doing well. The plant leads the industry in the excellence of its product. Hundreds of luxury fiberglass boats, shrink-wrapped in white plastic, look like beached Shamu whales before they are trucked off. But the industry depends on disposable recreational dollars and I worry over the large numbers of workers who will be made redundant when the next recession comes.

Next door to Bayliner is Pipestone's second largest employer, the Ellison Meat Company, which packages beef and pork for retail outlets. Wages are modest and a few town fathers worry privately that a possible influx of Hispanic workers might force them even lower in the future.

Without a consistent and growing economic base, the seasonal festivals, the quality of life, the solid work ethic, the safe neighborhoods, the good education, and the small-town charm may be all frosting and no cake. I desperately wanted Pipestone revived because I wanted its youngsters to replicate the childhood odyssey of my youth.

The life-blood of the hinterland that used to nourish the town was drying up. Factory farms were exploding in the southland with thousands of animals under cover in football-field-size buildings. American diets were changing. People were eating less beef and pork but more fish and chicken. The hearty staples upon which the America of my childhood had fed—butter, cheese, lard, whole milk, eggs, red meat, bacon—were out of vogue. A new pseudo-religion stalked the land as people religiously read the labels on cans. They looked for the good stuff—dietary fiber, vitamins, calcium, iron, and all the rest—while eschewing saturated fat, sodium, nitrates, cholesterol, sugar and everything deemed "unnatural." Zealots had convinced millions that red meat was bad for them and that the corn-fed feedlots had compounded the problem by producing beef with too much fat. An old timer reflected that consumers want meat so tender they "don't have to chew it." Vegetarianism, a new cult and passion, was gaining devotees. Americans were eating less for enjoyment and more as an insurance policy to ward off an early visit from the grim reaper.

Even if Pipestone had been immune to such momentous dietary and cultural changes, my town would have changed. In Pipestone stores the eggs on sale were apt to come from chicken factories in Arkansas, the vegetables from truck farms in California, Texas, or Mexico, the pork chops from hog production facilities in Iowa, the beefsteak from feedlots in Nebraska or Colorado, the cheese from factories in Wisconsin.

The rich tapestry of small proprietors and the agrarian infrastructure of my youth had all but disappeared.

One third of the farm homes that Father and I had visited on missions of mercy had been abandoned. They were gradually sinking into the soil or being blow away. Those that remained seemed lifeless, their individuality and personalities had vanished. They were farms without animals, daily chores, or character. You could drive for miles and not see chickens, ducks, sheep, hogs, horses, or even cows. Pheasants and Hungarian partridge had diminished in concert with the destruction of their habitat. The range of crops I knew as a youth had been reduced to a near monoculture of corn and soybeans. Farmers now sit inside air-conditioned $150,000 combines, insulated from the field, sky, perhaps even their own mortality, listening to tapes with stereophonic sound. Fewer chores make for fewer farmer tans. Now farmers can do in an hour what it used to take Bert Vander Slice and Lee DeGriselles days, if not weeks, to accomplish.

I lamented the demise of the family-sized farm and an entire genus of American I had known as a boy. For while I knew that a farmer is not inherently more noble, law-abiding, or ethical than an urbanite, I saw that he is different because he is shaped solely by heroic attempts to coerce growth from plants and animals. The Greeks were correct, I believed, in holding that agriculture is the "best tester of good and bad men." The life of a yeoman is physical and concrete, yet spiritual and mystical. Like Aristotle and Jefferson, I worry about the human cost of the increasingly empty countryside and what it means for the future of our democratic institutions. "I think our governments will remain virtuous for many centuries," wrote our third president, "as long as its people are chiefly agricultural. When citizens get piled up upon one another in large cities, as in Europe, they will become as corrupt." The statistics were shocking. During the past 15 years 2,000 family farms *vanished every week;* 2,000 acres of their land were *lost to urbanization each day!*

Many of the county landmarks of my boyhood had vanished. For the sake of efficiency, the Minnesota Highway Department had routed #23 around Russell, Ruthton, and Holland. I missed slowing down and seeing familiar churches, banks, cafes, and general stores. What is the trade-off between efficiency and change that does damage to the inner life? A raw-boned farmhouse on a bleak hillside north of Holland, was gone as was a weather-beaten schoolhouse behind a grove. Familiar shelter-belts and windbreaks had been pushed over, grubbed out, and burned. Should we miss them? Yes, because they are the cairns and buoys by which we circumnavigate the social landscape. Without them amnesia threatens and we may forget where or who we are. The restless march of mechanization and the passing of one generation to another was ending a way of life that I had known and loved.

In the early 90s I drove into an abandoned farmyard on the northern edge of the county. I felt like a trespasser, perhaps not unlike a medieval peasant transgressing the sanctuary of his cathedral. The driveway was lined with a double row of wind-bent Russian olive trees. It was a road that led nowhere, to a field of crumpled dreams. It was all there—a spavined barn, bladeless windmill, crumpled stock tank, rusting machinery, broken down fences—a farm corpse left without a decent burial. The graffiti-etched house with broken windows beckoned. The slab of concrete on the back stoop had a couple of kids' handprints in it. An enormous cottonwood in the front yard with big roots knuckling up through the soil had served as a protective umbrella for life below. The roots were skinned smooth from kids sitting on them. I imagined games of pick-up sticks, marbles, and mumblety-peg on the smooth dirt in between.

I stuck my head in a window and immediately got a whiff of the 1930s, a slice of the past and out of time. Large chunks of plaster had broken loose and lay on the floor. Strips of wall paper with a floral print of red and white flowers with green stems had torn loose. Shattered furniture, old magazines, broken dishes, crockery, and cutlery littered the floor. The red brick-patterned linoleum was worn through except near the chimney, where the cast-iron stove had once stood. A hawkish auction dealer had probably gotten it for a song when the family sold out.

I tripped back in time to a June evening in the Great Depression—kerosene lamps giving off their soft glow, fireflies and June bugs hitting the screens, the sweet narcotic of red clover wafting through the house, WNAX radio of Yankton giving crop reports, father reading the newspaper, mother at the kitchen sink, kids coloring or playing with a cat. *A unique and irreplaceable family had been here, with all their solitary begetting, living, struggling, praying, celebrating, and dying! I was on hallowed ground! A Promethean struggle against the relentless forces of nature, evil, disease, and death had taken place in this humble abode.* I dropped my head in a silent prayer for their courage. My mind continued to play out the tableau. Had they been happy? Did their babies live and grow to adulthood? Was a child killed or injured in an accident? Had they escaped the Summer Terror? Did family concord or discord reign? Did they have a church and a faith to sustain them in times of darkness? Did insanity, depression, or untimely death strike unawares? Had Father ever crossed their threshold?

But it was getting dark and the wind was coming up. My reverie came to a close. I drove away saddened by the flux and fragility of life.

In its attempt to help, government policy was "culling out" the small farmer. "Get big or get out" was the cry of the experts. The Green Revolution was taking hold and government planners wanted, like Karl Marx, to free people from the "drudgery" of growing food. "You have high test scores," counselors told bright grandkids of those I worked with on the threshing rig. "You could choose one of a half dozen different professions." It was triage by flattery and only barely concealed the contempt for those who stayed in a place that modernity had passed by.

The government had corrupted the character of those now living in the homes where Father had taken his medical ministrations. The U.S. Department's "Payment In Kind" (PIK) program gave farmers a year's corn crop without expense, time, or risk. Set-aside payments meant "farming without working." It was like a lottery except the government paid you to play. The lesson was as old as history—the corrupting power of money. In trying to protect the farmer, the government had sullied his soul. On visits to Pipestone, it seemed to me that the chins of farmers were marginally closer to their chests than had been the case when I knew them as a child. Did not Euripides say, "not much to look at—a farmer."

The sense of isolation, of being exploited, neglected, passed by, of being part of a dying culture was pervasive. A farmer of 60 years with a crusted face and hornlike hands who would not whimper when he lost a finger in a grinder would become wet-eyed before a 25-year-old finance major from Mankato State who cut off his credit. The few survivors know that family farming is over in America, yet they will not give up. They know the pathologies of nonfarming urban America and want no part of it. Two cultures are in collision. I was reminded of the Latin cynic who ridiculed the rough calluses of the Roman farmers by scoffing that "he must be in the habit of walking on his hands." Not to worry. The America of the future will have far fewer callused hands.

"I'm sorry I can't fill this magnificient church that your Father and Red Klaus built," said the United Methodist pastor. He shook his head in defeat as I mumbled something about it not being his fault. The population of the county was now below 10,000. The base for sustaining a full array of social services was about gone. The Episcopalians had closed down their services and rented their building to a rival denomination. Thus the "rural flight" away from the *Coteau des Prairies* that began in the 1930s continues today. In 1995 births in neighboring South Dakota totaled fewer than 10,500—fewer than in any year of the Depression.

The average age of the members of Pipestone mainline churches had gradually inched into the late 50s.

Those who are left frequent the bars, barbershops, and coffee shops as they wait for the sun to warm the land. Many exist in a quiet despair because economically and psychologically their way of life is no longer working. Farmers think about the "good money" they made in the 1940s and 50s. But it's not working like that now. Unacquainted with the workings of the American economy, they feel the failure as a personal fault. Others had long since joined migration of snowbirds to Arizona and Florida in their fifth-wheelers and motor homes. Whatever their address, whether they left or stayed the winter, they drew their sustenance more from Washington than they did the soil.

But more worrisome for me than Pipestone's economic regression was America's moral decline. In my lifetime the percentage of illegitimate births had gone from 3 percent to over 30 percent; children with single mothers, from 4 percent to 25 percent; imprisonment for violent crime rose from 10 to 80 inmates per 100,000 of our population. SAT scores have plummeted as average daily TV viewing has risen to seven and one/half hours. As barns of the heartland were being pulled down, prisons were being constructed. Social pathologies that were a bare whisper during my childhood now thunder across our land like the Great Northern # 42 rocketing through town.

Have we forgotten a truth as old as Plato; that a city or a nation is only a crowd of citizens. But if each of them has renounced his private virtue, how can they build a public good?

During the Depression we lived nobly, however poor we might have been. Wickedness was attributed to flaws in individual characters, not to society's shortcomings. Debt was ignoble. Marriage was a sacrament. Divorce was disgraceful. Stigmas were viewed as the protective and necessary constraints that keep behavior within the channels that ennoble society. Pregnancy meant expulsion from school, and the boy responsible for the impregnation had to make "an honest woman" of the girl. The suggestion that women might resent being called "ladies" would have confounded me. Couples did not keep house before marriage and there could be no wedding until the girl's father had approved. Gentlemen removed their hats in a woman's presence and stood when a woman entered the room. Relationships between the sexes were precise. No one questioned the duty of men crossing the seas to fight for their country while girls wrote cheerful letters, sent cookies, and remained pure. Girls let you touch them here *but not there* and explained that they were saving themselves for marriage. Later the rules would change. But we didn't know it then.

The spiritual and moral axis of life has grown dim. Now the institutions of social control have been weakened and people, especially young people, have embraced an ethos that values self-expression over self-control. The moral canopy that structured my inner life is in tatters. Our society now places less value than before on what we owe to others as a matter of moral obligation; less value on sacrifice as a moral good; less value on social conformity and respectability; and less value on correctness and restraint in matters of physical pleasure and sexuality.

I am grateful, nevertheless, that the Pipestone of the Great Depression is my true home. That impression will never change nor can it be taken from me. I was blessed, moreover, by having been born in Pipestone rather than moving there from some urban Vanity Fair. As a result I wasn't dissatisfied, as I might have been, with everyday things that were a fraction or so better somewhere else.

A child's memory, it is said, is open for a second and then snaps shut and rolls forward, blank and flat, preserving the image until the summons of Death. Such is the miracle of memory that during the past half-century, in times of reflection, I have brought up a legion of those childhood images. Through the distance of space, time, and experience, I review these mental photographs and understand them as they were made; fleeting memories of vanishing places in a land that had, through love and longing, become my own.

Or to use another metaphor, I always carried Pipestone around with me the way a box turtle bears its own protective shell. Whenever a faint sense of angst arose, I found myself closing my eyes and walking the familiar streets of Pipestone, made weightless by the buoyancy of my nostalgia. In truth, I had a Norman Rockwell childhood—I was known, I was protected, I was loved, I counted for something. If there is anything worth calling theology, it is listening to people's stories, listening to them and cherishing them. The best thing about a small town is that I had grown up knowing everyone. And I had left Pipestone before discovering that this virtue is considered by some to be its worst vice.

Only after leaving did I realize that my Pipestone mentors were like the noble Romans—they sought the good of their *polis*. They were rooted and settled. They could not conceive of rights without responsibility. Many were the descendants of those who homesteaded in the county. Residence provided continuity. Wealth was understood to carry civic obligation and not as cause for a display of narcissism. My mentors drew from, while at the same time deepening, the roots of community, family, faith, and country. They knew that shame, guilt, and stigmas were necessary to keep behavior within the well-defined river contours of behavioral and cultural rectitude. Alas, we now live amid a nation of wanderers—many who skip across the world and web via cyberculture. For the new intellectual aristocracy, the traditionalism and prudence of the village heartland are seen as remote and small-minded. We seem to have lost touch with the virtues of self-reliance and honest toil and rely instead on millions of technocrats who want to "reinvent government" rather than deepen citizenship.

But the tribal village is eternal in the spirit of a boy. It was Aristotle who said that friendships are formed by shared delights. For me, the old Pipestone is more real than the present one. It molded impulses and patterns that continue to guide me. It aroused longings I will have until I die. It stimulated obsessions that continue to haunt me. For Pipestone was my place where, within the mystery and terror of life, I knew I was loved. There were those unique persons on farms, in school, in shops, on Main Street, at church, and in the homes along familiar streets who shaped me. However humble their attainments might be, they were neither conned nor impressed by externals. I knew that honor was a gift that a man made to himself; that money was transitory, but honor wasn't. They taught me that I had to keep a sense of myself; that my character is all that I have and, in the end, the sole property that is really mine. They knew that men, to be heroes, need idealization.

They embodied standards and expectations of virtue and integrity, duty and honor, civility and promise-keeping that I wanted to achieve. Pipestone was the embodiment of both the support and challenge that, as a timid youngster, I needed to become strong and to face a frightening yet fascinating future.

Epilogue: The Great Depression— A Legacy of Values

Since I wrote the first edition of *The Magical Years,* the demographic trends revealing the decay of the American heartland have continued to accelerate. Up and down the Great Plains, the country's spine, from North Dakota to Texas, small towns are declining. In some cases, literally dying out. The remarkable prosperity of the past few decades never reached the legions of "Our Town" Pipestones. According to the 2000 census, nearly 60 percent (250 of 429) of the counties on the Great Plains lost population in the 1990s. The emptying out of the nation's rural breadbasket is all the more surprising considering the population resurgence in cities and suburbs. Yet the degeneration of a large swath of our country's midsection—covering a 317,320-square-mile area spread over parts of 10 states—has not seeped into the conscience of urban America. City dwellers still perceive our agricultural villages as oases from society's maddening stew of gridlock, smog, and crime. Where else can a visitor leave a car unlocked, not to mention *running,* on a quick trip to the post office? Farmers in small towns are considered the ultimate entrepreneurs, our national icon of autonomy. Yet, 42 percent of Midwestern farmers earn less than $20,000 annually.

"We're going to have to start importing pallbearers," commented a grizzled old farmer, in a county where deaths exceeded births by fivefold. "It's like the parting of the Red Sea," reflected another octenagarian. "There are rivers of people flowing out of the rural Plains." "The handwriting is on the wall," mused a hoary elder as he saucered his coffee. "Every little town in this whole area is going down. I don't see any way to bring them back. If the founders of this town saw what was happening, they'd turn over in their graves."

During the past three years, I have done a great deal of speaking on the Great Depression before a wide variety of organizations. My audiences have, in large measure, supported my impressions of that cataclysmic decade. Time and again I have heard something like the following: *"I wouldn't take anything for the experience that I gained as a result of having lived through the Depression and World War II. But never again do I want to undergo such hard and tragic years!"*

One has to beware, therefore, of *"senioritis,"* the emotional and psychic nostalgia that afflicts many of us during our sunset years. The human psyche often does strange things to childhood and adolescent remembrances. The warm and heartfelt occurrences are, like a balloon full of helium, not only enlarged but embellished. The painful afflictions and hurtful memories on the other hand are, like a splinter or wound that the body encapsulates and walls off from healthy tissue, decreased and minimized.

There were, however, several positive and negative values that found their origins in the Great Depression. In drawing such distinctions among them, I want to be descriptive between "then and now." I trust the comments that follow will not seem moralistic or be considered a homily. First, several positive values that stem from the Depression:

POSITIVE VALUES OF THE GREAT DEPRESSION

FRUGALITY

I believe that one of the major values that separates today's seniors from the "Boomer" and "X'er" generation is the value of frugality. Like the wolf in the fable of the "Three Little Pigs," scarcity was ever at the door of tens of millions during that decade. As I stated in the earlier chapters, families then saved literally everything. I knew a Pipestone family who, after pushing their antiquated 'rust-bucket' of a car to the town dump, ripped out all of the upholstery and braided the strips into rugs. "On Sunday we had a decent meal," reflected an old codger who had survived 80 Minnesota winters. "The rest of the week we had leftovers."

The values of the third millennium, of hedonism over heroism and consumerism over parsimony, stand in stark contrast to the moral universe I knew in the 1930s. Consequently, I worry over the effect that long periods of opulence might have on the American collective soul. *Most major religions warn that long periods of affluence often produce individuals who are spiritually and morally flabby.* Such is the American paradox: moral and spiritual ennui in a time of material abundance and sensate gratification.

Near the gated community in Arkansas where we—and many other retirees—spend our winters, there is a modest restaurant called "The Shack." Gastronomes would undoubtedly label it a "greasy spoon," a hole-in-the-wall, or a dump. By Arkansas standards, however, it ranks high, having won an award for serving the best hamburgers in southwestern Arkansas. They are far superior to anything served by

McDonalds or Burger King, yet cost only $1.95. Large shakes are $1.25 and the Tuesday special, a spaghetti dinner for $3.25, includes a large salad and Texas toast. The ambiance on a razorback or red-neck scale of one to ten would be about a seven. Nevertheless, the wait to be seated is often quite long even if one comes at 5:00 P.M.

Judging from the BMWs, Cadillacs, Lincoln Town cars, Lexus,' and Park Avenue Buicks that dot its chuck-holed gravel parking lot, the Shack's patrons are notably affluent. Why do they patronize the place? Because the survivors of the straightened times of the Depression are still compulsive bargain-seekers. They simply cannot jettison the parsimonious values of their upbringing. Even when patronizing an elite restaurant, many feel guilty if they do not select the cheapest item on the menu.

In recent years I have attended several 50-year wedding anniversaries of my relatives and friends. On such occasions I hear a common refrain regarding the testimonials that children and grandchildren make regarding their parents and grandparents: *"They are extremely thrifty, but at the same time, are amazingly generous!"* On the surface these two values, parsimony and altruism, seem contradictory. But it is an established fact that spendthrifts are prohibited from being philanthropic. The virtue of financial beneficence is dependent upon being parsimonious. That which is not spent is invested. Those who lived through the Depression intuitively know the mathematics of compound interest. The Puritan value of thrift benefited not only the heirs of those who lived through the Depression, but also the common good.

For the most part seniors today are well off. A tour of a few of the gated "golden ghettos" in Florida, California, and Arizona will convince any doubting Thomas of that fact. Or check the ages of the passengers of the cruise lines in the Caribbean. If we are judged by Gandhi's or Hubert Humphrey's maxim that a society is judged by how it takes care of its seniors, we have made remarkable strides since the Depression. To be sure, Social Security played an important role in providing for those in retirement. Nevertheless, the virtue of thrift is primarily responsible for the fact that, today wealth is skewed to those over 50. In terms of deciles, the most prosperous currently are those working shortly before retirement, age 55–65. The next wealthiest, 65–75; the third most affluent, 75–85.

The Depression, therefore, simply reinforced and expanded the numbers of those in the moral heritage of Benjamin Franklin. America is unique among the democratic and industrialized nations because, instead of charging an omnicompetent State to provide for the common good, our Founding Fathers encouraged citizens to create, in Alexis de

Tocqueville's words, "private little platoons" to promote the "common welfare." Tens of thousands of private institutions—from the Salvation Army to Dorothy Day Centers, from Harvard College to a black Baptist nursery school—are thus benefited.

Contrast if you will, the thrift and values of present day seniors with the values of all too many of their grandchildren. Alas, narcissism, materialism, sensuality, and hedonism are all too familiar among the youngsters. As I pen these words, a popular television program is, *Who Wants To Be A Millionaire?* Whereas gambling was almost universally condemned as immoral during the Depression (in spite of a bit of harmless Catholic bingo), today casinos dot the landscape. In the 1930s, gambling was deemed to violate the means/ends principle: one should not hope to get rich without honest work. Now all but a few of our states have joined a national lottery whose purse often exceeds one hundred million dollars. Television anchor persons treat lottery numbers as news comparable to the weather and sports.

Americans who survived the Great Depression and the Second World War knew that suffering and privation were an integral part of life.

INVENTIVENESS AND CREATIVITY

The world of my childhood was barren of "Toys 'R Us" and "Children's Palaces." Parents did not sign a contract with a children's "fun house" where a birthday party took place, replete with video games, party hats, whistles, and cake for so much a head. Plastic plates and paper hats and tablecloths are all for two-income families. No sweat. Let others clean up the mess! Nor were there any McDonalds with two-story, "green-house" glass play areas, generic-type "playgrounds" that coerced parents to stop for "fun and games."

Kids used to *build things*—now they *buy them*.

During the Depression children reached into themselves to create their own toys, go-carts, crystal radio sets, and games. Now we purchase "things" for entertainment. I suspect it was more fun to create something new. "Daddy. I'm *bored!*" is a refrain parents and grandparents often hear today.

I am not a knee-jerk anti-technology freak. But children today watch on average seven hours of television a day, mesmerized by a medium that dulls creativity and enhances either passivity or aggression.

A Protected and Extended Childhood and Adolescence

In spite of the wholesale economic privation of the Depression, children of that era were not prematurely deprived of their innocence. The "Our Town" homes of that era were cocoons without television, the Internet, or X-rated movies to erode the natural wonder and purity of heart. While life was economically harsh, our culture had yet to suffer the erosion of civility, modesty, and decorum.

When I was in grade school I rushed home to listen to heroic radio serials of the genre of Louis L'Amour. Sex was pianissimo and the protagonists exerted a moral influence to restrain the forces of evil. Alas, both in degree and in kind, the moral landscape has changed today. Our culture is steeped in sex, violence, and profanity. I am surprised that as a society we allow youngsters to watch *Beavis and Butthead, South Park,* and *Married With Children.* Each new cycle of CDs and television series "pushes the envelope" regarding violence and sex. Today, adolescent females are especially prone to psychic and moral damage. Obsessing over body image and dating and even having sex at a younger and younger age is a formula for disaster.

Students of literature and readers of Shakespeare recall the famous passage from *As You Like It* (II.vii) that depicts the seven ages of man. According to the pessimistic Jaques, every age is afflicted with the melancholy that defines the human condition. In Jaques's view human life is repetitious, tedious, and predictable, lacking in adventure, romance, and mystery:

> *Then the lover, sighing like [a] furnace*
> *All the world's a stage,*
> *And all the men and women merely players:*
> *They have their exits and their entrances;*
> *And one man in his time plays many parts,*
> *His acts being seven ages. At first the infant,*
> *Mewling and puking in his nurse's arms*
> *And then the whining schoolboy*

This famously morose speech, ironically, occurs in a play that is more full of wonder than of melancholy. But Jaques ends as follows:

> *Last scene of all,*
> *That ends this strange eventful history,*
> *Is second childishness and mere oblivion,*

*Sans teeth, sans eyes, sans taste, sans
everything.*

Alas, the modern world, in my view has listened too well to Jaques. It lacks a vision of human life as a series of unfolding experiences that lead to a great climax that illuminates the harmony between the parts and the whole. Modernity constantly meddles with the grand design, depreciating the significance of certain ages such as childhood and old age and exaggerating other periods (youth?!) as the epitome of happiness.

Ironically, in spite of the material poverty of my childhood, the Great Depression was to me a time of wonder, expectancy, and hope. Even though we're dressed in Depression hand-me-down garb, you see that wonder in the eyes of my brother and me on the cover of this book. Alas, modernity too often robs today's children of that carefree, happy-go-lucky, magical time of being "boy eternal." Aggressive sex education and legions of chicken-little, the sky-is-falling doomsters predicting environmental collapse rob our young of their innocence. Putting children in daycare centers deprives them of the loving bonding and attention of their mothers, and easy divorce denies them the security and stability of home. Television and computer games destroy the resourcefulness of imagination.

During my childhood, schools were not centers of ideological conflict that involved feminism, "inclusive" language, and homosexuality. My school allowed me to be a child and did not prematurely subject me to death and dying courses, "safe" sex, AIDS education, and "alternative" families and lifestyles. My tender years were not assaulted with the anxieties and problems that beleaguer a later age in life, nor was I constantly exposed to inappropriate subject matter. In my later adolescence, love was allowed to awaken, bloom, and ripen in nature's good time, subject to the virtues of purity, modesty, and chastity, as I discovered the nature of manhood and later the demands and rewards of fatherhood.

During the 30s the Heartland morality was supported, or at least not undermined, by Hollywood, the media, members of the "chattering class," and other elites. The film industry's Hays Commission established some appropriate criteria for what was decent and moral in movies. Alas, today Hollywood and television constantly push the filth "envelope." As I write these words, the picture voted best of the year depicts the suburbs as a subvertly dysfunctional place where fathers salivate over their daughter's friends; the next-door neighbor, a retired Marine, beats his wife and collects Nazi memorabilia; and the only sane, healthy, and wealthy people in the neighborhood are a homosexual couple.

Today, for legions of our youth, the mystery of love and the delicacy of courtship are lost. Adolescence has become for too many a time for sexual experimentation and "safe sex." From the Presidential Oval Office to the movie sets of Hollywood, our culture gives way to the deadly sin of lust. To return to Shakespeare, our culture has destroyed the playfulness and mirth of such happy lovers as Orlando and Rosalind in *As You Like It.*

It is instructive to compare photographs of high school students during the Depression and the 1940s, individually or in concert, with those of today. (Or, to simply observe adolescents in a shopping mall or leaving high school.) The attire of today's young people is shocking: jeans either too tight or several sizes too large, skimpy shorts, belly-buttons showing, no belts, shirttails out, tattoos, ear piercing in abundance. The girls, particularly, seem to have lost respect for themselves. It's pitiful to watch many of them with their stomachs hanging out over their jeans and their shirts stretched tight across their generous bosoms. *Does an external slovenliness betray a spiritual vacuousness? Is the etiology of such cloddish and churlish dress to be found in permissive parents and in school administrators who fear their charges?*

Tragically, our culture has been thoroughly sexualized. During my adolescence had someone used the term "rape" I would have automatically assumed he was speaking about a legume, a cabbage-like plant, that was grown for cattle fodder. Undoubtedly instances of sexual harassment occurred, but back then our society was not so consumed by all things sexual. Today children are taught, almost before they are toilet-trained, to fear strangers and to distinguish between "good" and "bad" touching. No longer can teachers hug their charges who suffer from emotional and moral trauma. In grade school they are exposed to information about condoms, homosexuality ("Tommy has two daddies!") "safe" sex and, thanks to Oval Office antics of our recent president, even oral sex.

During my childhood, innocence—with all of its wonder and fascination about the world and its people—was a precious psychic treasure. Then our innocence was given up gradually and at the proper stages. The end result? Less cynicism, less bitterness, and less distress too early in life. Alas, in today's world I have encountered a legion of students who have not as yet reached their 17th birthday for whom the adage, "sweet sixteen," tragically, cannot apply. *"They have had it all"—sex with multiple partners, liquor, drugs, broken relationships, parental faithlessness and more—far to early in life.* Madison Avenue and Hollywood have "pushed the envelope" of the permissible so far that boundaries are about gone.

The songs of the 1930s and 40s nourished our romantic and nostal-gic affections. The following—*There's A Long, Long Trail*—is but a sam-ple that asked our generation not to expect instant gratification:

There's a long, long trail a-winding
Into the land of my dreams,
Where the night-in-gales are singing
And a white moon beams.
There's a long, long, night of waiting
Until my dreams all come true;
Till the day when I'll be going, down that
Long, long trail with you.

Another was *Don't Sit Under the Apple Tree (With Anyone Else But Me)* that focused on the need for fidelity and trust:

Don't sit under the apple tree, with anyone else but me,
Anyone else but me, Anyone else but me.
          No! No! No!
Just remember that I've been true to nobody else but you;
          So just be true to me
I'm so afraid that the plans we made, Underneath those moonlit skies
Will fade away and you're bound to stray, If the stars get in your eyes.
So, don't sit under the apple tree, With anyone else but me;
          You're my L - O - V - E.

Other songs in this genre are In the *Good Old Summertime, By the Light of the Silvery Moon, Look For the Silver Lining, On the Sunny Side of the Street, Oh, What a Beautiful Morning, When You Wish Upon A Star, Cruising Down the River,* and *Swinging on a Star.* The majority of the members of what Tom Brokaw calls "The Greatest Generation" know the lyrics to all of them by heart.

Now compare those lyrics to the nihilistic, hate-filled, and violent images that have taken up lodged in the minds of many youngsters today. In the mid-1980s, when Tipper Gore realized that her three daughters were being exposed to lyrics that included profanity and vio-lence and in some cases actually encouraged rape, she ask the industry to label tapes and CDs so that parents could screen them. She was pil-loried by Hollywood and the rock music industry as a bigot who want-ed to censor freedom of expression. She learned her lesson. As her husband came to national prominence, the music industry contributed millions to Al Gore's various campaigns and Tipper's moral outrage ceased.

Like a fine piece of Dresden china that has been smashed and crudely glued back together, many adolescents carry deep wounds that will last a lifetime.

THE NORMATIVE FAMILY WAS LARGELY INTACT

The traditional family provided the soil for the growth of character, discipline, and future empowerment. Today, far too many families have been abandoned by "dead-beat" dads, alimony-escaping fathers. Although Gloria Steinhem's sneering dismissal of traditional marriage "A woman needs a man like a fish needs a bicycle," was uttered many years ago, its effect still poisons the minds of young girls.

Through the 1950s, the role of fatherhood was appreciated and supported by all facets of society. When Vice President Quayle in 1996 criticized a popular TV sitcom whose title character, Murphy Brown, had a baby out of wedlock, he was assailed by legions of critics for his so-called puritanical hang-ups. Two years later, however, an article in *The Atlantic Monthly* indicated that Quayle was right in recognizing that the seed-bed of many of our social pathologies is fatherless families. Recently the head of the National Broadcasting Company indicated that his company *did not have a single series in 1998 wherein the focus was on a normative and traditional family.* He promised to do better in the future.

As to the nurture of primary communities, it is clear to me that the god of liberalism has failed. Government cannot create families, it can only assist them. When it arrogates to itself the idea of running families, schools, cities, it makes them worse. It destroys more than it builds. The giveaway philosophy of the nanny state contradicts my deeply held Christian belief that God invests humans with free will. That philosophy devalues the selflessness of good deeds and of charity. One has to be careful not to have the omnicompetent State take over for the Almighty.

One third of all our country's children go to sleep each night in fatherless homes. Eighty-five percent of the juvenile offenders in long-term correctional facilities today grew up without a father in the household. During the Depression juvenile crime, promiscuity, drug abuse, and school truancy were but a shadow of what they are today because Depression-era families as a rule did not manifest "life without father." Thanks to radical feminists, opinion-makers from the "chattering class," and amoral Hollywood elites, fatherhood is widely denigrated today. At the same time, legions of single mothers testify that they can barely cope with their sons.

In interviewing members of the "Greatest Generation," Tom Brokaw has discovered that most of them still have the same spouse. (That is, if they haven't lost a husband or wife to cancer, heart disease, and the like.) But when Brokaw queries them regarding their children, they usually respond with some variation of the following: *"Fortunately, our children (the Boomers) are doing well. They have a financial security that was unknown to us. But tragically, many of them have not found the marital happiness that we have had."*

Statistics prove this observation. Now there is one divorce for every two marriages; then, there was but one divorce out of every six couples who went to the altar.

Perhaps the Bible is right in asserting that a certain amount of suffering, sacrifice, and privation is necessary not only to firm up one's character, but also to put a marriage on a solid foundation.

NEGATIVE VALUES
FROM THE GREAT DEPRESSION

RELIGIOUS CONFLICT AND SUSPICION

As I have stated earlier, the *Kulture Kampf* that existed during my upbringing was exceedingly unfortunate. The Pipestone prism was a venue too constricted to allow full appreciation of the richness of the American melting pot. Ethnic and religious enclaves produced narrow parochialisms, which exacerbate suspicion and hostility.

Sociobiologists claim that xenophobia (fear of the stranger or the alien) has some genetic origin. Alas, community cohesiveness—parochial or national—has often been built on hatred of those whose difference is religious, ethic, or racial. During the Vietnam era, hatred was directed at "our own" who grew beards, wore tattered clothes, and who let their hair grow long enough for a pony tail.

Modernity, of course, is the solvent of tradition—patterns of belief and behavior that are both ennobling and restrictive. While my village's religious and moral traditions were restrictive, they also gave me roots and a strong sense of belonging within a larger and often chaotic world.

RACIAL AND ETHICAL MYOPIA

It was not until I entered the Navy Air Corps in 1944 that I discovered that the "Arsenal of Democracy" was not democratic and that the war against Germany and Japan was fought with a Jim Crow military. Black Americans were stevedores, assigned to the scullery and relegated to the "scut" jobs. Only during the final stages of the war, when our manpower reserves were drawn down, did we finally allow a few blacks to become pilots and commanders of Sherman tanks. Later I was ashamed to discover that in Texas, black soldiers had to eat "take-out" food at military commissaries, while Italian and German P.O.W. officers dined with their American peers.

Between the end of the war and the summer of 1946, when I was discharged, I served as a Naval Shore patrolman and rode transcontinental trains between Chicago and the west coast. In Chicago we were housed in a nice hotel in the loop that had a swimming pool on the 18th floor. One afternoon one of my mates came storming into my room and exclaimed, *"Did you know they let nig.... swim in the pool? Today is the last time I'll swim in that water!"* He was a Kansas farm boy who had seen very little of the world.

Even worse was the internment of 120,000 Japanese-American citizens shortly after the Japanese attack on Pearl Harbor. Even liberals such as President Roosevelt, Governor Earl Warren, and Supreme Court Justice William Douglas signed and/or supported the infamous Executive Order 9066 without due process of law. Tragically, even democracies are not immune to the destruction of freedom when they feel threatened. Alas, then skin pigmentation was a basis for judging loyalty and disloyalty.

In spite of this, nearly 80 percent of the Nisei generation registered for the draft. While German-Americans and Italian-Americans served in integrated military units, Japanese-Americans were assigned to a separate fighting team—the 442nd Regimental Combat Team. Daniel Inouye, now a United States Senator, had his right arm blown off by a German rifle grenade in Italy. He belonged to the most decorated unit in our military history. Yet, on his way back to Hawaii, he continued to experience racial rejection. Entering a barbership with his empty right sleeve pinned to his army jacket covered by ribbons and medals for his military heroism, Captain Inouye was told: "We don't serve Japs here."

While I remember no African-Americans in Pipestone, there were several Jewish families. But when Jewish adolescents became of marriageable age, their families usually moved to the Twin Cities so that they might find a suitable marriage partner. During the Depression, anti-Semitic jokes were widely told without censure. The popularity of one of my few Indian classmates, George Brown, was probably due to the fact that he was an outstanding football player. Nevertheless, the larger world was out of sight. Our citizens viewed our small town mores and culture as a suitable template for the larger world. Theoretically, America was a "great melting pot" of all nationalities and races. But according to the prescribed menu of Anglo-Saxon chefs, it was difficult to "homogenize" certain races.

Racism in the heartland was covert and uninformed, not overt and experiential. Our xenophobia arose from Pipestone's narrow prism rather than from malice. In that sense World War II was a significant "break-out" experience. The rural womb was forever sundered, and legions of farm and village folk who previously had traveled little more than 50 miles from home were suddenly exposed to the rich diversity of folk and places with strange sounding names. America would never be the same again.

AN INORDINATE FEAR OF DESTITUTION

In spite of the Protestant's cardinal principle of *sola grati (by grace alone), "works-righteousness"* was the ethic of much of the country during the Depression. We conformed to our Sunday liturgical worship, but on the other six days of the week we "worked to beat hell." For many people today *"retirement equals redirection."* During the Depression, it was equated with uselessness, being a "tax-eater," or on the "garbage heap," being a "no-good."

The omnipresence of poverty put a straight-jacket on just about anything one did for pleasure or enjoyment that cost money. Many simply could not enjoy the fruits of their labor if that enjoyment entailed spending money.

During my childhood, parents often charged their children to prove themselves "worthy." Kids were told to jump through the "hoops" and "measure up"; life is tough and there are no "freebies." Only after children had performed to an acceptable standard, did love and acceptance follow. Today, many psychologists concur with the insights of Jesus, St. Paul, and Martin Luther. A Deity who grants unconditional love releases a spontaneous loving-obedience in the recipient. Parents who continue to sacrifice and suffer for their children in spite of the graceless response of the latter, ultimately prime the pump for their "loving back."

In sum, during the Depression too many parents were still stuck in the Old Testament ethos.

Today we are just as "judgmental" as folks were in the Depression, only the focus has enlarged. During my youth the "village pentagon" of authority—pastor, teacher, parent, lawyer, physician—focused on personal failings rather than social evils. The prevailing adage—"Correct one's manners and everything will turn out all right"—was almost universally believed. We were judged *microcosmically* for private failings rather than for such super-human and demonic social viruses as racism, unemployment, sexism; urban America suffered *macrocosmically.*

STEREOTYPED WOMEN'S ROLE

Married women during the Depression were relegated to lives consumed by *Kucke, Kinder,* and *Kirche*—kitchen, children, and church. The hearth and children were their altar. Personal disappointment, if not disaster, awaited anyone who attempted to escape the biological role that God and nature intended. Spousal abuse went largely undetected. Once, during an examination, Father discovered black and blue bruises on the body of one of his patients, the wife of a German farmer. "Why don't you leave him?" Father asked. *"But I love him!"* was the answer.

Leaving a loveless marriage during the Depression was almost impossible for most women. The financial barriers were insurmountable, to say nothing of the social censure that would invariably have resulted. The parental mantra to their troubled married daughters then was: "You made your own bed, now sleep in it!" Communal pressure to marry was intense. I remember a single female relative in her early 50s who once cried: *"I don't care who he was or what he (did to me). If I had it to do over, I would even have married a bum or a drunkard!"*

The vocations for single women were narrow—teaching, nursing, secretarial work, Christian missions, and perhaps a few others. The audacious few who entered traditional male vocations faced ridicule. *"She's a hen medic,"* was the barb many male physicians (including my Father) used in speaking about women who dared to transgress their domain. Was he threatened by them? We will never know, but he was not alone in judging someone by her gender rather than by merit.

Today, 70 years after the Depression, women are at liberty to choose just about any profession. Moreover, they are free to remain unmarried and childless without bearing the onerous label of being an "old maid" or a "spinster." Thanks to effective birth control, women now can decide whether they wish to become mothers and bear children. We can be thankful that the feminist movement has destroyed traditional chauvinist barriers and allowed talented women to join their male counterparts. The sum total of American personal talent has been immeasurably enriched as a result. It is a revolution still not accepted in many traditional and third-world portions of the globe.

Gender discrimination in medicine, law, and in corporate America is almost a thing of the past. The problematic issue facing third millennium women, however, is how to successfully integrate marriage and childbearing within their vocational career. Responsible articles in women's magazines are honest enough to admit that it is an almost intractable problem, and that "no one can have it all," so "sacrifices have to be made." As long as women bear, suckle, and nurture children, this will continue to be a thorny issue and their careers are fated never to be completely isomorphic with those of men.

AMERICAN CULTURE AT THE BEGINNING OF THE THIRD MILLENNIUM

Before bringing this epilogue to a close I wish to make several observations concerning American culture. Recently the residents in a New York skyscraper noticed cracks appearing in the wall of their 57th floor penthouse apartment. Subsequently, occupants on other floors complained of similar ruptures. An architect was called in for a consultation. After a careful analysis, he warned: "I cannot fix your problem. *The origin of those cracks is in the footings and foundation of your building."*

In spite of American material plenty and affluence, there are some worrisome cultural "cracks" that have widened in the past 40 years. Our decline can be quantified by the following seven cultural indicators: Since 1960 *average TV viewing time has increased from 5.06 to 7.04 hours; illegitimate births from 5.3 percent to 30.1 percent of all births; average SAT scores have declined from 975 to 890; the percentage of children living with single mothers has increased from 8 percent to 25 percent; the number of children on welfare has increased from 3.5 percent to 13 percent of all children; the violent crime rate (per 100,000 persons) has increased from 16.1 percent to 80.1 percent; and the median prison sentence for "serious crime"(murder, rape, aggravated assault, burglary, theft, etc.) has declined from 22.5 to 8.0 years.*

What is shocking is just how precipitously American life has declined in the past 40 years, despite the enormous government efforts to improve it. In spite of massive amounts of federal and state spending, social regression continues. There is a vast body of evidence suggesting that government Great Society "remedies" have reached the limit of their success. Alexander Solzhenitsyn observed that the West has been undergoing "an erosion and obscuring of high moral and ethical ideals. The spiritual axis has grown dim." John Updike concurs: "The fact that, compared to the inhabitants of Africa and Russia, we still live well cannot ease the pain of feeling we no longer live nobly."

Let me be more specific about the moral regression of the past several decades:

AMERICAN LIFE HAS COARSENED SINCE THE GREAT DEPRESSION

In comparison with today, our clothes and food during that era were coarse, even crude and unrefined. But middle class values were intact. Our habits were not vulgar, rude, and unpolished. Alas, today American habits have significantly changed. Former U.S. Senator Patrick Moynihan coined the phrase, *"defining deviancy down"* to describe a process by which we change the meaning of "moral" to fit what we are doing anyway. To put it philosophically, we are allowing "descriptive ethics"(our present behavior) to change "normative ethics"(what philosophers, the Bible, and reason teach as correct and right action). Put another way, my favorite historian, the British author Arnold Toynbee, would say that our recent history reveals the *proletarianization* of the dominant minority.

Toynbee's monumental *Study of History* tracks the etiology of the disintegration of civilizations. He affirms that one of the consistent symptoms of societal decline is that the elites of a nation—the *"dominant minority"*—begin to imitate those at the bottom of society. The growth phase of America, for example, was led by a creative minority with a strong, self-confident sense of style, virtue, and purpose. The uncreative minority followed along through *mimesis,* a mechanical and superficial imitation of great and inspired originals. But we have moved from the moral exemplars such as George Washington, Abraham Lincoln, and Theodore Roosevelt to the Richard Nixons and Bill Clintons. We are witnessing the aftermath of a collapse of the gentleman's code of the elites, creating a vacuum in which the underclass behavior takes on the element of a code.

Civilizations, Toynbee avers, do not disintegrate because of external force. The Roman Empire, for example, did not perish because the Barbarians—the Goths, Vandals, and Huns—were militarily superior to the Roman legions. During the era of the Republic, Roman citizens gave exemplary service and sacrifice to both *patria* and *familia* (state and family). During the senescence of the Empire, however, values declined with the result that the populace demanded ever increasing allotments of welfare and entertainment ("bread and circuses"). Toynbee believes, therefore, that societies fail because of internal moral rot. Over a period of time termites can weaken the wooden beams of a magnificent log building. So too, an extended period of moral fecklessness and lassitude can destroy a powerful nation.

The code of the gentleman was a Depression-era internal method for tracking how one measured up to a standard accepted by those whose approval was sought. To be an American gentleman meant one was loyal, respectful, courteous, brave. and true. When you were wrong, you owned up to your trespass and took your punishment like a man. A real man did not take advantage of women. He was gracious in victory and a good sport in defeat. A handshake was more binding than any legal document. When your ship went down, you put the women and children in lifeboats, and waved good-bye with a smile.

A placard in front of an Arkansas Baptist church reads: *A Good Conscience Makes A Soft Pillow."* A bad conscience is the awareness that we have not behaved as we should. In classic philosophy, the term "virtues" was applied to organized ways that men modulated and con-trolled their restless lives. The cardinal virtues—courage, temperance, justice, and prudence—were not relative or pertinent to just one society, one epoch, or one culture. Timeless and universally needed, virtue is a necessity because of the nature of man and his common physical and social contexts.

Psychiatrist John Rosemond suggests that the etiology of today's ill-mannered youth is due to "boomer parents not lowering *the boom enough!"* Depression-era parents were unconcerned with the issue of fairness (used in this case to refer to the perception that there is "equi-ty" between misbehavior and its consequence) when it came to disci-pline. Rather, old-fashioned parents wanted to nip misbehavior in the proverbial bud, which was generally accomplished through a lowering of the proverbial "boom." Depression era parents realized that the size of a given misbehavior should not dictate the size of the punishment. After all, any misbehavior, no matter how small, can become a major problem if allowed to flourish; ergo, the "boom."

Modern parents tend to believe that many of the old-fashioned parenting practices should be avoided, as they are supposedly damaging to self-esteem. In a sense, that is according to the dictates of Dr. Benjamin Spock. But Depression-era parents wanted to raise humble, modest children. Intuitively, before the term became popular, they realized that kids whose self-esteem was based on a lack of rules and discipline were likely to be obnoxious little brats. Ergo, "the boom." Like my peers, as a kid I was boomed a lot and had my mouth washed out on several occasions by Mother for using a "naughty" word. I didn't like it, but in talking with people my age, we all agree that in retrospect, these psychologically incorrect disciplinary events (PSIDEs) eventually proved to be blessings in our lives.

Frankly, lots of people my age were never spanked. Instead, the first time they violated curfew, they were grounded for a semester; the first time they talked back to their dads, they were made to chop and carry firewood for an entire week; the first time they rode their bikes where they had been told not to, their bikes were taken away for a month; the first time they goofed off in class, they were made to write long letters of apology to the teacher and every classmate. And so on. No, spanking was not the secret to rearing reasonably well-behaved children. The not-so-secret secret was the disciplinary "boom." The post-WW II kids are not the "boomers." Our parents were.

During the Depression the ethos of virtue, with its rules and norms, was still fairly well in place. Alas, now it's the subject of jokes and excuses. With the disintegration of the code of the gentleman, the parallel code of the lady has also collapsed.

The vacuum has been filled with what sociologist Charles Murray has called the "thug code:" Take what you want, respond violently to anyone who antagonizes you, gloat when you win, despise courtesy as weakness, treat women as receptacles, take pride in cheating, deceiving, or exploiting successfully. It's the code of hip-hop, perhaps the inarticulate values of underclass males since time immemorial. Alas, now they are front and center as a result of the collaboration of some of America's best creative and merchandising talent. Today there is no common understanding of vulgarity and the Depression-era contempt for the indecent and lewd has all but vanished. The tolerance in public discourse of four-letter words, now common in Hollywood films, television sit-coms and even women's magazines, shows how far we have fallen. As I pen these words, two of the five films up for an Academy Oscar in 2001 each had actors saying the "F" word more than 65 times.

Over 40 years ago Newton Minow, then the FCC chairman, coined the phrase "vast wasteland" to describe television programmage. Today, critics say it has deteriorated to the point of being a "toxic dump."

Truancy, vulgarity, and promiscuity in America are not new. But up until a few decades ago they were publicly despised and largely confined to the "mud sill" of society—groups we called "low-class" or "trash." Respectfulness toward and imitation of underclass behavior extend to other classic symbols and signs that once were used to distinguish nice people from riffraff. The hooker look in fashion, tattoos, and body-piercing abound as much as does wearing jeans to church. No one in the public eye calls any kind of dress "cheap" or "sleazy" anymore.

Shortly before her death in 1985 my Mother told me that she would have feared raising her children in our amoral culture. She spoke for legions of grandparents.

Sexual behavior? As late as 1960 sleeping with one's boyfriend was "low class," done furtively, and usually with the girl the boy expected to marry. Behavior today that is considered normal was considered sluttish during the Depression. Notice the words that are used to describe intimacy: what once was called "making love," then shifted to "having sex" and is now "hooking up"—like airplanes refueling in flight. How is it possible that the supreme physical, even sacramental act, of love that often generates new human life is almost universally degraded in society today? During the 1930s if a person used vulgar language, we labeled him as an unlettered and coarse simpleton. Language that floods into our living rooms today was not even heard in the saloons during my childhood.

Family? The language of living together conveys the change in status over the years. People used to "shack up," now they co-habit. The woman used to have a bastard, then an illegitimate child; now she has a nonmarital birth. American elites are twisting in apology for every failing they can concoct, disavowing what is best in our culture, and imitating what is worst. Since the Depression many of the inner-city poor have drifted from the bourgeois virtues that reigned during that time. Yet their emulation of such values was the engine that powered many of them up into the middle class. Tragically, in a society as rich and opportunity-filled as ours, the long-term poor now seem to possess few of the habits that advancement requires. Fifty years ago no futurist predicted the disappearance of the two-parent family.

With our elites running as fast as they can from making any value judgments about illegitimacy, it will be no easy task to marshal the moral authority to revive marriage. Yet, that is the daunting task that faces all persons of good will at the beginning of the new millennium.

Fashion? Again, the underworld is in vogue. Designers strive for the "homeless" look, the "prison-garb" look, and the "red-light-district" look. At Minnesota's Mall of America, there are legions of skimpy little dresses for skinny little girls in animal prints more suited for streetwalkers than hopscotchers. On national television, people unhesitatingly bare the most vulgar and grotesque moments of their lives for Geraldo Rivera and Jerry Springer.

Film? During my youth clerics were depicted in heroic roles. Today film directors often portray priests and pastors as fools, drunkards, homosexuals, or lechers.

Popular Music? Recent decades have witnessed popular music's downward spiral into violence, obscenity, misogyny, and race hatred. I worry about the corrupting effect of its more brutal and sexually explicit lyrics. I am reminded that the greatest thinkers of the past—from Plato to Aristotle to Rousseau and Nietzsche—engaged each other across the centuries in a dialogue regarding the power and danger of music. The ancient Greeks assigned music a crucial role in education. Rhythm and harmony, they maintained, take hold of the youthful soul long before reason does, and our character is largely shaped by the tastes we develop in early life. I agree with Plato and Aristotle that children should be exposed to only the right kinds of music, with a view to controlling the passions and cultivating a love of moderation. *The elders of the Depression were faithful to the ideal—Statescraft as Soulcraft!* We performed the classical works of the Western canon. Our martial offerings stayed within the controlled energy of the marches of John Phillip Sousa. Our high school "swing band" tried to replicate the "Big Band" sound of Glenn Miller, with no need for pelvic grinds. Nor did anyone in public education suggest that band or choir was merely a "frill," the first thing to be pruned in case of financial exigency. Intuitively, the citizens of Pipestone agreed with the musical philosophy of the classical philosophers.

During the Enlightenment, thinkers like Hobbes, Locke, and Montesquieu abandoned the focus on virtue, and redirected politics toward the modest goals of peace, security, and prosperity. In doing so, they shut their eyes to the influence of music on culture. Finally, Rousseau and Nietzsche rediscovered the power of music to inspire and elevate the soul. *But they sought to inflame rather than moderate the passions.* The fruit of their sad legacy is with us today. The spiritual shallowness of modern liberalism is driving our young to seek fulfillment in ever more violent musical experiences, which they falsely hope will give meaning to their empty lives.

Frankly, I side with Plato and Aristotle and long for a new kind of music that will calm youthful passions, ennoble the reason, and deepen the soul.

THE CLINTON LEGACY: A PARADIGMATIC EXAMPLE OF ELITES WHO HAVE BEEN INFECTED BY THE "SICKNESS OF PROLETARIANIZATION"

During the Depression, "Grifters" was a term used to describe fast-talking con artists who roamed the countryside, profiting at the expense of the poor and the uneducated, always one step ahead of the law, moving on before they were held accountable for their schemes and half-truths. The phrase White Trash, or Poor White Trash, with its racial sub-texts, has long bothered me, but on reading about the Clintons, it seems there may be a valid sociological category that could be called Rich White Trash—to denote a privileged class that hasn't fully developed the inner code that allows most of us to restrain our natural grabbiness.

For millions, Clinton debased and corrupted a unique capacity—marital love, a sacramental gift if you will—that men and women have been given. Our children and grandchildren learned that when it comes to breaking a moral law, it is not the sin but the spin that is important. Clintonian, post-Monica ethics focused on the personal destruction of others in order to shift the blame. Our youth discovered that oral sex is really not sex. Already weakened by Hollywood, pop culture, and rap musical groups, children were exposed to sexual realities traditionally left to later stages of maturity. Our young people discovered that *moral performance* is not as important as *public performance*. In a strange inversion of morality, our children learned that the real sinner is not one who commits the wrong, but the one who calls it "wrong."

There was nothing aimless about the Clintons' wanderings; every move was calculated, part of their grand scheme to claw their way to the top. When one considers pardons for political friends and donors, "renting-out" the Lincoln bedroom for large political contributions, abuse of women, gifts to the White House taken by the Clintons for their personal use, and the attempt to lease extravagant penthouse offices with taxpayer money—in sum: their noisome and graceless exit from office—it is not to be doubted that the Clintons were our First Grifters. George Will has stated that while Bill Clinton was not our poorest president, he was the poorest man to occupy the presidency. Our survival as a culture requires that we somehow contrive to get well from the collective sickness that the Clintons dramatized in Arkansas and in Washington.

WEAKENING OF INSTITUTIONAL FOUNDATIONS

Just as culture is the seedbed of politics, our social institutions are the incubators of cultural attitudes. Community and charitable institutions have promoted social cohesion, assimilation, and service to the community. Alas, as we enter the third millennium, all of these traditional institutions are in decline. Entropy affects the P.T.A., the Jaycees, Kiwanis, Rotary, the Red Cross, and almost any service organization one can name. Volunteering, except among the elderly parents of the baby boomers, is down and philanthropy has dramatically sunk as a proportion of national income. The American Legion and Veterans of Foreign Wars, like their members, are in their dotage. An increasing percentage of Americans are not only disconnected from contributing to the common good, but prefer to live in physically separated "gated" communities, condos, and apartment buildings.

THE DECLINE OF THE MAINLINE CHURCHES

Liberal Protestantism enters the third millennium worried and enervated. Its geographical religious base, the village and agricultural heartland, has been devastated by demographic trends. Many denominations have lost 35 percent of their membership in the past four decades. With the average age of the mainline membership in the high 50s, a wag suggests that going to church reminds him "of being a chapter of the AARP at prayer." Much like the body of the Native American enervated by tuberculosis, the spirit of the mainline today is debilitated. Mainline critics claim some liberal clergy seem more attached to social and political ideologies than classical Biblical doctrine. Moreover, like the effect of canister from Union artililery at Gettysburg on General Picket's Virginians, controversy over the issue marital "unions" and ordination of homosexuals, is tearing huge gaps in mainline membership.

As a result, the mainline is awash with feelings of pain, cynicism, depression, and distrust. Yet, the evangelical tide within the Christian theological spectrum continues. Fifty years ago mainline Protestant missionaries outnumbered those from evangelical churches by 9 to 4. Today, evangelicals outnumber mainliners by 40 to 3.

In 1900, the beginning of what American Protestants christened as "the Christian Century," 80 percent of Christians were either Europeans or North Americans. Today 60 percent are citizens of the "Two-Thirds World"—Africa, Asia, and Latin America. There are *10 times more* Episcopalians in Nigeria than there are in the United States. The future, in more ways than one, belongs to the nations of color.

Critics hold that the mainline bought into the radical moral and cultural changes of the '60s and early '70s, believing that they were permanent. Alas, such changes are now seen as ephemeral, and today the mainline seems caught in a time warp and cannot return to the theological fundamentals. Legions of members are dismayed over their church's acceptance of alternative sexualities but hesitate to proclaim the bodily resurrection of Jesus Christ. At the same time evangelical churches, having resisted the acids of relativism and "what-is-happening-now" modernity, are growing like the Canadian thistles Lee DeGriselles and I hoed in the 1940s. The more you chopped at them, the more they multiplied. In spite of a woeful shortage of priests and nuns, Roman Catholicism is showing surprising vigor and is growing in membership. Pentecostalism, which began in 1907, now counts over 420 million adherents worldwide and is growing at a rate of 20 million a year. The "sectarian cycle" paradigm has been proved once again; that is, as sects become acculturated, they lose their zeal and become churches. Thus, the aphorism of Puritan divine Cotton Mather: *"Religion brought forth Prosperity, and the Daughter destroyed the Mother."*

THE FAILURE OF PUBLIC EDUCATION

Today, there is a disease—functional illiteracy—that is as destructive of children's futures as the "Summer Terror," the polio epidemic of the 1930s and '40s. It has overtaken one-third of America's children. Functional illiteracy claims two thirds of our inner city black children by the time they enter the fourth grade. Literacy officials in Arkansas report that *54 percent of adult Arkansans cannot read beyond the second grade level!* Tragically, we already have a cure for illiteracy, but it is being administered to far too few.

Imagine that a plague were sweeping the land, infecting our most vulnerable citizens. And imagine that the American Medical Association advocated abolishing, or at least boycotting and undermining, the screening measures that would detect the progress of this disease. Public outcry would surely follow such an abdication of professional responsibility. Yet, that is exactly the position of the National Education Association, the union that brokers the narrow interests of the teachers. The NEA has consistently opposed national standardized tests designed to take the educational temperature of students suffering from the plague of low achievement. If the NEA recognized the evidence that well-prepared teachers can help poor students achieve, it would be obligated to take the lead in weeding out bad teachers and changing work rules to ensure that the best teachers are in the most challenging schools. Tragically, union leaders prefer the tyranny of low expectations.

In his groundbreaking expose, *Why Johnny Can't Read,* Rudolf Flesch uncovered a worrisome fad in education: schools had begun to replace time-honored and proven methods of teaching methods with the "look-say" method, the precursor of today's "whole language." These methods, Flesch argued, had no scientific basis and did not help children learn to read. Now the evidence is clear: schools need to return to "phonics, phoneme awareness, fluent word recognition, vocabulary, and comprehension." Yet most state education agencies, schools of education, and school districts continue to advocate reading strategies that don't work. Many of these institutions march under the banner of "balanced instruction" but, in fact, they continue to push the flawed "whole language" methods at the expense of phonics. According to Mr. William Bennett, the former secretary of education, this is the educational equivalent of treating polio with aspirin. "We would never stand for such malpractice in medicine, and we should not tolerate it in education."

In the past few decades we have witnessed the decline of *mind-culture,* the traditional role of the school. Schools today increasingly serve a *therapeutic purpose.* As I pen these words many principals have eliminated dodgeball, ostensibly to avoid wounding the psyches of the more corpulent, less agile, pupil. In many gym classes all forms of competition are eliminated and everyone gets a trophy. Increasingly schools have eliminated the position of valedictorian because it makes other children feel inferior. Like most areas in life, school may be a cruel place but attempts to enforce a rigid egalitarian outcome are not only foolish but fated to fail. Whenever feelings become more important than the mind, we diminish the central purpose of education.

During my youth, of course, it was not expected that every adolescent needed a high school diploma. There was still plenty of work that necessitated big biceps and a strong back. There was little shame attached to leaving school to improve the family's financial condition. Other students lacked either the motivation or intellectual ability to continue. Teachers did not obey the gospel of "social pass." Nor did they put up with undisciplined students whose behavior destroyed the progress of an entire class. To "mainstream" the retarded would have been considered ridiculous.

Today's adherence to a forced and rigid egalitarian ideology for all pupils has devastated the environment where students are challenged to perform.

Today, in stark contrast to the lip service they give to public education, a significant segment of our elites have abandoned the public school. Like every recent Democratic president with the exception of Jimmy Carter, Bill Clinton sent his daughter to the posh Sidwell Friends (Quaker) School. The engine of the melting pot that served my generation well is in now in decay. Both materially, morally, and intellectually, public schools (dubbed by their critics as "government schools") continue to be abandoned. The parents of the "Greatest Generation" are shocked that their grandchildren attend schools that need metal detectors and employ police officers as monitors. Seventy-five percent of our urban poor who earn less than $15,000 per year want vouchers so their children can escape failing schools. But for most liberals, "choice" pertains only to abortion, not educational freedom. Today's parents are the first generation to believe its children will receive an inferior education to theirs.

Moreover, public educators have shifted to an anti-conservative orientation. Historical illiteracy is rampant; only 22 percent of our universities require *any kind of history course.* But ignorance is only half the equation. Jacques Barzun warns in his best-selling book, *From Dawn to Decadence,* "when the nation's history is poorly taught, ignored by the young, and proudly rejected by qualified elders, awareness of tradition consists only in *wanting to destroy it.*" Patrick Garry, author of *A Nation of Adversaries: How the Litigation Explosion is Reshaping America,* finds that too many students learn nothing about the past "except when it was wrong. Their teachers are not only ignoring history, they are attacking it. For many the teaching of history has become merely another form of political advocacy against the pillars of American heritage." When teaching does not promote the objective study of history but rather promulgates select political goals, as Roger Kimball argues in *The Long March,* "everything is sucked through the sieve of politics and the ideology of victimhood."

Hostility toward history and the past was the sad legacy of the 1960s counter-culture movement. The generation whose motto was *"don't trust anyone over 30,"* always confident of its own moral supremacy, had little respect for the accumulated wisdom of the ages. Perhaps that is why

Bill Clinton, unlike his predecessors, rarely spoke of previous presidents except to apologize for their mistakes.

THE ADVENT OF NEW AGE SELF-ACTUALIZATION

Our culture reveals a recent growth of a therapy-culture consumerism, an ethos that has edged out the Depression focus on civic duty and moral responsibility. Novels now explore interior lives and many popular magazines—*People, Self,* and *O, The Oprah Magazine*—are consumed with self. We now have a cappuccino culture of customized choice. David Frum notes in *How We Got Here* that ours is a permissive and hedonistic culture "that is engulfed in its own feelings and contemptuous of intellectual rigor, that gives priority to the self over the community and believes the inner life of each self to be of infinite interest to all others, that distrusts government yet expects beneficence from it, and that is permeated at all levels by a potent sense of entitlement."

Self-pity replaces self-sacrifice, and an obsession with personal freedom replaces the focus on the collective ethos of the past. *"I kicked some butt"* is the credo of self-actualization, not "I sacrificed for the common good."

In spite of the tremendous advances of women, blacks, and other minorities since the Depression, the gospel of victimology now causes many leaders of such groups to deny their successes. Alas, the professional pessimism of the victimologists grants them the balm of moral absolution. I worry that the reigning ideology of "diversity" in practice is converted into division and separateness where we judge people by the pigmentation of their skin. When I left academia shortly before the end of the 20th century, a sizable number of my colleagues held that we lived in a racist purgatory in which all black effort is a Sisyphean affair where even keeping one's head above water is a victory. I affirm that blacks, women, Latinos and others are not eternal victims. We need to focus on the American Credo that, as a Kiwanian, I repeat every week: *"One Nation,* Under God, *Indivisible . . ."*

In 1994 I asked members of a college senior seminar that I taught what they thought was the "most important decision that they would ever have to make in their lives." Nearly all the students answered in terms related to self-fulfillment. "Deciding which career to pursue," "Figuring out which graduate school to attend," Choosing where I should live." Only one student answered differently, "Deciding who should be the mother of my children." For this "eccentric" opinion, and especially the quaint way it was put, he was immediately attacked by nearly every other member of the class, men and women alike.

Moreover, the emotive and intuitive, rather than the rational and intellectual, now seem to dominate. As a society we seem engulfed in our own feelings and translate political issues into the simple language of love and hate. "It is a society in which the local school," reports Frum, "which may have a leaking roof, has a resident team of counselors."

Traditionally, political scientists have warned that emotion is best left out of the political arena. At least, it should be held on a short tether. The role of government is to address narrow and specific grievances, not to serve as an omnicompetent nanny that assuages permanent emotional desires. Love, generosity, and compassion are virtues best practiced by private individuals, not public bureaucracies. Today, however, we have confused having feelings with governing. Presidents are elected nowadays, not because they've thought through Social Security reform, but because *"he felt our pain."* Empathy, "healing," and "journeys" is a politics of empathy that masquerades as a policy agenda.

Materialism is the defining ethos of our era—not only in the property sense, but in the moral sense as well. All issues are reduced to the sensate. Teen-age smoking is tightly regulated, but teen sex is largely ignored. Regular attendance at a health club is an index of well-being, but faithful participation at a church or synagogue is not. Our therapeutic culture dictates that one should openly confess all emotional traumas but keep silent regarding one's Christian convictions. A political candidate's college grades can be examined, but not her moral beliefs or history. Vice is now a disease while virtue is classed as intolerance. Guilt is now wedded to smoking, paying the retail price, getting a tan, and eating red meat or a high-calorie muffin rather than to false witness or betrayal. Pornography is free speech while opposition to reparations for blacks and affirmative action is race-hate. Prenatal health care is a moral issue but abortion is not.

One of the debilitating features of modern life is the endless push for and consumption of ever more goods and services. Our reigning vice is envy, the insidious drive that is apt to destroy gracious activity and the just assessment of others. "All man's miseries derive from not being able," said Pascal, "to sit quietly in a room alone."

As I mentioned in the preface, there is danger in writing during one's gray-haired years. There may be a generic tendency among seniors to magnify the pathologies and minimize the virtues of the generations that are to replace them. I certainly do not wish to end this study on a dyspeptic note. But I see many signs of *primitivism* in our society. That is, a rejection of the ideals of the best of western culture.

I am reminded that Tacitus too, was worried as he observed the noble and courageous Germans as they took over from his decadent Romans. By "decadent" Tacitus and I mean a society that has fallen away from any sense of high purpose or unity in its culture. While I do not see our culture in a "free-fall," as I stated earlier, there are worrisome cracks in our institutions. Too many members of American society today seek only more "toys," to enhance their pleasure and convenience.

It is my earnest hope that the afflictions that bedevil us are soon arrested before they further weaken the moral bedrock of our society. Deliverance is not to be found in the material, secular, or political sectors of life. Our social and civic institutions—families, churches, schools, neighborhoods, and civic associations—have traditionally taken on the responsibility of providing our children with love, order and discipline—of teaching self-control, compassion, tolerance, civility, honesty and respect for property and authority. Government, even at its best, can never be more than an auxiliary in the development of character. We need, rather, a revival of morally and spiritually strong individuals, families, and religious communities. If that happens, we may have some assurance that the social pathogens of the last few decades will be contained.

SELECTED BIBLIOGRAPHY

Amato, Joseph & Meyer, John W. *The Decline of Rural Minnesota*. Marshall, Minnesota: Crossings Press, 1993.

Amerson, Robert. *From the Hidewood: Memories of a Dakota Neighborhood*. St. Paul: Minnesota Historical Society Press, 1996.

Behr, Edward. *Prohibition: Thirteen Years That Changed America*. New York: Arcade Publishing, 1996.

Benjamin, Walter W. "The Methodist Episcopal Church in the Postwar Era," *The History of American Methodism*, Vol II. Nashville: Abingdon Press, 1964.

Benjamin, Walter W. "The Great Steel Strike: 1918-1919" in A *Miscellany of American Christianity*, Stuart Henry, ed. Durham: Duke University Press, 1959.

Benjamin, Walter W. *War & Reflection*. White Bear Lake: Red Oak Press, 1997.

Blankenhorn, David. *Fatherless America:* New York: Basic Books, 1995.

Bly, Carol. *Backbone*. Minneapolis: Milkweed Editions, 1985.

Bly, Carol. *Letters From The Country.* New York: Harper & Row, 1981.

Bode, Carl, ed. *The Portable Thoreau*. New York: Penguin Books, 1947.

Breathnach, Sarah Ban. *Simple Abundance*. New York: Time Warner, 1995.

Brokaw, Tom. *The Greatest Generation*. New York: Random House, 1998.

Brokaw, Tom. *The Greatest Generation Speaks:* Letters & Reflections. New York: Random House, 1999.

Bryson, Bill. *The Lost Continent: Travels in Small-Town America,* New York: Harper & Row, 1989.

Caldwell, Erskin. *Afternoons in Mid-America*. New York: Dodd, Mead & Company, 1976

Connell, Evan S. *Son of the Morning Star: Custer and The Little Bighorn,* New York: North Point Press, 1984.

Covici, Pascal, ed. *The Portable Steinbeck,* New York: The Viking Press, 1943.

Dickerson, James, R. *Home on the Range: A Century on the High Plains,* Lawrence: University of Kansas Press, 1995

Elson, Robert. *Prelude to War.* Alexander, Virginia: Time-Life Books, 1977.

Folwell, William, W. *A History of Minnesota*. St Paul: Minnesota Historical Society, Vol. II, 1924; Vol. III, 1926.

Frankl, Viktor E. *Man's Search For Meaning,* New York: Pocket Books Press, 1959.

Frazier, Ian. *Great Plains.* New York: Penguin Books, 1989.

Freud, Sigmund. *The Future of an Illusion,* New York: Doubleday Press, 1953.

Gabler, William G. *Death of the Dream: Classic Minnesota Farmhouses*. Afton, MN: Afton Historical Society Press, 1997.

Hamilton, Carl. *In No Time At All*. Ames, Iowa: Iowa State University Press, 1974.

Hanson, Victor, Davis. *Field Without Dreams: Defending the Agrarian Idea*. New York: Free Press, 1996.

Higgs, Robert. "Regime Uncertainty: Why the Great Depression Lasted So Long and Why Prosperity Resumed After the War," *The Independent Review,* Volume I, Number 4, Spring 1997.

Hildebrand, John. *Mapping the Farm: The Chronicle of a Family.* New York: Vitage Press, 1995.

Hill, Stan. *Confessions of an 80 Year-Old Boy,* White Bear Lake, Minnesota: The Red Oak Press, 1994.

Hoffer, Eric. *The True Believer,* New York: Harper & Row, 1951.

Horn, Huston. *The Old West: The Pioneers.* New York: Time/Life Books, 1974.

Hull, William, H. *The Dirty Thirties,* Minneapolis: Stanton Publication Services, 1989.

Horowitz, David. *Radical Son: A Generational Odyssey.* New York: The Free Press, 1997.

Jennings & Brewster. *The Century.* New York: Doubleday, 1988.

Johnson, Paul. *A History of the American People.* New York: HarperCollins, 1997

Keegan, John. *Fields of Battle: The Wars for North America.* New York: Alfred Knopf, 1996.

Keillor, Garrison. *Lake Wobegon Days,* New York: Viking Penguin Inc., 1985.

Kennedy, David W. *Freedom From Fear.* New York: Oxford University Press, 1999.

Kershaw, Ian. Hitler: *1889-1936 Hubris.* New York: W. W. Norton & Company, 1998.

Kohn, Howard., *The Last Farmer: An American Memoir.* New York: Harper & Row, 1988

Laycock, George. *The Mountain Men.* New York: Lyons & Burford,   1988.

Lewis, Sinclair. *Babbitt,* New York: New American Library, 1922.

Lewis, Sinclair. *Arrowsmith,* New York: Modern Library, 1925.

McCrossen, Alexis. *Holy Day, Holiday.* University of Cornell Press, 2000.

Merchant, Tom, ed. "Rails Across the Prairie," Westbrook, Minnesota: Sentinel News Inc., 1989.

Mitchell, Jim. *A Nickel For Bread,* Sioux Falls: Prairie Grove Books, 1990

Milner, E.R. *The Life and Times of Bonnie and Clyde.* Carbondale: Southern Illinois University Press, 1996.

Niebuhr, Reinhold, *Moral Man and Immoral Society,* New York: Charles Scribners, 1932.

Norris, Kathleen. *Dakota: A Spiritual Geography.* New York: Ticknor & Fields, 1993.

Potter, Merle, *101 Best Stories of Minnesota.* Minneapolis: Schmitt Publications, 1956.

Rambow, David, ed. *Coteau Heritage,* "The Sacred Pipestone Quarries," *Coteau Heritage:* Journal of the Pipestone Historical Society, Volume 2, Number 2, 1989.

Rambow, David, ed. "Pipestone County Pioneer Doctors: The First Fifty Years," *Coteau Heritage, Journal of the Pipestone County Historical Society.* Volume 5, Number 1, January 1993.

Reed, Benjamin, F. *History of Kossuth County Iowa.* Chicago: S.J. Clark Publishing Company, 1913

Ricketts, Harry. *Rudyard Kipling: A Life.* New York: Carroll & Graf, 1999.

Rolvaag, O.E. *Giants in the Earth.* New York: Harper & Row, 1927.

Shirer, William. *Berlin Diary,* 1934-1941. Sphere Books, ed., London, 1970.

Shirer, William, L. *The Nightmare Years: 1930-1840.* New York: Bantam Books, 1984.

Shirer, William, L. *The Rise and Fall of the Third Reich.* Simon and Schuster, 1959.

Smiley, Jane. *A Thousand Acres.* New York: Fawcett Columbine, 1991.

Takaki, Ronald. *Double Victory: A Multicultural History of America in World War II* New York: Little, Brown, and Company. 2000.

Townsend, Peter. *Duel of Eagles.* London: Butler & Tanner Limited, 1970.

Updike, John. *In The Beauty of the Lilies,* New York: Ballantine Books, 1996.

van Bockel, Jacob. *Holland Heritage.* N.P. van Bockel Publishing. 1982.

van Bockel, John. *Another Time.* N.P. 1999.

Veblen, Thorstein. *The Theory of the Leisure Class.* New York: Viking Compass, 1967.

Ward, Geoffrey C. *The West: An Illustrated History.* New York: Little Brown and Company, 1996.

Warren, Donald. *Radio Priest: Charles Coughlin, The Father of Hate Radio,* New York: The Free Press, 1996.

Watkins, T.W. *The Hungry Years.* New York: Henry Holt & Co. 1999.

Winston, Diane. *Hot & Righteous: The Urban Religion of The Salvation Army.* Cambridge: Harvard University Press, 1999.

INDEX OF NAMES

ABOUT THE AUTHOR

Walter W. Benjamin was three years old when the Great Depression began in 1929. Like millions of others his life was shaped by the decade that followed. The son of a country physician, Benjamin served in the Navy Air Corps in World War II, received his Ph.D. in ethics at Duke University, and spent most of his career at Hamline University in St. Paul, Minnesota. Dr. Benjamin specialized in medical and business ethics and his essays have appeared in such periodicals as *The Wall Street Journal, The New England Journal of Medicine, Post-Graduate Medicine, Corporate Report, The Internist,* and *Humane Medicine,* as well as *Newsweek, The Washington Post,* and *The Chicago Tribune.* He is the author of *War & Reflection* (Red Oak Press).

Professor Benjamin was a British-American-Canadian Association lecturer in Great Britain in 1996. He spoke before the business and medical faculties and students at the Universities of Manchester, London, Oxford, Edinburgh, Birmingham, Durham and others during a 21-day lecture tour.